Approaching Difficulties in Literacy Development: Assessment, Pedagogy and Programmes

This Reader, along with the companion volume *Understanding Difficulties in Literacy Development: Issues and Concepts* forms part of *Difficulties in Literacy Development* (E801), a course belonging to the Open University MA in Education programme.

The Open University Masters in Education

The Open University Masters in Education is now firmly established as the most popular postgraduate degree for education professionals in Europe, with over 3000 students registered each year. It is designed particularly for those with experience of teaching, the advisory service, educational administration or allied fields. Specialist lines in management, applied linguistics, special needs/inclusive education and lifelong learning are available within the programme. Successful study on the MA entitles students to apply for entry into the Open University Doctorate in Education programme.

Details of this and other Open University courses can be obtained from the Student Registration and Enquiry Service, The Open University, PO Box 197, Milton Keynes MK7 6BJ, United Kingdom: Telephone: +44 (0) 845 300 6090; e-mail: general-enquiries@open.ac.uk.

Alternatively, you may wish to visit the Open University website at http://www.open.ac.uk, where you can learn more about the wide range of courses and packs offered at all levels by The Open University.

Approaching Difficulties in Literacy Development: Assessment, Pedagogy and Programmes

Edited by
Felicity Fletcher-Campbell, Janet Soler
and Gavin Reid

Los Angeles | London | New Delhi
Singapore | Washington DC

The Open University
Walton Hall
Milton Keynes
MK7 6AA
United Kingdom
www.open.ac.uk

SAGE Publications Ltd
1 Oliver's Yard
55 City Road
London EC1Y 1SP

SAGE Publications Inc.
2455 Teller Road
Thousand Oaks, California 91320

SAGE Publications India Pvt Ltd
B 1/I 1 Mohan Cooperative Industrial Area
Mathura Road
New Delhi 110 044

SAGE Publications Asia-Pacific Pte Ltd
33 Pekin Street #02-01
Far East Square
Singapore 048763

Library of Congress Control Number: 2008944007

British Library Cataloguing in Publication data

A catalogue record for this book is available from the British Library

ISBN 978-1-84860-770-5
ISBN 978-1-84860-771-2 (pbk)

Typeset by C&M Digitals (P) Ltd, Chennai, India
Printed and bound in Great Britain by TJ International Ltd, Padstow, Cornwall
Printed on paper from sustainable resources

Mixed Sources
Product group from well-managed
forests and other controlled sources
www.fsc.org Cert no. SGS-COC-2482
© 1996 Forest Stewardship Council
FSC

Contents

Acknowledgements

We should like to thank the authors who contributed their chapters, as well as colleagues within and outside The Open University who helped with the preparation of the manuscripts. Special thanks are due to the following people for their assistance in the production of this book:

Kathy Simms (course secretary)
Theresa Nolan (course manager)
Gill Gowans (copublishing executive)

Chapter 1
From: Goswami, U., 'Reading, Dyslexia and the Brain', *Educational Research*, 50 (2), 2008, pp. 135–48. Reprinted by permission of the publisher (Taylor & Francis Group, http://www.informaworld.com).

Chapter 2
From: Scarborough, H.S., 'Connecting Early Language and Literacy to Later Reading (Dis)abilities: Evidence, Theory and Practice', in S.B. Neuman and D.K. Dickinson (eds) *Handbook of Early Literacy Research*, pp. 97–110 (New York: Guilford Press, 2001). Copyright © 2001 by Guilford Press. Reprinted by permission of Guildford Press via the Copyright Clearance Center.

Chapter 4
From: Cain, K., Oakhill, J. and Lemmon, K., 'Individual Differences in the Inference of Word Meanings From Context: The Influence of Reading Comprehension, Vocabulary Knowledge and Memory Capacity', *Journal of Educational Psychology*, 96 (4), 2004, pp. 671–81. Copyright © 2004. Reproduced with permission of the American Psychological Association.

Chapter 5
From: Purcell-Gates, V., Degener, S.C., Jacobson, E. and Soler, M., 'Impact of Authentic Adult Literacy Instruction on Adult Literacy Practices', *Reading Research Quarterly*, 37 (1), 2002, pp. 70–92. Reprinted with permission of the International Reading Association.

Chapter 6
From: Wheldall, K. and Pogorzelski, S., 'Is the PhAB Really Fab? The Utility of the Phonological Assessment Battery in Predicting Gains Made by Older Low-Progress Readers Following Two Terms of Intensive Literacy Instruction', *Educational Psychology*, 23 (5), 2003, pp. 569–90. Reprinted by permission of the publisher (Taylor & Francis Group, http://www.informaworld.com).

Chapter 7
From: Simpson, J. and Everatt, J., 'Reception Class Predictors of Literacy Skills', *British Journal of Educational Psychology*, 75 (2), 2005, pp. 171–88. Reproduced with permission from the *British Journal of Education Psychology*, © The British Psychological Society.

Chapter 8
From: Johnston, P. and Costello, P., 'Principles for Literary Assessment', *Reading Research Quarterly*, 40 (2), 2005, pp. 256–67. Reprinted with permission of the International Reading Association.

Chapter 9
From: Mortimore, T., 'Dyslexia and Learning Style – a Note of Caution', *British Journal of Special Education*, 32 (3), 2005, pp. 145–8. Copyright © 2005 NASEN. Reproduced with permission of Blackwell Publishing Ltd.

Chapter 10
From: Norwich, B. And Lewis, A., 'Mapping a Pedagogy for Special Educational Needs', *British Educational Research Journal*, 27 (3), 2001, pp. 313–29. Reprinted by permission of the publisher (Taylor & Francis Group, http://www.informaworld.com).

Chapter 11
From: Goodwyn, A. and Findlay, K., 'Shaping Literacy in the Secondary School: Policy, Practice and Agency in the Age of the National Literacy Strategy', *British Journal of Educational Studies*, 51 (1), 2003, pp. 20–35. Copyright © 2003 Society for Educational Studies (SES). Reproduced with permission of Blackwell Publishing Ltd.

Chapter 12
From: Meacham, S.J., 'Headwoman's Blues: Small Group Reading and the Interactions of Culture, Gender and Ability', in A.I. Willis, G.E. Garcia, R. Barrera and V.J. Harris (eds) *Multicultural Issues in Literacy Research and Practice*, pp. 49–67 (Mahwah, NJ: Lawrence Erlbaum, 2003). Copyright 2003 by Lawrence Erlbaum. Reprinted by permission of Lawrence Erlbaum via the Copyright Clearance Center.

Chapter 13
From: Tett, L., 'Excluded Voices: Class, Culture and Family Literacy in Scotland', *Journal of Adolescent & Adult Literacy,* 44 (2), 2000, pp. 122–8. Reprinted with permission of the International Reading Association.

Chapter 14
From: Glynn, T. and McNaughton, S., 'Trust Your Own Observations: Assessment of Reader and Tutor Behaviour in Learning to Read in English and Māori', *International Journal of Disability, Development and Education*, 49 (2), 2002, pp. 161–73. Reprinted by permission of the publisher (Taylor & Francis Group, http://www.informaworld.com).

Chapter 15
From: Hurry, J. and Sylva, K., 'Long-Term Outcomes of Early Reading Intervention', *Journal of Research in Reading*, 30 (3), 2007, pp. 227–48. A journal of the United Kingdom Literacy Association.

Chapter 16
From: Lea, M.R. and Street, B.V., 'Student Writing in Higher Education: An Academic Literacies Approach', *Studies in Higher Education*, 23 (2), 1998, pp. 157–72. Reprinted by permission of the publisher (Taylor & Francis Group, http://www.informaworld.com).

Chapter 17
From: Kerr, H., 'Dyslexia and Adult Literacy: Does Dyslexia Disempower?', in M. Hamilton, L. Tett and J. Crowther (eds) *Powerful Literacies*, pp. 69–79 (Leicester: National Institute of Adult Continuing Education, 2001). Reproduced with kind permission of the authors and NIACE. Copyright © NIACE 2001 (www.niace.org.uk/publications).

Chapter 18
From: Melhuish, E.C., Phan, M.B., Sylva, K., Sammons, P., Siraj-Blatchford, I. and Taggart, B., 'Effects of the Home Learning Environment and Preschool Center Experience upon Literacy and Numeracy Development in Early Primary School', *Journal of Social Issues*, 64 (1), 2008, pp. 95–114. Copyright © 2008 The Society for the Psychological Study of Social Issues. Reproduced with permission of Blackwell Publishing Ltd.

Introduction

Felicity Fletcher-Campbell

This volume starts from the clear premise that, first, literacy is a contested concept and, second, that acquiring literacy is a complex process. The manifestation of difficulties in literacy does, in fact, help us to understand the acquisition of literacy far more helpfully than if no difficulties existed. In cases where literacy is acquired unproblematically, the process can, beguilingly, appear almost developmental. But, when, in a society which places a high value on literacy (whatever its specific definition), literacy is acquired with difficulty, we begin to scrutinize the process to see where the barriers are being constructed: we do not pause to analyse something which poses no challenges. It is within this scrutiny that acquiring literacy is seen to be complex and, hence, that difficulties in literacy parallel this complexity. This volume considers the complexity of literacy difficulties and, in so doing, shows how research into literacy difficulties has to be multi-faceted and multi-disciplinary and involve a range of research approaches and methods. This research brief is necessary to accommodate the wide range of issues that can, potentially, explain literacy difficulties and suggest strategies and interventions to ease those difficulties.

It is significant that in the collection of articles in this volume, no one commentator or researcher claims dominance of the field in understanding literacy difficulties. The articles are evidence-based but remind us that any research has its limitations – not least because any good research study has a very precise, focused research question. Even if the research is robust and rests on a secure methodological approach, it can yield ambiguous findings or the findings can be misinterpreted. When this misinterpretation or ambiguity becomes enshrined in policy, then trouble follows. We find, in this volume, suggestions of how literacy research, and the neglect of the recognition that research always takes places in a context, may, ironically, have contributed to literacy difficulties in that unhelpful strategies and interventions have been implemented. The authors in this present volume commonly show how a previous research study needs revisiting or a single finding needs specific focus in order to refine it; or how the choice of methodology affects the findings; or how the findings must be read in the light of other considerations. In some cases, more seems to have been learnt about literacy as the years have progressed – and, here, the rare longitudinal studies are particularly welcome. In others, the same points are being made as were made previously – not always to revitalize or confirm them but because previous lessons have not been heeded or political imperatives have not had time to gather up the existing evidence.

The volume is divided into five sections, each of which focuses on one of the functions involved in addressing literacy difficulties.

Part 1 asks the 'So What?' question which is indispensable for linking theory to practice. It is important to remember that this linkage is a two-way process. Theorists have a duty to point out the implications for practice, while practitioners have a duty to challenge and evaluate their practice in the light of theory and research findings. However, it is in the day-to-day observation of practice that flaws, or lack of refinement, in theory can be detected and practitioners can thus participate in theory generation and refinement by considering 'what fits' and 'what does not fit'. Theorists then have an obligation to listen to them.

Part 2 turns to the assessment of literacy difficulties. The chapters do not consider assessment merely as a skill but, rather, as an activity inextricably linked to pedagogy. While how an assessment is undertaken is of critical importance – mismanagement can generate frail or misleading data – yet assessment is only of value if the 'So What?' question is asked and acted upon. And this 'So What?' goes far deeper than is implied in assessment for categorization ('dyslexic' or 'not dyslexic'; 'extra time in exams' for 'normal treatment') which may be about access and equity but is not directly about literacy difficulties.

Part 3 takes the next logical step: Pedagogy and Planning. But planning inevitably has to take account of the external environment. The vast majority of practitioners operate within a set of parameters dictated not by 'pure theory' (what practice would be like in an ideal world uncontaminated by variables) but by political frameworks, themselves designed according to political, socio-economic and cultural requirements and values. In this third part, thus, the relevant issues widen to embrace ethnicity, culture, and issues within education such as the 'specialness' of special educational needs teaching, and 'learning styles'. Each of these begs the question of what are 'literacy difficulties' and gives a reminder of two more important points, which reinforce the complexity of 'literacy' and 'literacy difficulties' – that literacy does not exist in a vacuum and that teaching literacy will be influenced by a range of classroom practices that have been generated through other lineages.

It is easy to allow media attention to restrict the consideration of literacy difficulties and to create the impression that it is a phenomenon mostly resident in primary or lower secondary education. Part 4 widens the scope, bringing in articles from Scotland and New Zealand, a study which examines the persistence (or otherwise) of literacy difficulties as the environment changes, and an article which increasingly challenges the understanding of 'literacy' (and hence literacy difficulties) the further that learners proceed from the relatively confined school curriculum and enter higher education.

Finally, but, arguably, of most importance, Part 5 examines how changes in practice are brought about and asks the uncomfortable question of for whose benefit 'labels' are attached to learners who find acquiring literacy difficult. There are no answers here. The only way that the reader can arrive at a resolution is to ponder over all the chapters in this Reader and its companion volume and come to his/her own decision, grounded in the evidence presented and his/her evaluation of the robustness of that evidence.

This volume presents a range of perspectives and approaches. The articles were selected because they demonstrated the complexity of literacy difficulties, were up to date, and were 'arguable with'. For literacy evolves and transmutes: in a decade there will be new considerations untouched in this volume. We hope that readers will be motivated to participate in, and contribute to, this evolution.

Part 1

Goswami uses recent developments in neuroscience to answer 'old' questions about approaches to reading across languages. The data presented here reinforce the idea of complexity and the need to have multiple approaches to literacy difficulties. There are messages in this chapter that can be transferred outside the field of neuroscience. For example, the importance of oral language is easy to forget when focusing on script-based difficulties and

Goswami gives a timely reminder about the importance of rigorous research methods and the fact that as research methods develop, so new findings can be presented.

Learning to read is not like suddenly being able to ride a bike – once you have the skill, a few wobbles and you are off for life. Learning to read is, as the title of OU course E801 reminds us, a developmental process – not an event – and this process involves proximal abilities and skills. In Chapter 2, Scarborough draws attention to this and also presents evidence that reading difficulties persist through an individual's life: early intervention may be necessary but not sufficient. And 'predictors', often courted by policy-makers, are frail: often, all that can be done is to identify instances of 'high risk' and remember that there are always exceptions. Again, here is one of our recurrent messages – simplistic interpretations of data must be avoided: for example, it is not enough just to identify 'family history' as a 'cause' of difficulties in a child; difficulties in previous generations may have been rooted in genetic factors or may have been rooted in socio-cultural factors.

The next chapter, by Ellis, gives an indication of what happens when data are misinterpreted by being taken out of context and dissociated from other paradigms: 'any study driven mainly by one paradigm can only offer limited insights'. The fact that one group of learners made exceptional progress with a particular method of teaching reading does not mean that other groups will fare similarly. Ellis points to other areas of educational research – specifically, what is known about the management of change and curriculum innovation. She points out that the background features of a particular study must be examined in full before the process of that study is implanted elsewhere – for example, any curriculum innovation is affected by such factors as related staff development, support structures, management and leadership from above, and the availability of advice during implementation.

The report of Cain et al. is a useful example of, first, what can be achieved in a carefully conducted small-scale investigation and, second, how assessment tests can be used in a focused way to answer a very specific research question (rather than just to produce a cumulative assessment of an individual). This is a lesson well worth heeding.

Finally in this section, the focus turns to adult literacy and large-scale research. Purcell-Gates et al. adopt a social practice perspective and discuss the importance (and greater efficacy) of 'authentic' practice – that is, practice grounded in learners' day-to-day context and concerns – as opposed to decontextualized skill acquisition.

Part 2

In this part, the usefulness of two assessment instruments (PhAB and DEST) in common use in English schools is discussed before attention turns to literacy assessment more generally.

In Chapter 6, Wheldall and Pogorzelski question the value of making distinctions between dyslexic low-progress readers and non-dyslexic low-progress readers. This raises issues about when distinctive pedagogy for groups of learners displaying different behaviours with regard to literacy difficulties should be applied. Does the cause of reading difficulties matter or should attention focus on imaginative and effective interventions? The chapter questions whether categorization can be predictive of response to an intervention programme and addresses the critical question of whether learners 'just catch up' without specific systemic intervention. In passing, it might be noted that Wheldall and Pogorzelski's proportion of severe dyslexics is low – just three to five per cent of the 25 per cent of learners with difficulties (and thus about one per cent of the total population). Some of the criteria that the authors use in relation to PhAB can be transferred elsewhere – for example, PhAB gives a diagnosis but is deemed less informative for practice. There is the suggestion that it may not be necessary to use PhAB to categorize learners in order to determine interventions as interventions may be effective for all learners in this study. There are challenges for teachers in this chapter as there are in Chapter 7, which considers DEST's usefulness as a predictor in comparison with other school-based assessment. The authors consider that individual items in the assessment instrument may serve a better purpose than the test as a whole. This suggestion relates to expert practitioners' ability to focus on one specific learner behaviour within the administration of a test and produce another test to look at that particular behaviour in detail. This places assessment under the Assessment For Learning banner rather than as a means to the ends of categorization for administrative purposes. One message for teachers may be that they should have confidence in tried-and-tested school-based assessment (provided that evidence to prove its efficacy has been collected systematically) rather than assume that a commercial test is superior.

Finally in this section, Johnston and Costello locate literacy assessment in society, pointing out that literacy involves democratic interaction. Any focus on a narrow sample of 'literate behaviour' will distort teaching. Different instruments will have different meanings according to different cultural and societal assumptions and values which may give more information about power relations than anything to do with 'literacy skills'. The messages here are timely, following the more technical considerations of the specific instruments in the first two chapters in this section.

Part 3

Mortimer's chapter warns against making ungrounded assumptions about the capacity of other general interventions (here, the case of preferred learning styles) to enhance the learning of students with dyslexia. We must always look at the quality of the evidence before we incorporate any intervention into our pedagogy. This highlights the close relationship between practice and theory. Practice that is not theoretically justified is dangerous.

Challenging assumptions further, Norwich and Lewis question the notion of a 'common curriculum' (where 'curriculum' includes 'pedagogy'). Their chapter shows an argument in action and, usefully, it is an argument which does not arrive at answers easily, following our Reader theme of complexity and supporting the hypothesis that continua of teaching approaches may be the most appropriate model for those with literacy difficulties, giving the opportunity for different weights and balances using common ingredients rather than a choice between distinctive diets.

The focus then turns to a specific policy example with the chapter by Goodwyn and Findlay, which powerfully illustrates that literacy is a contested concept, driven as much by politics as research into the acquisition of skills which literacy needs. The authors here also show not only how official rhetoric around literacy policy can be internally inconsistent and espouse different philosophical positions, but also how the policy, in all its manifestations, can be variously interpreted by the practitioners involved in its implementation. This is a reminder that, as researchers into literacy difficulties, we must always clarify what 'version' of literacy is practised in the context in which we are working.

This reminder is apposite for Meacham's chapter from the USA which examines the construction of literacy in a richly diverse, multi-ethnic environment. In addition to the insights it gives us about 'literacy' and 'literacy difficulties', the article has two important features. First, it shows the workings of a research project that was very complex on account of the vast range of intervening variables. Second, it shows how extended metaphor can be employed to support data analysis.

Part 4

In Chapter 13, Tett explores the manifestation of different literacies in different cultures, noting how one 'literacy' can predominate to such an extent that it disenfranchises those whose identity is grounded in a culture with a different literacy. Those using the dominant literacy can adopt a medical perspective regarding users of other literacies, seeing them as deficient in their language use. The article shows the relationship between pedagogy and the content of the curriculum, and suggests that an emancipatory pedagogy is needed to free some learners of their lack of confidence in themselves which results from their self-perception of being a user of what they have been taught is a 'deficient' literacy. The author's insistence on 'authenticity' can be transferred to a myriad of contexts in which small-scale practitioner research is conducted at masters level.

The chapter by Glynn and McNaughton investigates both the cultural influences on literacy and the implementation of a specific programme for literacy difficulties, emphasizing 'the inseparable linkages between language learning and cultural learning'. Interestingly, these authors are able to use a methodology first tried in a study they conducted nearly three decades previously. Research which is able to build on experience and test conceptual frameworks over time, in changing contexts, is extremely valuable. Similarly, Hurry and Sylva can 'look back' as they report a longer-term investigation of Reading Recovery. The importance of this time frame comparison is highlighted by the fact that, while immediate gains were reported for children engaged in the intervention, longer-term effects were far less distinct. This reminds us that, as researchers, we can 'construct' evidence by virtue of the methodological frames that we use. Early intervention, however good, may be inadequate on its own and support may need to be available to some students for a far longer time. If we relate this practical finding to what we know about the causes of literacy difficulties (see, for example, chapters in the companion volume to this), this may not surprise us.

The final chapter in this part gives evidence of variation within a literacy or related literacies – in this case, academic literacies. Students can be confused by the very different sets of expectations and conventions assumed by different members of staff and subject areas within higher education – largely because different fields of investigation have their own cultures and histories. Different perspectives, representing different statuses in the power hierarchy, validate different responses from students and render these responses acceptable or unacceptable.

Part 5

The final part starts with a chapter taking up the theme of inclusion, exploring the dilemma between 'labelling', following identification, as, on the one hand, in useful gaining of access to resources and helping the learner to position him/herself; and, on the other, promoting 'learned helplessness' on the part of those identified, so that the label becomes an instrument of disempowerment and strengthens the suggestion of a fixed state of inability. This is the dilemma faced by numerous teachers in a wide range of contexts day by day. Finally, Melhuish et al. report on a large-scale study of the effects of learning activities in the home. This study goes far beyond those which suggest a link between a child's achievement and socio-economic background. It focuses on the learning activities (which can include activities which teach the child how to learn) and suggests that it is these, rather than the background characteristics themselves, that influence a child's level of achievement. This is important in terms of planning effective interventions (which it suggests should be collaborative).

Part 1

Theoretical Understandings: Implications for Practice

1

Reading, Dyslexia and the Brain

Usha Goswami

[…]

How universal are the neural demands made by learning to read in different languages? What are the core neural systems involved, and what goes wrong in the dyslexic brain? Current neuroimaging technologies are able to throw light on research questions such as these, as will be illustrated below. In some instances, neuroimaging technologies can contribute unique information that behavioural methodologies are simply unable to provide. This includes information about the time processes in reading, and information about the parts of the brain that are affected by remedial packages for developmental dyslexia. Some neuroimaging methodologies can gather data without requiring overt attention on the part of the child. These methodologies are particularly powerful for contributing to our understanding of the biological basis of developmental dyslexia.

The history of research on developmental dyslexia has been dominated by visual theories of the disorder, ever since Hinshelwood (1896) described it as 'congenital word blindness'. Historically, theories of reading development also assumed that visual processing was core to individual differences in the acquisition of reading. In the 1970s, for example, there was much discussion of 'Phonecian' versus 'Chinese' reading acquisition strategies. It was assumed that children who were learning to read character-based orthographies like Chinese required excellent visual memory skills in order to distinguish between the visually complex characters that represented spoken words. Hence, visual memory or 'logographic' strategies were assumed core to reading acquisition of languages like Chinese and Japanese. Children who were learning to read languages like Greek or Italian, which were alphabetic and transparent (each letter corresponding to one, and only one, sound) appeared to require code-breaking skills. It was assumed that once the brain had learned the symbol–sound code, reading should be largely a process of phonological assembly. Many experiments were conducted with children learning to read in English, to compare the contribution of 'Chinese' versus 'Phonecian' acquisition strategies (e.g. Baron 1979). Dual-route models of reading, originally developed using data from adults, were applied to children who were learning to read (Stuart and Coltheart 1988). It was assumed that, developmentally, children could choose to learn to read by either Chinese or Phonecian strategies.

From: *Educational Research*, 50 (2), 2008, pp. 135–48.

These ideas about individual differences have not gone away (e.g., Stein and Walsh 1997; Stuart 2006), but they are looking increasingly dated with the advent of brain imaging. Neuroimaging has also shed light on the processes underpinning the development of reading in deaf children, whom it was once assumed had no choice but to rely on visual memorisation strategies (e.g., Conrad 1979). Essentially, neuroscience is showing that despite the apparently different demands on the brain made by learning to read English, Greek or Chinese, and the apparently different processing strategies used by children who are deaf or who are dyslexic, reading across orthographies depends on the adequate functioning of the phonological system. Even for languages like Chinese, which would appear reliant on visual processing, it is oral language skills that underpin the acquisition of reading.

As I show in this review, brain imaging studies demonstrate that reading begins primarily as a phonological process. In the early phases of learning to read, it is the neural structures for spoken language that are particularly active. As reading expertise develops, an area in the visual cortex originally named the 'visual word form area' (VWFA) becomes increasingly active (Cohen and Dehaene 2004). This area is not a logographic system, even though it is very close to the visual areas that are active during picture naming. The VWFA is also active during nonsense word reading, and as nonsense words do not have word forms in the mental lexicon, the VWFA is thought to store orthography–phonology connections at different grain sizes (Goswami and Ziegler 2006a). Deaf readers rely on the same phonological system for reading as everyone else (MacSweeney et al. 2005). Children with developmental dyslexia show selective under-activation of key phonological areas of the brain, but targeted phonology-based interventions improve levels of activation in these areas, 'normalising' neural activity (Simos et al. 2002).

Learning to read: behavioural data

Many behavioural studies in developmental psychology show the critical role of 'phonological awareness' in learning to read (for a recent review, see Ziegler and Goswami 2005). Phonological awareness is thought to develop via language acquisition. Between the ages of 1 and 6 years, children acquire words at an exponential rate. For example, the average 1-year-old might have a productive vocabulary of around 50–100 words, but by the age of 6 the average child's receptive vocabulary will contain around 14,000 words (Dollaghan 1994). In order for the brain to represent each word as a distinct and unique sequence of sounds, each entry in the 'mental lexicon' must incorporate phonological information along with information about meaning. For example, there must be implicit knowledge of the sounds that comprise a particular word, and the order in which they occur. Phonological awareness is essentially the child's ability to reflect on this implicit knowledge, and to make judgements based on it. Hence, phonological awareness is typically measured by a child's ability to detect and manipulate component sounds in words, for example, by deciding whether words rhyme, or by removing the initial sound from a spoken word.

The syllable is the primary processing unit across the world's languages (Port 2006). In fact, there is an apparently language-universal sequence in the development of phonological awareness, from syllable awareness, through 'onset-rime' awareness to 'phoneme' awareness. Syllables ('university' has five syllables, 'coffee' has two syllables) can be segmented into sub-parts called onsets and rimes. The onset is the sound or sounds before the vowel, such as the 'spr' sound in 'spring' and the 'st' sound in 'sting'. The rime is the vowel and any subsequent sounds in the syllable, such as the 'ing' sound in 'spring' and 'string'. The phoneme is the smallest unit of sound that changes meaning. 'Spring' and 'string' differ in meaning because the second sound is different in each word ('p' versus 't' respectively). In many of the world's languages, onsets and rimes are the same as phonemes. This is because the dominant syllable structure across the world's languages is consonant–vowel (CV). Relatively few words in English are CV syllables (5% of English monosyllables follow a CV structure: see De Cara and Goswami 2002). Examples of English words comprised of CV syllables are 'go', 'do' and 'yoyo'.

Behavioural studies across languages have shown that phonological sensitivity at all three linguistic levels (syllable, onset-rime, phoneme) predicts the acquisition of reading (for a review, see Ziegler and Goswami 2005). Furthermore, it has been demonstrated that training phonological awareness has positive effects on reading acquisition across languages, particularly when it is combined with training about how letters or letter sequences correspond to sounds in that language (e.g., Bradley and Bryant 1983; Schneider, Roth, and Ennemoser 2000). Children with developmental dyslexia across languages appear to have specific problems in detecting and manipulating component sounds in words (called a 'phonological deficit': see, e.g., Snowling 2000). For example, they find it difficult to count the number of syllables in different words, to recognise rhymes, to distinguish shared phonemes and to delete phonemes or substitute one phoneme for another (Korean: Kim and Davis 2004; German: Wimmer 1996; Greek: Porpodas 1999; Hebrew: Share and Levin 1999; for a comprehensive review, see Ziegler and Goswami 2005). Dyslexic children are developing some awareness of phonology, but this is a slow and effortful process. Deaf children also develop phonological codes, for example, via lip reading ('speech reading') and vibrational cues. This is the case even if signing is their native language. Phonology is essentially the smallest contrastive units of a language that create new meanings. In signed languages, phonology depends on visual/manual elements, with handshapes, movements and locations combined to form signs (Sandler and Lillo-Martin 2006). For deaf children too, individual differences in phonological awareness are related to reading acquisition (e.g., Harris and Beech 1998).

Reading and learning lo read: neuroimaging data

To date, most neuroimaging studies of reading have been conducted with adults (see Price and McCrory 2005 for a recent synthesis). This was partly due to the methodologies available. The most popular methods for studying the brain during the act of reading depended on imaging techniques like functional magnetic resonance imaging (fMRI) and positron emission tomography (PET). The fMRI technique measures changes in blood flow in the brain, which take approximately 6–8 seconds to reach a maximum value (i.e. maximum activity will be measurable 6–8 seconds after reading a particular word). fMRI works by measuring the magnetic resonance signal generated by the protons of water molecules in brain cells, generating a BOLD (blood oxygenation level dependent) response. The fMRI method is excellent for the localisation of function, but because changes in brain activity are summated over time, it cannot provide information about the sequence in which different neural networks become engaged during the act of reading. In PET, radioactive tracers are injected into the bloodstream and provide an index of brain metabolism. Because of the use of radioactive tracers, PET is not suitable for studying children.

More recently, the value of the electroencephalogram (EEG) methodology for studying reading is being recognised. Neurons communicate on a millisecond scale, with the earliest stages of cognitive information processing beginning between 100 ms and 200 ms after stimulus presentation. EEG methods can measure the low-voltage changes caused by the electrochemical activity of brain cells, thereby reflecting the direct electrical activity of neurons at the time of stimulation (e.g., at the time of seeing a word). Initially, EEG methods were less widely used in the neuroscience of reading, because it is difficult to localise function using EEG. However, developmentally, information about the time course of processing is very important. Data from EEG studies suggest that the brain has decided whether it is reading a real word or a nonsense word within 160–180 ms of presentation, for children and adults across languages (Csepe and Szucs 2003; Sauseng, Bergmann, and Wimmer 2004).

Adult studies of reading based on PET and fMRI have focused on a relatively small range of reading and reading-related tasks, and studies of children using fMRI have followed suit. Typical tasks include asking participants to read single words and then comparing brain activation to a resting condition with the eyes closed; asking participants to pick out target visual features while reading print or 'false font' (false font is made up of meaningless symbols matched to letters for visual features like the 'ascenders' in the letters b, d, k); making phonological judgements while reading words or nonsense words (e.g., 'do these items rhyme?': leat, jete) and making lexical decisions (e.g., pressing a button when a word is presented, and a different button when a nonsense word is presented). Adult experiments show a very consistent picture concerning the neural networks that underpin skilled reading (e.g., Price et al. 2003; Rumsey et al. 1997; for comments on divergence, see Price and McCrory 2005). Word recognition in skilled readers appears to depend on a left-lateralised network of frontal, temporoparietal and occipitotemporal regions, whatever language they are reading (see Figure 1.1).

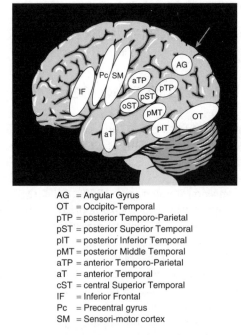

AG   = Angular Gyrus
OT   = Occipito-Temporal
pTP = posterior Temporo-Parietal
pST = posterior Superior Temporal
pIT = posterior Inferior Temporal
pMT = posterior Middle Temporal
aTP = anterior Temporo-Parietal
aT   = anterior Temporal
cST = central Superior Temporal
IF   = Inferior Frontal
Pc   = Precentral gyrus
SM   = Sensori-motor cortex

Figure 1.1   A schematic depiction of some of the neural areas involved in reading (left hemisphere depiction) (from Price and McCrory 2005)

However, there is some additional recruitment of visuo-spatial areas for languages with non-alphabetic orthographies (e.g., left middle frontal gyrus for Chinese: see meta-analysis by Tan et al. 2005). The frontal, temporoparietal and occipitotemporal regions essentially comprise the language, auditory, cross-modal and visual areas of the brain. At a very simple level, semantic and memory processing is thought to occur in temporal and frontal areas, auditory and phonological processing in temporal areas, articulation in frontal areas, visual processing in occipital areas and cross-modal processing in parietal areas.

Although there are still relatively few neuroimaging studies of children reading, the studies that have been done show a high degree of consistency in the neural networks recruited by novice and expert readers. For example, work by Turkeltaub and colleagues has used fMRI and the false font task to compare neural activation in English-speaking participants aged from 7 to 22 years (Turkeltaub et al. 2003). Importantly, 7-year-olds can perform the 'false font' task as well as adults, hence changes in reading-related neural activity are likely to reflect developmental differences rather than differences in reading expertise. Turkeltaub et al. (2003) reported that adults performing their task activated the usual left hemisphere sites, including left posterior temporal and left inferior frontal cortex. They then restricted the analysts to children below 9 years of age. Now the main area engaged was left posterior superior temporal cortex. This region is traditionally considered the focus of phonological activity, and is thus thought to be active during grapheme–phoneme translation. As reading developed, activity in left temporal and frontal areas increased, while activity previously observed in right posterior areas declined. This pattern was interpreted as showing that reading-related activity in the brain becomes more left-lateralised with development.

In further analyses focusing just on the younger children, the researchers investigated the relationships between three core phonological skills and word processing. The three core phonological skills are usually taken to be phonological awareness, phonological memory and rapid automatised naming (RAN). I will focus on the phonological awareness findings here. Turkeltaub et al. (2003) calculated partial correlations between activated brain regions and each of these three measures while controlling for the effects of the other two measures. They reported that the three different measures correlated with three distinct patterns of brain activity. Brain activity during phonological awareness tasks appeared to depend on a network of areas in left posterior superior temporal cortex (phonology and grapheme–phoneme translation) and inferior frontal gyrus (articulation). The level of the children's phonological skills modulated the amount of activity in this network. As noted earlier, the left posterior temporal sulcus was the primary area recruited by young children at the beginning of reading development. Therefore, neuroimaging data suggest that phonological recoding to sound rather than logographic recognition is the key early reading strategy. Activity in the inferior frontal gyrus increased with reading ability. This area is also a key phonological area (Broca's area), important for the motor production of speech. Left inferior frontal gyrus is also activated when deaf children perform phonological awareness tasks silently in fMRI studies (MacSweeney et al. 2005).

An fMRI study of 119 typically developing readers aged from 7 years to 17 years by Shaywitz and colleagues found a similar developmental pattern (Shaywitz et al. 2007). Instead of the false font task, this study used a rhyme decision task (e.g., 'do these items rhyme?': leat, kete), and a visual line orientation task (e.g., 'Do [\\V] and [\\V] match?'). Shaywitz and his colleagues reported that networks in both left and right superior and middle frontal regions were more active in younger readers, with activity declining as reading developed. In contrast, activity in the left anterior lateral occipitotemporal region increased. This region includes the putative visual word form area (VWFA). Hence, both Turkeltaub et al. (2003) and Shaywitz et al. (2007) found decreased right hemisphere involvement as reading developed, but found this for somewhat different neural networks. The difference in the behavioural tasks used (e.g., false font versus rhyme judgement) may explain some of these differences.

Overall, therefore, current neuroimaging data support a 'single route' model of reading development, based on a process of developing orthographic–phonological connections at different grain sizes (Ziegler and Goswami 2006). Reading is founded in phonology from the beginning (Goswami and Ziegler 2006b). The VWFA becomes more active as reading develops, reflecting the development of an orthographic lexicon containing both whole words and fragments of familiar words such as orthographic rimes (Pugh 2006). The VWFA is not a logographic or visual lexicon, able to support 'Chinese' processing or the 'direct route' from printed word to meaning postulated by 'dual-route' theory. Neuroimaging studies of typically developing readers show that the neural networks for spoken language play an important developmental role in reading from the outset.

Neuroimaging studies of dyslexia

The networks recruited for reading

Neuroimaging studies of adult readers with developmental dyslexia suggest that there is a typical activation in the three important neural sites for reading, namely the left posterior temporal regions, the left inferior frontal regions and the left occipitotemporal regions (such as the VWFA). These data suggest both problems with the phonological aspects of reading and with the efficient development of an orthographic lexicon (e.g., Brunswick et al. 1999). These fMRI and PET studies typically rely on tasks such as word and nonsense word reading (e.g., 'valley', 'carrot', 'vassey', 'cassot'), and the 'false font' task. Again, the experimental picture is largely one of convergence across orthographies. For example, adult dyslexics in Italian, French and English all showed activation of a left-lateralised neural network based around posterior inferior temporal areas and middle occipital gyrus (Paulesu et al. 2001). This was a cross-language comparison within one study. However, issues of experimental design become critical when comparing individual imaging studies across languages. When studying any kind of disability, it is crucial to equate participant groups for their overall ability in the actual tasks being used to acquire the neuroimaging data. For example, it is impossible to interpret group differences in brain activity if the dyslexics are worse at reading the nonsense words being used than the control adults. In this case, differences in neural activation could simply reflect different skill levels (i.e., behavioural differences in reading performance). Similarly, it is critical to use the same criteria for acquiring images of the brain in different studies if interpretations about cross-language differences are being drawn (e.g., Ziegler 2005). Otherwise, apparent language-based differences could simply reflect differences in the significance thresholds or other experimental criteria used to acquire the images by different research groups.

Neuroimaging studies of children with developmental dyslexia report a very similar pattern to adult data (e.g., Shaywitz et al. 2002, 2007; Simos et al. 2000). For example,

Shaywitz et al. (2002) studied 70 children with dyslexia aged on average 13 years, and compared them to 74 11-year-old typically developing controls (although the controls were not matched for reading level). Using fMRI, the children were scanned while performing a variety of reading-related tasks. These were letter identification (e.g., are t and V the same letter?); single letter rhyme (e.g., do V and C rhyme?); non-word rhyming (e.g., do leat and jete rhyme?); and reading for meaning (e.g., are corn and rice in the same semantic category?). Brain activity in each condition was contrasted with activity in a baseline condition, the line orientation task (e.g., do [\\V] and [\\V] match?). Shaywitz et al. (2002) reported that the children with developmental dyslexia showed under-activation in the core left temporoparietal networks, with older dyslexics showing over-activation in right inferior frontal gyrus. The children with developmental dyslexia also showed increased activation in right temporoparietal networks. One drawback of the study, however, was that there were group differences in behavioural performance in some of the component tasks. In the non-word rhyming measure, for example, the controls (79%) were significantly better than the children with dyslexia (59%). This means that some of the differences found in brain activation could reflect differing levels of expertise rather than differences core to having developmental dyslexia. In a subsequent study of an expanded sample, Shaywitz et al. (2007) used in-magnet non-word reading ability as a covariate to control for this problem. Shaywitz et al. compared 113 dyslexic children aged 7–18 years to the 119 typically developing readers discussed above in the non-word rhyme and visual line orientation tasks. Compared to the typically developing children, the dyslexic children showed no age-related increase in the activity of the VWTA. Instead, activity in the left inferior frontal gyrus (speech articulation) and the left posterior medial occipitotemporal system both increased, and reading did not become left-lateralized, with continued right hemisphere involvement.

There are also a few studies in the literature exploring the neural networks recruited for reading by dyslexic children in other languages. A study of 13 German dyslexic children aged 14–16 years was reported by Kronbichler et al. (2006). They used a sentence verification task (e.g., 'A flower needs water – TRUE), in an fMRI design, to try and replicate natural reading. A false font task provided the control task. Consistent with studies of English dyslexics, they found reduced activation of left occipitotemporal networks and increased activation of left inferior frontal areas. A study of eight Chinese children with developmental dyslexia reported by Siok et al. (2004) claimed biological disunity, however. Their fMRI study used a homophone judgement task, in which the children had to decide whether two different Chinese characters made the same sound (an English homophone is week – weak), and a character decision task, in which the children saw one Chinese character and had to decide whether it was a real word or not. The first task was intended to measure orthography–phonology connections, and the second orthography–semantic relations. Siok et al. (2004) reported that the Chinese dyslexics did not demonstrate the reduced activation in left temporoparietal regions that would typically be found in developmental dyslexia in English during the homophone judgement task. Instead, an area involved in visuo-spatial analysis showed reduced activity, the left middle frontal gyrus. Siok et al. (2004) used this latter finding to argue that the biological marker for developmental dyslexia in Chinese was reduced activation of left middle frontal gyrus. However, the design of this study does not yet permit this conclusion. A control group matched for reading level is also required. Reduced activation in left middle frontal gyrus when making homophone judgements in Chinese might be expected for the level of reading achieved by the children with dyslexia. If this were to be the case, then increased involvement of net-works for visuo-spatial analysis as reading develops would be part of typical reading development in Chinese, rather than a unique biological marker for developmental dyslexia.

Developmental differences in the time course of neural activation

While fMRI studies can provide important information about the neural networks sup-porting reading in typically developing versus dyslexic readers, they do not provide infor-mation about the time course of neural processing. This is important, as in typically developing readers, words are distinguished from non-words within around 180 ms, sug-gesting early contact with the VWFA and semantic sites. It seems likely that this process would be delayed in developmental dyslexia. Similarly, it seems possible that cognitive processes such as grapheme–phoneme conversion might take longer in developmental dyslexia.

A longitudinal study of 33 English-speaking children using magnetic source imaging (MSI) compared brain activation in a letter–sound task (the child sees a letter and has to provide its sound) and a simple non-word reading task (e.g., 'lan') at the end of kinder-garten and again at the end of grade 1 (Simos et al. 2005). Magnetic source imaging depends on a combination of magneto-encephalography (MEG) and MRI. The MEG measures the magnetic fields generated by the electrical activity in the brain rather than the electrical activity itself (the latter is measured by EEG). These magnetic fields are tiny; they are one billion times smaller than the magnetic field generated by the electricity in a lightbulb. By combining this information with MRI scans, both the time course and spa-tial localisation of brain activity is possible. Of the 33 children studied, 16 were thought to be at high risk of developing dyslexia.

Simos et al. (2005) reported that the high-risk group were significantly slower to show neural activity in response to both letters and non-words in kindergarten in the occipi-totemporal region (320 ms compared to 210 ms for those not at risk). The high-risk group also showed atypical activation in the left inferior frontal gyrus when performing the letter–sound task, with the onset of activity *increasing* from 603 ms in kindergarten to 786 ms in grade 1. The typically developing readers did not show this processing time increase. Comparing the onset of activity of the three core neural networks for reading, Simos et al. (2005) reported that low-risk children showed early activity in the left occipitotemporal regions, followed by activity in temporoparietal regions, predominantly in the left hemi-sphere, and then bilateral activity in inferior frontal regions. In contrast, high-risk children showed little differentiation in terms of the time course of activation between the occipi-totemporal and temporoparietal regions. High-risk children who were non-responsive to a phonological remediation package also being administered (*n* = 3) were distinct in show-ing earlier onset of activity in inferior frontal gyrus compared to the temporoparietal regions. Given the current dearth of time-course studies by other research groups in either English or in other languages, it is difficult to interpret these differences in terms of the cognitive components of reading. Nevertheless, Simos et al. (2005) comment that the increased inferior frontal activation probably reflects the role of compensatory articulatory processes. As noted earlier, deaf children also show increased inferior frontal activation during phonological processing tasks. This may indicate that children with phonological difficulties rely more heavily on networks for articulation when phonological processing is required.

The neural effects of remediation

Although there are a variety of remediation packages for dyslexic children based on different theories of developmental dyslexia, the most effective packages across languages appear to be those offering intensive phonological intervention (e.g., Bradley and Bryant 1983; Schneider, Roth, and Ennemoser 2000). Simos and his research group (2002) used magnetic source imaging to explore neural activation in eight children with developmental dyslexia who had received 80 hours of intensive training with such a package and who had shown significant benefits from the remediation (Simos et al. 2002). MSI scans were taken during a non-word rhyme matching task (e.g., 'yoat', 'wote') both before the intervention and following remediation. Simos et al. (2002) reported that prior to the intervention, the dyslexic children showed the expected hypoactivation of left temporoparietal regions. Following the intervention, all eight children showed a dramatic increase in the activation of left temporoparietal regions, predominantly in the left posterior superior temporal gyrus (the networks supporting grapheme–phoneme recoding in typically developing readers: see Turkeltaub et al. 2003). These activation profiles were very similar to those of eight controls who also participated in the MSI study, but who did not require remediation. Nevertheless, even after remediation, neural activity was delayed in the children with dyslexia relative to the controls. The peak in left superior temporal gyrus activity occurred at 837 ms on average for the dyslexic children, and at 600 ms for the controls. The data were taken to show a normalization of brain function with remediation. Nevertheless, Simos et al. (2002) commented that even with intensive remediation, children with dyslexia are slow to achieve the reading fluency shown by non-dyslexic children.

Shaywitz and Shaywitz (2005) used retrospective examination of the large sample of children with developmental dyslexia reported in Shaywitz et al. (2002) to compare the different developmental trajectories for children at risk for reading difficulties. Shaywitz and Shaywitz (2005) distinguished three groups within this sample when they were young adults. The first was a group of persistently poor readers (PPR), who had met criteria for poor reading in both the 2nd/3rd and the 9th/10th grades. The second was a group of accuracy-improved poor readers (AIR), who had met criteria for poor reading in the 2nd/3rd grades but who did not meet criteria in the 9th/10th grades. The third was a control group of non-impaired readers (C), who had never met criteria for poor reading (the participants had been studied since the age of 5 years). Shaywitz and Shaywitz (2005) reported that both the PPR and the AIR groups showed hypoactivation of the core left hemisphere sites when required to manipulate phonology. For example, in a nonsense word rhyming task, both groups of young adults still showed relative hypoactivity in neural networks in left superior temporal and occipitotemporal regions. However, the groups were distinguished by their neural activity when reading real words. The AIR group still demonstrated under-activation in the usual left posterior areas for real word reading, whereas the PPR group activated the left posterior regions to the same extent as controls (this was an unexpected finding).

Shaywitz and Shaywitz (2005) then carried out further analyses based on connectivity. Connectivity analyses examine the neural areas that are functionally connected to each other during reading. The connectivity analyses suggested that reading achievement depended on memory for the PPR group, and not on the normalised functioning of the left posterior regions. The unimpaired controls demonstrated functional connectivity between left hemisphere posterior and anterior reading systems, but the PPR group demonstrated functional connectivity between left hemisphere posterior regions and right prefrontal areas associated with working memory and memory retrieval. Shaywitz and Shaywitz (2005) speculated that the PPR group were reading primarily by memory. As the words used in the scanner were high-frequency, simple words, this is quite possible. However, this design choice complicates the interpretation of the neural differences found, as the PPR group may not be able to use memory strategies to read less frequent or less simple words. For such stimuli, the PPR and AIR groups may show similar neural profiles. It may also be important that the PPR group had, in general, lower IQ scores than the AIR group. Prospective longitudinal studies comparing patterns of neural activation and connectivity in dyslexic children as high-frequency words become over-learned would clearly be very valuable.

Different technologies, different research questions: the promise of brain imaging for understanding reading and developmental dyslexia

As will be clear from the foregoing review, most studies of reading development and of developmental dyslexia have relied on fMRI. These studies have provided excellent data regarding the neural networks underpinning reading in typically developing and dyslexic readers. They have also shown that the functional organisation of the networks for reading is similar in typical development and in dyslexia. Children with developmental dyslexia do not recruit radically different neural networks when they are reading. Rather, they show hypoactivation of crucial parts of the network of areas involved in word recognition, and an atypical pattern of continuing right hemisphere involvement. Although highly informative, these studies are essentially correlational studies. They can answer research questions about the neural demands made by learning to read in different languages, and they can answer research questions about the core neural systems involved for dyslexic and typically developing readers. They can also answer research questions about the patterns of connectivity between different neural networks. However, they cannot answer research questions about what 'goes wrong' in the dyslexic brain, although they can help to rule out hypotheses (e.g., about the visual basis of developmental dyslexia; see Eden and Zeffiro 1998).

Neuroimaging methods that provide data on the time course of neural processing, such as MEG (MSI) and EEG, can begin to answer causal questions. As might be expected, it has been shown using MSI that neural activation is delayed in core components of the network of areas recruited for reading by children at risk for dyslexia. However, behavioural studies showing that children with developmental dyslexia are slower to read words aloud make the same point. When EEG or MSI techniques show that core components of the reading network are activated in a different order in dyslexia compared to typical reading, this is more informative with respect to causality. For example, Simos and his colleagues have shown atypically earlier onset of activity in inferior frontal gyrus (articulation) compared to the temporoparietal regions in three children at high risk for dyslexia who appear to be non-respondent to a phonological remediation package. If robust with larger samples and diagnosed dyslexics, such findings could suggest that there are different neuro-developmental routes to word recognition for dyslexic children compared to controls. Nevertheless, these different neuro-developmental routes are not the cause of dyslexia. Rather, they illustrate the response of a dyslexic brain to being trained to learn to read.

In my view, the most informative studies with respect to causation in developmental dyslexia are longitudinal prospective studies that use brain imaging to study basic sensory processing in at-risk children, with a view to understanding the causes of the phonological deficit. Here, the most promising studies to date are those investigating basic auditory processing using methodologies sensitive to the time course of auditory processing at the millisecond level. For example, a large-scale Finnish study (the Jyväskylä Longitudinal Study of Dyslexia (JLD): see Lyytinen et al. 2004a) has followed babies at familial risk for dyslexia since birth. A large variety of behavioural and EEG measures has been taken as the children have developed. EEG measures of auditory sensory processing (evoked response potentials to speech and non-speech cues) have been found to distinguish the at-risk babies from controls even during infancy (e.g., Lyytinen et al. 2005). For example, infants at risk for developmental dyslexia were less sensitive to the auditory cue of duration at six months of age (Richardson et al. 2003). The infant participants had to discriminate between two bisyllabic speech-like stimuli with a varying silent interval (e.g. 'ata' versus 'atta'). Duration discrimination was still impaired when the same children were 6.5 years of age (Lyytinen et al. 2004b).

English children with developmental dyslexia are also impaired in this duration discrimination task (Richardson et al. 2004). In addition, English children are impaired in discriminating the rise time of amplitude envelopes at onset, which is an important auditory cue to the onset of syllables in the speech stream (Goswami et al. 2002; Richardson et al. 2004). Finnish adults with developmental dyslexia also show rise time processing impairments, and individual differences in rise time sensitivity predicted up to 35% of unique variance in phonological tasks like rhyme recognition (Hämäläinen et al. 2005). In the English studies, individual differences in rise time sensitivity predict unique variance in both phonological awareness measures (around 20%: Richardson et al. 2004) and in reading and spelling measures (around 25%: Goswami et al. 2002). We are currently collecting EEG data comparing rise time discrimination in English children with and without dyslexia. Data so far suggest that children with developmental dyslexia indeed show atypical auditory processing of rise time stimuli, with Nl amplitude (an EEG measure of sound registration) failing to reduce as amplitude envelope rise times become extended (Thomson, Baldeweg, and Goswami 2005). This suggests that neural responses in the dyslexic brain do not distinguish between different rise times, at least for the auditory processing comparisons used in our study (15 ms versus 90 ms rise times).

Conclusion

Different neuroimaging methodologies contribute complementary data regarding the neural networks underpinning reading acquisition and developmental dyslexia. While fMRI studies can identify the core neural systems involved in reading, EEG and MEG methodologies are required to investigate the time course of activation of the different networks that contribute to word recognition, and to investigate potential sensory precursors of the phonological deficit. With respect to key questions in education, each neuroimaging method can contribute different kinds of data. For example, when evaluating the claims made for different kinds of remediation package for developmental dyslexia, fMRI will be useful in assessing whether interventions affect the core neural networks for reading, or affect a different kind of network (e.g., motivational systems). When evaluating claims that the core cognitive difficulty in developmental dyslexia lies in forming a high-quality phonological representation, methodologies that can explore the time course of sensory processing such as EEG will be most useful. Neuroimaging methods are of optimal use when they can provide experimental data that is not available from behavioural investigations. For example, it is possible in principle to identify neural markers of risk for developmental dyslexia that can be measured in pre-verbal infants and in older children without requiring their explicit attention (Szücs and Goswami 2007). It is these areas of neuroscience that are likely to be of most potential benefit to educators.

References

Baron, J. 1979. Orthographic and word-specific mechanisms in children's reading of words. *Child Development* 50: 60–72.

Bradley, L., and P.E. Bryant. 1983. Categorising sounds and learning to read: A causal connection. *Nature* 310: 419–21.

Brunswick, N., E. McCrory, C.J. Price, C.D. Frith, and U. Frith. 1999. Explicit and implicit processing of words and pseudowords by adult developmental dyslexics: A search for Wernicke's Wortschatz. *Brain* 122: 1901–17.

Cohen, L., and S. Dehaene. 2004. Specialization within the ventral stream: The case for the visual word form area. *NeuroImage* 22: 466–76.

Conrad, R. 1979. *The deaf school child.* London: Harper & Row.

Csepe, V., and D. Szucs. 2003. Number word reading as a challenging task in dyslexia? An ERP study. *International Journal of Psychophysiology* 51: 69–83.

De Cara, B., and U. Goswami. 2002. Statistical analysis of similarity relations among spoken words: Evidence for the special status of rimes in English. *Behavioural Research Methods and Instrumentation* 34, no. 3: 416–23.

Dollaghan, C.A. 1994. Children's phonological neighbourhoods: Half empty or half full? *Journal of Child Language* 21: 257–71.

Eden. G.F., and T.A. Zeffiro. 1998. Neural systems affected in developmental dyslexia revealed by functional neuroimaging. *Neuron* 21: 279–82.

Goswami, U., J. Thomson, U. Richardson, R. Stainthorp, D. Hughes, S. Rosen et al. 2002. Amplitude envelope onsets and developmental dyslexia: A new hypothesis. *Proceedings of the National Academy of Sciences of the United States of America* 99: 10911–16.

Goswami, U., and J.C. Ziegler 2006a. Fluency, phonology and morphology: A response to the commentaries on becoming literate in different languages. *Developmental Science* 9, no. 5: 451–3.

Goswami, U., and J.C. Ziegler 2006b. A developmental perspective on the neural code for written words. *Trends in Cognitive Sciences* 10, no. 4: 142–3.

Hämäläinen, J., P.H.T Leppanen, M. Torppa, K. Muller, and H. Lyytinen. 2005. Detection of sound rise time by adults with dyslexia. *Brain and Language* 94: 32–42.

Harris, M., and J.R. Beech 1998. Implicit phonological awareness and early reading development in prelingually deaf children. *Journal of Deaf Studies and Deaf Education* 3, no. 3: 205–16.

Hinshelwood, J.A. 1896. A case of dyslexia: A peculiar form of word-blindness. *Lancet* 2: 1451.

Kim, J., and C. Davis. 2004. Characteristics of poor readers of Korean Hangul: Auditory, visual and phonological processing. *Reading and Writing* 17, no. 1–2: 153–85.

Kronbichler, M., et al. 2006. Evidence for a dysfunction of left posterior reading areas in German dyslexic readers. *Neuropsychologia* 44: 1822–32.

Lyytinen, H., T. Ahonen. and T. Guttorm, et al. 2004a. Early development of children at familial risk for dyslexia. Follow-up from birth to school age. *Dyslexia* 10: 146–78.

Lyytinen, H., M. Aro, and K. Eklund. et al. 2004b. The development of children at familial risk for dyslexia: Birth to school age. *Annals of Dyslexia* 5, no. 4: 185–220.

Lyytinen. H., et al. 2005. Psychophysiology of developmental dyslexia: A review of findings including studies of children at risk for dyslexia. *Journal of Neurolinguistics* 18: 167–95.

MacSweeney, M., D. Waters, M. Brammer, B. Woll, and U. Goswami. 2005. Phonological processing of speech and sign in the deaf brain'. Poster presented at the Cognitive Neuroscience Society, March, New York.

Paulesu, E., et al. 2001. Dyslexia: Cultural diversity and biological unity. *Science* 291, no. 5511: 2165–7.

Porpodas, C.D. 1999. Patterns of phonological and memory processing in beginning readers and spellers of Greek. *Journal of Learning Disabilities* 32: 406–16.

Port, R. 2006. The graphical basis of phones and phonemes. In *Second language speech learning: The role of language experience in speech perception and production,* ed. M. Munro, and O. Schwen-Bohm. Amsterdam: John Benjamins.

Price, C.J., M.-L. Gorno-Tempini, K.S. Graham, N. Biggio, A. Mechelli, K. Patterson, and U. Noppeney. 2003. Normal and pathological reading: Converging data from lesion and imaging studies. *NeuroImage* 20, suppl. 1: S30–S41.

Price, C.J., and E. McCrory. 2005. Functional brain imaging studies of skilled reading and developmental dyslexia. In *The science of reading: A handbook,* ed, M.J. Snowling and C. Hulme. 473–96. Oxford: Blackwell.

Pugh, K. 2006. A neurocognitive overview of reading acquisition and dyslexia across languages. *Developmental Science* 9: 448–50.

Richardson, U., P.H.T. Leppänen, M. Leiwo, and H. Lyytinen. 2003. Speech perception of infants with high familial risk for dyslexia differ at the age of 6 months. *Developmental Neuropsychology* 23: 385–97.

Richardson, U., I. Thomson, S.K. Scott, and U. Goswami. 2004. Auditory processing skills and phonological representation in dyslexic children. *Dyslexia: An International Journal of Research and Practice* 10, no. 3: 215–33.

Rumsey, I. M., B. Horwilz. B.C. Donohue, K. Nace, J.M. Maisog, and P. Andreason. 1997. Phonological and orthographic components of word recognition: A PET rCBF study. *Brain* 120: 739–59.

Sandler, W., and D. Lillo-Martin. 2006. *Sign language and linguistic universals.* Cambridge: Cambridge University Press.

Sauseng. P., J. Bergmann. and H. Wimmer. 2004. When does the brain register deviances from standard word spellings. An ERP study. *Cognitive Brain Research* 20: 520–32.

Schneider, W., F. Roth, and E. Ennemoser. 2000. Training phonological skills and letter knowledge in children at-risk for dyslexia. A comparison of three kindergarten intervention programs. *Journal of Educational Psychology* 92: 84–95.

Share, D., and I. Levin. 1999. Learning to read and write in Hebrew. In *Learning to read and write: A cross-linguistic perspective.* In *Cambridge Studies in Cognitive and Perceptual Development,* ed. M. Harris and G. Hatano. 89–111. New York: Cambridge University Press.

Shaywitz, B.A., et al. 2002. Disruption of posterior brain systems for reading in children with developmental dyslexia. *Biological Psychiatry* 52, no. 2: 101–10.

Shaywitz, B.A., et al. 2007. Age-related changes in reading systems of dyslexic children. *Annals of Neurology* 61: 363–70.

Shaywitz, S.E., and B.A. Shaywitz. 2005. Dyslexia (specific reading disability). *Biological Psychiatry* 57: 1301–9.

Simos, P.G., J.I. Breier. J.M. Fletcher, E. Bergman, and A.C. Papanicolaou. 2000. Cerebral mechanisms involved in word reading in dyslexic children: A magnetic source imaging approach. *Cerebral Cortex* 10: 809–16.

Simos, P.G., et al. 2002. Dyslexia-specific brain activation profile becomes normal following successful remedial training. *Neurology* 58: 1203–13.

Simos, P.G., et al. 2005. Early development of neurophysiological processes involved in normal reading and reading disability: A magnetic source imaging study. *Neuropsychology* 19, no. 6: 787–98.

Siok, W.T., C.A. Perfetti, Z. Jin, and L.H. Tan. 2004. Biological abnormality of impaired reading is constrained by culture. *Nature* 43: 71–6.

Snowling, M.J. 2000. *Dyslexia.* Oxford: Blackwell.

Stein, J., and V. Walsh. 1997. To see but not to read: The magnocellular theory of dyslexia. *Trends in Neuroscience* 20: 147–52.

Stuart, M. 2006. Teaching reading: Why start with systematic phonics teaching? *Psychology of Education Review* 30, no. 2: 6–17.

Stuart. M., and M. Coltheart. 1988. Does reading develop in a sequence of stages? *Cognition* 30: 139–81.

Szücs, D., and U. Goswami. 2007. Educational Neuroscience: Defining a new discipline for the study of mental representations. *Mind, Brain and Education* 1, no. 3: 114–27.

Tan, L.H., A.R. Laird, K. Li, and P.T. Fox. 2005. Neuroanatomical correlates of phonological processing of Chinese characters and alphabetic words. A meta-analysis. *Human Brain Mapping* 25, no. 1: 83–91.

Thomson, J.M., T. Baldeweg, and U. Goswami. 2005. 'Developmental trajectories of auditory perception in dyslexia: an ERP study'. Poster presented at the 1st Course, International School on Mind, Brain and Education, July, Sicily, Italy.

Turkeltaub, P.E., L. Gareau, D.L. Flowers, T.A. Zeffiro. and G.F. Eden. 2003. Development of neural mechanisms for reading. *Nature Neuroscience* 6, no. 6: 767–73.

Wimmer, H. 1996. The nonword reading deficit in developmental dyslexia: Evidence from children learning to read German. *Journal of Experimental Child Psychology* 61: 80–90.

Ziegler, J.C. 2005. Do differences in brain activation challenge universal theories of dyslexia? *Brain and Language* 98: 341–3.

Ziegler, J.C., and U. Goswami. 2005. Reading acquisition, developmental dyslexia, and skilled reading across languages: a psycholinguistic grain size theory. *Psychological Bulletin* 131, no. 1: 3–29.

Ziegler, J.C., and U. Goswami. 2006. Becoming literate in different languages: similar problems, different solutions. *Developmental Science* 9, no. 5: 429–53.

2

Connecting Early Language and Literacy to Later Reading (Dis)abilities: Evidence, Theory, and Practice

Hollis S. Scarborough

As recently as 20 years ago, learning to read was not thought to commence until formal instruction was provided in school. Accordingly, reading disabilities were largely considered to be an educational problem with no known antecedents at earlier ages. It is now abundantly clear that reading acquisition is a process that begins early in the preschool period, such that children arrive at school having acquired vastly differing degrees of knowledge and skill pertaining to literacy. Attention has thus turned to whether preschool differences in language and literacy development are reliable prognostic indicators, and perhaps direct causes, of later reading (dis)abilities. I review and discuss the available evidence from longitudinal research that has examined such issues, with particular attention to at-risk populations such as offspring of parents with reading disability and preschoolers diagnosed with early language impairments.

The multifaceted nature of reading and its acquisition

Skilled readers are able to derive meaning from printed text accurately and efficiently. Research has shown that in doing so, they fluidly coordinate many component skills, each of which has been sharpened through instruction and experience over many years. Figure 2.1 illustrates the major 'strands' that are woven together during the course of becoming a skilled reader. It is customary to consider separately the strands involved in recognizing individual printed words from those involved in comprehending the meaning of the string of words that have been identified, even though those two processes operate (and develop) interactively rather than independently. (For a fuller review of this material, see the recent report of the Committee on the Prevention of Reading Difficulties in Young Children, 1998.)

Most children who have trouble learning to read in the early school years stumble in mastering the 'word recognition' strands. In English orthography, the spellings of spoken words are governed largely by the 'alphabetic principle,' the notion that our written

From: Neuman, S.B. and Dickinson, D.K. (eds) *Handbook of Early Literature Research,* pp. 97–110 (New York: Guilford Press, 2001).

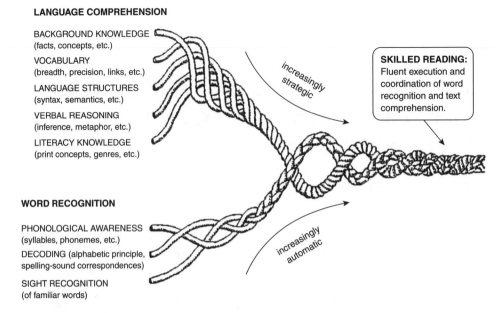

LANGUAGE COMPREHENSION

BACKGROUND KNOWLEDGE
(facts, concepts, etc.)

VOCABULARY
(breadth, precision, links, etc.)

LANGUAGE STRUCTURES
(syntax, semantics, etc.)

VERBAL REASONING
(inference, metaphor, etc.)

LITERACY KNOWLEDGE
(print concepts, genres, etc.)

increasingly strategic

SKILLED READING:
Fluent execution and
coordination of word
recognition and text
comprehension.

WORD RECOGNITION

PHONOLOGICAL AWARENESS
(syllables, phonemes, etc.)

DECODING (alphabetic principle,
spelling-sound correspondences)

SIGHT RECOGNITION
(of familiar words)

increasingly automatic

Figure 2.1   Illustration of the many strands that are woven together in skilled reading

symbols (letters or graphemes) systematically represent the smallest meaningful speech elements (phonemes) that make up the pronunciation of a word. It stands to reason that grasping the alphabetic principle will be difficult if a child does not yet appreciate that spoken words consist of phonemes, because without this 'phonemic awareness' the child cannot truly understand what letters stand for (Liberman, 1973).

Recognizing printed words further requires that one learn and apply the many correspondences between particular letters and phonemes, so that the pronunciation of a printed word can be figured out ('decoded'); matching the derived pronunciation to stored information about spoken words in one's mental lexicon enables the identity of the printed word to be recognized. Phonological decoding is the most reliable guide to word recognition, but there are also plenty of exceptions (words such as 'of,' 'two,' 'choir,' and 'yacht') whose spellings must, wholly or in part, be memorized outright. Finally, skilled reading requires that the processes involved in word recognition become so well practiced that they can proceed extremely quickly and almost effortlessly, freeing up the reader's cognitive resources for comprehension processes.

Although most reading disabilities are associated with deficits in phonemic awareness, decoding, and sight recognition of printed words, reading skill can also be seriously impeded by weaknesses in the 'comprehension' strands, particularly beyond second grade when reading materials become more complex. Even if the pronunciations of all the letter strings in a passage are correctly decoded, the text will not be well comprehended if the child (1) does not know the words in their spoken form, (2) cannot parse the syntactic and semantic relationships among the words, or (3) lacks critical background knowledge or inferential skills to interpret the text appropriately and 'read between the lines.' Note that in such instances, 'reading comprehension' deficits are essentially *oral* language limitations.

A daunting fact about reading (dis)abilities is that differences among schoolchildren in their levels of reading achievement show strong stability over time, despite remedial efforts that are usually made to strengthen the skills of lower achievers. (For a review, see Scarborough, 1998). Only about 5–10% of children who read satisfactorily in the primary grades ever stumble later, and 65–75% of children designated as reading disabled early on continue to read poorly throughout their school careers (and beyond). In light of this continuity, there has been increasing interest in whether children at risk for reading disabilities might be identifiable at early ages, so that steps could be taken to prevent or ameliorate their difficulties in learning to read in school. Of course, early intervention requires that we know what early signs to look for in order to identify which preschoolers are most likely to develop reading disabilities. That topic is reviewed next.

Predicting reading achievement from kindergarten measures

Most research on the prediction of future reading abilities has involved samples who were first tested just prior to the start of schooling (in the United States, usually in the kindergarten year) and who were then followed up after having received 1 or 2 years of reading instruction. In a recent meta-analysis (Scarborough, 1998), I examined the findings from 61 samples, in which a wide variety of predictors had been used by the researchers. Table 2.1 summarizes those results for three sets of skill variables: those involving the processing of print itself, assessments of various facets of oral language proficiency, and measures of nonverbal skills.

Table 2.1 Average correlations between kindergarten predictor variables and later reading scores, based on a meta-analysis of findings from 61 research samples

Predictor variable	No. of samples	Mean *r*	Median *r*
Measures requiring the processing of print			
Rudimentary reading: letter–sound knowledge or entire 'readiness' battery	21	.57	.56
Letter identification: naming of upper and lower-case letters	24	.52	.52
Print concepts: familiarity with the mechanics and purposes of book reading	7	.46	.49
Measures of oral language proficiency			
General language index: expressive and receptive skills	4	.46	.47
Phonological awareness	27	.46	.42
Expressive ('naming') vocabulary	5	.45	.49
Sentence or story recall	11	.45	.49
Rapid serial naming speed	14	.38	.40
Verbal IQ	12	.37	.38
Receptive language (syntactic)	9	$\leq$.37	.40
Receptive vocabulary	20	.33	.38
Expressive language skills	11	.32	.37

(Continued)

Table 2.1   (Continued)

Predictor variable	No. of samples	Mean *r*	Median *r*
Verbal memory (digit or word list recall)	18	.33	.33
Receptive language (semantic)	11	.24	.25
Speech production (pronunciation accuracy)	4	—	.25
Speech perception (phoneme discrimination)	11	.22	.23
Measures of nonverbal abilities			
Visual memory	8	.31	.28
Nonverbal IQ	8	.26	.25
Motor skills	5	.25	.26
Visual discrimination	5	.22	.20
Visual–motor integration	6	.16	.13

Note. Data from Scarborough (1998).

It is reassuring that the results from prediction studies dovetail nicely with what has been learned from research on the cognitive requirements of skilled reading and the acquisition of its various 'strands'. That is, although visual and motor skills of entering students have been a traditional focus of readiness testing, performance on such nonverbal tasks actually provides little prognostic information about future reading difficulties. On the other hand, rudimentary skills that tie in to the 'word recognition' strands – especially letter identification and phonological awareness – are among the best predictor measures. Likewise, early differences in the sorts of verbal abilities that make up the 'comprehension' strands – most notably vocabulary, sentence/story recall, and concepts of print – have also been reliable predictors of later reading.

On average, however, the correlations of individual kindergarten predictor measures with future reading achievement are not nearly as strong ($r \leq .57$) as the correlations between first- or second-grade reading scores and those earned 1 to 4 years later ($r = .75$). In efforts to improve predictive accuracy, some researchers have combined kindergarten predictor variables to compute a multiple correlation with reading outcome scores in their samples. When this has been done, the results (mean $R = .75$) suggest that the predictability of future reading ability is about as strong from kindergarten onward as it is from grade to grade once formal reading instruction has commenced.

In short, the results of kindergarten prediction studies suggest that the important cognitive–linguistic strands that must be coordinated in learning to read are rather securely in place before formal school instruction begins, such that children who arrive at school with weaker verbal abilities and literacy knowledge are much more likely than their classmates to experience difficulties in learning to read during the primary grades. This raises the next question: How far back in development can the roots of the various strands be traced?

Predicting reading from infant and preschool measures

Developmental relationships between language and literacy abilities have been studied from early ages in three kinds of samples: preschoolers with early language impairments, offspring of adults with reading disabilities, and unselected samples of infants or preschoolers. These studies of younger children are particularly valuable because, unlike most kindergarten prediction research, the children's progress has typically been observed over several years prior to the start of schooling. Such longitudinal research makes it possible to discern developmental patterns in the acquisition of reading-related skills that may both shed light on theoretical questions and provide a foundation for designing early diagnostic and preventive programs. Very briefly, the highlights of each body of work are as follows.

Early language impairment

Several dozen follow-up studies have been conducted to look at the short- and long-range outcomes of preschoolers who were diagnosed (and, in most cases, treated) at speech-language clinics (e.g., Aram & Hall, 1989; Bishop & Adams, 1990; Catts, Fey, & Tomblin, 1997; Rescorla, 1999; Stothard, Snowling, Bishop, Chipchase, & Kaplan, 1998). Virtually every such study has confirmed that preschoolers with language impairments are indeed at considerable risk for developing reading disabilities (as well as for continued oral language difficulties) at older ages.

Family incidence of reading disability

The fact that reading disabilities tend to 'run in families' has been established for nearly a century, with higher incidence noted among the relatives of affected schoolchildren than in the families of their normally achieving classmates. Although family aggregation had not previously been examined in a prospective way, I reasoned that having a parent or older sibling with a reading disability should place a preschooler at risk for experiencing similar difficulties, and that if there are some early antecedents to reading disabilities, these could be discovered by following such at-risk youngsters from an early age. Accordingly, I undertook such a study in 1979 and showed that offspring of parents with reading problems were indeed at much higher risk for difficulty in learning to read, and that these children differed on language measures from otherwise-similar peers at ages as young as 30 months (Scarborough, 1989, 1990, 1991a, b; Scarborough, Dobrich, & Hager, 1991). Recently, outcome results for several similar studies have been reported that tend to converge with these findings (Byrne et al., 1998; Elbro, 1999; Gallagher, Frith & Snowling, 1999; Lyytinen et al., 1999; Pennington, Lefly, & Boada, 1999). Risk estimates depend, of course, on the criteria used to diagnose reading disabilities in adults and children; averaging across studies, approximately 40% of offspring of affected parents, but less than 10% of other children (of otherwise similar backgrounds), develop a reading disability (Scarborough, 1998).

Unselected infant/preschool samples

Rather than looking at particular at-risk populations, some researchers have sought to examine preschool differences in relation to future prereading and reading skills in entire groups of children from the same preschools or birth cohorts (e.g., Bryant, Maclean, Bradley, & Crossland, 1990; Maclean, Bryant, & Bradley, 1987; Molfese, 1999; Shapiro et al., 1990; Walker, Greenwood, Hart, & Carta, 1994; Whitehurst, 1999). As in the research on selected at-risk pre-school samples, these studies have found reliable associations between early abilities and later prereading skills and/or reading achievement.

Findings in common

Although it is customary to review these three bodies of literature separately, here I want to focus on the commonalities among their findings. In reading these various literatures over the years, I have been struck by the fact that the relationship between early language and literacy development and later reading achievement has appeared to be similar in many respects and not contradictory in any major way, despite the differing goals and sampling procedures of the three kinds of studies. What follows is a list of some empirical results that have been observed in at least two of the three kinds of research samples. (There is a wealth of additional detail to be found in each individual investigation, but a comprehensive review of that material is beyond the scope of this chapter.)

1. In these studies of younger children, as in the kindergarten prediction research summarized earlier, nonverbal skills generally have been unrelated to concurrent or future language and literacy levels, whereas verbal skills have been much better predictors. Even in infancy (birth to age 2 years), pediatric ratings of language milestones predict later reading achievement better than do perceptual-motor indices (Shapiro et al., 1990). Similarly, recent studies have found that electrophysiological responses of infants' brains to language – but not nonverbal – stimuli are correlated with language and reading abilities in subsequent years (Lyytinen et al., 1999; Molfese, 1999).

2. Somewhat surprisingly, in most cases, the magnitudes of the longer-term correlations between preschool language abilities (at ages 2 to 4 years) and school-age outcomes have been about as large as the corresponding shorter-term associations (in Table 2.1) between kindergarten scores and subsequent achievement.

3. During the preschool period, most verbal skills have tended to be well correlated with each other, both concurrently and predictively (e.g., Anthony, Lonigan, Dyer, & Bloomfield, 1997; Chaney, 1992; Rescorla, 1999; Scarborough, 1990, 1991a, b) and have been good prospective predictors of kindergarten-age differences in phonological awareness, letter knowledge, print concepts, and other relevant skills (e.g., Bryant et al., 1989, 1990; Byrne et al., 1998; Lonigan, Burgess, Anthony, & Barker, 1998; Scarborough, 1990; Whitehurst, 1999) as well as with subsequent reading achievement. These predictive correlations have often tended to be weaker for measures of speech than for other aspects of language production and for measures of receptive rather than expressive language (e.g., Bryant et al., 1989, 1990; Chaney, 1992; Gallagher et al., 1999; Lonigan et al., 1998; Pennington et al., 1999; Shapiro et al., 1990).

4. When several domains of developing language (phonological, syntactic, lexical, etc.) have been examined within a sample, the successful predictors of future reading abilities usually have not been confined to a single linguistic domain (e.g., Catts, Fey, Zhang & Tomblin, 1999; Rescorla, 1999; Scarborough, 1989, 1990; Walker et al., 1994). It is often the case, furthermore, that reading outcomes have been best predicted by different sets of language variables at different ages within longitudinal samples (e.g., Gallagher, Frith, & Snowling, 1999; Lyytinen et al., 999). Figure 2.2, which shows some findings from my longitudinal sample,

illustrates this phenomenon. At the youngest ages, syntactic and speech production abilities were most deficient, relative to those of the comparison group, in the group of youngsters who subsequently developed reading disabilities. Later in the preschool period, however, the groups differed instead in vocabulary and phonological awareness skills.

5. Similarly, when longitudinal data have been examined for individual children with weak early language skills, deficit profiles have actually been observed to change over time within individuals during the preschool years (e.g., Bishop & Edmundson, 1987; Scarborough & Dobrich, 1990). For example, a 3-year-old with across-the-board weaknesses in syntactic, lexical, and phonological skills might show a narrower range of deficits (e.g., in just one domain) a year later.

6. Even when their early language deficits have lessened considerably in severity (or have disappeared entirely) by the time of school entry, children with a family history of reading disability and/or a history of early language impairment nonetheless remain at high risk for developing reading problems at a later age (Fey, Catts, & Larrivee, 1995; Rescorla, 1999; Scarborough & Dobrich, 1990; Stothard et al., 1998).

7. Despite the relationship that has been found between preschool language problems and school-age reading problems, exceptions to this trend have been seen in every sample. That is, some children with early language deficits did not develop reading disabilities, and some children who became poor readers had not appeared to be behind in their preschool language development.

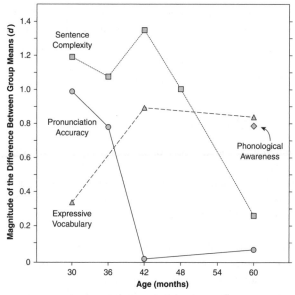

Figure 2.2   Changes over time in the aspects of language that differentiated preschoolers who became disabled readers from those who did not (Scarborough, 1990, 1991a). Effect sizes for the differences between the group means are shown for sentence complexity (Index of Productive Syntax), expressive vocabulary (Boston Naming Test), pronunciation accuracy (percentage of consonants correctly produced) and phonological awareness (matching of rhymes and initial phonemes).

Taken all together, these results suggest that there is a great deal of continuity between early developmental differences and later ones. On the other hand, the data also suggest that the pattern of across-age continuities is not entirely simple or straight forward but, instead, presents some complexities that might be overlooked were it not for the fact that these phenomena have been observed by different researchers in various kinds of samples. Some implications of these common findings for theory and practice are discussed next.

Theoretical issues: present and future

All the research reviewed previously has concerned the issue of how language development is related to the acquisition of literacy. Various researchers have recast and narrowed this broad question in different ways, such as: What are the consequences of early language impairment? Are preschool language disorders and later reading disabilities two manifestations (differing, perhaps, in severity) of the same clinical condition at different ages? What are the preschool antecedents of reading disability, and which ones play a causal role in its development? What preschool developments are necessary and sufficient for successful reading acquisition? And so forth. Although these differences in emphasis have guided the selection of research subjects by various investigators, the data from all such studies are pertinent to explaining language–literacy connections of all sorts. For that reason, I feel that looking at the commonalities among findings is helpful in addressing theoretical issues.

Given the wealth of evidence now available from longitudinal studies of early language and literacy, one would think that clear answers to the questions of interest would be rather easy to derive. This is not the case, however. Why has it been so difficult to answer these questions? There are undoubtedly a host of reasons. Here, I want to focus on a few factors that, in my opinion, may have impeded the derivation of firm conclusions from the extant data.

Correlation versus causality

We all have been taught that the existence of a relationship between two variables does not mean that one variable necessarily causes the other. Establishing causation requires experimental research in which it is demonstrated that manipulating the presumed cause (X) does indeed lead to changes in the presumed effect (Y). Such an experimental result, moreover, does not rule out the possibility of reciprocal, rather than just unidirectional, causation (i.e., that Y simultaneously exerts a causal influence on X).

With regard to reading disabilities, experimental training studies with beginning students have shown that there is a reciprocal causal relationship between attaining phonological awareness and learning to decode print (Ehri & Wilce, 1980; Perfetti, Beck, Bell, & Hughes, 1987). For the other verbal abilities that are good predictors of future reading achievement from kindergarten age (Table 2.1) or earlier, however, little evidence is available yet to determine their causal status. Some language skills may indeed play a causal role in the development of reading, but some may only be 'correlates' or 'markers' that are characteristic of children who will have trouble learning to read but that are not the reason those children have difficulty. In fact, there are indications that preschool training that successfully ameliorates early speech/language impairments is not effective in reducing such children's risk for later reading problems, as it ought to be if those language weaknesses are a causal impediment to learning to read (Fey et al., 1995; Stark et al., 1984).

At present, the most widely held view as to the cause of reading disabilities is that affected children have a core phonological deficit (often of constitutional, usually genetic, origin) that impedes the development of phonemic awareness and hence interferes with discovering the alphabetic principle and with learning to decode (e.g., Liberman, Shankweiler, & Liberman, 1989; Stanovich & Siegel, 1994). Powerful and parsimonious though this theory is, it has been challenged for failing to account readily for several empirical trends. For example, training programs designed in accordance with the phonological deficit hypothesis have not been completely effective in preventing and treating reading disabilities (e.g., Torgesen, Wagner, & Rashotte, 1997). Also, some children who successfully overcome their initial difficulties in learning to decode in response to such instruction nevertheless start to fall behind again in reading at a later point (Slavin et al., 1996). Of greater relevance to our preschool focus [...] are the correlational data reviewed earlier. That is, several facets of verbal ability other than phonological awareness have been shown to be equally strong predictors of later reading, not just from kindergarten age but also at much younger ages. Similarly, phonological awareness itself seems to be predicted as well by previous lexical and syntactic abilities as by phonological ones. Findings such as these suggest that the phonological core deficit hypothesis may not account fully for the development of reading disabilities.

In response, proponents of the phonological deficit hypothesis have argued cogently that deficits in other aspects of developing language all stem from more fundamental weaknesses in the phonological domain. That is, even though other sorts of language deficits are predictive of future reading difficulties, they are just correlates (or secondary symptoms) rather than true causes of reading disability (Shankweiler & Crain, 1986). The developmental patterns and relative strengths of the correlations, however, do not readily accord with this explanation. (Consider, for example, the data in Figure 2.2.) Also, results of a recent genetic analysis of the heritability of phonological awareness, general language abilities, and reading skills were inconsistent with this account (Hohnen & Stevenson, 1999).

An alternative approach has been to propose moving from a single-deficit to a double-deficit (or, in principle, a multiple-deficit) model of reading disability. These are subtyping hypotheses, according to which some children's reading difficulties stem from phonological deficits, whereas others' have their roots in different language weaknesses, solely or in conjunction with phonological deficits (e.g., Bowers & Wolf, 1993; Manis et al., 1999). There is no consensus as to the nature of the additional deficit(s), however, and empirical support for the hypothesized subtypes is fairly limited. Moreover, proposed qualitative differences have tended to be confounded with severity of impairment. Although the notion of subtyping is appealing, research spanning several decades has been rather unsuccessful in revealing consistent subgroupings of disabled readers, and I am not sure that the latest subtyping hypotheses will stand the test of time.

It is possible, however, to imagine a single-deficit model of reading disabilities that incorporates the strengths of the phonological-deficit hypothesis and also accounts for the preschool correlational data reviewed in this chapter. To do so requires, however, that we stop thinking about causality only in terms of a 'chain' of events that influence each other in turn (e.g., successive deficits in phonological processing, attaining phonological awareness, grasping the alphabetic principle, and, finally, learning to read). As illustrated in Figure 2.3, although some disorders progress in this manner (e.g., the disease glaucoma), others do not. The observable symptoms of syphilis, for instance, do not constitute a causal chain. Instead, the root cause is a persisting bacterial infection, which produces different symptoms at different stages of the disease. Note that knowing which type of causal model accounts for a disorder has important implications not just for theory but also for its treatment. For a causal chain, successive treatment of any symptom along the way will prevent the emergence of all successive stages of the disease. In contrast, for a syphilis-like disorder, effective treatment of a symptom will not halt the progression of the disorder; instead, it is necessary to identify and treat the underlying condition.

It is possible also to entertain a hybrid model that incorporates both an underlying condition (e.g., a genetic predisposition to have difficulty learning certain kinds of linguistic patterns) that is the root cause of a series of different symptoms and some causal influences

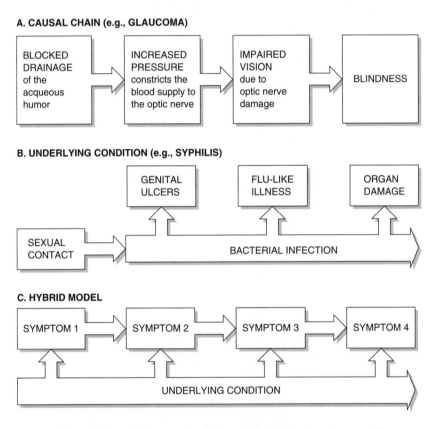

Figure 2.3   Models of possible causal relationships in the developmental progression of a condition or disorder. (In variations of the hybrid model, some horizontal arrows could be absent.)

between symptoms. With regard to reading disabilities, for instance, suppose that successive 'symptoms' include deficits in early syntactic proficiency, phonological awareness, and decoding of print, respectively. Although there are sizable correlations among all three measures, the syntactic deficit might have no causal influence on the subsequent development of the other two deficits, but the weakness in phonological awareness would indeed be an important ('proximal') cause of difficulty in learning to decode. If so, if a child is affected by the underlying condition, treatment of an early syntactic impairment would not reduce the child's risk for reading disability, but training in phonological awareness would be of benefit in eliminating or ameliorating the child's difficulty in learning to decode. It would still be possible, however, that the underlying condition would continue to exert its influence on other strands during later stages of reading acquisition, leaving the child at risk for future difficulties despite having attained adequate skill in decoding. All these predictions from the model are consistent with the research that I have reviewed earlier.

Differences in severity of the underlying impairment, furthermore, would lead to differences in the number and severity of symptoms that are exhibited. Extrinsic factors (especially the quality of reading instruction) are sure to play a causal role too. Hence, anomalous cases (successful reading achievement by a child who had previously been diagnosed with a language impairment, and conversely, only subclinical weaknesses in early language in a child who later exhibited a reading disability) can be accommodated by the model, albeit not without costs in terms of parsimony.

Nonlinear growth and an 'ascendancy' hypothesis

To explain the changing preschool deficit profiles that have been observed may require another break from traditionally linear ways of thinking about developmental disorders. It is fairly well established that growth in some (perhaps all) components of language consists of spurts and plateaus at particular times rather than steady incremental advances. If so, then a delay in acquisition will mean that spurts and plateaus will occur at a somewhat older age than usual, as illustrated by the dashed growth curve in Figure 2.4. In such a case (depending, of course, on the durations of plateaus and the degree of delay), there may be ages at which the performance levels of delayed and nondelayed cases will be virtually identical, a phenomenon that Scarborough and Dobrich (1990) termed 'illusory recovery.' It provides a simple explanation for the otherwise puzzling fact, noted earlier, that language and reading problems often (re)emerge at older ages in children who had appeared to have overcome their preschool language impairments by the time they entered school.

In more general terms, when growth of a skill is nonlinear, deficits in that skill will be most readily detectable during periods when normal development undergoes a spurt (e.g., when rapidly developing children are reaching the postspurt plateau, and growth of the slower developing children may just be starting to accelerate). Spurts in particular language skills occur at different ages, on average (e.g., the well-known vocabulary spurt, typically occurring at about 18 months, precedes the period of rapid acquisition of morphology and syntax from age 2 to 4 years). Therefore, at any given time, conditions for detecting individual or group differences in a skill will be best when that skill is normally 'ascendant.' According to this ascendancy hypothesis, furthermore, the milder the language defay (i.e., the smaller the horizontal distance between the dashed and solid curves in Figure 2.4), the more transient and domain-specific the pattern of observed deficits will be. A severe delay, in contrast, will be characterized by a more persistent and across-the-board deficit profile. (Note that what looks like a qualitative

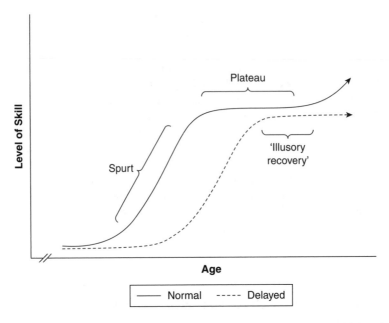

Figure 2.4   Illustration of how nonlinear development of language skills might lead to periods of 'illusory recovery' by children who had previously appeared to be delayed. Data from Scarborough and Dobrich (1990).

difference, or subtype, would really be a quantitative severity difference.) If this ascendancy hypothesis correctly captures the measurement situation for early language skills, then the notion that a single underlying language disorder could manifest itself as a series of deficits in different aspects of language, each correlated with the next, is precisely what would be expected for mild-to-moderate severity levels.

   In sum, I believe that greater power and flexibility in theorizing about the relationships between language and literacy development can be obtained by considering alternatives to causal chains and linear growth assumptions. I have not tried to construct a full theory but, rather, to illustrate how some interesting phenomena seen in the available literature can perhaps be explained more satisfactorily than at present.

Practical implications: present and future

With regard to diagnosis, the risk factors that have been identified by the correlational research on preschoolers and kindergartners provide the best current guidelines for designing screening batteries to identify those young children who are most likely to develop reading disabilities. As noted earlier, researchers who have assessed kindergartners on various subsets of such variables have attained high multiple correlations with subsequent reading scores. Figure 2.5 shows how well such screening batteries have succeeded in the typical study of this sort, in which 89% prediction accuracy has been obtained in samples of about 200 children. For most purposes, this is a reasonably satisfactory level of success. Note, however, that virtually every study has obtained few 'miss' errors (i.e., children not identified as at risk by the screen but who became disabled readers) but a sizable proportion of 'false alarms') (children identified by the screen as being at risk, but who later achieved

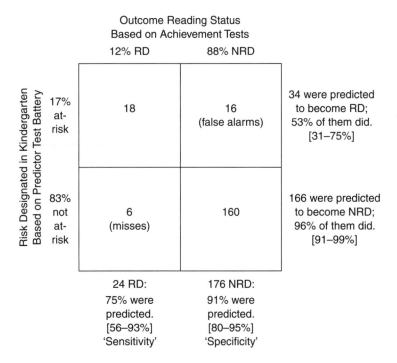

Figure 2.5   **Typical results obtained by combining kindergarten-age measures to predict later reading in samples of about 200 children. The ranges of values across studies are shown in brackets. RD, reading disabled; NRD, not reading disabled. Based on data from Scarborough (1998, Table A–7).**

adequately on the reading measure). If early intervention is targeted at all children designated as at risk, this means that about half of those receiving it might not actually be in need of it. At present, this is the most serious concern associated with using such screens, not just because the costs of intervention are substantially raised but also because the possible negative educational and psychological consequences of mislabeling 'false alarms' are not known. If this issue is handled sensibly, though, I think a good case can be made that early identification and intervention are warranted.

The available data also indicate that diagnosing risk is more problematic at younger ages. The observations that language deficit profiles change over time within individual preschoolers (as well as between groups, as in Figure 2.2) means that assessment at a single time point may be misleading as to how broad a child's language impairment might be. In the future, I believe that diagnostic improvements can be achieved by giving increased consideration to the possibility of nonlinear growth in skills, to the ascendancy hypothesis (stronger detectibility of individual differences during expected growth spurts), and to the occurrence of 'illusory recovery.'

With regard to intervention, the data also provide some guidance as to what developing skills should be fostered in at-risk youngsters. First, although equating correlation with causality is a false inference, the opposite – that a lack of correlation implies a lack of causal influence – is usually a reasonable conclusion. Hence, for the purpose of preventing later reading problems, there is no reason to provide training in skills that poorly predict future reading achievement.

Second, among the stronger predictors, only phonological awareness has yet been demonstrated to play a causal role in learning to read. A successful intervention program would thus certainly include training in this skill. And, because connecting phonological awareness with letter knowledge has been shown to enhance the acquisition of the alphabetic principle, this too should be a focus. The best candidates for additional components of an intervention program are those suggested by the correlational research, namely, print concepts, retention of verbal material, and oral language skills (especially expressive vocabulary). Although there is no guarantee that training in these skills will facilitate reading acquisition, this important causal question can be investigated through follow-up studies of the efficacy of intervention programs.

Finally, especially with regard to younger at-risk preschoolers (especially those with a diagnosis of language impairment and those with a family history of reading disability), interventions based on an accurate causal model are likely to be most effective in reducing risk for later reading problems. Simply addressing these children's current 'symptoms' through conventional speech–language therapy apparently does not reduce such risk, probably because weaknesses in speech and language do not causally impede reading acquisition, at least over the short term. Hence, as Fey (1999) has urged, proactive training of known 'proximal' causal factors (such as phonological awareness) may be required. If and when evidence accrues for the existence of an underlying 'root' cause of reading ability differences, strengthening that factor would clearly be an important facet of any early intervention program.

[...]

References

Anthony, J.L., Lonigan, C.J., Dyer, S.M., & Bloomfield, B. (1997, April). *The development of phonological processing in preschool-aged children: Preliminary evidence from confirmatory factor analysis*. Paper presented at the meeting of the Society for Research in Child Development, Washington, DC.

Aram, D.M., & Hall, N.E. (1989). Longitudinal follow-up of children with preschool communication disorders: Treatment implications. *School Psychology Review*, 18, 487–501.

Bishop, D.V.M., & Adams, C. (1990). A prospective study of the relationship between specific language impairment, phonological disorders and reading retardation. *Journal of Child Psychology and Psychiatry*, 31, 1027–1050.

Bishop, D.V.M., & Edmundson, A. (1987). Specific language impairment as a maturational lag: Evidence from longitudinal data on language and motor development. *Developmental Medicine and Child Neurology*, 29, 442–459.

Bowers, P.G., & Wolf, M. (1993, March). *A double-deficit hypothesis for developmental reading disorders*. Paper presented at the meeting of the Society for Research in Child Development, New Orleans.

Bryant, P.E., Bradley, L., Maclean, M., & Crossland, J. (1989). Nursery rhymes, phonological skills and reading. *Journal of Child Language*, 16, 407–428.

Bryant, P.E., Maclean, M., Bradley, L.L., & Crossland, J. (1990). Rhyme and alliteration, phoneme detection and learning to read. *Developmental Psychology*, 26, 429–438.

Byrne, B., Fielding-Batsley, R., Hindson, B., Mackay, C., Newman, C., & Shankweiler, D. (1998, April). *Early intervention with children at risk for reading disability: A mid-term report*. Paper presented at the conference of the Society for the Scientific Study of Reading, San Diego, CA.

Catts, H.W., Fey, M., & Tomblin, B. (1997, April). *The language basis for reading disabilities*. Paper presented at the meeting of the Society for the Scientific Study of Reading, Chicago.

Catts, H.W., Fey, M., Zhang, X., & Tomblin, B. (1999). Language bases of reading and reading disabilities: Evidence from a longitudinal investigation. *Scientific Studies of Reading, 3,* 331–361.

Chaney, C. (1992). Language development, metalinguistic skills, and print awareness in 3-year-old children. *Applied Psycholinguistics, 13,* 485–514.

Committee on the Prevention of Reading Difficulties in Young Children (1998). *Preventing reading difficulties in young children.* Washington, DC: National Academy Press.

Ehri, L., & Wilce, L.S. (1980). The influence of orthography on readers' conceptualization of the phonemic structure of words. *Applied Psycholinguistics, 1,* 371–385.

Elbro, C. (1999, April). How quality of phonological representations of lexical items predicts phono-logical processing of spoken and written language. In B.E. Pennington (Chair), *Longitudinal studies of children at family risk for dyslexia: Results from four countries.* Symposium conducted at the meeting of the Society for Research in Child Development, Albuquerque, NM.

Fey, M.E. (1999). Speech-language pathology and the early identification and prevention of reading disabilities. *Perspectives, 25,* 13–17.

Fey, M.E., Catts, H.W., & Larrivee, L.S. (1995). Preparing preschoolers for the academic and social challenges of school. In M.E. Fey, J. Windson, & S.E. Warrent (Eds.), *Language intervention: Preschool through the elementary years* (pp. 3–37). Baltimore: Brookes.

Gallagher, A., Frith, U., & Snowling, M. (1999, April). Early literacy development in children at genetic risk of dyslexia. In B.F. Pennington (Chair), *Longitudinal studies of children at family risk for dyslexia: Results from four countries.* Symposium conducted at the meeting of the Society for Research in Child Development, Albuquerque, NM.

Hohnen, B., & Stevenson, J. (1999). The structure of genetic influences on general cognitive, lan-guage, phonological, and reading abilities. *Developmental Psychology, 35,* 590–603.

Liberman, I.Y. (1973). Segmentation of the spoken word and reading acquisition. *Bulletin of the Or-ton Society, 23,* 65–77.

Liberman, I.Y., Shankweiler, D., & Liberman. A.M. (1989). The alphabetic principle and learning to read. In D. Shankweiler & L. Y. Liberman (Eds.), *Phonology and reading disability: Solving the reading puzzle.* Ann Arbor: University of Michigan Press.

Lonigan, C., Burgess, S.R., Anthony, J.L., & Barker, T.A. (1998). Development of phonological sensitivity in 2- to 5-year-old children. *Journal of Educational Psychology, 90,* 294–311.

Lyytinen, H., Hietala, A., Leinonen, S., Leppanen, P., Richardson, U., & Lyytinen, P. (1999, April). Early language development among children with familial risk for dyslexia. In B.F. Pennington (Chair), *Longitudinal studies of children at family risk for dyslexia: Results from four countries.* Symposium conducted at the meeting of the Society for Research in Child Development, Albuquerque, NM.

Maclean, M., Bryant, P.E., & Bradley, L.L. (1987). Rhymes, nursery rhymes and reading in early childhood. *Merrill-Palmer Quarterly, 33,* 255–282.

Manis, F., Seidenberg, M.S., Stallings, L., Joanisse, M., Bailey, C., Freedman, L., Curtin, S., & Keafing, P. (1999). Development of dyslexic subtypes: A one-year follow up. *Annals of Dyslexia, 49,* 105–134.

Molfese, D.L. (1999, April). Predicting reading performance at eight years of age from auditory brain potentials recorded at birth. In V.J. Molfese (Chair), *Longitudinal studies of reading abil-ities: Biological and educational influences on development and persistence.* Symposium con-ducted at the meeting of the Society for Research in Child Development, Albuquerque, NM.

Pennington, B.F., Lefly, D.L., & Boada, R. (1999, April). Phonological development and reading outcomes in children at family risk for dyslexia. In B.F. Pennington (Chair), *Longitudinal studies of children at family risk for dyslexia: Results from four countries.* Symposium conducted at the meeting of the Society for Research in Child Development, Albuquerque, NM.

Perfetti, C.A., Beck, L., Bell, L., & Hughes, C. (1987). Phonemic knowledge and learning to read are reciprocal: A longitudinal study of first grade children. *Merrill-Palmer Quarterly, 33,* 283–319.

Rescorla, L.R. (1999, July). *Outcomes of late talkers: Academic and language skills at age 13.* Paper presented at the meeting of International Association for the Study of Child Language, San Sebastian, Spain.

Scarborough, H.S. (1989). Prediction of reading disability from familial and individual differences. *Journal of Educational Psychology,* 81, 101–108.

Scarborough, H.S. (1990). Very early language deficits in dyslexic children. *Child Development,* 61, 1728–1734.

Scarborough, H.S. (1991a). Early syntactic development of dyslexic children. *Annals of Dyslexia,* 41, 207–220.

Scarborough, H.S. (1991b). Antecedents to reading disability: Preschool language development and literacy experiences of children from dyslexic families. *Reading and Writing,* 3, 219–233.

Scarborough, H.S. (1998). Early identification of children at risk for reading disabilities: Phonological awareness and some other promising predictors. In B.K. Shapiro, P.J. Accardo, & A.J. Capute (Eds.), *Specific reading disability: A view of the spectrum* (pp. 75–119). Timonium, MD: York Press.

Scarborough, H.S., & Dobrich, W. (1990). Development of children with early language delays. *Journal of Speech and Hearing Research,* 33, 70–83.

Scarborough, H.S., Dobrich, W., & Hager, M. (1991). Literacy experience and reading disability: Reading habits and abilities of parents and young children. *Journal of Learning Disabilities,* 24, 508–511.

Shankweiler, D., & Crain, S. (1986). Language mechanisms and reading disorders: A modular approach. *Cognition,* 24, 136–168.

Shapiro, B.K., Palmer, F.B., Antell. S., Bilker, S., Ross, A., & Capute, A.J. (1990). Precursors of reading delay: Neuro developmental milestones. *Pediatrics,* 416–420.

Slavin, R.E., Madden, N A., Dolan, L.J., Wasik, B.A., Ross, S., Smith, L., & Dianda, M. (1996). Success For All: A summary of research. *Journal of Education for Students placed at Risk,* 1, 41–76.

Stanovich, K.E., & Siegel, L.S. (1994). Phenotypic performance profiles of children with reading disabilities: A regression-based test of the phonological-core variable-difference model. *Journal of Educational Psychology,* 86, 24–53.

Stark, R., Bernstein, L., Condino, R., Bender, M., Tallal, P., & Carts, H. (1984). Four year follow-up study of language-impaired children. *Annals of Dyslexia,* 34, 49–68.

Stothard, S., Snowling, M., Bishop, D., Chipchase B., & Kaplan, C. (1998). Language-impaired preschoolers: a follow-up into adolescence. *Journal of Speech, Language and Hearing Research,* 41, 407–418.

Torgesen, J.K., Wagner, R.K., & Rashotte, C.A. (1997). Prevention and remediation of severe reading disabilities: Keeping the end in mind. *Scientific Studies of Reading,* 1, 217–234.

Walker, D., Greenwood, C., Hart, B., & Carta, J. (1994). Prediction of school outcomes based on early language production and socioeconomic factors. *Child Development,* 65, 606–621.

Whitehurst, G.J. (1999, April). The role of inside-out skills in reading readiness of children from low-income families. In C.J. Lonigan (Chair), *From prereaders to readers: The role of phonological processing skills in at risk and typically developing children.* Symposium conducted at the meeting of the Society for Research in Child Development, Albuquerque, NM.

3

Policy and Research: Lessons from the Clackmannanshire Synthetic Phonics Initiative

Sue Ellis

[…]

The Synthetic Phonics experiment in Clackmannanshire, Scotland has, it seems, had a significant impact on literacy policy in England. The Westminster Select Committee Enquiry into Teaching Children to Read concluded, 'In view of the evidence from the Clackmannanshire study … we recommend that the Government should undertake an immediate review of the National Literacy Strategy' (Education and Skills Committee, 2005b: 23). The outcome of that review, the Rose Report, devoted four pages to the Clackmannanshire study and recommended that all English children be taught to read using systematic synthetic phonics, taught discretely as the prime approach in learning to read (DfES, 2006).

In Scotland, the Clackmannanshire experiment has not been ignored, but has not generated the highly charged debates or radical policy and curriculum overhauls seen south of the border. In contrast to the reaction in England, the Scottish HM Inspectorate of Education (HMIe) report concluded: 'Whilst this programme had made a strong impact on pupils' ability to sound out, spell and recognise words, further work was required to link these skills to other aspects of reading such as comprehension' (HMIe, 2006: 4).

This [chapter] does not seek to discredit synthetic phonics or the work in Clackmannanshire. Instead, it explores why Scotland and England responded in such different ways to this study. It argues that differences in the way literacy policy is determined in Scotland, and a greater knowledge of the wider funding and policy context, can explain the more measured response from Scottish policy makers. Further, it argues that consideration of the national and local staff development context provides another story about the study, one that sits alongside the psychology research with its focus on individual performance and teaching programmes. A third story arises from consideration of the national test data for the cohort of pupils in the Clackmannanshire trial. Together, these three stories highlight the complex relationships and tensions between academic research, curriculum development and policy development in literacy.

To do this, the [chapter] draws on publicly available sources: HMIe inspection reports, national test results, Clackmannanshire Council Reports and reports on the Learning and

From: *Journal of Early Childhood Literacy*, 7 (3), 2007, pp. 281–97.

Teaching Scotland (LTS) website, which provides national curriculum advice for Scotland. It also draws on evidence from interviews with staff working in Clackmannanshire schools during the intervention period. In this way, the [chapter] attempts to explain the national policy context and piece together exactly what the local authority actually did, and describe what some teachers and head teachers felt was important and useful.

The Clackmannanshire study

Clackmannanshire local authority was formed in 1994, when Scottish local government was reorganized into 32 local authorities. It is the smallest local authority in Scotland, managing 3 secondary schools and 19 primary schools, some of which are very small. Twenty-four per cent of its primary pupils in 2004 had a free school meal entitlement (compared to a national average of 21%) but this varies hugely from 5 per cent to 58 per cent between schools. Across the county, therefore, there are pockets of wealth and prosperity and some areas of very significant deprivation (HMIe, 2006).

The Clackmannanshire experiment was carried out by Joyce Watson and Rhona Johnston of St Andrews University. The seven-year longitudinal study, which so impressed the Westminster Select Committee, was one of three linked studies on phonics. The studies addressed the academic debates among psychologists about how young children set about learning the connections between letters and sounds, the knowledge and skills that are needed, the optimum pace and sequence of letters/sounds, and when these should be taught. Proponents of analytic phonics (e.g. Goswami, 2005) argue for a developmental sequence in which rhyming skills help children draw analogies between words to crack the alphabetic code. This, they suggest, better suits the irregular 'deep' orthography of English. Others (e.g. Stuart, 2006) argue for synthetic phonics, where the key to cracking the alphabetic code lies in teaching children to recognize and blend (or synthesize) individual letter-sound correspondences as early as possible, avoiding distractions such as rhyme.

The first study took place in 1992–3 (before Clackmannanshire was formed) and was part of the research for a PhD. It is described variously as a study of 'methods of teaching reading and spelling' and 'research examining how phonics was taught' in 12 schools (Watson and Johnston, 1998). This study described the phonics teaching and examined the content, pace and impact of the programmes. It reported serious reading gains as soon as teachers began showing children how to decode CVC (consonant, vowel, consonant) words. It also reported that a class following an accelerated analytic phonics programme made greater gains than those on slower phonics programmes.

The second study was also designed to address a theoretical issue: '… whether synthetic phonics was more effective than analytic phonics merely because letter sounds were taught at an accelerated pace' (Johnston and Watson, 2004: 343). It was a 10-week intervention, and the 92 children were tested up to the end of their first year of school.

For 10 weeks, three groups of children were extracted for two 15-minute sessions of extra tuition a week. One group had sight vocabulary training only (i.e. no additional phonics tuition beyond that included in the normal class programme), another was taught two letters a week in an initial position in words (the 'analytic phonics' group) and the third group was also taught two letters a week but in the initial, middle and final position (the 'synthetic phonics' group). Children from four classes were randomly assigned to groups to control for possible effects of different class teachers and reading programmes. Because the lead researcher was also the teacher for the extracted groups, this was not a typical randomized controlled trial. From this study, Watson and Johnston concluded that synthetic phonics led to better reading, spelling and phonemic awareness and that the advantage lay in showing children how to sound and blend letter sounds to pronounce unfamiliar words (Watson and Johnston, 1998).

The third study is the one that will be discussed in this [chapter]. It created huge media excitement and policy debate in England and further afield (Department for Education and Skills [DfES], 2006; National Inquiry into the Teaching of Literacy [NITL], 2005). Johnston and Watson (2005a) report that it involved around 300 children and was jointly funded by Clackmannanshire Council and the Scottish Executive. It began in 1997–8 and was given additional funding in 1999. This study is important and deserves attention because it is one of very few longitudinal phonics studies to follow a cohort of children to the end of their primary career.

This cohort study sought to contribute to psychologists' understanding of the reading process by comparing the effects of phonemic awareness, analytic phonics and synthetic phonics instruction on reading and spelling. One hypothesis was that 'if training in phonological awareness is essential for young children learning to read, the analytic phonics programme with phonological awareness training should be more effective than the other two programmes' (Johnston and Watson, 2004).

The first phase of the longitudinal project was a 16-week programme implemented with 13 classes in eight schools. Five 'synthetic phonics' classes did 20 minutes of whole-class synthetic phonics per day. They were taught six letter sounds in eight days in initial, middle and final positions, together with the formation of the letters. They were taught to sound and blend letters and were shown how to use this to both read and spell words. Four 'phonemic awareness/ analytic phonics' classes did 10 minutes a day of phonemic awareness training without reference to print and a separate 10 minutes of analytic phonics, covering just one sound per week. A control 'analytic phonics' group of 4 classes did 20 minutes a day of analytic phonics, also covering one sound per week. The class teachers did all teaching.

After 16 weeks, tests on word reading showed the analytic and phoneme awareness/analytic groups were reading one month behind their chronological age. The synthetic phonics group were seven months ahead of their chronological age, and seven months ahead of the other two groups. In spelling, the synthetic phonics group was eight months ahead of the analytic phonics group and nine months ahead of the analytic phonics/phoneme awareness group. Watson and Johnston (1998: 7–8) concluded that synthetic phonics was a more effective teaching method than analytic phonics.

In the second phase, those classes initially not given synthetic phonics followed the synthetic phonics programme, completing it by the end of their first year at school. Towards the end of their second year, all 13 classes were re-tested. The reading and spelling averages for all groups were well above their chronological age and there was no significant difference in word reading or comprehension between the three original groups, although there was a significant difference in favour of the original synthetic phonics group for spelling.

This cohort was followed through to the end of their primary school career. The report on this seven-year longitudinal study was summarized and published by the Scottish Executive (Johnston and Watson, 2005a). The children were, on average, three years and six months ahead of chronological age in decoding words. They were one year and nine months ahead in spelling and were three and a half months above the expected level for their chronological age in comprehension. The report concluded that synthetic phonics was a highly effective teaching method that produced long-lasting effects.

The full research report was published on the Scottish Executive Education Department's (SEED) website (Johnston and Watson, 2005b). This gave more detail about the study (although not an abstract, a timeline or a participant flow diagram, all of which would have been helpful). This detailed some aspects less central to the synthetic/analytic phonics debate; for example, boys had less positive attitudes towards reading than girls.

The longitudinal study had huge press coverage in both Scotland and England, mostly focused on the three and a half year gain in decoding single words.

The national context in Scotland

One key to understanding Scotland's very different reaction to the Clackmannanshire study lies in the way that Scottish education policy is organized and developed. In Scotland, there is no central, legally enforced national curriculum. Instead, there are non-statutory curriculum guidelines and the minister in charge of education is legally required to set National Priorities for education, and to review these from time to time. The National Priorities are few (there are currently five) and fairly broad. For example, one current priority is: 'To raise standards of educational attainment for all in schools, especially in the core skills of literacy and numeracy, and to achieve better results in national measures of achievement, including examination results' (SEED, 2007: 1). Performance outcomes and measures sit alongside each priority to provide a common measure for standards and quality. Each local authority is expected to interpret and deliver the curriculum guidelines and National Priorities in a way that meets local needs. The Director of Education for each local authority must present and explain the authority's literacy policy to local councillors and use the performance measures and other nationally agreed performance indicators to evaluate how effectively it is working.

This devolved decision-making has two effects. First, it removes the literacy curriculum (although not literacy itself) from national political debate. This means that parliamentary politicians, who have excellent understandings of how to deliver soundbites and capture media attention, but often know less about literacy teaching or interpreting statistical evidence, cannot make political capital by aligning themselves with a particular teaching approach; they simply have no locus in such decisions. Directors of Education, answerable to locally elected councillors and working to agreed and common evaluation and performance structures determine how the literacy guidelines are interpreted and delivered. Whereas in England the Conservative MP, Nick Gibb, could use parliamentary questions about Clackmannanshire to challenge Labour's education policy, in Scotland he would have met the standard Scottish Executive response: 'We do not have a statutory curriculum in Scotland, so we do not prescribe to local authorities how they have to teach a particular subject' (Andalo, 2005: 3).

Second, devolved decision-making locates discussion about the literacy curriculum firmly in the hands of those who have to deliver it. This results in a more measured and nuanced professional debate about literacy teaching and literacy learning. It also fosters appreciation of the hard work, commitment and imagination that underpins any successful curriculum innovation. Wholesale dismissal of the Clackmannanshire study would be regarded as both discourteous and unwise. Rather, the reaction of teachers and policy makers at local authority level has been to see what lessons might be learned and ideas adapted and applied to their own, parallel innovations. This process of curriculum development by 'evolution rather than revolution' (Humes and Bryce, 2003) is highly pragmatic, driven by 'what works in this context' rather than by theoretical constructs. It is an approach that contrasts strongly with the concerns with 'programme fidelity' expressed in the Rose Review.

Moss and Huxford (2007), in their analysis of the phonics debate in England, maintain that 'Phonics in the policy context is not the same as phonics in the research context or phonics as a focus for a political campaign'. Each interprets the question of how to raise literacy achievement in a different way, works to different timelines and recognizes different evidence. In each context, what phonics 'stands for' varies, and is differently positioned in relation to the various tiers at which national policy decisions are made and interpreted. The devolved and evolutionary approach to literacy policy in Scotland possibly curtails the number of different things phonics can 'stand for' and aligns it more closely to learning, in a smaller, more localized policy space. This may explain why there are fewer struggles around it.

The national funding context for the longitudinal Clackmannanshire study

Although decisions about the curriculum are devolved, the Scottish Executive uses ring-fenced funding to encourage local authorities and schools to attend to particular issues. In 1997, £20m was made available nationally, on a matched-funds basis, for early intervention initiatives to raise literacy and numeracy attainment in the first two years of school. For a country the size of Scotland (population 5,102,400), this represents a large amount of money, tightly targeted on the early years school curriculum. All 32 local authorities submitted bids for specific projects. The bids were assessed by HMIe and those that addressed too narrow an aspect of literacy were advised to widen their focus and address a number of strands. In 1998, Helen Liddell, then Minister for Education, used the Excellence Fund to extend the funding to £60m over 5 years. This enabled local authorities to support further curriculum change as children moved into their third year of school and to 'roll out' the most successful initiatives to other schools.

This, then, was the funding context for the longitudinal Clackmannanshire phonics study: it was one part of a broader literacy development project that was specifically designed to raise the attainment of the children during the first three years of school. It took place within a big national project and was funded by money that was additional to the local authority's normal education budget.

The first year of Clackmannanshire's project involved the eight intervention schools in two main initiatives. One was the synthetic phonics study and the other introduced new core reading schemes and library books into the schools (Robertson, 2005). After the first year, the local authority was keen that the pupils in the experimental phonics cohort built on their knowledge and skills during their second year of primary education. They used the early intervention money to develop a Primary 2 literacy programme that focused more heavily on developing thinking and comprehension skills. This new programme entailed a new evaluation.

Lesley Robertson, the local authority advisor responsible for the project reported to the Clackmannanshire Learning and Leisure Committee of 27 October 1999: 'It was agreed with the University of St Andrews to construct another research programme whereby the progress of pupils in P2 classes involved in the second phase of the programme could be evaluated with the same academic rigour as in the first phase. In broad terms this approach meant that the children continued to build on their basic reading and spelling skills while at the same time, a large part of the teaching programme could be focused on the acquisition of thinking and comprehension skills. The teaching programme began in September 1998 and the evaluation exercise was carried out in 1999' (Robertson, 1999: 2).

Clackmannanshire also used the early intervention funding to provide home–school liaison teachers in four of the intervention schools. These teachers provided classroom support for children; made home visits to support literacy development outside school; and established story clubs, library visits, after-school homework clubs and parent groups. They also created libraries and borrowing services in the schools (Clackmannanshire Council, 2003).

At national level, there was considerable interchange of ideas across Scotland. Every local authority was running its own intervention projects and HMIe organized a national event for coordinators, head teachers and teachers to encourage professional networks and promote cross-fertilization of ideas. Local authorities organized further individual and joint conferences for staff and the national evaluation team set up two opportunities for sharing initiatives and classroom practice (Fraser et al., 2001).

The staff development context

It is quite clear that at no point did the local authority just give the schools a phonics scheme and tell them to get on with it. The curriculum development process was sensitive to the local context and ensured that those responsible for implementation were intellectually engaged and committed. The teachers developed the deep and grounded understanding that we know is essential for effective and responsive teaching (Blackmore, 1998). The staff development provided in conjunction with the researchers from St Andrews University was systematic, coherent and delivered with conviction. It provided specific content knowledge about phonics and teaching literacy as well as offering practical advice about structuring lessons, using the resources, making learning purposeful, motivating children and the importance of noticing and building on success. Teachers discussed how to plan and deliver phonics and literacy lessons that were focused and interactive, with clear learning purposes, explicit links to previous learning and opportunities for children to apply their knowledge and to reflect on what had been learnt.

The Clackmannanshire staff I interviewed were highly enthusiastic about the training they had been given. One head teacher explained:

The professional development they provided really shifted the culture and expectations. I had good, experienced staff working in my school but the previous [professional development] programmes had all offered a straight choice between pottery and computing ... everything was a 'how to' course. Before, there'd been nothing on core curriculum subjects like literacy, and nothing to engage the brain.

The teachers particularly liked the clear focus on just one new aspect of content knowledge: one teacher told me 'it [the course] was … very clear. You just had one single thing to master. They didn't suggest loads of different ideas so that you had to divide your attention when you went back, or have to work out what should be your main priority'. Another said, 'The CPD gave you wonderful confidence. They said "just do this and do it really well". Because we were all doing the same thing … [we] … all had common problems and could support each other'.

Although all the teachers I spoke to spent longer than the 20 minutes originally suggested as the length of a phonics lesson – some (e.g. Macnair, 2006) reported lessons lasting as long as an hour – all appreciated the clear and practical advice about lesson delivery, the pace of teaching and the importance of providing opportunities for pupils to practise and apply their learning. Writing in *The Scotsman,* Lesley Robertson, the staff tutor for Clackmannanshire's early intervention and phonics initiative, says, 'In attempting to define the success of the programme, we believe that a significant component of the methodology is the explicit modelling of the thinking process by the teacher' (Robertson, 2005: 4).

When school reforms fail, the head teacher is often to be seen supporting the reform from a distance, rather than directly leading it (Datnow et al., 2002). In Clackmannanshire, the new approaches were explained in detail to the head teachers and senior management teams before they were explained to the teachers. This ensured commitment and informed support from these crucial managers. One teacher said, 'Follow-through in school was fantastic. My head teacher was really interested and enthusiastic. The expectations were high, but I had clear targets, with encouragement and support to get there'.

The teachers involved in the first few project cohorts were clearly excited about being at the cutting edge of research and felt empowered to actively shape the project and suggest ways to develop the materials to better support children's learning. For example, the teachers suggested introducing physical movement into lessons to allow children to release some energy and reduce frustrations arising from the amount of time spent sitting still. The report to councillors on Clackmannanshire's Learning and Leisure Committee acknowledges this: 'The Scottish Office had indicated an interest in contracting with the University of St Andrews to produce a CD Rom containing the materials [that were] developed in conjunction with teachers in Clackmannanshire' (Robertson, 1999: 1).

Alongside the phonics programme was a rigorous system for monitoring the progress of individual pupils and providing support to those who needed it with catch-up groups and homework clubs for anyone who seemed to be falling behind. Johnston and Watson (2005b) point out that none of the children in the original synthetic phonics group required additional support, but that some who had originally been part of the other two groups did require this support. The head teachers and some teachers I interviewed were strongly in favour of the additional support system. One experienced class teacher was less enthusiastic; she felt that children who struggled in the phonics lessons might experience more enjoyment and easy success in PE or Art but were taken out to do more phonics. This, she felt, created an early, negative experience of school.

The system, from the time it was first set up, also monitored and supported the staff. Lesley Robertson, the local authority advisor, was a talented administrator but was also dedicated and knowledgeable about teaching phonics and literacy. She worked closely with the researchers and the teachers and had huge credibility with the head teachers and senior management staff in schools. One head teacher said, 'It was great to have someone on the end of a phone who you could ring up with any questions – even questions about an individual child, and you knew you could have a sensible discussion with someone who was knowledgeable and could give you good advice about what to try'.

The decision to focus on one cohort of pupils and introduce new resources, study programmes and Continuing Professional Development (CPD) to the teachers as this cohort moved into their class ensured that teachers got a clear message of what was expected, that the CPD was provided at the point of need and that school managers knew what they should expect to see happening in class. Other early intervention projects in Scotland provided CPD to the Primary 1 and Primary 2 teachers together. This meant that the Primary 2 teachers had to adapt the new ideas for a cohort of pupils who had received no intervention programme before trying it properly with the intervention cohort a year later. In effect, they had a year to forget what they had been told. In the Clackmannanshire model, the Primary 2 teachers were given the relevant CPD only when the intervention cohort arrived as their class. Everyone accepted that this cohort of pupils was bringing a different set of knowledge and skills and the Primary 1 teachers were keen to offer focused support and advice. This itself created an internal pressure: a Primary 2 teacher reported embracing the initiative mainly because her Primary 1 colleague was so interested to see how she was building on the children's previous work.

A rolling programme of courses about teaching literacy and phonics was established to 'catch' teachers transferred to Primary 1 or Primary 2 classes halfway though the year. If no courses were running in the first four to six weeks of taking over a class, the new teacher was sent to other schools to observe how that stage was taught. One head teacher told me: 'The whole thing was organised and managed so that no-one in the system was left unsupported'.

Clackmannanshire was not the only local authority to introduce synthetic pnonics as part of its early intervention strategy. Others also tried, but with less success, which alone makes Clackmannanshire worthy of attention. This was undoubtedly a well-designed intervention and the design features fit with a lot of what we now know about successful staff development and curriculum reform: it had an authentic beginning and systematically built ideological commitment in the key staff. It was understood as a long-term initiative rather than a short-term 'cure', was supported by policy development at all levels and had internal feedback loops to monitor and support progress (Datnow et al., 2002).

The different contexts and aims of policy and research

Rhona Johnston (2006) has argued that none of this additional information about staff development and other initiatives can explain the advanced phonic decoding skills that the Primary 7 cohort displayed – on average three and a half years ahead of their chronological age. She is quite right, which makes this a valuable and interesting result for those who study the psychology of reading. However, it also illustrates one of the tensions that can arise from using tightly focused psychology research to inform policy development. The researchers and policy makers are driven by different questions and recognize different evidence as legitimate. For parents and policy makers, there is no practical advantage to children being able to sound out complex individual words as an isolated skill. The pragmatic policy task is to design and implement a literacy curriculum that creates readers who are significantly better at reading for meaning; people who can visualize as they read, infer meaning, recognize key ideas, new knowledge and contradictions and who are able to use and apply what they read to real life situations.

Pawson (2005) suggests that different perspectives value different kinds of questions and different kinds of evidence. The tightly focused questions that drive academic research can be problematic for policy makers who must attend to contextual features and evidence that researchers often consider unreliable, irrelevant background information or simply 'noise' to be screened out. He suggests that instead of focusing on single programmes and asking' what does and doesn't work', policy makers should embrace complexity by asking 'what works, for whom and in what circumstances' (Pawson, 2005).

'What works' for psychology researchers working in a tightly delineated and relatively slow-moving domain of phonics research may not work for policy makers, teachers or curriculum developers, who must work to different timescales and across a range of contexts and forms of evidence (Moss and Huxford, 2007). For example, one source of evidence that policy makers use about 'what works' is national test results. In Scotland, children sit a national test in reading or writing when the teacher judges them to have attained a 5–14 Level. This means that small groups of children, or even individuals, will be sitting tests at different points throughout the year. The system is set up to reflect what children can currently do, rather than what they could do at some arbitrary point decided by a national exam board. Moreover, it is biased in favour of the child and teacher judgement; if a child does badly in the test but the teacher has robust evidence from classroom work that the child has attained the level, they can award it.

For experimental psychologists, the Scottish 5–14 national test items are imperfect: they are not standardized, they are administered by the classroom teacher and are not externally marked. Yet from a policy maker's perspective, they are valuable because they reflect real-life literacy expectations and mirror the literacy demands of normal classroom practice, which is rarely true of psychology tests.

In Scotland, national testing is not compulsory, but national test results are used by many local authorities, including Clackmannanshire, as part of their internal monitoring and evaluation procedures. Local authorities monitor when children attain each level and are told how their own results rank against comparator local authorities. HMIe also comment on test results when they inspect local authorities and schools. For example, the HMIe (2006) inspection report on Clackmannanshire reports that, in primary schools, the 'performance in all three areas (reading, writing and mathematics) was below the average for comparator authorities and national averages' (HMIe, 2006: 4).

The official expectation is that most children will have attained Level D by Primary 7, the last year of primary school. In practice, this yardstick is rather long; the percentage of children attaining levels early has steadily increased since the system was introduced and most local authorities expect many (but not all) children to have achieved Level D by the end of Primary 6.

The national test results are shared with children and parents but the government does not centrally collect them, or publish 'league tables' of schools or local authorities. In 2005, however, *The Sunday Times (Scotland)* used the Freedom of Information Act to request the Primary 7 national test results for every school and local authority in Scotland (Fracassini et al., 2005). Table 3.1 summarizes the Primary 7 national test results for the eight schools involved in the early intervention study. It details the percentage of children in Primary 7 awarded Level D for the year before the research cohort, the research cohort and the year after the cohort.

The percentage of Free School Meal (FSM) entitlement is a broad indicator of the socio-economic status of families in the school. Literacy attainment is linked to this and, in Scotland, pupils in the bottom quarter of the socio-economic index are more than twice as likely to be among the bottom 25 per cent for reading attainment (SEED, 2002). The school roll indicates the size of the school. It is the total number of children attending the school and can only hint at the number of children in a particular year-group. Reporting results in terms of pupil percentages is always problematic: in small schools with small year-groups, the under- or over-performance of just one or two children can create a relatively large percentage 'swing' from year to year. The percentage results for bigger schools are more robust.

Obviously, firm conclusions cannot be drawn from these data. However, they do raise some questions for policy makers. Despite all schools getting a synthetic phonics input,

Table 3.1   Reading attainment in P7 (% pupils Level D or above)

School	School roll	Percentage free school meal entitlement in 2003/4	Reading attainment in P7 (% pupils Level D or above)		
			Year: 2003/4	Year: 2002/3 (intervention cohort)	Year: 2004/5
A	488	14	69	70	82
B	409	22	80	84	79
C	229	56	47	78	n/a
D	155	76	47	73	66
E	146	41	57	44	72
F	114	45	44	20	21
G	63	33	70	91	75
H	277	17	87	77	77

Notes: National average for P7 pupils at Level D or above in 2003/4 = 74.5%; National average for free school meal entitlement in 2003/4 = 21%.

there appears to be variability in national test achievement between the eight schools in the study. This does not, as one might expect, reflect the FSM entitlement. Some of the schools are doing very well indeed: in 2003–4, schools C, D and G had FSM entitlements way above the national average, 56 per cent, 76 per cent and 33 per cent respectively, yet are attaining, and in two cases exceeding, national averages – stunning results. Others, schools E and F for example, with similar catchments, are doing less well.

The largest school in the cohort, School A, serves the most advantaged catchment area with a FSM entitlement of 14 per cent, well below the national average. Yet its results are only in line with national attainment. Even 82 per cent attainment in the following year (2004–5) is disappointing. Schools with similar catchments in local authorities such as East Renfrewshire were at this time regularly attaining in the region of 90 per cent or more.

There are two points that emerge from this brief analysis. First, it seems there may be patterns of school-level variation that could be interesting and important for policy makers but are not made apparent by a psychology research paradigm that focuses on individual achievement scores and programmes of study.

Second, the national test results should not be seen as a direct challenge to the raft of standardized test results reported for the Clackmannanshire study. The psychology tests and national tests have emerged from different paradigms and measure different things. This analysis merely shows that one cohort's reading achievement can look quite different under different lenses. A potential problem for policy makers and teachers in England is that the lens used by the Westminster government to measure success in reading bears more similarity to the Scottish 5–14 tests than to the raft of reading tests used by the Clackmannanshire researchers.

Moss and Huxford (2007) argue that literacy problems are not couched within a single paradigm's field of reference. Perhaps the real lesson from this broader examination of the Clackmannanshire study is that any study driven mainly by one paradigm can only offer limited insights. Other Scottish local authorities deliberately created multi-paradigm projects in response to the national early intervention initiative. West Dunbartonshire, serving the second poorest area in Scotland (Clackmannanshire, as the eighth poorest area, is slightly better-off), designed possibly the most successful intervention and based it on a 'literacy for all' agenda. The starting point was that curriculum change is about contexts and staff as well as programmes and teaching content: 'Civil servants working under the directives of politicians don't bring about inspiration and revolution, and revolution is what is needed if you're going to turn things right around' (MacKay cited in Smith, 2007). The West Dunbartonshire intervention was not driven by a desire to know which theory works the best, but by the need to address a raft of complex, real-world literacy issues. Phonics is an important part of the early literacy programme but teachers draw on both analytic and synthetic approaches. The Hanen (2002) programme is also used to train staff to support and promote children's language and communication and there is an important emphasis on noticing and celebrating literacy achievement (MacKay, 2006).

Moss and Huxford (2007) argue that different groups within the phonics community in England have increasingly manoeuvred to control the policy space around early literacy. It is important that academics and policy makers continue to respect the insights afforded by a multi-disciplinary approach to literacy policy, even when some aspects of the system do not naturally promote such a view. One of the psychologists on the Rose Review famously told the Westminster Select Committee of Enquiry into Reading, 'The research on reading goes on in psychology departments'. The chairman asked, 'So we should listen to psychologists more than educational researchers?' and she replied, 'Yes' (Education and Skills Committee, 2005a: 5, Q. 38–9). The evidence in this [chapter] suggests that the Select Committee and those who produced the Rose Review might have been well advised to ignore her reply and listen to both. This, it seems, is what policy makers in Scotland have chosen to do. [...]

References

Andalo, D. (2005) 'Reading Scheme Will Not Be Rolled Out in Scotland', *Guardian* (3 June): 3, URL: http://education.guardian.co.uk/schools/story/0.,1498836.00.html.

Blackmore, J. (1998) 'The Politics of Gender and Educational Change', in A. Hargreaves. A. Liberman, M. Fullen and D. Hopkins (eds) *International Handbook of Educational Change*, pp. 460–81. Norwell, MA: Kluwer Academic.

Clackmannanshire Council (2003) *My Mum Likes School: Evaluation of the Effectiveness of Home School Liaison Work in Increasing Parental Involvement in Four Core Schools*. Clackmannan: Clacks Council Early Learning Initiatives.

Datnow, A., Hubbard, L. and Mehan. H. (2002) *Extending Educational Reform: From One School to Many*. London: Routledge Falmer.

Department for Education and Skills (DfES) (2006) *Independent Review of the Teaching of Early Reading: Final Report,* 'The Rose Review'. London: DfES.

Education and Skills Committee (2005a) *Eighth Report: Witnesses Monday 15 November 2004: Dr Morag Stuart.* London: United Kingdom Parliament, URL (consulted 16 May 2005): http://www.parliament.the-stationery-office.co.uk/pa/cm200405/cmselect/cmeduski/121/12111.htm

Education and Skills Committee (2005b) *Teaching Children to Read: Eighth Report of Session 2004–5.* London: HMSO.

Fracassini, C., Farquharson, K. and Marney, H. (2005) 'Focus: Secrecy that Fails Scotland (Or What the Executive, Unions, Councils – and Even Some Parents – Don't Want You To Know). *Sunday Times (Scotland)* (13 November), URL (March 2006): http://www.timesonline.co.uk/article/0.,2090–1870190_1.00.html

Fraser, H., MacDougall, A., Pirrie, A. and Croxford, L. (2001) 'Early Intervention in Literacy and Numeracy: Key Issues From the National Evaluation of the Programme', *Interchange* 71. Edinburgh: SEED.

Goswami, U. (2005) 'Synthetic Phonics and Learning To Read: A Cross-Language Perspective', *Educational Psychology in Practice* 21 (4): 273–82.

Hanen (2002) *Learning Language and Loving it: A Guide to Promoting Children's Social. Language, and Literacy Development in Early Childhood Settings (Second Edition).* Canada: Weitzman and Greenberg.

HM Inspectorate of Education (HMIe) (2006) 'Pilot Inspection of the Education Functions of Clackmannanshire Council in October 2005', SEED. Edinburgh, http://www.hmie.gov.uk/documents/inspection/ClackmannanINEA 2Pilot.html

Humes, W.M. and Bryce, T.G.K. (2003) 'The Distinctiveness of Scottish Education', in T.G.K. Bryce and W.M. Humes (eds) *Scottish Education: Second Edition Post-Devolution,* pp. 108–18. Edinburgh: Edinburgh University Press.

Johnston, R.J. and Watson, J.E. (2004) 'Accelerating the Development of Reading, Spelling and Phonemic Awareness Skills in Initial Readers', *Reading and Writing* 17: 327–57.

Johnston, R. and Watson, J. (2005a) 'A Seven Year Study of the Effects of Synthetic Phonics Teaching on Reading and Spelling Attainment', *Insight* 17. Edinburgh: SEED.

Johnston, R. and Watson J. (2005b) *The Effects of Synthetic Phonics Teaching on Reading and Spelling Attainment: A Seven Year Longitudinal Study.* Edinburgh: SEED.

Johnston, R. (2006) Personal Communication, 8 April.

MacKay, T. (2006) *The West Dunbartonshire Literacy Initiative: The Design, Implementation and Evaluation of an Intervention Strategy to Raise Achievement and Eradicate Illiteracy – Phase I Research Report.* Dunbarton: West Dunbartonshire Council.

Macnair, L. (2006) 'Inside the Classroom: Three Approaches to Phonics Teaching (Synthetic Phonics – How I Teach It)', in M. Lewis and S. Ellis (eds) *Phonics: Practice, Research and Policy,* pp. 45–59. London: Sage.

Moss, G. and Huxford, L. (2007) 'Exploring Literacy Policy-Making From the Inside Out', in L. Saunders (ed.) *Exploring the Relationship between Educational Research and Education Policy-Making*. London: Routledge Falmer.

National Inquiry into the Teaching of Literacy (NITL) (2005) *Teaching Reading: Literature Review*. Melbourne: Australian Government, Department of Education, Science and Training.

Pawson, R. (2005) *Evidence-based Policy: A Realist Perspective*. London: Sage.

Robertson, L. (1999) *Report to Learning and Leisure Committee of 27 October 1999,* Clackmannanshire Early Learning Initiative: Third Progress Report. Clackmannan: Clackmannanshire Council, URL (consulted March 2006): http://72.14.203.104/search?q=cache:jHEYgXxY578J:ltscotland.org.uk/images/clalocevall_1cm4–122377.pdf

Robertson, L. (2005) 'Why Synthetic Phonics was a Natural Winner', *Scotsman* (27 April), URL (consulted March 2006): http://thescotsman scotsman.com/education, cfm

Scottish Executive Education Department (SEED) (2002) *Programme for International Student Assessment: Scottish Report.* Education and Young People Research Unit. Edinburgh: SEED

Scottish Executive Education Department (SEED) (2007) *National Priorities for Education.* Edinburgh: SEED, URL (consulted March 2007): http://www.nationalpriorities.org.uk/schools/priority 1.html

Smith, C. (2007) 'One Man's Quest To Eradicate Illiteracy', *Independent* (8 March), URL (consulted March 2007): http://education.independent.co.uk/carreers_advice/article.2336440.ece

Stuart, M. (2006) 'Teaching Reading: Why Start With Systematic Phonics Teaching', *The Psychology of Education Review* 30 (2): 6–17.

Watson, J.E and Johnston, R.S. (1998) 'Accelerating Reading Attainment: The Effectiveness of Synthetic Phonics', *Interchange* 57. Edinburgh: SEED.

4

Individual Differences in the Inference of Word Meanings From Context: The Influence of Reading Comprehension, Vocabulary Knowledge, and Memory Capacity

Kate Cain, Jane Oakhill and Kate Lemmon

[…]

Since the early days of research on reading, a strong relation between reading ability and vocabulary knowledge has been acknowledged. However, the precise nature of the relation between these skills, the mechanisms by which vocabulary learning takes place, and the conditions to facilitate such learning are still far from clear. We report two studies that investigate the relation between children's text comprehension, their ability to acquire new word meanings, and the factors that influence vocabulary acquisition from written contexts.

Reading comprehension ability and word knowledge are highly correlated in both children and adults (Carroll, 1993). Theoretical explanations for this relation fall broadly into two camps, those that posit a causal relation with vocabulary influencing reading ability and those that propose a common variable underlying the development of these two skills. In support of the direct causal relation, Beck, McKeown, and colleagues found that instruction in word meanings improved comprehension and recall of texts containing the taught words (see Beck & McKeown, 1991, for a review). Stahl and Fairbanks's (1986) meta-analysis of vocabulary instruction research found modest but facilitatory effects even for standardized assessments of reading comprehension, which did not contain the target words. The proposed reason for this direct relation is that the size or richness of an individual's vocabulary or the speed of access to vocabulary items affects reading comprehension ability (see Daneman, 1988, or Perfetti, 1994, for reviews).

These aspects of an individual's vocabulary knowledge will affect text comprehension for most individuals under certain circumstances. However, not all research supports a direct causal relation between vocabulary knowledge and reading comprehension. Prior knowledge of a topic or relevant vocabulary can influence understanding of a text (Spilich, Vesonder, Chiesi, & Voss, 1979; Wittrock, Marks, & Doctorow, 1975), but limited vocabulary knowledge does not always lead to comprehension difficulties (Freebody & Anderson, 1983) and vocabulary knowledge per se does not appear to be sufficient to ensure adequate

From: *Journal of Educational Psychology*, 96 (4), 2004, pp. 671–81.

comprehension of extended discourse (Pany, Jenkins, & Schreck, 1982). However, the major limitation of these causal theories is that they do not specify a mechanism for how vocabulary-related differences arise in the first place.

In our opinion, a more useful framework for studying the relation between vocabulary knowledge and reading comprehension is provided by theories proposing a common skill or mechanism that contributes to the determination of both. Vocabulary knowledge not only predicts reading comprehension level, it is also a good predictor of verbal IQ. Consequently, it has been proposed that the ability to acquire new information from context is the skill that mediates the relation between reading comprehension and verbal IQ and also reading comprehension and vocabulary knowledge (Jensen, 1980; Nippold, 2002; Sternberg & Powell, 1983). In an extension of this hypothesis, Daneman (1988) proposed that processing capacity, in part, determines the ability to learn from context.

Adults' ability to infer new word meanings from context is related to independent assessments of their vocabulary knowledge and memory capacity (Daneman & Green, 1986), but there is some debate over the importance of this skill for children. Children's acquisition of word meanings through context can be slight, with a likelihood of learning the meanings of 15% of unknown words encountered during undirected reading (Swanborn & de Glopper, 1999). Vocabulary gains through context can appear small when compared with the acquisition of word meanings through direct instruction (Jenkins, Matlock, & Slocum, 1989). Thus, although some researchers advocate instruction in the use of contextual cues (Nippold, 2002), others argue for a systematic program of vocabulary instruction (Biemiller & Slonim, 2001).

These two types of instruction need not be mutually exclusive. Direct instruction in word meanings might add those items directly to an individual's vocabulary, but the ability to use those words in all of their nuances is more likely to arise from repeated exposures, through which their meanings are refined (Jenkins et al., 1989; Nagy & Scott, 2000). If word meanings are learned incrementally, a reader might require both direct instruction and exposure to that word in multiple contexts to fully fix its meaning in his or her lexicon. A meta-analysis of studies investigating vocabulary teaching suggests that the most effective method of vocabulary instruction involves the presentation of words both in context and with definitions (Stahl & Fairbanks, 1986).

Differences between written and spoken language indicate that inference from written contexts might be important for vocabulary development. Written language is lexically richer than spoken language and may, therefore, provide a greater number of learning opportunities than are available in spoken contexts (Cunningham & Stanovich, 1998). Avid readers encounter considerably more words each year than their less well-read peers (Anderson, Wilson, & Fielding, 1988), and measures of 9–11-year-olds' exposure to print predicts significant growth in vocabulary (Echols, West, Stanovich, & Zehr, 1996). Practice at reading is likely to lead to more efficient access of word meanings. Regular reading can also provide instances *to* acquire, refine, and consolidate vocabulary knowledge through inference from context.

One text variable that affects a student's ability to acquire new word meanings from context is the distance between the target word and its cue (Carnine, Kameenui, & Coyle, 1984). In naturalistic texts, readers may have to integrate information from several idea units spaced throughout the passage rather than from a single adjacent idea unit in order to derive a complete meaning of an unknown word. Increasing the distance between the different pieces of information to be integrated increases the processing demands for the reader, which will adversely affect individuals with smaller memory capacity (Daneman, 1988; Daneman & Green, 1986). There is some evidence that 4th- to 6th-grade children's ability to learn from context is more strongly related to their working memory capacity than their chronological age (Cull's study; as cited in Daneman, 1988). In Cull's study, the distance manipulation was achieved by placing contextual cues either before or after the word to be learned, which may have led to different processing strategies. Thus, there is clearly a need to investigate the relation between memory capacity and inference from context without such a confound, an aim of the work reported here.

In relation to comprehension skill, distance between pieces of information to be integrated in a text adversely affects less skilled comprehenders' ability to resolve anaphors, detect inconsistencies, and infer new word meanings from context (Cain, Oakhill, & Elbro, 2003; Ehrlich & Remond, 1997; Oakhill, Hartt, & Samols, 2003). Less skilled comprehenders also experience working memory limitations (Yuill, Oakhill, & Parkin, 1989), suggesting that their difficulties with distance arise because of processing difficulties. The relation between memory skills and the ability to derive word meanings from context was explored further in the current study.

Children with better language skills demonstrate superior performance on vocabulary learning tasks. Four-year-olds with larger vocabularies learn more words in experimental storybook reading tasks than those who start out knowing fewer words (Ewers & Brownson, 1999; Sénéchal, Thomas, & Monker, 1995), However the probability of learning new words from context differs dramatically between good and poor readers (Nicholson & Whyte, 1992; Swanborn & de Glopper, 2002). Shefelbine (1990) found that 6th-grade students with the poorest vocabulary knowledge at outset learned the fewest words from context, even though they had the greatest room for improvement. He proposed that children with smaller vocabularies face two difficulties in expanding their vocabulary: (a) They have to learn more words, and (b) their understanding of the words they already know is less well developed.

Larger vocabulary size may indicate more efficient memory for word learning. Two different components of memory are implicated in word learning: phonological short-term memory, which is assessed by measures such as forward digit span and concerns the passive storage of verbal information, and verbal working memory capacity, which is assessed by tasks that involve the simultaneous storage and processing of verbal information, such as reading span (Gathercole, 1998).

Children with good phonological short-term memory are better able to accurately represent the sound structure of a new word, which may facilitate setting up a stable lexical entry for this new word (Gathercole, Hitch, Service, & Martin, 1997). The relation between verbal working memory capacity and vocabulary knowledge may be more complex. College students' vocabulary knowledge is related to their working memory capacity (Daneman & Green, 1986). Therefore, Daneman (1988) proposed that working memory processing capacity plays an important role in vocabulary acquisition. Others argue that semantic skills contribute to (verbal) working memory performance (Nation, Adams, Bowyer-Crane, & Snowling, 1999; but see Cain, Oakhill, & Bryant, 2004).

This review demonstrates a need to understand more fully the role that inference from context plays in children's vocabulary development and the different text and reader variables that affect this process. We report two studies that investigated schoolchildren's ability to infer the meanings of novel vocabulary items from context in relation to one text variable: the proximity of the target word and its useful context, and three reader variables: reading comprehension skill, prior vocabulary knowledge, and memory skills.

Study 1

The aim of this study was to investigate whether skilled and less skilled comprehenders differ in their ability to infer the meanings of novel vocabulary items from context. We manipulated the processing demands of the task by changing the proximity of the novel word and its useful context (near vs. far). It was predicted that children with weak reading comprehension skills would perform particularly poorly in the far condition, when the novel word and context were not adjacent and the processing demands of the task were high. An independent assessment of working memory capacity was taken. We predicted that the less skilled group would obtain significantly lower scores on this measure and that working memory capacity would be related to performance on the vocabulary inference task.

Method

Participants

Two groups of 9–10-year-olds participated in this study: 12 skilled comprehenders (7 girls, 5 boys) and 13 less skilled comprehenders (6 girls, 7 boys). Participants were recruited from urban schools with socially mixed catchment areas on the south coast of England. The majority of participants were from lower middle-class families. All were Caucasian, spoke British English as their first language, and had no known behavioral problems or learning difficulties.

Two tests were used to select participants: the Gates–MacGinitie Primary Two Vocabulary Test (Level 4, Form K; MacGinitie & MacGinitie, 1989), which provides an index of a child's ability to read and understand written words out of context, and the Neale Analysis of Reading Ability – Revised British Edition (Form 1; Neale, 1989), which provides scores for word reading accuracy in context and text comprehension. The Gates–MacGinitie is a group-administered test. It was completed by 227 children and was used to screen out exceptional readers: Children who obtained either very high or very low scores were excluded, and the remaining 74 average readers were assessed using the Neale Analysis.

The selected children obtained reading accuracy ages that were within 12 months of their chronological age. The 13 less skilled comprehenders obtained reading comprehension ages that were below their chronological ages and at least 8 months below their reading accuracy age (mean comprehension – accuracy difference = –24 months). In this way, we were able to exclude any child whose weak comprehension skills had arisen from word reading difficulties. The 12 skilled comprehenders obtained comprehension ages that were at or above that predicted by their reading accuracy age (mean difference = 11 months).

A series of tests were conducted to confirm the group matching. An alpha level of .05 is used throughout this [chapter]. The skilled and less skilled groups differed significantly with regard to their reading comprehension age, as measured by the Neale Analysis [$Ms =$ 128.5 and 94.8 months, SDs = 9.9 and 10.2, respectively), $t(23)$ = 8.43, $p < .01$. The skilled and less skilled group did not differ significantly with regard to their age ($Ms =$ 117.5 and 118.9 months, SDs = 4.2 and 3.1, respectively), $t(23) < 1$: Neale Word Reading Accuracy (Ms = 117.3 and 118.7 months, SDs = 9.0 and 7.0, respectively), $t(23) < 1$; Gates–MacGinitie scores (Ms = 35.3 and 34.5, SDs = 2.1 and 2.2, respectively), $t(23) < 1$: or the number of stories that they had read on the Neale Analysis (Ms = 5.5 and 5.6. SDs = 0.5 and 0.7, respectively), $t(23) < 1$. The latter measure was necessary to ensure that the difference in comprehension scores did not arise because the less skilled group had read fewer stories and, therefore, obtained lower comprehension scores simply because they had attempted fewer comprehension questions.

In addition, the groups were matched for Neale Word Reading Accuracy age using the regressed Neale Word Reading Accuracy scores to take into account the possibility that the two groups were selected from populations that differed in their reading-aloud ability. Adopting the most unfavorable assumption (that the mean accuracy age score of the population that the less skilled comprehenders was drawn from was equivalent to their comprehension age score and that the mean accuracy age score of the population from which the skilled group was drawn from was equal to their comprehension age score), we calculated regressed accuracy scores for all children. The reliability coefficients for the Neale Word Reading Accuracy score are 90 for ages 96–119 months and .84 for ages 120–143 months. The skilled and less skilled groups did not differ significantly with regard to regressed Neale Word Reading Accuracy (Ms = 118.0 and 116.0 months, SDs = 8.1 and 6.5, respectively), t(23) = 1.02, p = .32. It is therefore unlikely that the Neale comprehension differences, or any differences on the experimental task, arose from differences in word reading ability.

Materials and procedure

Vocabulary inference from context task.   Eight short stories were written, each containing a made-up word with a novel meaning (i.e., not a synonym of a known word). The meaning of the unknown word could be derived from information contained in one or two sentences that occurred either immediately after the unknown word (near condition) or after some additional filler sentences (far condition). Thus, there were two versions of each story. An example of both versions of a story is shown in Table 4.1.

The child was read the following instructions:

Table 4.1   Example of text used in the vocabulary learning from context task

Introduction	Informative context	Filler text	Ending
Lucy was taking her dog, Ben, to the park. First she had to find Ben's *wut.**	Her dad suggested taking a football, but that was not quite right. Their football was far too big to play catch with, and it had lost its bounce.	She searched all the rooms in the house, even the kitchen. During her hunt, she found all sorts of things: her hair band that had been missing for a month, an overdue library book, and even her grandma's false teeth!	Lucy decided that she had to be more tidy in the future.

Note: In the far condition, the filler text appeared where marked by the asterisk (*). The text as presented to the children was continuous, not blocked as above, and the novel word was not italicized in the text that the children saw. The information provided by the table headings (e.g., introduction, informative context, etc.) is included here for illustrative purposes only and was not included in the version presented to the children. Acceptable responses included the following: a ball (1 point): a small and/or bouncy ball (2 points).

Today I have brought along some stories that I would like you to read out loud to me. The person who wrote them got a bit stuck at times and didn't always know the right word to put in, so they've put a funny word in the story instead. I want you to tell me what you think the word means. If you have any ideas when you get to the word, then tell me what you think the word means then. But don't worry if you haven't got any ideas. At the end of each story, I will ask you to explain the meaning of the word. For example, if I asked you what a bed was, you might tell me that it was 'a long piece of furniture that we sleep in.'

Children read the story up to the end of the sentence in which the unknown word appeared. The remainder of the text was kept covered with a piece of paper. The tester then asked the child what he or she thought the strange word might mean (e.g., 'What do you think a *wut* might be?'). Responses were recorded verbatim and scored later. The child then completed the story. At the end, the child was asked, 'What do you think a *wut* might be? You can stick with your first idea or you can change your mind.' Each child read four stories in each condition, and the set was counterbalanced as completely as possible within group.

Working memory task.   This task was similar to the Listening Span Test developed by Daneman and Carpenter (1980) and used with children by Siegel and Ryan (1989). The tester read aloud sentences that were missing their final word. The final word completion was constrained by the sentence context, and the task was to complete the sentence with a single word and remember that word for later recall. Children completed three trials at three levels of difficulty in which the number of trials (and, thus, the number of final words to be recalled) was increased: three sentences, four sentences, and five sentences. One point was awarded for each final word recalled in its correct position.

Results

The reliability of our experimental measures was assessed by calculating Chronbach's alpha over items. The reliability coefficients were both acceptable: Working Memory Listening Span task, $\sigma = .68$; Vocabulary Inference task, $\alpha = .79$.

Vocabulary inference task

Points were awarded for the quality of the definition of the unknown word: 0 points for an incorrect response, 1 point for a partially correct definition, and 2 points for a complete definition. Examples of responses and points allocated are shown in Table 4.1. All responses were scored by two independent raters, and disputes were resolved by discussion.

For each condition (near, far), a use of context score was calculated by subtracting the score obtained before the useful context from that obtained after context. These scores were analysed in a two-way analysis of variance (ANOVA), with skill group (skilled, less skilled) and proximity (near, far) as factors. There was a main effect of skill group, $F(1, 23) = 18.01, p < .01$, because the skilled comprehenders obtained higher scores than the less skilled group in general *(Ms = 4.8 and 2.7, SDs = 1.3 and 1.2, respectively;* $\eta^2 = .27$). There was a marginal effect of proximity, $F(1. 23) = 3.68, p = .07$, because scores obtained in the near condition tended to be higher than those obtained in the far condition *(Ms = 4.1 and 3.2, SDs = 1.9 and 2.1, respectively;* $\eta^2 = .04$). These two factors were involved in a significant interaction, $F(1. 23) = 6.21, p = .02, \eta^2 = .07$). Planned comparisons were conducted to determine whether the proximity manipulation affected the performance of each skill group differently, as predicted. The scores obtained by the skilled group in the near *(M = 4.7, SD = 1.6)* and far *(M = 4.9, SD = 1.4)* conditions did not differ significantly, $t(11) < 1$. For the less skilled comprehenders, there was a significant difference between the scores obtained in the near condition *(M = 3.6, SD = 2.2)* and the far condition *(M = 1.7, SD =1.4)*, $t(12) = 2.67$, $p = .02$.

Working memory task

The total number of items recalled in their correct order was calculated for each participant. The skilled group recalled significantly more items *(M = 19.8. SD = 4.8)* than did the less skilled group *(Ms = 15.5, SD = 3.4)*, $t(23) = 2.62$, $p < .02$, $d = 1.04$. However, the working memory scores were not significantly correlated with performance in either condition (near, $r = .17$, $p > .10$; far, $r = .32$, $p < .12$).

Summary and discussion

Children with weak reading comprehension skills were less able to infer the meanings of novel vocabulary items from context than were their skilled peers. The less skilled group's performance was affected by the proximity of the useful context and the novel word. They were much less likely to provide an appropriate meaning of the novel word when it was separated from the context by filler text. The skilled group was not affected by this manipulation. Although the interaction between the two factors was significant, the measurement of effect size shows that comprehension ability accounted for the greater proportion of the variance in performance on the vocabulary inference task.

Consistent with previous work (Cain et al., 2003), there was a relation between inference from context and reading comprehension skill, this time with an older sample of children. Contrary to previous research by Stothard and Hulme (1992), less skilled comprehenders had weak verbal working memory skills relative to the skilled group. However, other studies have found working memory differences between skilled and less skilled comprehenders (e.g., Yuill et al., 1989), and the Stothard and Hulme study may have lacked discriminatory power because of floor levels of performance. The estimate of effect size demonstrates that the difference in working memory scores between the skill groups was substantial. The less skilled group's performance on the vocabulary inference task was poorer in the condition that had the higher working memory demands, but working memory capacity and performance on the vocabulary inference task were not significantly correlated.

There were several limitations to the study, which prompted further investigation. The small number of participants (25) meant that the study lacked power. It is important to investigate the relation between memory and vocabulary inference with a more powerful design because of Daneman's (1988) claim that working memory capacity may account for individual differences in contextual learning (see also Biemiller & Slonim, 2001). Indeed, in the current study, the skilled comprehenders were not adversely affected by the proximity manipulation and obtained higher working memory scores than the less skilled group.

We did not check children's memory for the literal or factual content of the stories from which they inferred the novel vocabulary items. Thus, group differences may have arisen because the less skilled comprehenders had poorer memory for the text per se, rather than a specific difficulty with inferring new word meanings from context. The skilled comprehenders also made more lucky guesses in their initial explanations of the novel word. The mean total of lucky guesses for the skilled group and less skilled groups did not differ significantly *(Ms* = 1.8 and 1.2, *SDs* = 1.1 and 1.2, respectively), *r*(23) = 1.28, *p* = .21. However, the skilled comprehenders may have taken advantage of some unintended contextual clues before the target context was encountered, thereby reducing the pool of possible target meanings of the novel words and enabling them to use the context more efficiently when encountered.

We can interpret our results in (at least) two ways: (a) Less skilled comprehenders have difficulties in inferring the meanings of new words from context, or (b) less skilled comprehenders have a more fundamental deficit with vocabulary acquisition in general. That is, less skilled comprehenders might simply find it hard to set up and/or maintain an integrated representation of a new label and its meaning. A second study was conducted to distinguish between these two hypotheses by including a direct instruction task (where participants are explicitly taught the meanings of new vocabulary items) to relate to performance on the vocabulary inference task. In addition, the study was designed to investigate individual differences in vocabulary knowledge, as well as comprehension, in relation to mechanisms for vocabulary learning.

Study 2

The first aim of this study was to explore how individual differences in both comprehension level and vocabulary knowledge affect the ability to learn new word meanings. Children with weak vocabulary skills learn fewer new vocabulary items from context than their more skilled peers even though they have the greatest room for gain (Shefelbine, 1990). We compared the performance of three groups: (a) skilled and (b) less skilled comprehenders matched for vocabulary knowledge and (c) less skilled comprehenders with weaker vocabulary skills than the two other groups. This design was used to determine whether children with poor comprehension and weak vocabulary experience a greater vocabulary learning deficit than the type of less skilled comprehender who participated in Study 1.

All children completed two experimental measures of vocabulary learning: the inference from context task used in Study 1 and a direct instruction task. In the latter, children were taught the meanings of novel words explicitly by reading out the new word together with its meaning. Two measures were derived: an ease of learning score, calculated from the number of repetitions required to learn the novel words, and a delayed recall score. From these scores, we can determine whether children who experience difficulties on the inference from context task also experience difficulties in setting up an integrated representation of a new label and its meaning (ease of learning) and/or find it hard to maintain this information over time (delayed recall).

Poor phonological short-term memory can lead to vocabulary learning difficulties by impairing the ability to retain a new phonological label and establish a new lexical entry for that word. We assessed short-term memory in order to relate it to performance on the direct instruction task (although previous work has found no difference between skilled and less skilled comprehenders on measures of short-term phonological memory; Oakhill, Yuill, & Parkin, 1986).

We included two measures of working memory capacity: the listening span measure used in Study 1 and a counting span measure (Case, Kurland, & Goldberg, 1982). The latter task measures processing capacity without the element of sentence comprehension evident in the listening span task. Thus, we were able to examine whether processing capacity in general, as opposed to processing capacity for text, was related to performance on the vocabulary inference task. We predicted that both measures of working memory would be related to comprehension skill and also to task performance on the vocabulary inference task, particularly in the far condition where the processing demands are greatest. In addition, we could test whether the weak vocabulary group experienced a greater impairment on the verbal working memory task than the comparison group of less skilled comprehenders (see Nation et al., 1999).

We included two memory questions after each text. These required recall of information stated explicitly in the text. Thus, we were able to investigate whether the less skilled comprehenders were specifically impaired in their ability to infer the meanings of novel vocabulary items from context, or whether they were more generally impaired in their memory for the text from which the inference has to be drawn. In order to assess the relative influence of word meaning acquisition, memory capacity, and memory for the text on the vocabulary inference task, we controlled for these measures in our statistical analyses.

Method

Participants

Three groups of 9–10-year-olds participated in this study: one group of skilled comprehenders, one group of less skilled comprehenders, selected in the same way as those who participated in Study 1, and another group of less skilled comprehenders with weaker vocabulary skills relative to both other groups (weak vocabulary group). Participants attended urban schools with socially mixed catchment areas near the city of Nottingham, England. The majority of participants were from lower middle-class families. Eighty-three percent of the sample were Caucasian; the rest were British Asian. All spoke British English as their first language and had no known behavioral problems or learning difficulties.

The following tests were used in the selection process: Form 1 of the Neale Analysis of Reading Ability – Revised (NARA-11; Neale, 1997) and the Gales–MacGinitie Primary Two Vocabulary Test (Level 4, Form K; MacGinitie & MacGinitie, 1989), both used in Study 1. In addition, we administered: the Graded Nonword Reading Test (GNWRT, Snowling, Stothard, & McLean, 1996), which measures children's decoding ability; the British Picture Vocabulary Scale – Second Edition (BPVS; Dunn, Dunn, Whetton, & Burley, 1997), which assesses receptive vocabulary; and the Word Association subtest from the Clinical Evaluation of Language Fundamentals – Revised (CELF-R; Semel, Wiig, & Secord, 1987), which measures semantic fluency. Group characteristics are reported in Table 4.2.

The 12 less skilled comprehenders (7 girls, 5 boys) and the 12 skilled comprehenders (9 girls, 3 boys) did not differ significantly on the vocabulary measures, Gates–MacGinitie, $t(22) < 1$; BPVS, $t(22) = 1.93$, $p = .07$; CELF-R Word Association subtest, $t(22) < 1$, on the measures of word reading and decoding ability, regressed NARA-11 Word Reading Accuracy scores, $t(22) = 1.34$, $p = .19$; GNWRT scores, $t(22) < 1$, or on chronological age, $t(22) < 1$. The less skilled comprehenders obtained significantly lower NARA-11 comprehension scores than those of the skilled group, $t(22) = 9.77$. $p < 01$.

The group of less skilled comprehenders with weak vocabulary skills (5 girls, 7 boys) obtained comparable regressed NARA-II Word Reading Accuracy scores with those obtained by the other groups (both $ts < 1.0$). The weak vocabulary group obtained lower

NARA-II comprehension scores compared with the skilled group, $t(22) = 9.45$, $p < .01$, but did not differ from the less skilled comprehender group on this measure, $t(22) = 1.22$, $p = .23$.

The weak vocabulary group was selected to have poorer vocabulary skills than the other groups, Gates–MacGinitie: skilled versus weak vocabulary group, $t(22) = 5.42$, $p < .01$, less skilled versus weak vocabulary, $t(22) = 6.13$.$p < .01$; BPVS: skilled versus weak vocabulary, $t(22) = 531$, $p < .01$, less skilled versus weak vocabulary, $t(22) = 6.13$, $p < .01$. Group differences on the Word Association task only reached significance for the comparison between the skilled comprehenders and the weak vocabulary group, $t(22) = 2.11$, $p < .05$. The other group comparisons did not reach significance (both $ts < 1.0$).[1]

Table 4.2   Group characteristics for Study 2

Measure	Skilled comprehenders		Less skilled comprehenders		Weak vocabulary group	
	M	SD	M	SD	M	SD
Chronological age	115.0	3.5	116.3	4.3	115.6	4.5
Gates–MacGinitie (max. = 45)	31.5	2.7	34.1	2.2	30.2	0.5
BPVS	108.8	2.6	106.3	3.8	100.2	5.0
CELF–R	42.0	7.8	18.7	7.5	36.0	5.8
GNWRT (max. = 24)	19.4	2.2	18.4	4.1	19.3	2.9
Reading accuracy	125.5	7.3	125.7	6.8	129.9	11.5
Reading comprehension	127.7	9.9	96.7	5.6	92.1	8.5
Number of stories	6.0	0.0	6.0	0.0	5.8	0.4

Note: n = 12. Means in the same row that do not share superscripts differ at $p < .05$ in the t tests. max. = maximum: Gates–MacGinitie = Gates–MacGinitie Vocabulary subtest; BPVS = British Picture Vocabulary Scale (standardized scores); CELF–R = Word Association subtest from the Clinical Evaluation of Language Fundamentals – Revised; GNWRT = Graded Nonword Reading Test; Reading accuracy and reading comprehension = age-equivalent (in months) scores obtained on the Neale Analysis of Reading Ability – Revised (NARA-II); number of stories = stories completed on NARA-II.

Materials and procedure

Sixteen stories, each with a different novel word, were used in this study. Each story contained contextual clues from which the target definition could be inferred. Eight of these stories had been used in Study 1: the other eight were written for this experiment. Texts used in the first study were modified to reduce the opportunity for fortuitous guesswork before the target context was encountered. Pilot work indicated that, for all texts, the meanings of the novel words could only be determined from the useful context (i.e., none of them were guessed correctly).

The 16 novel word items were divided into four groups of four words. Four lists of experimental items were created, using a Latin square rotation so that each list comprised eight novel words to be presented in stories and eight different novel words to be presented in the direct instruction task. Thus, each child was presented with different words in the two tasks, which were administered in separate sessions.

Vocabulary direction instruction task.   For this task, a procedure adapted from Cain, Oakhill, Barnes, and Bryant (2001) was used. Children were told the following:

Today I want you to pretend that there is a make-believe place called Gan, which is different from where we live. Some things on Gan have different names from the names that we use. I am going to tell you about these things, and I want you to try to remember what they are.

Eight novel words and their meanings were then read aloud, for example, 'A small bouncy ball is called a *wut*.' After the eight items had been read aloud, children were tested for their verbal recall of the novel word meanings with specific questions, for example, 'On Gan, what is a *wut?*' This test provides an index of how easily participants acquired the meanings of the novel words. Wrong answers were corrected immediately and the questions to test these items repeated after the complete set of items had been presented, so that only items that were recalled incorrectly were presented more than once. A delayed test of memory for these items was administered after a short filler task (forward digit span).

Vocabulary inference from context task.   The procedure followed was the same as that used in Study 1, with two additional questions after each story to assess memory for facts in the text.

Short-term memory.   A forward digit span task was administered using lists of digits that increased in length, starting with two digits. Four trials were presented for each list length, with items recalled in order of presentation. Testing ceased when two or more trials of a certain list length were incorrectly recalled. The score entered into the analysis was the total number of trials correctly recalled before testing ceased (Pickering & Gathercole, 2001).

Working memory.   Two assessments of working memory capacity were administered: The listening span measure used in Study 1 and a counting span task modified from Pickering and Gathercole (2001). In each task, children completed four trials with two three, four, and five items per trial (sentences or dots).[2]

Results

The reliability of our experimental measures was assessed by calculating Chronbach's alpha over items. In all cases, the reliability coefficients were acceptable: listening span = .72, counting span = .65, vocabulary direct instruction tasks (for Lists 1–4) = .79 – .87, vocabulary inference (for Lists 1–4) = .78 – .84, vocabulary inference task memory questions = .76. The forward digit span retest reliability coefficient was .82 (Pickering &. Gathercole, 2001). We present the analysis of each assessment individually, followed by the results of a set of multiple regressions designed to determine the relative contribution made by the memory and learning variables to performance on the vocabulary inference task.

Performance on the individual tasks

Direct instruction task.   An ease of learning score was calculated by awarding 1 point for each item correctly recalled the first time, 2 points for items requiring a second presentation trial, 3 points for three trials, and so forth. The score obtained was the sum of the learning trials required until perfect recall was achieved. This score reflects ease of learning the word definitions: 8 denotes perfect learning and recall, and higher scores indicate that the definitions of some words had to be repeated. Means (with standard deviations) for the skilled, less skilled, and weak vocabulary group were 16.5 (4.9), 17.3 (3.8), and 22.6 (8.7), respectively. A delayed memory score was calculated from responses after the filler task, using the 0–2 point scale described in Study 1 for the context task. This score reflects ability to retain the taught word definitions. In order, the means (with standard deviations) for the skilled, less skilled, and weak vocabulary group were 9.2 (3.9), 7.8 (3.7), and 7.0 (2.8), respectively.

These two scores were treated as the dependent variables in two separate one-way ANOVAs, with skill group (skilled, less skilled, weak vocabulary) as a between-subjects factor. In the ease of learning analysis, there was a significant effect of skill group. $F(2. 33) = 3.44. p < .05, \eta = .208$. The weak vocabulary group required significantly more repetitions than both the skilled comprehenders, $t(22) = 2.42. p < .05, d = 0.86$, and the less skilled group, $t(22) = 2.09. p < .05, d = 0.79$, both large effects. The skilled and less skilled groups did not differ on this measure, $t(22) < 1$. In the analysis of the delayed recall scores, the effect of skill group was not significant, $F(2,33) = 1.19, p = .10$.

Vocabulary inference from context task: Memory for literal and factual content.   The responses to the questions tapping memory for literal and factual content were scored as either correct or incorrect, and the total was calculated (maximum = 16). These scores were entered into a one–way ANOVA, with skill group as a between-subjects factor. The skilled, less skilled, and weak vocabulary groups obtained comparable means (and standard deviations) of 14.1 (1.3), 13.5(2.0), and 13.3 (1.5), respectively. The effect of skill group was not significant, $F(2, 33) = 1.04, p = .20$.

Vocabulary inference from context task: Vocabulary learning scores.   Each definition of a novel vocabulary item was awarded a score of 0–2 points following the same scoring criteria described above. The difference between the scores obtained before and after the useful context was calculated. In the near condition, the means (and standard deviations) for skilled, less skilled, and weak vocabulary groups were 4.17 (1.95), 3.92 (1.93), and 2.75 (1.45), respectively. In the far condition, the means (and standard deviations) for skilled, less skilled, and weak vocabulary groups were 4.08 (1.37), 2.21 (1.72), and 1.04 (1.57), respectively. These scores were entered into a two-way ANOVA, with skill group (skilled, less skilled, weak vocabulary) and proximity (near, far) as factors. There was a highly significant effect or skill group, $F(2, 33) = 7.97, p < .01, \eta^2 = .22$, and a highly significant effect of proximity, $F(1, 33) = 15.57, p < .01, \eta^2 = .09$, qualified by a significant interaction, $F(2, 33) = 3.37, p < .05, \eta^2 = .04$. Planned comparisons revealed that the skilled comprehenders performed comparably in both conditions, $t(11) < 1$, whereas both the less skilled and the weak vocabulary group obtained lower scores in the far relative to the near condition, $t(11) = 3.26, p < .01$, and $t(11) = 3.42, p < .01$, respectively.

Short-term memory.   The forward digit span mean scores (and standard deviations) for the skilled, less skilled, and weak vocabulary groups were 13.92 (2.50), 14.91 (3.08), and 14.75 (1.91), respectively. These data were treated as the dependent variable in a one-way ANOVA, with skill group as a between–subjects factor.[3] The effect of skill group did not reach significance, $F(2, 32) < 1$, and this variable is not included in any further analyses.

Working memory.   The mean scores (and standard deviations) obtained on the listening span task were 29.58 (10.55), 14.75 (7.86), and 16.08 (8.12) for the skilled, less skilled, and weak vocabulary groups, respectively. These data were entered into a one-way ANOVA, with skill group as a between-subjects factor. There was a highly significant effect of skill group, $F(2, 33) = 6.32, p < .01, \eta^2 = .12$. Planned comparisons revealed that the skilled group obtained significantly higher scores than the less skilled comprehenders, $t(23) = 3.25, p < .01, d = 1.27$, and the weak vocabulary group, $t(23) = 2.88, p < .01, d = 1.11$. The difference between the two poor comprehender groups was not significant, $t(23) < 1$.

In the counting span task, the skilled, less skilled, and weak vocabulary groups obtained mean scores (and standard deviations) of 42.75 (8.75), 36.92 (7.96), and 38.58 (7.87), respectively. A one-way ANOVA did not reveal a significant effect of skill group, $F(2, 33) = 2.56$, $p = .09$.

Relations between the different assessments

We conducted three sets of fixed-order hierarchical multiple regression analyses to address two crucial questions: (a) Do either comprehension or vocabulary skills explain unique variance in the vocabulary inference task over and above the contribution made by ease of vocabulary learning (assessed by the direct instruction task), factual memory for the text, or working memory? (b) Do comprehension and vocabulary predict independent variance in performance on the vocabulary inference task?

To explore the contribution made by ease of learning, and the further contributions made by comprehension and vocabulary ability, to performance on the near condition of the vocabulary inference task, we conducted a pair of analyses as follows. In the first analysis of the pair, ease of learning scores were entered in the first step, vocabulary scores in the second, and comprehension in the third. In the second analysis of the pair, the order of Steps 2 and 3 was reversed. A parallel set of analyses was conducted, with performance in the far condition as the dependent variable. A second comparable set of analyses was conducted, with memory for the text controlled for in the first step and a third set with working memory performance entered in the first step. We report results for each of the learning and memory variables in turn. For brevity, we only report significant results.

Ease of learning.   Neither ease of learning nor reading comprehension ability was a significant predictor of performance in the near condition. The only variable that predicted significant variance in the near condition was vocabulary in the following analysis: Step 1, ease of learning, $R^2 = .004$, *ns*; Step 2, vocabulary, $\Delta R^2 = .119$, $p < .05$; Step 3, comprehension, $\Delta R^2 = .022$, *ns*. Although vocabulary predicted a substantial proportion of variance in this analysis, it did not explain significant variance in the paired analysis, when entered in the third step after comprehension.

A different pattern of data was found for the analyses in which performance in the far condition was the dependent variable. Again, ease of learning did not account for significant variance at the first step ($R^2 = .004$, *ns*). When entered at the second step, vocabulary predicted unique variance ($R^2 = .156$, $p < .02$) and comprehension predicted additional variance when entered at the third step ($R^2 = .140.p < .02$) With the order of Steps 2 and 3 reversed, only comprehension predicted unique variance: Step 2, comprehension, $R^2 = .276$, $p < .01$; Step 3, vocabulary, $\Delta R^2 = .020$, *ns*. The increment in R^2 indicates that comprehension skill predicted a substantial proportion of variance in performance in the far condition.

Memory for the text.   Neither memory for the text, vocabulary knowledge, nor reading comprehension ability explained significant variance in performance in the near condition of the vocabulary inference task. The comprehension and vocabulary variables did explain independent variance, with comprehension being the stronger predictor. For Analysis 1: Step 1, memory for the text, $R^2 = .016$, *ns*; Step 2, vocabulary, $\Delta R^2 = .205$, $p < .01$; Step 3, comprehension, $\Delta R^2 = .141$, $p < .02$. When the order of Steps 2 and 3 was reversed, comprehension explained a sizeable proportion of the variance when entered at Step 2 ($\Delta R^2 = .322$, $p < .01$), but vocabulary did not explain further variance when entered at Step 3 ($\Delta R^2 = .023$, *ns*). As before, the increment in R^2 indicates that comprehension skill predicted substantial variance in performance in the far condition.

Working memory.   Comparable with the previous analysis, neither working memory, vocabulary knowledge, nor reading comprehension ability explained significant variance in performance in the near condition of the vocabulary inference task. In the prediction of scores obtained in the far condition, comprehension was found to explain a greater proportion of variance than did vocabulary ability. In addition, working memory explained significant variance. For Analysis 1: Step 1, working memory, $\Delta R^2 = .191$, $p < .05$; Step 2, vocabulary, $\Delta R^2 = .112$, $p < .05$; Step 3, comprehension, $\Delta R^2 = .075$, $p = .062$. When the order of Steps 2 and 3 was reversed, comprehension explained unique variance when entered after working memory at Step 2 ($\Delta R^2 = .164$, $p < .01$). Vocabulary did not explain further variance when entered at Step 3 ($\Delta R^2 = .022$, *ns*).

Working memory capacity explained variance in the ability to infer the meanings of vocabulary items in the far condition, and it was also related to comprehension level. These analyses also demonstrate a less substantial increment in R^2 attributable to comprehension skill, when entered after working memory scores. To determine whether working memory made a unique contribution to performance on this task over and above the variance attributed to comprehension and vocabulary, we conducted a final analysis. Comprehension and vocabulary were both entered at the first step and explained a sizeable proportion of the variance *($R^2 = .361$, $p < .01$)* Working memory did not explain any significant variance when entered at the second step after these variables ($\Delta R^2 = .017$, *ns*), indicating that the effect of working memory capacity was mediated by the variance it shared with reading comprehension skill.

Summary and discussion

In the direct instruction task, children with both weak vocabulary and comprehension skills required more repetitions to learn the definitions of new words than both skilled comprehenders and less skilled comprehenders with good vocabulary skills. The size of these effects was substantial. However, the three groups' ability to retain this knowledge was comparable, at least over a short delay. It should be noted that children were only likely to remember the partial definition, indicating that the meanings for the new vocabulary items were not fully represented in long-term memory. There was no evidence from the multiple regression analyses that performance on the direct learning task was related to the ability to infer word meanings from context.

In the vocabulary inference task, there was a sizeable effect of comprehension skill. Furthermore, both groups of less skilled comprehenders were adversely affected by the distance manipulation: They were less able to infer the correct definition of a novel word from its useful context in the far condition. As in Study 1, the skilled comprehenders' performance was not affected by the distance manipulation. However, the two groups of less skilled comprehenders were as able as the skilled comprehenders to answer the memory questions after each story, and there was no evidence from the multiple regression analyses that memory for the text affected performance on the vocabulary inference task.

Both groups of less skilled comprehenders had comparable working memory skills and performed more poorly on the verbal working memory assessment than did the skilled comprehenders. A relation between vocabulary knowledge and verbal working memory was not found. The multiple regression analyses indicate that the impaired memory capacity of the less skilled comprehenders was a major determinant of their poor performance in the far condition of the vocabulary inference task.

Both groups of less skilled comprehenders were impaired on the vocabulary inference task, but only the weak vocabulary group was impaired on the direct instruction task.

These two tasks appear to be tapping different skills. From the multiple regression analyses, we can conclude that performance on the direct instruction and the vocabulary inference tasks was relatively independent: The ease of learning measure did not explain significant variance in the vocabulary inference task. Individual differences in vocabulary knowledge and comprehension skill were more important predictors. Comprehension ability was consistently related to performance in the far condition, partly because of the variance it shared with working memory capacity. Initial vocabulary knowledge was a less important predictor of performance and did not predict unique variance in performance when entered after reading comprehension level.

General discussion

Our understanding of the relations between reading comprehension skill, vocabulary knowledge, and vocabulary acquisition is extended in several ways by these results. Children with weak reading comprehension skills were consistently poorer at inferring the meanings of novel vocabulary items from context, relative to their same-age skilled peers. A major source of difficulty was the processing demands of the task. Poor comprehenders with weak vocabulary skills relative to their peers experienced additional sources of difficulty in learning new vocabulary items, namely, in the acquisition of word meanings through direct instruction and vocabulary inference in general. These findings and their implications are discussed, in turn.

Children with text comprehension problems are poor at generating a range of inferences (Cain & Oakhill, 1999; Cain et al., 2001; Oakhill, 1982, 1984). They are particularly impaired at making inferences that are necessary to construct a well-integrated and coherent representation of the meaning of a text. We have shown that less skilled comprehenders are also poor at using inferential processing to work out the meanings of single new words when explicitly directed to do so, particularly when the processing demands of the task are high.

There was no evidence that less skilled comprehenders with good vocabulary skills experienced more widespread difficulties with vocabulary acquisition: Their scores on the direct instruction task were comparable with those of the skilled comprehended. However, the poor comprehenders with weak vocabulary skills were impaired on the direct instruction task, requiring a greater number of repetitions to learn new word meanings. Their subsequent retention of this information was comparable with that of the other groups. There was no evidence for phonological short-term memory deficits in either group of less skilled comprehenders. The weak vocabulary group's difficulties in learning new words might lie in the setting up of new lexical entries, a proposal that warrants further investigation.

One possible source of impaired performance on the vocabulary inference task is memory limitations. Both groups of less skilled comprehenders performed poorly on the working memory assessments relative to the skilled group. Furthermore, the comprehension scores explained unique and sizeable variance in the far condition of the vocabulary inference task, which appeared to be related to its high processing demands and the variance shared between reading comprehension ability and working memory. Working memory capacity might influence vocabulary acquisition from context because it is a crucial factor in an individual's ability to integrate different information across a text (Daneman, 1988). It appears to be an important determinant of performance for the less skilled comprehenders with good vocabulary skills.

There may be different underlying reasons for the weak vocabulary group's difficulties on the inference task. This group derived the least number of definitions on the vocabulary inference task in both conditions (although they were not significantly poorer on this task than were the less skilled comprehenders). Initial vocabulary knowledge explained performance on this task over and above ease of learning, measured by the direct instruction task. Thus, the weak vocabulary group's difficulties on the vocabulary inference task appear to be independent of their difficulties on the direct instruction task. They may have lacked strategic knowledge about how to derive words from context. McKeown (1985) found strategy knowledge differences between 5th graders with good and poor vocabulary skills: Those with high vocabulary knowledge had a more sophisticated understanding of the relation between context and new words than did the children with low vocabulary skills and were more likely to use more than one piece of information to constrain the meanings of new words.

McKeown's (1985) study and our own used paradigms to assess deliberate learning from context, in which the reader is explicitly requested to derive the meaning of the target item. These tasks contrast with an incidental learning paradigm, in which participants are not aware of the purpose of the task and learning is measured later. Deliberate learning paradigms do not reflect natural reading, where word learning is incidental to the purpose of reading. However, their great strength is their ability to measure an individual's potential. As Swanborn and de Glopper (1999) stated, 'Knowing how to derive word meanings from context is a necessary condition for incidental word learning' (p. 279). We have identified a group of poor readers who lack proficiency in this basic skill. Programs of instruction in learning word meanings from context meet with relative success (Fukkink & de Glopper, 1998) and can benefit even poor readers (Stahl & Fairbanks, 1986). Work is now needed to establish whether the performance of the two different groups of less skilled comprehenders can be improved through training in the knowledge and use of skills required to infer words from context.

We compared the performance of two groups of poor comprehenders, with good and poor vocabulary skills. Many researchers of reading comprehension difficulties regularly match their skilled and less skilled groups on measures of vocabulary knowledge as well as word reading (e.g., Cain et al., 2001; Ehrlich & Remond, 1997; Stothard & Hulme, 1992). However, these children may experience difficulties in learning new word meanings under certain conditions. Teachers and caregivers can and do facilitate word learning for younger children by highlighting unknown vocabulary in shared reading experiences (Elley, 1989; Sénéchal, Cornell, & Broda, 1995). As children get older and become independent readers, such opportunities diminish and the ability to infer from context may become an increasingly important means of vocabulary learning. We propose that poor comprehenders with good vocabulary skills may have acquired the same apparent vocabulary skills as their skilled peers through direct instruction and possibly inference from context in considerate texts, where new words and contextual clues to the meaning of those words are in close proximity. As children become more independent readers and move from reading books with controlled vocabularies, the opportunities for word learning from context will increase. The less skilled comprehenders' vocabularies might not increase at the same rate as those of the skilled comprehenders, who have greater opportunities for learning from context because of their more efficient processing capacities and because they may have more reading experience. The other group of poor comprehenders, those who already have weak vocabulary skills, face additional difficulties in acquiring vocabulary. These children appear to lack the strategic knowledge needed to infer the meanings of new words and also appear to require more encounters with new words to consolidate lexical entries. We found support for both of the hypotheses outlined in the *Summary and discussion* section of Study 1: Some less skilled comprehenders' primary deficit lies in inferring the meanings of new words (particularly in inconsiderate contexts), whereas other less skilled comprehenders experience an additional difficulty, that of setting up a representation between a new label and its meaning.

In the introduction, we outlined different accounts of the relation between vocabulary knowledge and reading comprehension. We have examined how they may be related because they both develop through shared skills and processes, namely, inference making and working memory. A direct (and causal) link between vocabulary and reading comprehension is implied by models of reading that emphasize the importance of fluency and automaticity of access to word meanings on text comprehension (see Daneman, 1988, and Perfetti, 1994, for reviews). We did not explore the latter hypothesis in the current work, and the available evidence for such a relation is equivocal. Some studies find semantic deficits in populations of poor comprehenders (Nation & Snowling, 1999), whereas others do not (Yuill & Oakhill, 1991). In Study 2, the skilled and less skilled comprehenders did not differ on the measure of semantic fluency (Word Association subtest from CELF-R) that has discriminated groups in other work (Nation & Snowling, 1998).

A complex relation between vocabulary and comprehension level is apparent. It is important that researchers differentiate vocabulary knowledge from ease of access to that knowledge when they investigate this relation. Some training programs result in gains in vocabulary knowledge, but not all of them lead to corresponding increases in comprehension skill (e.g., Mezynski, 1983). Different factors such as instruction method and reader variables affect the efficacy of vocabulary instruction (Stahl & Fairbanks, 1986); thus, the failure of some training studies might be because the period of instruction was not sufficiently extensive to improve fluency and access to the word meanings. There is evidence that both the number of words known by an individual and the ease with which word meanings can be accessed influence text comprehension. Further work is now needed to tease apart the contribution made by word knowledge and access to that knowledge in relation to comprehension skill.

There are several limitations to the current study. As discussed above, we did not assess incidental learning for the vocabulary items; rather, children's attention was directed to the target word. Thus, performance on this task does not necessarily reflect a child's ability to learn new word meanings from text in everyday reading situations: It most probably overestimates their ability. Further research is needed to investigate whether skilled comprehenders also show an advantage in the incidental learning of new words. Second, as noted above, children were likely to infer the partial rather than the full meanings of the unknown words. This was probably a consequence of our design, which only provided children with a single exposure. Other work has demonstrated that children benefit from repeated exposures to new words in context (Jenkins et al., 1989). Future work should address whether good and poor comprehenders differ in the number of exposures they require to fully learn a new vocabulary item and/or whether good comprehenders' advantage in the current study was the result of a superior fast-mapping mechanism. Third, our paradigm did not enable the assessment of causal relations. Although we speculate that inference from context, a skill associated with good reading comprehension, is a plausible facilitator of vocabulary growth, longitudinal investigations are necessary to test this hypothesis.

In summary, children with reading comprehension deficits are poor at inferring the meanings of novel word items from context. Although there is some disagreement about the relative importance of learning from context as a means of vocabulary acquisition (e.g., Biemiller & Slonim, 2001), there is a wealth of research to support a strong relation between leisure reading and vocabulary knowledge (e.g., Cunningham & Stanovich, 1998). In light of that research and our current findings, we agree with the suggestions of researchers such as Nagy and Scott (2000) and Nippold (2002) that there is a role for instruction in the use of contextual cues in the curriculum to aid the increase and consolidation of vocabulary knowledge. A deficit in learning from context may impede the vocabulary development of children with weak comprehension skills as they become independent readers. Clearly, there is a need to study the relation between learning from context, comprehension skill, and vocabulary acquisition over time.

Notes

1　Two less skilled comprehenders were absent from this test session.
2　We included the easier two-level trials in the second study, because we were not sure at the outset whether the less skilled comprehenders with weak vocabulary skills would have significantly greater working memory impairments than the other two groups.
3　One less skilled comprehender was absent from this test session.

References

Anderson, R.C., Wilson, P.T., & Fielding, L.G. (1988). Growth in reading and how children spend their time outside of school. *Reading Research Quarterly, 13,* 285–303.

Beck, I., & McKeown, M. (1991). Conditions of vocabulary acquisition. In R. Barr, M.L. Kamil, P. Mosenthal, & P.D. Pearson (Eds,), *Handbook of reading research* (Vol. 2, pp. 789–814). Mahwah, NJ: Erlbaum.

Biemiller, A., & Slonim, N. (2001). Estimating root word vocabulary growth in normative and advantaged populations: Evidence for a common sequence of vocabulary acquisition. *Journal of Educational Psychology, 93,* 498–520.

Cain, K., & Oakhill. J.V. (1999). Inference making ability and its relation to comprehension failure. *Reading and Writing, 11,* 489–503.

Cain, K., Oakhill, J.V., Barnes, M.A., & Bryant, P.E. (2001). Comprehension skill, inference-making ability, and their relation to knowledge. *Memory and Cognition, 29,* 850–859.

Cain, K., Oakhill, J., & Bryant, P. (2004). Children's reading comprehension ability: Concurrent prediction by working memory, verbal ability, and component skills. *Journal of Educational Psychology, 96,* 31–42.

Cain, K., Oakhill, J.V., & Elbro, C. (2003). The ability to learn new word meanings from context by school-age children with and without language comprehension difficulties. *Journal of Child Language, 30,* 681–694.

Carnine, D., Kameenui, E.J., & Coyle, G. (1984). Utilization of contextual information in determining the meaning of unfamiliar words. *Reading Research Quarterly, 19,* 188–204.

Carroll, J.B. (1993). *Human cognitive abilities: A survey of factor analysis studies.* New York: Cambridge University Press.

Case, R., Kurland, D.M., & Goldberg, J. (1982). Operational efficiency and the growth of short-term memory span. *Journal of Experimental Child Psychology, 33,* 386–404.

Cunningham, A.E., & Stanovich, K.E. (1998). What reading does for the mind. *American Educator, 22* (1 & 2), 8–15.

Daneman, M. (1988). Word knowledge and reading skill. In M. Daneman, G., MacKinnon, & T.G. Waller (Eds.), *Reading research: Advances in theory and practice* (Vol. 6, pp. 145–175). San Diego, CA: Academic Press.

Daneman, M., & Carpenter, P.A. (1980). Individual differences in working memory and reading. *Journal of Verbal Learning and Verbal Behavior, 19,* 450–466.

Daneman, M., & Green, I. (1986). Individual differences in comprehending and producing words in context. *Journal of Memory and Language, 25,* 1–18.

Dunn, L.M., Dunn, L.M., Whetton, C., & Burley. J. (1997). *British Picture Vocabulary Scale – Second Edition.* Windsor, England: NFER-Nelson.

Echols, L.D., West, R.F., Stanovich, K.E., & Zehr, K.S. (1996). Using children's literacy activities to predict growth in verbal cognitive skills: A longitudinal investigation. *Journal of Educational Psychology, 88,* 296–304.

Ehrlich, M.F., & Remond, M. (1997). Skilled and less skilled comprehenders: French children's processing of anaphoric devices in written texts. *British Journal of Developmental Psychology, 15,* 291–309.

Elley, W.B. (1989). Vocabulary acquisition from listening to stories. *Reading Research Quarterly,* 14, 174–187.

Ewers, C.A., & Brownson, S.M. (1999). Kindergarteners' vocabulary acquisition as a function of active vs. passive storybook reading, prior vocabulary, and working memory. *Reading Psychology,* 20, 11–20.

Freebody, P., & Anderson, R.C. (1983). Effects on text comprehension of differing proportions and locations of difficult vocabulary. *Journal of Reading Behavior, 15,* 19–39.

Fukkink, R.G., & de Glopper, K. (1998). Effects of instruction in deriving word meanings from context: A meta-analysis. *Review of Educational Research, 68,* 450–469.

Gathercole, S.E. (1998). The development of memory. *Journal of Child Psychology and Psychiatry,* 39, 3–27.

Gathercole, S.E., Hitch. G.F., Service, E., & Martin, A.J. (1997). Phonological short-term memory and new word learning in children. *Developmental Psychology, 33,* 966–979.

Jenkins, J.R., Matlock, B., & Slocum, T.A. (1989). Two approaches to vocabulary instruction: The teaching of individual word meanings and practice in deriving word meaning from context. *Reading Research Quarterly, 24,* 215–235.

Jensen, A. (1980) *Bias in mental testing.* New York: Free Press.

MacGinitie, W.H., & MacGinitie, R.K. (1989). *Gates-MacGinitie Reading Tests.* Chicago: Riverside.

McKeown, M.G. (1985). The acquisition of word meaning from context by children of high and low ability. *Reading Research Quarterly, 20,* 482–496.

Mezynski, K. (1983). Issues concerning the acquisition of knowledge: Effects of vocabulary training on reading comprehension. *Review of Educational Research, 53,* 253–279.

Nagy, W.E., & Scott, J.A. (2000). Vocabulary processes. In M.L. Kamil, P.B. Mosenthal, P.D. Pearson, & R. Barr, (Eds.). *Handbook of reading research* (Vol. 3, pp. 269–284). Mahwah, NJ: Erlbaum.

Nation, K., Adams. J.W., Bowyer-Crane, C.A., & Snowling, M.J. (1999). Working memory deficits in poor comprehenders reflect underlying language impairments. *Journal of Experimental Child Psychology, 73,* 139–158.

Nation, K., & Snowling, M.J. (1998). Semantic processing and the development of word-recognition skills: Evidence from children with reading comprehension difficulties. *Journal of Memory and Language, 39,* 85–101.

Nation, K., & Snowling, M.J. (1999). Developmental differences in sensitivity to semantic relations among good and poor comprehenders: Evidence from semantic priming. *Cognition, 70,* 81–83.

Neale, M.D. (1989) *The Neale Analysis of Reading Ability – Revised British Edition.* Windsor, England: NFER-Nelson.

Neale, M.Y. (1997) *The Neale Analysis of Reading Ability – Revised (NARA-II).* Windsor, England: NFER-Nelson.

Nicholson, T., & Whyte, B. (1992). Matttew effects in learning new words while listening to stories. *National Reading Conference Yearbook, 41,* 499–503.

Nippold, M.A. (2002), Lexical learning in school-age children, adolescents, and adults: A process where language and literacy converge. *Journal of Child Language, 29,* 474–478.

Oakhill, J.V. (1982). Constructive processes in skilled and less-skilled comprehenders' memory for sentences. *British Journal of Psychology, 73,* 13–20.

Oakhill, J.V. (1984). Inferential and memory skills in children's comprehension of stories. *British Journal of Educational Psychology, 54,* 31–39.

Oakhill, J.V., Hartt, J., & Samols, D. (2003). *Comprehension monitoring and working memory in good and poor comprehenders.* Manuscript submitted for publication.

Oakhill, J.V., Yuill, N.M., & Parkin, A. (1986). On the nature of the difference between skilled and less-skilled comprehenders. *Journal of Research in Reading, 9,* 80–91.

Pany, D., Jenkins, J.R., & Schreck, J. (1982). Vocabulary instruction: Effects of word knowledge and reading comprehension. *Learning Disability Quarterly, 5,* 202–215.

Perfetti, C.A. (1994). Psycholinguistics and reading ability. In M.A. Gemsbacher (Ed.), *Handbook of psycholinguistics* (pp. 849–891). San Diego, CA: Academic Press.

Pickering, S.J., & Gathercole, S.E. (2001). *The Working Memory Test Battery for Children.* London: Psychological Corporation.

Semel, E., Wiig, E.H. & Secord, W. (1987). *Clinical Evaluation of Language Fundamentals – Revised.* San Diego, CA: Psychological Corporation.

Sénéchal, M., Cornell, E.H., & Broda, L.S. (1995). Age-related differences in the organization of parent–infant interactions during picture-book reading. *Early Childhood Research Quarterly, 10,* 317–337.

Sénéchal, M., Thomas, E., &, Monker, J.A. (1995). Individual differences in 4-year-old children's acquisition of vocabulary during storybook reading. *Journal of Educational Psychology, 87,* 218–229.

Shefelbine, J.L. (1990). Student factors related to variability in learning word meanings from context. *Journal of Reading Behavior, 22,* 71–97.

Siegel, L.S., & Ryan, E.B. (1989). Development of working memory in normally achieving and subtypes of learning disabled children. *Child Development, 60,* 973–980.

Snowling, M.J., Stothard, S.E., & McLean, J. (1996). *Graded Nonword Reading Test.* Bury St. Edmunds, England: Thames Valley Test Company.

Spilich, G.J., Vesonder, G.T., Chiesi, H.L., & Voss, J.F. (1979). Text processing of domain-related information for individuals with high and low domain knowledge. *Journal of Verbal Learning and Verbal Behavior, 18,* 275–290.

Stahl, S.A., & Fairbanks, M.M. (1986). The effects of vocabulary instruction: A model-based meta-analysis. *Review of Educational Research, 56,* 72–110.

Sternberg, R.J., & Powell, J.S. (1983). Comprehending verbal comprehension. *American Psychologist, 38,* 878–893.

Stothard, S.E., & Hulme, C. (1992). Reading comprehension difficulties in children: The role of language comprehension and working memory skills. *Reading and Writing, 4,* 245–256.

Swanborn, M.S.L., & de Glopper, K. (1999). Incidental word learning while reading: A meta-analysis. *Review of Educational Research, 69,* 261–285.

Swanborn, M.S.L., & de Glopper, K. (2002). Impact of reading purpose on incidental word learning from context. *Language Learning, 52,* 95–117.

Wittrock, M.C., Marks, C., & Doctorow, M. (1975). Reading as a generative process. *Journal of Educational Psychology, 67,* 484– 489.

Yuill, N., & Oakhill, J. (1991). *Children's problems in text comprehension: An experimental investigation.* Cambridge, England: Cambridge University Press.

Yuill, N.M., Oakhill, J.V., & Parkin, A.J. (1989). Working memory, comprehension skill and the resolution of text anomaly. *British Journal of Psychology, 80,* 351–361.

5

Impact of Authentic Adult Literacy Instruction on Adult Literacy Practices

Victoria Purcell-Gates, Sophie C. Degener, Erik Jacobson and Marta Soler

When adult learners go to school to learn to read and write better, what do they do with this learning? Do they read and write more and different kinds of texts in their out-of-school lives? If such changes in literacy practices occur for adult literacy students, which dimensions of their literacy instruction can we suggest are related to such changes?

This study examined two dimensions of adult literacy instruction, hypothesized as possibly related to increases in the types of texts and frequencies with which adult literacy learners engage in reading and writing activities in their lives outside of school. The outcome of this study has both theoretical and instructional significance. Theoretically, it contributes to a social practice view of literacy (Barton & Hamilton, 1998) that considers literacy to be best understood as a set of social practices associated with different domains of life that are purposeful and embedded in broader social goals and cultural practices. The questions pursued by this study explore the relationships, if any, between these social and cultural practices and adult literacy instruction. In other words, with this study, we began to explore what we refer to as the *actualization* of literacy instruction: the playing out in practice of what has been attended to by focused formal instruction.

This study can be viewed as a measure of instructional outcome for adult literacy students. As such, it addresses a real need to empirically explore the theoretical claim, or inference, that particular types of adult literacy instruction are more effective than others. Rather than conducting the traditional outcome assessment of change in literacy skill, or achievement, as measured by norm-referenced or criterion-referenced tests (with all of the attendant difficulties with validity and reliability, particularly for adult learners), we have assessed *directly the* impact of targeted aspects of instruction on the ultimate end-goal of all literacy instruction – actual reading and writing practices of the students. One way to think of this is to accept that the assessment of reading and writing skill level is settling for an interim measure of instructional outcome because no one would argue that a final test score is the instructional end point. Rather, it must be used to infer actual *use* of that reading and writing skill, and it is this *use,* or *practice,* of reading and writing that is the ultimate outcome, or goal, of literacy instruction.

The study of adult learners' literacy practices is further motivated by the cognitive argument that literacy skills – like all skills – must be practised to become automatic, and that this practice is achieved in out-of-school contexts to a large degree by increased frequencies of reading and writing or by reading and writing different types of texts in addition to those

From: *Reading Research Quarterly,* 37 (1), 2002, pp. 70–92.

already commonly written and read. Automaticity (LaBerge & Samuels, 1974) in reading refers to fluent and effortless – in the sense of not requiring conscious attention – word recognition. Readers must attain automaticity in word recognition before they can attend to the actual purpose of reading – comprehension. The cognitive demands of reading and writing words change according to their written contexts, and it cannot be assumed that automatic recognition of a word in one context ensures automatic recognition in another. Written contexts reflect variation in genre, textual form, and syntax. Examining the different types of textual contexts inherent in different reading and writing practices (e.g., reading lists, novels, mortgages; writing essays, personal letters, notes) is thus required to explore the degree to which adult learners are practicing their newly acquired literacy skills with the implication that an outcome of this activity is increased automaticity of written language processing.

Finally, this study, with its emphasis on increases in frequencies of literacy practices as well as in types of texts read and written by adults, builds on and informs the body of research undertaken by the first author. Specifically, she was interested in exploring whether or not different types of adult literacy instruction would positively change literacy practices following studies that showed (a) it is possible to attend adult literacy classes for years and not read and write more in one's life (Purcell-Gates, 1995; 1996b), (b) children of adults who read and write more frequently and read and write a wide array of texts begin school with higher levels of emergent literacy knowledge (Purcell-Gates, 1996b), and (c) children who begin school with higher levels of emergent literacy knowledge are more successful at learning to read and write in school than those with lower levels (Purcell-Gates & Dahl, 1991).

Theoretical frame

This study was conducted within a sociocultural theory of literacy development that views literacy as situated within sociocultural contexts and literacy use as a cultural practice. Within this, the term *literacy culture* can be used to reflect all of the ways in which persons – within individual families and homes as well as within different sociocultural communities – use print, practise literacy, and engage in literacy practices. This implies the construct of multiple literacies, socially situated (Street, 1989). It also implies the social practice theory of literacy described previously (Barton & Hamilton, 1998).

It must be noted that the definition of *literacy practice* we use differs slightly from that put forth by Barton and Hamilton (1998) in their ethnography of literacy practice in Lancaster, England. Barton and Hamilton, coming from a social theory perspective, defined *literacy practices* as

> the general cultural ways of utilizing written language which people draw upon in their lives. In the simplest sense literacy practices are what people do with literacy. However, practices are not observable units of behavior since they also involve values, attitudes, feelings and social relationships … This includes people's awareness of literacy, constructions of literacy and discourses of literacy, how people talk about and make sense of literacy. These are processes internal to the individual; at the same time, practices are the social processes that connect people with one another, and they include shared cognitions represented in ideologies and social identities. (pp. 6–7)

Barton and Hamilton (1998) stated that while literacy practices are unobservable, the associated literacy events and texts are observable units. Literacy events, for these researchers, were activities where literacy had a role and included both texts and talk around those texts.

While finding no fault with this definition of literacy practices and literacy events, we have chosen to focus on the central part of these: texts and the reading and writing of these texts. This differs partly because, while Barton and Hamilton (1998) come from a social theory perspective, the senior author of this report comes from a sociopsycholinguistic perspective. As previously described, this study is motivated by interest in the cognitive and linguistic effects of reading and writing different types of written texts. Thus, for this study, we focused on the texts that are involved in uses of written language. Therefore, when we use the term *literacy practices,* we are referring to the reading and writing of specific texts for socially situated purposes and intents. This excludes, but assumes, the unobservable aspects of literacy practices as discussed by Barton and Hamilton. Given the design and purpose of this study, it was impossible to capture those (e.g., values, attitudes, feelings, social relationships, constructions and discourses of literacy) as data, directly or indirectly.

Further, given that the purpose of this study was to search for a relationship between instruction and change in literacy practices, we acknowledge the slightly different operationalization of *literacy practices,* but reject this as a limitation.

Related literature

Theoretical biases for adult literacy instruction

While very little empirical research exists on the outcomes of different types of adult literacy instruction (Wagner & Venezky, 1995), the prevailing belief among academics and adult literacy program and policy leaders is that instruction that is (a) collaborative, dialogic, and responsive to the lives and needs of the learners (Auerbach, 1993; Freire, 1993; Horton, as cited in Glen, 1996; Purcell-Gates & Waterman, 2000) and (b) uses authentic, or real-life, literacy activities and materials is best for adult learners (Auerbach, 1995; Fingeret, 1991; Lytle, 1994; Stein, 2000). Thus, we focused on these two dimensions of adult literacy instruction in this study of the relationships between instruction and change in literacy practices.

Authentic, real-life materials and activities
As noted by Lytle (1994), adult literacy programs differ in their emphasis on teaching predetermined sets of skills, or alternately, on building the literacy practices of everyday life. This is reflected in the contents of adult literacy textbooks, which range from life skills and problem solving to phonics and word family drills. For this report, literacy work grounded in the life of the student outside of the classroom was considered real-life literacy. We also use the term authentic to describe these outside-of-school literacy practices and materials.

We recognize the debate over the term authentic as it applies to literacy events and to literacy instruction (S. Stahl, personal communication, April 26, 2000). While we acknowledge that school activities such as workbook skills can be viewed as authentic within a particular frame of pedagogy and genre, we use the term authentic for this investigation to reflect literacy uses found in social contexts outside of schools. In other words, we consider as authentic those literacy events that researchers (Barton & Hamilton, 1998; Purcell-Gates, 1996a; Taylor, 1985; Taylor & Dorsey-Gaines, 1988; Teale, 1986) have documented as mediating people's social and cultural lives.

The distinction between real-life and school-only literacy activities and materials appears to be important in light of research that has found students learn most efficiently when instructional materials reflect and incorporate students' prior experiences (Fingeret, 1991; Scribner, 1997). Classroom activities using generative themes taken from the lives of adult learners have been seen to facilitate their acquisition of literacy (Freire, 1993; Glen, 1996; Purcell-Gates & Waterman, 2000). This perspective recognizes that adult learners have a wealth of experience on which to draw (Freire, 1993; U.S. Congress, Office of Technology Assistance, 1993). Given their many responsibilities (as parents or workers), adult literacy students have a limited amount of time for attending classes and studying. These students desire skills that they can use in the current contexts of their lives (Freire, 1993; U.S. Congress, Office of Technology Assistance, 1993) and often express a desire to use materials geared toward their day-to-day experiences as adults and parents (Nwakese & Seiler, 1993).

The use of real-life literacy materials and activities in adult literacy programs is supported by research that documents the powerful role of context in learning. For example, workplace literacy programs teach literacy skills as they are needed within specific work contexts. Compared to programs that concentrated on more general literacy, adult programs that incorporated job-related materials were associated with larger increases in both job-related and general literacy (Sticht, 1988). Other studies suggest that much of the growth made by participants in general literacy programs is likely to be lost if recently learned skills are not applied, and thus practiced, in real-life situations (Brizius & Foster, 1987). Transferring skills between contexts is extremely difficult, however, and rarely accomplished by learners to the degree often assumed by educators (National Center on Adult Literacy [NCAL], (1995). Thus, it would make sense to involve learners in real-life literacy practices in the classroom to ease the transference problem.

However, the concept of *real life* can actually be decontextualized in ways that reduce the effectiveness of its inclusion in adult literacy programs. Once activities and materials are mass-produced and mass-prescribed, they become increasingly distanced from the lives of individual students. Given the diversity of life situations among adult learners, this could easily happen in the adult literacy classroom. For example, a thematic unit centered around the use of checkbooks would be considered a real-life activity by most middle-class people. However, it would not be contextually relevant for students who do not have checking accounts, have never had checking accounts, and have no realistic plans for opening checking accounts in the near future (Lerche, 1985).

One way some practitioners avoid this inappropriate use of real-life activities and materials is to respond to their individual students' literacy needs and elicit student-generated, student-provided, or student-requested texts. Hunter and Harman (1985) concluded that maximum use of this type of material was associated with higher levels of student achievement. Other researchers claim that student writing based on their own lives is associated with increases in writing skills (D'Annunzio, 1994; Stascz, Schwartz, & Weeden, 1994).

Student/teacher power relationships

Dialogic, collaborative, educational practice includes the student as a participant and partner in the goals, activities, and procedures of the class and program. This is in contrast to the more typical practice wherein students cede authority and power to the teacher (or underlying program structure) for decisions regarding their learning. Freire (1993) referred to this latter type of education as a banking model of education, where the student is the passive recipient of the teacher's knowledge. This retains the student's object status, according to Freire, and precludes real learning or any significant changes in the lives of the students. To be truly liberatory, Freire maintained, an education must begin with the solution of the teacher–student contradiction, by reconciling the poles of the contradiction so that both are simultaneously teachers and students. Further, Freire (1997) asserted that dialogic relationships are inherent in human nature and a requirement for learning and knowing.

Despite the belief of many literacy educators that collaborative relationships among teachers and students represent an effective way to reach diverse students (Risko & Bromley, 2000), there has been little research with regard to the influence of the structure of literacy instruction on adult students' acquisition of literacy (Lytle, 1994). However, this distinction between collaborative and teacher-directed power relationships appears to be important. Studies have shown that student learning is enhanced when students are active partners (U.S. Congress, Office of Technology Assistance, 1993) involved in decision making about their education program (Brizius & Foster, 1987). Purcell-Gates and Waterman (2000) attributed a great deal of the success of a women's literacy class in rural El Salvador to the dialogic nature of the relationship between the teacher – Waterman – and the students. The women – all survivors of an oppressed childhood and a brutal civil war and all of whom were basically nonliterate at the inception of the class – became effective readers and writers, assuming positions of leadership that required literate activity in their community.

Fingeret (1991) also called for dialogic practice and noted that curriculum development and teaching depend upon knowledge of students' cultures. In dialogic and collaborative practice, instructors can be educated by their students about the students' culture and history. Given the variety of cultures, many of them nonmainstream or immigrant, from which adult education students come, becoming educated about students' cultures and histories may be a crucial element in adult education teaching in the United States at this time (NCAL, 1995). For this study, we defined collaborative practice in terms of power sharing between teacher and student without, necessarily, the liberatory purpose inherent in Freirean-based definitions of dialogic practice (see Leistyna, Woodrum, & Sherblom, 1996).

Typology of self-reported descriptions of adult literacy instruction

As preparation for this study, we undertook a survey of adult literacy program directors across the United States (Purcell-Gates, Degener, & Jacobson, 2000). Using a short questionnaire, delivered by electronic mailing lists (listservs) and by mail to randomly selected programs representing all four National Institute for Literacy Regions of the U.S., we asked spokespersons of adult literacy programs to describe their programs. The questionnaire was structured to gain information about the two dimensions of interest: (a) the degree of collaboration between the teacher and the students, and (b) the degree to which the activities and materials in the classes reflect real-life literacy uses.

We received a total of 271 responses, representing programs across all regions of the U.S. Results showed a clear clustering of classes using materials and activities that are not authentic ('somewhat school-only' = 34%; 'highly school-only' = 41%; Total = 75%) and teacher directed rather than collaborative ('somewhat teacher directed' = 61%; 'highly teacher directed' = 28%; Total = 89%). A full 73% of the reporting practitioners described adult literacy classes that are teacher directed and involve their students primarily with activities and texts that are designed for only school-type settings and not for use in the out-of-school lives of the students.

Our typology study was not designed to test the efficacy of instruction that is both authentic and collaborative; rather it was designed to lay the groundwork for such inquiry with a description of the field of practice. The present study takes that next step and begins to explore outcomes of adult literacy instruction that can be described along these two dimensions.

Research questions

In summary, there are only some data and much theory about best practice for adult literacy instruction. There are good reasons to use change in literacy practices as an outcome of adult literacy instruction, given what we know about the need for practice of newly learned skills and about the emergent literacy benefits of many and varied uses of print in the lives of young children. No one has yet, however, systematically explored the relationships between types of literacy instruction and change literacy practices on the part of adult students. The research topics for this study, thus, were as follows: What are the relationships among (a) the degree to which adult literacy classes employ real-life literacy activities and materials, (b) the degree to which studens and teachers share decision making, and (c) changes in students' out-of-school literacy practices? The outcome measure was change in out-of-school literacy practices of the students, both in frequency per type of practice and in types of practices.

Method

Participants

Teachers and students were enlisted in this study through a process of snowball sampling. We initially contacted all respondents to the just completed typology study described above. Simultaneously, we put out calls over adult literacy electronic mailing lists, through National Center for the Study of Adult Learning and Literacy (NCSALL) contacts, databases, and publications. In addition, we began personally contacting state and regional adult education programs, asking for volunteers. To participate in the study, the site needed the following: (a) at least one teacher willing to participate; (b) at least three students from that teacher's class, or the student if it was a tutor–tutee arrangement, willing to participate; and (c) an identified local data collector, willing to be trained by us to collect the data over the course of the study.

In recruiting students, we sought to target adults who were working to improve their literacy skills. We considered students who were in the basic education levels, ranging from acquisition of basic literacy to acquisition of literacy skills needed to pass the Graduate Equivalency Degree (GED). We established two sets of criteria for a cutoff level for the English for Speakers of Other Languages (ESOL) students and for the native English-speaking students. ESOL students were only accepted into the participant pool if they did not possess high school diplomas or equivalents from their native countries. Further, they were not accepted if based on self-report they practised high levels of literacy in their native language. While many of these students were in ESOL classes, for our purposes, they needed to be working on their literacy skills as well as on learning to read, speak, and understand English. For native English-speaking students, possession of a high school diploma or its equivalent did not disqualify them from the study, but they needed to be in their adult class to improve their literacy skills. Participants were paid US$10 for each questionnaire interview.

The results of the analysis are based on the responses of 159 adult literacy students. Their ages ranged from 18 to 68. They attended adult literacy classes in 22 states, fairly evenly distributed across the mainland United States. The classes they attended represented the range of adult education class types including Adult Basic Education (ABE), English for Speakers of Other Languages (ESOL), classes specifically focused on helping adults gain their Graduate Equivalency Degree (GED), and different versions of family literacy classes. Their literacy levels ranged from preliterate to 11+ grade levels.

Design

This study was descriptive and correlational in design. Multiple methods were employed to describe adult literacy classes along the two dimensions named previously as well as to document (a) the full range of literacy practices engaged in by the adult learner participants, and (b) the changes, as self-reported, in literacy practices by the adult learner participants. For purposes of this study, *change* in literacy practices was operationalized to mean both the adoption of new types of literacy practices and increases in the frequencies with which familiar literacy practices are engaged. The relationships between the types of instruction experienced by the participants and any change in their literacy practices were captured through analysis of correlations.

Data collection instruments

Classroom data protocols

To type the classes along the two dimensions of interest, we developed three different protocols to allow us to triangulate our data. First, a 5-page Teacher Questionnaire was developed that incorporated short-answer questions, check-off items, and Likert scales. The items elicited information about specific literacy activities and their purposes, materials and texts read and written, the involvement of students in the decisions to use these materials, the extent to which teachers felt the activities and materials reflected real-life activities and materials, the extent to which the students collaborated in choosing these activities and texts, how student work was assessed and the extent to which students were involved in assessment, and the extent and type of student involvement in the overall program and program administration and policies.

Second, a protocol was developed for the data collector to use to describe the instruction along the two dimensions after observing a class in session. This protocol included holistic descriptions of the class sessions as well as individual items, including Likert scales, similar to those on the Teacher Questionnaire having to do with activities and materials used. Data collectors were instructed to first familiarize themselves with the content of the protocol and to take only field notes during the actual class observations. The protocol was to be filled in by the data collector immediately following the class observation.

Finally, a protocol was developed for the data collector to use in an interview with volunteer students, without the teacher present. This interview asked the students to describe the types of things they read and wrote in class and to rate the degree to which (a) they thought these activities and texts were real life, and (b) the degree to which they, the students, participated in choosing the activities and texts. The descriptions of class activities and texts were collected from the group discussion, with all contributions accepted. Responses to the Likert scale items were recorded via a vote procedure, where students individually voted for the response they felt most accurately captured their perceptions. The data collector filled in student responses to the questions on the protocol at the time of the interview.

The students who volunteered to take part in this group interview were not necessarily the same ones who responded to the at-home literacy questionnaires, with the exception of the tutor–tutee arrangements wherein the tutee was clearly the student who became the informant on literacy practices. In the case of whole-class set-ups, all students present on the day the data collector visited the class were invited to take part in the interview. This group may or may not have included the students from the class who had volunteered to be questioned in their homes.

With the use of the Teacher Questionnaire, the Class Observation Protocol, and the Student Interview Protocol, we collected information about the two instructional dimensions of interest to the study – teacher/student collaboration and authenticity of materials and activities – from three different perspectives: the teacher, the students, and the data collector observer of the class. This allowed us to triangulate the data to characterize the instruction associated with each student participant.

We piloted each of the three protocols in adult literacy classes not participating in the study. Each protocol was amended and adjusted as a result of this pilot work until we were satisfied that potential confusions inherent in the questions were clarified and that each question – or item – elicited the information we sought as it informed our research questions. In addition, the Class Observation Protocol was used by three members of the research team to observe three different adult literacy classes, filling it in as appropriate. These completed protocols, demonstrating different types of classrooms, were copied and included as models in the training material for each data collector.

Student home literacy questionnaire

To gather data for our dependent variable – information about change in the literacy practices of the adult learners – we developed an extensive questionnaire for use with each student. The items on the questionnaire asked about specific literacy practices such as reading coupons, writing personal letters, reading to a child, and so on. The questionnaire included 26 items pertaining to adult reading, 14 items pertaining to adult writing, 7 items pertaining to adult-with-child reading, and 3 items pertaining to adult-with-child writing.

The items on the questionnaire came, for the most part, from a participant-observation study of reading and writing in the homes and lives of 20 low-income families (Purcell-Gates, 1996b). Thus, they were derived from actual data to ensure grounded validity. To further ensure that we included all types of possible literacy practices, we piloted the questionnaire on five middle-income families. We added several items following this procedure.

For each item, the student was asked (a) In the past week, did you read/write X? (b) Can you show me or tell me about an example? (c) (If no) Have you ever read/written X? (d) (If yes) When was the first time you did this sort of reading/writing? (e) How often? (f) Do you still do this sort of reading/writing? Quotes and comments were also captured with each item. To provide a reliability check on the item of interest to us – change in literacy practice – we inserted between every fifth item a question that summarized the preceding five items and responses and asked specifically about change: 'I've just asked you about X, X, X, X, and X. Did you just *begin* to read any of these types of print (texts) after you began attending your literacy class? Specify which ones. Do you think you've read any of these items *more often* since you began attending your literacy class? Specify which ones.' At the end of the interviews, data collectors asked if the participants could think of anything else they had read or written during the last week or ever. They were then invited to walk through the house to discover or point out texts they had read or written. While the questionnaire is labeled as a home literacy one, it included items that are read and written outside of the home as well, such as signs, labels, song lyrics, and so on. For our purposes, home literacy refers to reading and writing that takes place in the lives of people outside of a literacy classroom, not only within the home itself.

The Student Home Literacy Questionnaire was piloted with 45 adult literacy students who were not participating in the larger study. During the piloting, we refined items, questions regarding demographic and personal information about the participants, and directions to the data collectors within the questionnaire. For participants who spoke mainly Spanish, we used a Spanish version of the questionnaire, translated by a native Spanish-speaking member of the research team. Spanish-speaking data collectors collected data from primarily Spanish-speaking participants.

While we had students in the participant pool who spoke languages other than Spanish, we provided data collectors only for the Spanish-speaking students. This was due to the difficulty of finding, and employing, data collectors who spoke other languages. Therefore, for the non-native English speakers, other than the Spanish speakers, a requirement for their inclusion in the study was that they speak and understand English well enough to answer the questionnaire items in English. We also had native Spanish speakers who participated completely in English. They were judged by the teacher and themselves to be fluent enough to do so.

Since there is no theoretical or empirical reason to suggest that the language in which the reading and writing occurs is related to the degree that young children in the home learn about emergent literacy concepts, our work with ESOL students focused on changes regarding specific text types, rather than the English skills they may have been acquiring and using. To ensure that newly acquired English language skills were not conflated with changes in literacy practice, a separate form of the Student Home Literacy Questionnaire was developed for all English for Speakers of Other Languages students. On this form, each literacy practice question was asked as it applied to engagement in that practice for each language spoken by the student. This allowed us to control for reported changes in literacy practice that represented only a shift into a new language.

Procedures

Site management: data collector training
Each of the four members of the research team took responsibility for overseeing the data collector training, collection of the data from the site data collector, and coding of the data from an assigned group of sites. Data collector training involved the research team member flying or driving to the adult literacy class site and meeting for approximately 4 hours with the data collector. At this meeting, the data collector was trained in the use of all of the data collection protocols and provided with instructions for mailing the data to the research team and for submitting expenses and pay vouchers. None of the data collectors were connected as teachers or administrators to the adult literacy program on which they were to collect data to help avert the tendency of responders to questionnaires to provide information they think you want to hear.

Site management: site maintenance
A major challenge for this study with its many far-flung sites was maintenance of a site. Following the data collector training, the individual research members maintained regular contact with their data collectors by phone or e-mail. The purpose of this regular contact was to help resolve issues of data collection as they arose, locate new classes or students as needed, communicate with teachers and program administrators as needed, and so on.

Two members of the research team served as data collectors as well as site managers for sites close enough to the university to be visited by car on a regular basis. A third member of the research team managed sites around the Chicago, Illinois, area because she was living there at the time. She also served as data collector for several of these sites. One member of the team was a Spanish national, and she managed most of the ESOL sites and translated all of the protocols into Spanish.

Class data collection
To collect the class data needed to type the individual classes along the two instructional dimensions of interest, the data collector first delivered the questionnaire to the teacher and arranged a time to observe a typical class, after which he or she would collect the questionnaire. During the class observation, the data collector assumed an unobtrusive position in the class and made notes on all that occurred as well as physical descriptions of the classroom, equipment, shelves, where students sat, and so on. During this visit, either during a break or right after the class, the data collector gathered a group of volunteer students to conduct the interviews. Following the observation, the data collector used the field notes to fill in the protocol for the observation. The data collector also read over the completed Teacher Questionnaire and arranged for a short interview with the teacher to clarify any ambiguous answers and to ask questions that may have arisen during the class observation.

Home Literacy Practices Questionnaire data collection
Data collectors conducted the literacy practices interviews in the homes of the participants. The context of the home was intentionally chosen to (a) remove the students from their

literacy classes to ameliorate the tendency of participants in self-report studies to give the interviewer what they think is expected (in this case information that the students may think will cast their classes in a positive light), and (b) help the students think about real-life literacy practices – rather than school-based ones – by placing them in the context in which many of those practices would have occurred and from which they could select examples. The interviews were repeated every 3 months for as long as the student was in the program up to four times or until the end of the data collection period, which stretched over 18 months (although students began with the study at different points, reflecting the snowball sampling nature of the study). Each interview/questionnaire took an average of 1 1/2 hours.

If a student changed classes during the course of the study, the data collector collected class data (with the same procedures and protocols) on the new class and the student/class pair was treated as a new site. This procedure was in response to the fact that the individual class was the unit of interest for this study, not an overall program. The questions on the Home Literacy Practices Questionnaire were then asked in reference to the class currently being attended by the student.

Other relevant student data

Following the collection of literacy practices data, all of the teachers were contacted and asked about the students' incoming literacy levels, attendance patterns, and number of hours per week the class was held. For literacy level, we sent the following request:

At what level of reading and writing would you say the student was when she or he joined this class? This is a subjective question and can be answered in several ways. If you can give a specific grade level (i.e., reading at a fifth-grade level), that would be great. Otherwise, more general terms like *low literate or nonreader* would also be helpful. Please indicate what evidence your response is based on (e.g., format assessment, teacher observation, prior reports). Note: If the student's native language is other than English, please tell us what level the student was in both first language and English.

Teachers assessed their students differently. Some gave a grade level, some used terms like *preliterate,* and others used Test of Adult Basic Education or Comprehensive Adult Student Assessment System test scores. As a research team, we created a 5-point scale for literacy level and together went over all the different teacher reports of student level and determined where on the 5-point scale students fell. Students received a 1 if they were considered preliterate; 2 if their reading was at grade levels 1–3; 3 for grade levels 4–7; 4 for grade levels 8–10; and 5 for grade levels 11 and higher.

For attendance, the teachers were given a 5-point scale for describing their students' overall attendance patterns: 1 = Rarely attends; 2 = Sometimes attends; 3 = Attends more often than not; 4 = Often attends; and 5 = Attends very regularly. All of this information was used in the final analysis.

Analysis

Class data

Data on the individual classes were coded and triangulated for typing along the two dimensions in the following way. Information from each of the three protocols was transferred to one coding sheet and into a matrix with the following headings: (a) Source (Class Observation, Teacher Questionnaire, Student Interview); (b) Activity/material (e.g., 'writing correspondence letters,' 'filling in worksheets,' 'reading children's books'); (c) Purpose (e.g., 'to thank guest speaker,' 'to practice grammar,' 'to encourage parents to read to their children'); and (d) Assigned (choices were 'by the teacher,' 'by the teacher and student together,' and 'chosen by the student'). All Likert scale numbers from each protocol were transferred to the coding sheet as well as responses to short-answer items. The coder then holistically assigned an authentic/school-only score as well as a collaborative/teacher-directed score to the class and placed the intersection of these onto a miniature dimensional grid located at the bottom of each coding sheet. This was later transferred to the central database.

Criteria for typing the classes are contained in Tables 5.1 and 5.2. Coders were advised to consider proportion of instructional time devoted to relevant types of activities and texts whenever possible when making decisions about assignment of class type.

Interrater reliability of the class typing was achieved and assessed in the following ways. First, to achieve initial agreement on class typing, the entire research team worked together to type five classes. During these sessions, we talked aloud about the criteria for each decision and came to agreement. After these sessions, each member of the team coded the classes from the collection of sites for which each was responsible. However, data collected by a research team member, as opposed to a data collector not on the team, was coded by another team member to ensure comparability of coding decisions across all sites.

Table 5.1   Criteria for typing classes along the authentic/school-only dimension

Type	Criteria
Highly authentic	Classes that use only realia, or texts that occur naturally in the lives of people outside of a classroom (e.g., newspapers, journals, novels, work manuals, driver's license materials). Further, the reading/writing activities that occur with these texts is the same as those that would occur with the texts outside of a learning situation. It is the confluence of these two factors that make programs highly authentic.
Somewhat authentic	Classes in this category may mention skills and may use some published textbooks and workbooks, but student work is heavily concentrated on real-life texts and issues. Classes in this category may use real texts with activities that mimic but are not the same as those that would occur with the text outside of a learning situation. For example, letters to the editor are written but not sent.
Somewhat school only	Classes are more highly focused on skills, with the majority of activities focused on phonics work, grammar work, and workbooks. Materials tend to be published textbooks and workbooks, though some mention may be made of authentic materials or activities such as Language Experience Approach, newspapers, or journals. This type of class tends to use facsimiles of real texts for learning to read these types of texts, for example, photocopies of newspaper articles that are not current and not necessarily about topics of interest to students.
Highly school only	Classes have a set curriculum with a focus on skills, phonics, or flashcards. Most, if not all, materials are from publishers, and there is almost no mention of authentic materials or activities. These classes most likely do not use real-life texts in any form. If they do, they are made up for teaching purposes and used only for skill learning (i.e., not for communicative purposes).

Table 5.2   Criteria for typing classes along the collaborative/teacher-directed dimension

Type	Criteria
Highly collaborative	Classes where students work with teachers to create the course, choose the materials, or design activities. Students are also involved in all aspects of the program; may serve on the board; make decisions regarding meeting times, class rules, class structure and location; and so on. Students may also work to publish newsletters and may help in recruiting new students.
Somewhat collaborative	Classes where student input is obviously influential on the activities of the class. These classes reflect an ongoing flexibility about the curriculum to allow for response to students' interests or expressed needs. There is collaboration in choosing course content and activities. Students are in charge of their own learning.
Somewhat teacher directed	Classes where students' goals, interests, or needs are taken into account when creating course content. Students have some input on class content, usually in the form of interest inventories, students' goals, or Individualized Educational Plans. Teachers encourage student input. Students typically choose from materials and activities that have already been selected by the teacher. Classes in this category consider themselves to be client driven though ultimate course decisions typically rest with the teachers. Teachers give needs assessments throughout the students' time in the class. Teachers and students periodically reflect on goals and whether or not the class is meeting them.
Highly teacher directed	Classes where students have little or no input into course content, activities, or materials. Students may be given a needs analysis when they start the program but needs are not continually reevaluated. Teachers may say that demographics of the students impact course content. Often a set curriculum is followed in these classes.

Second, an interrater reliability check was conducted by randomly selecting one third of the coded sites and recoding them. The recoding was done independently by the three research team members who had not coded the site originally, with the exception of those sites where the data collector was a team member. These were distributed to the two members of the team who had not originally coded the site or collected the data. Pairwise correlations of the results (Spearman's rank correlations) ranged from $r = .56$ to $r = .76$ for the Collaborative/Teacher-directed dimension and $r = .60$ to $r = .76$ for the Authentic/School-only dimension. Considering these interrater reliabilities too low, we initiated a third procedure.

The two team members with the highest overall agreement in the initial reliability check met and clarified criteria for typing the classes along the dimensions. With rewritten rubrics, they then each recoded one half of the entire class data set, again assigning sites for recoding to the team member who did not collect the data. An interrater reliability check (Spearman rank correlation) was run on the entire recoded class data set with the following results: Authentic/School-only dimension – $r = .86$; Collaborative/Teacher-directed dimension – $r = .78$.

Home Literacy Practices Questionnaire

Data from the Home Literacy Practices Questionnaire that were directly relevant to the research questions were transferred onto a coding sheet with the following matrix headings for each literacy practice asked about: 'Last week;' 'Ever;' 'Since class;' and 'More since class.' The coder marked a 0 for 'no' and a 1 for 'yes' in each of these columns. An asterisk (*) was used to indicate missing data and a 2 to indicate that the question was not applicable for that participant, given who they were (e.g., if they did not have children to read to) or their answers to previous questions (e.g., if they had already said yes to reading coupons, then the question 'Have you ever read coupons?' was not applicable). Coder decisions about the change columns ('Ever' and 'Since class') were based on the questions that asked about dates of beginning the class, dates that practices began, and the direct questions about beginning the practice or engaging in it more frequently.

Interrater reliability for the coding of the Home Literacy Practices Questionnaire was checked by randomly selecting 77 of the coded questionnaires from a total of 293 (26% of all coded questionnaires). Each of these selected questionnaires was recoded by another member of the research team. The completed code sheets were then compared for agreement of code at the individual question level. A total of 8,155 codes were examined. The overall rate of agreement between the original code and the second code was 94%.

Scaling responses to the questionnaire items

The final purpose of this analysis was to model changes in literacy practices using the theoretically derived predictors of (a) authenticity of instructional activities and texts and (b) the collaborative nature of the teacher/student relationship. Rather than perform analyses on individual literacy practices, the practices were placed on a common scale. This was done because the reliability of responses to individual survey items is very low, resulting in a less powerful analysis. When aggregating responses over the entire set of items answered by each respondent, the reliability of the resulting scale is much higher (Mehrens & Lehmann, 1991), resulting in a more powerful analysis.

Item Response Theory (IRT) methodology was used to place the literacy practices and respondents on a common scale. All IRT estimation was performed using BILOG. IRT methodology (Lord, 1980) also allowed us to achieve higher reliability of scores than we could achieve through Cronbach's alpha and, because the scaling spread the scores out, resulted in greater variation. All of this resulted in a more powerful analysis.

The scaling was done with data that was collapsed across all administrations of the Home Literacy Practices Questionnaire and with data that collapsed the new practices and increase in frequency data into one measure of change. Because of missing data, it was possible to estimate a change score for only 159 of the 173 respondents, a loss of 8% of the sample. The missing data were almost entirely the result of data collectors who did not understand that nonnative English speakers were to be asked about literacy practices in both English and their native languages, despite the ESOL-specific form that provided answer spaces for both English and native language responses for each item. Thus, incomplete and unuseable data were produced for a number of ESOL students.

The data on the resulting change scale fit the IRT model assumptions and had an estimated reliability of .94, with no literacy practices exhibiting statistically significant misfit. This procedure produced a single score for each respondent, estimating a *propensity to, or probability of change* for each literacy practice.

In addition to a change scale, IRT scaling was also conducted to create a scale of literacy practices engaged in by the students at the first administration of the Home Literacy Practices Questionnaire. This scaling procedure produced a single score for each respondent, estimating that respondent's *propensity to, or probability to engage in,* literacy practices. The estimated reliability of the scaled scores was .87.

Hierarchical Linear Modeling to model change

HLM was used to examine the instructional effects on the outcome of change in literacy practices. HLM allowed us to account for the classroom effect on error resulting from the fact that participants were nested within classrooms (Bryk & Raudenbush, 1992). A preliminary analysis showed that the intraclass correlation was .46, justifying our choice of HLM. In addition, HLM can handle unbalanced cell-sizes effectively, an advantage over ANCOVA. HLM, as well as controlling for individual classroom effects not of interest, also adjusts the degrees of freedom used to test class-level effects, thus providing more accurate, uninflated tests of their significance. All models were estimated using the HLM for Windows (version 4.0) computer program.

To account for the varying degrees of uncertainty in the estimation of the outcome variable, the inverse of the standard errors of each participant's outcome was used as weights. The inverse of the square of the standard errors was used as weights because the weights are assumed to be measures of certainty rather than measures of uncertainty. Thus, a weighted HLM model of *propensity to change* was estimated. To determine whether weighting had a large effect on the outcome of modeling, an unweighted model was also estimated. The models were essentially equivalent. Thus, we present only the results of the weighted model.

Respondent-level predictors of change

Change in literacy practices was assumed to be related to various predictors, both at the respondent level and at the classroom level. The respondent-level predictors investigated were the following:

- Attend: Attendance level
- LitLev: Incoming literacy level
- Gender: Gender of the respondent
- ESOL: English speaker of other languages status
- Tutor: Whether the respondent had a one-on-one tutor …
- Days: The number of days from the respondent's entry in the current adult education class to the time of the first administration of the survey

Classroom-level predictors of change

The following classroom-level predictors were investigated:

- Frequency: Hours of class per week
- Authenticity: Authentic nature of the classroom
- Collaboration: Collaborative nature of the classroom
- ESOL: Whether the classroom followed the ESOL format
- ABE: Whether the classroom followed the Adult Basic Education format
- FamLit: Whether the classroom followed the family literacy format

There were also some GED classrooms but not enough to estimate the effect of the GED format.

Unconditional and respondent-level models

To begin the modeling process, an unconditional model was estimated. In this model, only the overall mean change score (the intercept) and the variance of classroom effects were estimated. For this model, the percent of variation within and between classrooms was calculated.

Using the estimate (obtained from the unconditional model) of the variation within classrooms as a baseline comparison, a respondent-level regression model was estimated. Theoretically important respondent-level predictors were entered into the respondent-level model one at a time and then together. To determine whether these predictors should remain in the model, the following five criteria were considered: (a) the significance of each respondent-level predictor's regression weight, (b) the significance of the variance of each respondent-level predictor's regression weight across classrooms, (c) the unique percent increase in respondent-level variation explained by each respondent-level predictor, (d) the significance of chi-square difference statistics, and (e) the colinearity of each respondent-level predictor with all other predictors.

Classroom-level models

After the respondent-level model was finalized, it was used as a baseline comparison for models including classroom-level effects. First, a classroom-level model of the respondent-level intercept was developed. Next, classroom-level models of the respondent-level regression slopes were investigated.

Using the estimated classroom variation in intercepts as a baseline comparison, the base model was developed. Theoretically important respondent-level predictors were entered into the respondent-level model one at a time and then together. To determine whether these predictors should remain in the model, three criteria were considered: (a) the significance of each classroom-level predictor's regression weight, (b) the unique percent increase in classroom-level variation in the intercept explained by each classroom-level predictor, and (c) the colinearity of each classroom-level predictor with all other predictors at both the respondent and classroom levels.

Assessing the assumptions of HLM

The normality of the respondent-level residuals was checked by traditional statistical methods. Homogeneity of the respondent-level residuals (or difference between observed and predicted values) within each of the classroom units was tested with each run of the models. The normality of the residual variation in classroom-level prediction of respondent-level intercepts and slopes was checked by traditional statistical methods. Homogeneity of the residual variation in classroom-level prediction of respondent-level intercepts across all values of the classroom-level predictors was checked by inspecting scatter plots of classroom-level predicted values versus residuals. All of the assumptions were met.

Results

We will first present descriptive statistics for (a) the participants and (b) the classes typed along the two dimensions of authenticity and collaboration. Next, we will present the results of the IRT scaling of (a) literacy practices engaged in at the time of first interview and (b) literacy practice change reported as occurring after enrollment in the current literacy

Table 5.3 Descriptive statistics for categorical participant-level variables

Variable	Values	Original sample		Final sample	
		N	Percentage	N	Percentage
Attendance	1.0 – Rarely	8	4.6	7	4.4
	2.0 – Sometimes	12	6.9	12	7.5
	3.0 – More often than not	20	11.6	18	11.3
	3.5 – Between 3 and 4	2	1.2	2	1.3
	4.0 – Often	32	18.5	29	18.2
	4.5 – Between 4 and 5	1	0.6	1	0.6
	5.0 – Very regularly	98	56.6	90	56.6
	Total	173	100.0	159	100.0
Literacy level at beginning of class	1.0 – Preliterate	33	19.1	33	20.8
	2.0 – first–third grade	34	19.7	30	18.9
	3.0 – fourth–seventh grade	54	31.2	49	30.8
	4.0 – eighth–tenth grade	39	22.6	36	22.6
	5 0 – eleventh grade and up	13	7.5	11	6.9
	Total	173	100.0	159	100.0
Gender	Male	49	28.3	46	28.9
	Female	124	71.7	113	71.1
	Total	173	100.0	159	100.0
ESOL	No	100	57.8	98	61.6
	Yes	73	42.2	61	38.4
	Total	173	100.0	159	100.0
Tutor	No	129	74.6	118	74.2
	Yes	44	25.4	41	25.8
	Total	173	100.0	159	100.0

class. Finally, we will present the results of the HLM analysis designed to inform our research question: Is there a relationship between the degree of inclusion in adult literacy classes of authentic texts and materials, the degree of involvement of the students in the curricular and programmatic decisions of the class, and degree of change in the literacy practices of the students in their lives outside of school?

Participants and classes

Participants

Descriptive statistics for the participants are presented in Table 5.3 for the categorical variables and in Table 5.4 for the quantitative variables. Statistics from both the original sample and the final sample are presented to document our conclusion that losing 8% of the sample did not have much effect on the final results. To determine whether the highly positive skew of the predictor *Days* allowed outliers to have an inordinate effect on the results, a variable of *LogDays* was created by taking the natural log of the *Days* predictor. *LogDays* was approximately normally distributed. All models were estimated twice, once with *Days* and once with *LogDays*. Since the skewness of the original predictor had little effect on the estimation of the models, we present only the final model using the original *Days* predictor to enhance ease of interpretation.

Table 5.4 Descriptive statistics of quantitative, participant-level variables for final sample

Variable	N	M	SD
Attendance	159	4.2	1.2
Literacy level at start	1,159	2.8	1.2
Days attended class	157	435.2	521.4

Table 5.5 Descriptive statistics of categorical classroom-level variables

Variable	Values	N	Percent
Authenticity	1.0 – Highly school-only	13	16.9
	2.0 – Somewhat school-only	40	51.9
	3.0 – Somewhat authentic	21	27.3
	4.0 – Highly authentic	3	3.9
	Total	77	100.0
Collaboration	1.0 – Highly teacher directed	23	29.9
	2.0 – Somewhat teacher directed	39	50.6
	3.0 – Somewhat collaborative	12	15.6
	4.0 – Highly collaborative	3	3.9
	Total	77	100.0
ESOL	No	69	89.6
	Yes	8	10.4
	Total	77	100.0
Adult Basic Education	No	22	28.6
	Yes	55	71.4
	Total	77	100.0
Family literacy	No	68	88.3
	Yes	9	11.7
	Total	77	100.0

Authenticity and collaboration of the classes

Descriptive statistics for the classroom-level predictors are presented in Tables 5.5 and 5.6. The two instructional dimensions of authenticity and collaboration were highly correlated at $r = .71$. This relationship is displayed in Table 5.7.

Literacy engagement and change scales

Literacy practice engagement scale

The distribution of the scaled scores had a mean of 0 and a standard deviation of 1. The participants on the low end of the scale reported minimal engagement in literacy practices, while those on the high end reported substantial engagement. The scaling procedure produced three estimates for each literacy practice, displayed in Table 5.8: (a) a measure of the literacy practice's ability to discriminate between respondents with low and high *propensity to engage,* (b) a measure of the threshold of *propensity to engage* needed for a respondent to have a 50% chance of engaging in that literacy practice, and

Table 5.6   Descriptive statistics of quantitative classroom-level variables

Variable	N	M	SD
Frequency	77	7.0	6.0
Authenticity	77	2.2	0.8
Collaboration	77	1.9	0.8

Table 5.7   Results of class ratings along the two instructional dimensions of authenticity and collaboration*

	Highly teacher directed	Somewhat teacher directed	Somewhat collaborative	Highly collaborative
Highly authentic			1	2
Somewhat authentic	1	10	9	1
Somewhat school-only	11	27	2	
Highly school-only	11	2		

Note: *r = .71

(c) a measure of the fit of the literacy practice to the IRT model. None of the individual literacy practices exhibited statistically significant misfit, providing evidence that the IRT model fits the data. In addition, the literacy practices' estimated thresholds for engagement were spread out well along the scale, and their abilities to discriminate were reasonably high.

For the Discriminating ability column in Table 5.8, the higher values indicate higher discrimination between respondents with differing propensities to engage in the literacy practice. In the Threshold for engagement column, low values indicate low thresholds for engagement while high values indicate high thresholds.

The following example aids in understanding the scale. A hypothetical, below average on the scale of engagement, respondent receives a score of −1.50 on the literacy practice engagement scale. Such a respondent has a 50% probability of having engaged in *reading schedules and guides* because that practice's threshold for engagement is equal to the respondent's propensity to engage. The lower (or higher) the threshold for engagement, the higher (or lower) the probability that a respondent has engaged in that practice. For example, it is much more likely that the hypothetical respondent will have engaged in *reading calendars and tickets* because that practice's threshold (−2.88) is lower than the respondent's propensity to engage (−1.50), and the practice's discriminating ability (0.82) is reasonably high. Likewise, it is much less likely that the hypothetical respondent will have engaged in *writing instructions* because that practice's threshold (0.05) is much higher than the respondent's propensity to engage (−1.50), and the practice's discriminating ability (1.01) is reasonably high.

While the distribution of scores on this scale has a mean of 0 and a standard deviation of 1, all but two practices had thresholds of less than 0. This indicates that at the time of the first administration of the survey, most respondents had engaged in most of the literacy practices included in this survey.

Table 5.8   Results of IRT scaling of engagement in literacy practices at time one interview

Literacy practice	Discrim. ability	Threshold for engagement	Significance of misfit**
Reading labels, container print, signs	0.05*	–3.00*	*
Reading calendars, tickets	0.82	–2.88	1.00
Reading ads, coupons, fliers	1.07	–2.52	1.00
Reading bills, bank statements, receipts	1.16	–2.33	1.00
Writing names, labeling	1.13	–2.25	1.00
Reading books and stories	0.66	–2.16	0.55
Reading menus	0.82	–2.06	0.69
Reading addresses, phone books	1.70	–2.03	1.00
Reading postal letters	0.96	–1.90	0.62
Reading school communication	0.56	–1.85	0.32
Reading directions (e.g., recipes)	1.32	–1.74	0.64
Reading essays, info text, compositions	0.71	–1.52	0.79
Reading schedules, guides	0.85	–1.50	0.43
Writing messages, notes	1.53	–1.47	1.00
Writing postal letters	0.89	–1.42	0.12
Writing checks, money orders	0.98	–1.35	0.25
Writing on calendars, appointment books	1.21	–1.20	0.41
Writing lists	0.79	–1.16	0.19
Reading periodicals (eg., horoscopes, sports)	0.99	–1.13	0.54
Writing forms, applications	1.65	–1.05	0.48
Reading documents (e.g., lease, mortgage)	1.03	–0.94	0.66
Reading comics, cartoons	1.08	–0.58	0.65
Reading song lyrics	0.80	–0.24	0.91
Writing speeches, reflections, stories, poems	0.66	0.04	0.11
Writing instructions	1.01	0.05	0.39

Notes: *All respondents reported engaging in this practice. Thus, its discriminating ability is near zero, its misfit could not be estimated, and its threshold was set to –3.00 rather than the unreasonable value (–34.67) given by BILOG.

**The *p*-value or the fit statistic for each literacy practice. $p < .05$ indicates statistically significant misfit.

Literacy practice change scale

Along with each respondent's score, a standard error was produced, estimating the amount of uncertainty in the score. The scores and their accompanying standard errors were later used to model change in literacy practices. The resulting distribution of the scaled scores had, approximately, a mean of 0 and standard deviation of 1. The scaling procedure also produced three estimates, two for each literacy practice as well as one for measure of fit, displayed in Table 5.9. The practices' estimated thresholds for change were spread out well along the scale, and their abilities to discriminate were reasonably high. The respondents on the low end of the scale reported minimal change, while those on the high end reported substantial change. None of the individual literacy practices exhibited statistically significant misfit, providing evidence that the IRT model fits the data.

The following example aids in understanding the scale. A hypothetical respondent receives a score of 0.30 on the propensity to change in engagement scale. Such a respondent has an approximately 50% probability of exhibiting change in reading postal letters,

Table 5.9 Results of IRT scaling of change in level of engagement in literacy practices sorted by threshold

Literacy practice	Discrim. ability	Threshold for change	Significance of misfit**
Reading essays, info text, compositions	0.92	−0.29	0.12
Reading books and stories	1.15	−0.22	0.66
Reading labels, container print, signs	1.90	−0.10	0.83
Reading school communication	1.02	−0.09	0.77
Writing messages, notes	1.19	−0.08	0.82
Reading calendars, tickets	1.67	−0.06	0.65
Writing speeches, reflections, stories, poems	1.37	−0.03	1.00
Reading messages, notes	1.34	−0.01	0.77
Reading periodicals (e.g., horoscopes, sports)	1.24	0.14	0.85
Reading directions (e.g., recipes)	1.72	0.17	0.86
Writing instructions	1.00	0.18	0.45
Reading ads, coupons, fliers	1.33	0.21	0.78
Writing on calendars, appointment books	1.05	0.23	0.86
Reading bills, bank statements, receipts	0.96	0.23	0.11
Reading schedules, guides	1.11	0.27	0.40
Reading addresses, phone books	1.43	0.27	0.70
Reading postal letters	1.35	0.29	0.67
Writing checks, money orders	0.73	0.32	0.62
Writing lists	1.44	0.32	0.49
Reading song lyrics	1.63	0.33	0.40
Reading menus	1.59	0.37	0.48
Reading documents (e.g., lease, mortgage)	0.92	0.41	0.48
Writing postal letters	1.42	0.46	0.81
Writing names, labeling	1.45	0.47	0.82
Writing forms, applications	0.79	0.52	0.35
Reading comics, cartoons	1.05	0.69	0.77

** The *p* value of the fit statistic for each literacy practice. *p* < .05 indicates statistically significant misfit.

because that practice's threshold for change is nearly equal to the respondent's propensity to change. The lower (or higher) the threshold for change, the higher (or lower) the probability that a respondent will exhibit change. For example, it is much more likely that the hypothetical respondent will have changed in his or her engagement in *reading essays, information text, or compositions* because that practice's threshold (−0.29) is lower than the respondent's propensity to change (0.30), and the practice's discriminating ability (0.92) is reasonably high. Likewise, it is much less likely that the hypothetical respondent will have changed in his or her engagement in *writing forms and applications* because that practice's threshold (0.52) is much higher than the respondent's propensity to change (0.30), and the practice's discriminating ability (.79) is reasonably high.

While the distribution of scores on this scale has a mean of 0 and a standard deviation of 1, about two thirds of the literacy practices had thresholds of larger than 0. This indicates that most respondents had not reported change in most of the literacy practices included in the survey. This can also be taken to indicate that the validity threat in the tendency to give socially desirable responses in self-report questionnaire studies was not apparent in the data.

Table 5.10   Parameter estimates of final model of literacy practice change

Parameter	Weighted change scores		
	b*	b**	P
Intercept	0.393	0.043	0.079
LitLev	−0.279	−0.337	0.000
Days	0.00041	0.207	0.000
ESOL	−0.500	0.247	0.001
Authenticity	0.217	0.162	0.009

Notes: *unstandardized coefficient **standardized coefficient (or effect size)

Final HLM model

The final respondent-level model included three respondent-level predictors: (a) literacy level of the student upon entry to the class (LitLev), (b) whether or not the student was in an English for Speakers of Other Languages class (ESOL), and (c) the total number of days the student had attended the class prior to the first administration of the home literacy practices questionnaire (Days). The final classroom-level model of the respondent-level intercepts included only one predictor: the degree of authenticity of materials and activities in the class (Authenticity). No respondent-level slopes depended upon classroom membership or classroom characteristics, so no models were developed for the respondent-level slopes. All other respondent- and classroom-level predictors were not statistically significant, and no interaction terms were statistically significant either at the respondent level, the classroom level, or across levels.

The parameter estimates for the final model, using the natural days metric and weighted change scores, are presented in Table 5.10. Note that the most powerful predictors of literacy practice change were a student's literacy level on beginning the class and the number of days the student had attended the class at the time of the first interview. The lower the student's literacy level upon entry to the class, the more likely he or she was to report change in literacy practices. Further, the longer students had been attending their class, the more likely they would report change in their literacy practices. Both of these predictors were moderately related to change in literacy practices. The third respondent-level predictor, whether or not a student is an ESOL student, was negatively related to change in literacy practices.

Regarding classroom-level effects, students who were in classes with greater degrees of authenticity of activities and materials were more likely to report change in their literacy practices. This instructional dimension was moderately related to reported change in literacy practices.

As mentioned above, HLM adjusts the degrees of freedom used to test the classroom-level effects to produce uninflated significance tests. Because of this, the effective sample size for testing those effects is the number of classrooms in the study – 77. Even with this moderate sample size, the effect of authenticity of materials and texts in adult literacy instruction is statistically significant.

The residual variation between and within classrooms is estimated with each run of an HLM model. The residual variation between classrooms is tested for statistical significance with each run of an HLM model. In all methods of estimating the final model, the residual variation between classes was statistically significant, supporting the use of HLM methodology.

Summary of results

Regarding our research questions, the results show that, controlling for all other variables in the final model, the degree of authenticity in the activities and materials used in adult literacy instruction was statistically significantly related to the likelihood that adult literacy students in those classes will report change in frequency or type of out-of-school literacy practices. On the other hand, there was no statistical effect of the degree of collaboration between student and teacher on reported change in literacy practices. Finally, there were no statistically significant interaction effects, meaning that all statistically significant effects were simple, easily interpretable main effects.

Examining causal inferences

This study was correlational and not experimental in design, and we cannot claim a straightforward causal relationship between the degree of authenticity in adult literacy class activities and texts and change in frequencies and types of literacy practices of the students. However, because we controlled for all other influencing factors identified in the data, we did conclude tentative causality based on the logic of causal-comparative research (Hittleman & Simon, 1997). To examine this further, we conducted an analysis to examine the impact of the variable of authenticity on change in literacy practices.

To do this, we synthesized the two models upon which the results were based: the IRT model and the HLM model. By doing this, we could determine the predicted impact of increasing the authenticity in a classroom on the number of literacy practices reported as changed. We did this by mathematically predicting the increase in propensity to change given an increase in the degree of authenticity in a respondent's classroom. The results of this analysis are displayed in Figure 5.1 which shows that the predicted impact of moving from a highly inauthentic classroom to a highly authentic classroom is not as small as suggested by the effect size of .16 found in our analysis.

The upper panel of Figure 5.1 shows the additional number of literacy practices in which students are predicted to change in a more authentic classroom over and above the number of practices in which the same students are predicted to change in a highly school-only classroom. This panel shows that students who would change an average of 5 to 15 literacy practices in a highly school-only class would change in an additional 6 to 8 in a class rated as highly authentic. One can also see the predicted effect of moving a student from a highly school-only class to a somewhat school-only class (an average of 2 additional changed literacy practices) and to a somewhat authentic class (from 4 to 5 additional changed literacy practices).

The lower panel of Figure 5.1 translates the predicted increase in number of changed literacy practices to percent increases as a result of moving along the dimensional continuum from highly school-only to highly authentic. Here we see that students predicted to change in less than 5 literacy practices in a highly school-only class would demonstrate a 140 to 185% increase in changed literacy practices if moved to a highly authentic classroom. Further, the predicted increase in changed literacy practices is above 50% for the majority of students. Both panels demonstrate that the predicted effect on changed literacy practices

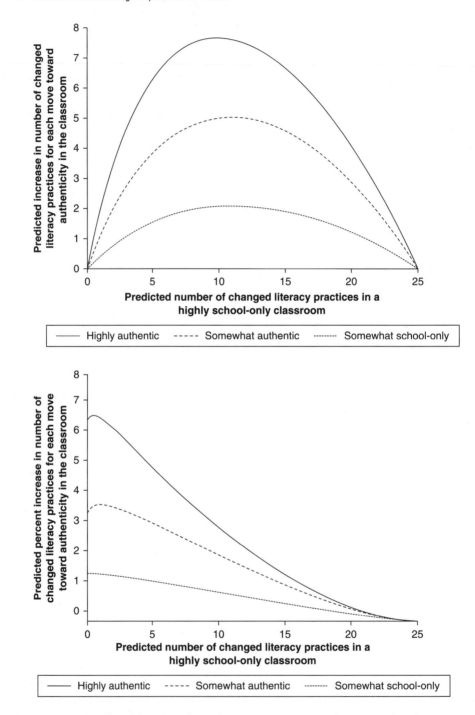

Figure 5.1   Predicted impact on students' literacy practices on moving from a class with little or no use of authentic texts and literacy activities to classes with increased degrees of authenticity

of moving to instructional contexts that include more authentic materials and activities is greatest for those students who would change least in a highly school-only classroom.

The tapering off to zero in the lower panel is an artifact of a ceiling effect. Because there were only 26 literacy practices – or text types – addressed in the questionnaire, students who are predicted to change in 25 literacy practices in a highly school-only classroom could only increase in one additional literacy practice no matter what type of classroom they would move to, resulting in a maximum of a 4% increase.

Discussion

Limitations

This study represents the first time anyone has attempted to examine literacy practice as an outcome of instruction within the adult basic education population. All of the difficulties of conducting systematic empirical research with adult education students also plagued this study, and the limitations thus produced must be acknowledged. First, all of the participants – teachers and students – were volunteer and not randomly selected. Thus we cannot claim true representation. Mitigating this, however, is the fact that the pattern of class types, considering the two dimensions of authenticity and collaboration, is remarkably similar to that found with the earlier typology study (Purcell-Gates, Degener, & Jacobson, 2000), which, while also relying on a volunteer sample, included many more programs. Further, the vast majority of the respondents in that study were randomly selected when we first sent out the surveys. We worked very hard to locate more classes in the authentic/collaborative quadrant to better answer our research question but were ultimately unsuccessful. Often classes would sound collaborative and authentic, only to prove not so after direct observation and teacher and student interviews.

A more serious threat to the issue of representation lies in the volunteer nature of the student participant pool. We acknowledge that students who are willing to accept researchers into their homes and to take the considerable time necessary to respond to the questionnaire items may very well be more motivated and involved in their literacy learning than those who are not. We take comfort in the fact, however, that these behavioral tendencies did not seem to be related to the type of classes in which they were participating, thus posing a reduced risk to interpretation of the results.

Readers must remember that this study was correlational and not experimental. Thus, we do not claim a firm statistical causal connection between particular types of literacy instruction and changes in literacy practices. However, given our careful analysis of the data, controlling for all other influencing factors, as well as our exploration of the predicted impact of the authenticity variable on the outcome variable of literacy practice change, we can conclude tentative causality. We believe that this type of design is close to being the best that researchers can do with this population of adult learners. Good experimentation requires random selection of program and random assignment of student to program. Adult students vary widely in their decisions to participate in adult education, how long they participate, motivations for participation, and so on. This variability reflects the diverse personalities, histories, life trajectories, and so on of adult students. It would be difficult, and perhaps impossible, to conduct a good experimental study within this context with a high enough N to produce valid and reliable results.

Dimension of teacher/student collaboration

We failed to find an effect on literacy practice change of the degree to which students and teachers shared power in decision making as regards curriculum and program governance. Although the logic of the hypothesis still holds – that students will engage in literacy more in their lives if they can truly influence what they learn to read and write in school – we could not detect a relationship. This could very well be the result of the way we operationalized and documented this dimension. A post hoc power analysis revealed that we did not have enough classrooms in the sample to detect a result if one existed.

It could also be that the operative elements of this dimension of collaboration cannot be measured in the ways we undertook. Clearly, one of the aspects of a dialogic relationship between teacher and student is affective in nature. While this could, and should, affect change in literacy practices in the long run, perhaps the best way to document this aspect is through ethnographic methods such as those conducted in the Purcell-Gates and Waterman (2000) study. Of course, it is also possible that there is no effect on literacy practice change from this dimension. This would not be to say that dialogic relationships between students and teachers are not worthy of striving for, just that one of the outcomes of that type of relationship is not literacy practice change.

Student-level factors related to change in literacy practice

The results of our analysis provide some very real insights into the different factors that are related to change in literacy practices by adult literacy students. Not surprising, but previously undocumented, are the relationships between individual student factors and literacy practice change. The factor with the strongest relationship to reported literacy practice change was that of the student's literacy level at the time he or she began attending the literacy class. This makes sense in that the degree to which a student *can* read would naturally affect the types of things he or she *will* read or the frequency of reading and writing events in that student's life. So, we see what we would expect: greater impact as regards change in literacy practices on those students who begin with lower levels of reading ability, regardless of instructional factors.

Related to this logic, we find that the second strongest determinant of reported literacy practice change is the amount of time a student has spent in a literacy class. The more time a student has to increase his or her reading ability, the more one is likely to see changes in what types of texts and how often that student reads and writes in life outside of the classroom. This finding lends added significance to efforts to increase students' persistence in attending adult literacy classes (Comings, Parrella, & Soricone, 1999). Clearly if we can find ways to make it possible and attractive for students to stay in classes, despite their pressing life responsibilities and their low self-esteem as previous school failures, we can expect to see significant outcomes accrue from these adults entering the literate world as readers and writers.

Finally, the less clear negative impact on reported literacy practice change of being an ESOL learner is also interesting. As a result of our ongoing struggle over the course of data collection to obtain useable data from ESOL students, we gained some perceptions of ESOL adult literacy students both by practitioners and by the students themselves.

First of all, a fascinating phenomenon emerged over the course of the study that can perhaps be described as a confusion, or blindness, which seems to confound ESOL status and literate status in the minds of many, particularly teachers. By this we mean that many teachers, when asked if certain students were 'nonliterate,' 'somewhat literate,' or 'highly literate,' would answer for ESOL students *as if* the question were being asked about being literate *in English*. This was so despite the explicit request to comment on the students' literacy levels in both their native languages and in English. Remember that we were limiting our student sample to those adults who were working to improve their literacy levels and we wanted to exclude adults who would be literate to at least a high school level. Therefore, we needed to know the literate status of the student volunteers before we included them in the participant pool, and we relied on teachers a great deal for this information. The confusion, or confounding, on the teachers' part of literate status and English literate status resulted in countless episodes where we had to drop individual ESOL participants when we ultimately learned that they were very literate in their native language and engaged in wide and frequent literacy practices in that language in their countries of origin.

Added to this difficulty was the fact that the ESOL students, perhaps due to the attitudes of the teachers toward students' native language literacy status, often described themselves as nonliterate or low literate when in fact they meant they could not read English very well. For many, it almost appeared as if they had left their native language literacy behind when they left their countries of origin and began again as newborn nonliterate persons. Many of the ESOL participants refused to even discuss what texts they read and wrote in their native language, even when it was apparent that we were counting those with the dual-language questionnaire items. Others would provide answers to some items as they pertained to their native literacy practices and not others. As described previously, all of this resulted in our inability to use their questionnaire data for the larger data pool on which we conducted the analysis.

Whether the resultant loss of participants and missing data contributed to the negative finding regarding ESOL status on our research questions is impossible to say. Regardless, this finding meant that ESOL students showed fewer changes in literacy practices after beginning their ESOL literacy classes than non-ESOL students. This could mean that those ESOL students who remained in the data pool – that is, answered questions about their native literacy practices and who were not judged (known by the teacher or self-revealed) to be highly literate in their native language – already engaged frequently in many different types of literacy practices *before* they began trying to learn to read and write English. However, this finding of a negative relationship is based on only a few of the many ESOL literacy students in U.S. adult education programs. All of the difficulties inherent in obtaining this ESOL data renders this finding of questionable generalizability.

Authentic reading and writing in the classroom

The results of this study suggest that the literacy practices of adults can change – in nature or in frequency – in response to adult literacy instruction that is reflective of real-life literacy practices. This finding is important on two levels. First, this is the first time that research has documented this for outside-of-school contexts, despite the widespread belief among academics that this type of instruction is best practice and despite the considerable lip service given to this principle by practitioners. It is important to have solid documentation for instructional beliefs to withstand the inevitable shifts that occur in the political and policy winds.

Second, this result demonstrates that despite the growing back-to-basics rhetoric, involving students in real-life or authentic literacy activities in the classroom is statistically significantly more related to growth and development of literacy practices than decontextualized skill work. Because this study controlled for the literacy level of students, it also suggests that there is no reading ability threshold at which this type of practice is inappropriate (see Freire, 1993).

Further, the predicted impact analysis demonstrated that those adult students who showed the least transference of reading and writing from school to their out-of-school lives in highly school-only classes would be the most positively affected by participating in classes with increasing amounts of authentic reading and writing. These are the adult students of most concern, naturally, and these findings support serious efforts to implement authentic literacy instruction in adult education programs.

The contributions of this study and its findings can be further explored by recalling the argument made above that measuring change in literacy practices can be viewed as a more proximal measure of instructional outcome than scores on tests of decontextualized literacy skills. The following argument is made to support this assertion. The goal of adult literacy instruction (or any literacy instruction) is to create literate beings who can and will use print for many and varied purposes. As such, the belief is that the resultant literate being will be more capable of negotiating the world and the different demands that life presents. We claim this as the goal of instruction because we do not believe that anyone would argue that literacy instruction is successful if the recipients of the instruction *can* read and write but *do not*. Given this argument, the actual outcome of literacy instruction is the *engagement* in many and varied literacy practices involving the reading and writing of many and varied texts. A measure of this literacy practice outcome – as was employed in this study – is, therefore, much more of a proximal one than is the measure of the *ability* to read and write in a general way as measured by skill assessments. The *ability to read and write* must precede or co-occur with the practice of reading and writing, but it is not yet, or alone, the actual *practice* of reading and writing. Thus, assessment of ability to read and write can be considered, relatively, as a distal measurement of instructional outcome.

The results of this study, therefore, represent a close and direct measure of outcome of adult literacy instruction. The results document that it is indeed beneficial, relative to the purposes of adult literacy instruction, to incorporate materials and literacy activities in the instructional program that reflect real-life texts and purposes for reading and writing them to the greatest degree possible. Reading newspapers to learn the news relevant to the students' lives and interests, writing letters that get sent to real people in the lives of the students, reading books and discussing them as readers who respond, writing notices and accounts for a newsletter that gets printed and read by real people … all of these types of activities can, according to the findings of this study, lead to substantive changes in the ways that students create literate lives outside of the classroom.

None of this precludes skill teaching or learning. As has been demonstrated elsewhere, teachers can weave important skill instruction into literacy instruction that focuses on authentic literacy use (McIntyre & Pressley, 1996; Pressley et al., 2001; Purcell-Gates, 1996a). None of the teachers in this study indicated that they taught no skills, and most of them who fell into the somewhat too highly authentic categories noted the use of some material that focused exclusively on skills. What was clear, however, was the impression that the skill teaching and student skill work were embedded in and served the purposes of the authentic reading and writing that the students were doing.

Complex texts

The scaling of the literacy practices that underwent change provides another interesting lens on the contributions of this study. This scale allows us to identify the types of practices that underwent greater frequencies of change among the participants and those that reflected fewer reported changes. As we see in Table 5.9, the two practices that were most affected by the changes that occurred in literacy use reported by the participants were reading essays, compositions, and text for information (i.e., expository text) and reading books and stories (i.e., fiction). These types of texts contain discourse at the greatest levels of 'writtenness' as defined and operationalized in the Purcell-Gates (1996b) study of emergent literacy and home literacy practices. What this implies is that those adult students who either adopted new literacy practices or read and wrote more frequently with different types of texts began to do this with more complex texts – using the term *complexity* in the sense of linguistic features that render texts more written than oral in nature (Chafe & Danielewicz, 1986).

This has interesting implications deserving of further research for our understandings of intergenerational literacy. This is so because earlier studies document that (a) frequency of literacy events as well as (b) the degree of complexity of texts written and read in the homes and lives of young children will predict the level of emergent literacy knowledge the children exhibit on entry into formal schooling (Purcell-Gates, 1996b). This, in turn, predicts quite well the degree of success these children will experience in learning to read and write in school (Purcell-Gates & Dahl, 1991). Further research could investigate more directly than has been done to date the implied hypothesis that children of adults who attend literacy classes that employ authentic texts and purposes benefit in terms of their emergent literacy experiences from their parents' increased reading and writing of more complex texts.

References

Auerbach, E.R. (1993). Putting the P back in participatory. *TESOL Quarterly, 27,* 543–544.

Auerbach, E.R. (1995). Deconstructing the discourse of strengths in family literacy. *Journal of Reading Behavior, 27,* 643–661.

Barton, D., & Hamilton, M. (1998). *Local literacies: Reading and writing in one community.* London: Routledge.

Brizius, J., & Foster, S. (1987). *Enhancing adult literacy: A policy guide.* Washington, DC: The Council of State Policy and Planning Agencies.

Bryk, A.S., & Raudenbush, S.W. (1992) *Hierarchical linear models.* Newbury Park, CA: Sage.

Chafe, W., & Danielewicz, J. (1986). Properties of spoken and written language. In R. Horowitz & S.J. Samuels (Eds.), *Comprehending oral and written language* (pp. 83–113). New York: Academic Press.

Comings, J.P., Parrella, A., & Soricone, L. (1999, December). *Persistence among adult basic education students in pre-GED classes* (NCSALL Rep. 12). Cambridge, MA: National Center for the Study of Adult Learning and Literacy, Harvard Graduate School of Education.

D'Annunzio, A. (1994). A nondirective combinatory model in an adult ESL program. In M. Radencich (Ed.), *Adult literacy: A compendium of articles from the Journal of Reading* (pp. 57–62). Newark, DE: International Reading Association. (ERIC Document Reproduction Service No. ED 373 268.)

Fingeret, A.H. (1991). Meaning, experience, literacy. *Adult Basic Education, 1,* 1–11.

Freire, P. (1993). *Pedagogy of the oppressed.* New York: Continuum.

Freire, P. (1997). *Pedagogy of the* heart. New York: Continuum.

Glen, J.M. (1996). *Highlander: No ordinary school* (2nd ed.). Knoxville, TN: University of Tennessee Press.

Hittleman, D.R., & Simon, A.J. (1997). *Interpreting educational research* (2nd ed.). Upper Saddle River, NJ: Prentice Hall.

Hunter, C.S.J., & Harman, D. (1985). *Adult illiteracy in the United* States. New York: McGraw Hill.

LaBerge, D., & Samuels, S. (1974). Toward a theory of automatic information processing in reading. *Cognitive Psychology, 6,* 293–323.

Leistyna, P., Woodrum, A., & Sherblom, S.A. (Eds.). (1996). *Breaking tree: The transformative power of critical pedagogy (Harvard Educational Review,* Reprint Series No. 27.) Cambridge, MA: Harvard Graduate School of Education.

Lerche, R.S. (1985). *Effective adult literacy programs: A practitioner's guide.* New York: Cambridge University Press.

Lord, F.M. (1980). *Applications of item response theory to practical testing problems.* Hillsdale, NJ: Erlbaum.

Lytle, S. (1994). Living literacy: Rethinking adult learner assessment. *Literacy, Practitioner, 2,* 1–2, 6–8.

McIntyre, E., & Pressley, M. (Eds.). (1996). *Balanced instruction: Strategies and skills in whole language.* Norwood, MA: Christopher-Gordon.

Mehrens, W.A., & Lehmann, I.J. (1991). *Measurement and evaluation in education and psychology.* New York: Harcourt Brace.

National Center on Adult Literacy (1995). *Adult literacy: The next generation* (NCAL Technical Rep. TR95-011). Philadelphia: Author.

Nwakese, P.C., & Seiler, L.H. (1993). Adult literacy programs: What students say. *Adult Learning, 5,* 17–18, 24.

Pressley, M., Wharton-McDonald, R., Allington, R., Block, C.C., Marrow, L., Tracey, D., Baker, K., Brooks, G., Cronin, J., Nelson, E., & Wood, D. (2001). A study of effective first-grade literacy instruction. *Scientific Studies of Reading, 5,* 35–58.

Purcell-Gates, V. (1995). *Other people's words: The cycle of low literacy.* Cambridge, MA: Harvard University Press.

Purcell-Gates, V. (1996a). Process teaching with direct instruction and feedback in a university-based clinic. In E. McIntyre & M. Pressley (Eds.), *Balanced instruction: Strategies and skills in whole language* (pp. 107–128). Norwood, MA: Christopher-Gordon.

Purcell-Gates, V. (1996b). Stories, coupons, and the *TV Guide*: Relationships between home literacy experiences and emergent literacy knowledge. *Reading Research Quarterly, 31,* 210–219.

Purcell-Gates, V., & Dahl, K. (1991). Low-SES children's success and failure at early literacy learning in skills-based classrooms. *JRB: A Journal of Literacy, 23,* 1–34.

Purcell-Gates, V., Degener, S., & Jacobson, E. (2000). Adult literacy instruction: Degrees of authenticity and collaboration as described by practitioners. *Journal of Literacy Research, 33,* 4, 571–93.

Purcell-Gates, V., & Waterman, R. (2000). *Now we read, we see, we speak: Portrait of literacy development in a Freirean-based adult literacy class.* Mahwah, NJ: Erlbaum.

Risko, V., & Bromley, K. (Eds.). (2000). *Collaboration for diverse learners.* Newark, DE: International Reading Association.

Scribner, S. (1997). *Mind and social practice: Selected writings of Sylvia Scribner.* New York: Cambridge University Press.

Stascz, B.B., Schwartz, R.C., & Weeden, J.C. (1994). Writing our lives: An adult basic skills program. In M. Radencich (Ed.), *Adult literacy: A compendium of articles from the Journal of Reading* (pp. 150–155). Newark, DE: International Reading Association.

Stein, S. (2000). *Equipped for the future content standards: What adults need to know and be able to do in the 21st century.* Washington, DC: National Institute for Literacy.

Sticht, T.G. (1988). Adult literacy education. *Review of Research in Education, 15,* 59–96.

Street, B. (1989). Literacy: 'Autonomous' vs. 'ideological' model. In M. Taylor & J.A. Draper (Eds.), *Adult literacy perspectives* (pp. 57–69). Toronto, ON, Canada: Culture Concepts.

Taylor, D. (1985). *Family literacy: Children learning to read and write.* Exeter, NH: Heinemann.

Taylor, D., & Dorsey-Gaines, C. (1988). *Growing up literate: Learning from inner-city families.* Portsmouth, NH: Heinemann.

Teale, W. (1986). Home background and young children's literacy development. In W.H. Teale & E. Sulzby (Eds.), *Emergent literacy: Reading and writing* (pp. 173–206). Norwood, NJ: Ablex.

U.S. Congress, Office of Technology Assistance. (1993). *Adult literacy and new technologies: Tools for a lifetime* (OTA-SET-550). Washington, DC: U.S. Government Printing Office.

Wagner, D., & Venezky, R. (1995, May). Adult literacy: The next generation. *Connections, 1,* 6.

Part 2

Assessing Literacy Difficulties

6

Is the PhAB Really Fab? The Utility of the Phonological Assessment Battery in Predicting Gains Made by Older Low-Progress Readers Following Two Terms of Intensive Literacy Instruction

Kevin Wheldall and Simmone Pogorzelski

[...]

In spite of convincing argument and evidence to the contrary (Wheldall, 1994; Wheldall & Beaman, 2000; Wheldall & Carter, 1996), there is an enduring belief that diagnosis of the cause of reading failure is instrumental in determining effective intervention and remediation. Reading researchers have been particularly concerned to distinguish dyslexic readers from other low-progress readers (Frith, 1995; Stanovich, 1988) since true dyslexics are deemed to be more resistant to instruction and in need of specific instruction more carefully tailored to meet their idiosyncratic needs. In spite of the best efforts of such researchers as Gundersen and Siegel (2001), Siegel (1999), Stanovich (1991, 1994, 2000), Stanovich and Siegel (1994) and Torgesen and Wagner (1998) to demonstrate that, for example, the discrepancy definition of dyslexia makes neither conceptual nor empirical sense, the belief persists that categorisation of sub-types of disabled readers is both possible and necessary. The purpose of the present [chapter] is neither to deny the existence nor the descriptive utility of the concept of dyslexia but to determine whether the categorisation of older low-progress readers into dyslexic and non-dyslexic groups is predictive of the likely gains in reading performance following intensive literacy intervention. Given the contemporary view of the central role of phonological processing in learning to read, and hence in the diagnosis of dyslexia (see below), this issue also is critically examined in the light of empirical findings.

There is considerable evidence to suggest that an underlying deficit in phonological processing skills is the primary cause of reading failure (Ball & Blachman, 1988, 1991; Bradley & Bryant, 1983; Share, 1995; Stanovich, 1991, 1994), which prevents students from learning and understanding the alphabetic principle required for fluent decoding and word recognition. Furthermore, it is believed that such a deficit is likely to be part of a

---

From: *Educational Psychology*, 23 (5), 2003, pp. 569–90.

larger more encompassing language disorder which, despite being present in early prereading skills, may fail to show up as a significant factor until after reading instruction formally commences (Bishop, 2001). Students who begin school with few phonological skills and little exposure to a text-rich environment will probably experience the most difficulty in grasping and utilising the alphabetic principle (Ball, 1996).

Phonological processing deficits are evident in a student's difficulty with short- and long-term memory tasks and their inability to access the phonological structure of language (Torgesen & Wagner, 1998). Tests to measure these processing deficits might include non-word and digit repetition tasks and rapid automatic naming (of digits, objects and colours) (Ball, 1996; Frith, 1995; Gallagher, 1995; Hulme & Snowling, 1992; Torgesen & Wagner, 1998). Students who have difficulty with these tasks also have difficulty understanding that words are made up of smaller component sounds, that is, they are poor in phonological awareness. Being poor in phonological awareness at an early age means students are unable to detect or generate rhymes and have little awareness of alliteration and syllables. Tests of phonological awareness for students who have already commenced formal reading instruction tap knowledge at the phoneme level (phonemic awareness) and require students to blend, segment and manipulate sounds within words (Adams, 1990; Ball, 1996; Share, 1995; Stanovich, 1992, 1994; Torgesen & Wagner, 1998). Recent research shows that students who demonstrate competence in phonemic awareness and sound symbol correspondences progress more rapidly in their reading development than students who do not have these skills (Adams, 1990; Report of the National Reading Panel, 2000; Share, 1995).

Researchers assert that phonological awareness and reading are either causally or reciprocally related (Adams, 1990; Ball & Blachman, 1991; Bradley & Bryant, 1983; Bruck, 1992; Hatcher, Hulme, & Ellis, 1994; McGuinness, McGuinness, & Donohue, 1995; Shankweiler, 1999; Share, 1995; Stanovich, 1994). In fact, both are correct to some extent. Phonological awareness is a crucial prerequisite skill for learning to read, as students who understand that words are made up of sounds are more likely to grasp the alphabetic principle and develop reading skills at a typical rate. Ball (1996, p. 82) contends that what starts off as a causal relationship shifts to one of 'mutual facilitation' as the commencement of reading instruction phonologically induces or 'bootstraps' reading development. In turn, learning to read increases a student's understanding that words are made up of smaller units of sound (phonemes).

There are a number of studies that demonstrate the reciprocity between letter–sound knowledge and phonological awareness (Ball & Blachman, 1988, 1991; Bradley & Bryant, 1983; Hatcher et al., 1994). These studies have highlighted what Hatcher et al. (1994, p. 42) termed the 'phonological linkage hypothesis' which, it is argued, demonstrates that training both these skills concurrently yields greater outcomes in reading gains than training either skill in isolation. Although there is no doubt that there is a relationship between phonological awareness and reading, there is some debate regarding the extent of reciprocity and the type of phonological skills that should be taught to both beginning readers and older low-progress readers. For instance, a number of researchers (Adams, 1990; Carnine, Silbert, & Kameenui, 1997; Ehri et al., 2001; Solity, Deavers, Kerfoot, Crane, & Cannon, 1999) claim that it is not necessary to train students in all phonological awareness activities to facilitate the acquisition and development of reading skills. It is argued that although some of these skills are related to reading, it is only blending and segmenting that directly parallel the act of reading and hence they are the only skills that need to be taught explicitly in conjunction with letter–sound knowledge (Solity et al., 1999). Such debate over the type of skills to be taught does not discount the importance of teaching phonological awareness skills to promote mastery of the alphabetic principle, but does question the notion of causality in reading disability. Thomas (2002), for example, highlights the tendency of researchers to overemphasise the importance of underlying processing variables that theoretically cause reading failure. It is more likely, contends Thomas, that the reason that phonological processing skills are so highly correlated with reading development is because these skills are so similar in nature.

What we do know is that students who are poor in phonological awareness will fail to develop competent reading skills unless they receive explicit, systematic and direct instruction in reading (Carnine et al., 1997; Shankweiler, 1999; Solity et al., 1999; Wheldall & Beaman, 2000). Students who have failed to learn to read initially will not catch up with their peers at a later date, but rather will fall further behind as a result of this initial failure (Wheldall & Beaman, 2000). This invariably leads to a 'negative spiral of cumulative disadvantage' for low-progress readers as their attempts to become competent readers are hindered by their initial lack of phonological skills (Stanovich, 1994, p. 281). Stanovich (1986, 1994, 2000) describes this consequence as the Matthew effect (the rich get richer and the poor get poorer) – the gap between good and poor readers increases not only in reading but also across all academic areas.

Support for a core deficit in reading disability has come from research showing that phonological deficits persist into adulthood (Ball, 1996; Bruck, 1992; Greenberg, Ehri, & Perin, 1997; Pratt & Brady, 1988; Shankweiler, Lundquist, Dreyer, & Dickinson, 1996; Stuart & Masterson, 1992; Yap & Van Der Leij, 1993). A number of researchers (Bruck, 1992, 1993; Fawcett & Nicolson, 1995; Felton, Naylor, & Wood, 1991; Gottardo, Siegel, & Stanovich, 1997; Shankweiler et al., 1996; Torgesen, Wagner, & Rashotte, 1997) contend that dyslexia that is phonologicaliy based is enduring even after years of intervention. Despite this evidence that a core phonological deficit is both specific and enduring for the dyslexic reader, there are a number of studies showing that when older low-progress readers (who are typically two to four years behind in their reading skills) receive instruction that directly targets core reading skills, reading is not only improved, but students are also able to catch up to their chronological age (Hempenstall, 1999; Lovett et al., 1994, Reynolds, 2000; Wheldall & Beaman, 2000). Additionally, there is evidence that effective reading instruction can lead to an improvement in phonological processing skills (Lovett et al., 1994; Pogorzelski & Wheldall, 2002).

The evidence outlined in this chapter suggests that students who are delayed in reading typically present with deficits in the phonological domain. The question arises whether this deficit is one of a biological nature or the result of experiential or environmental causes. We can assume that it is more likely that some students will develop reading skills at a typical rate if they come from a text-rich environment and also begin school with some phonological awareness skills (Ball, 1996). Tunmer, Chapman, Ryan, and Prochnow (1998) suggest that most children (approximately 75%) will develop an understanding of the alphabetic principle regardless of the type of instruction received. It is the other 25% that is of concern to reading researchers. Of this 25% it is thought that at least 3–5% of all children are severely dyslexic and will be those least likely to develop competent reading skills at a typical rate (Torgesen et al., 1997). In order to identify this group of dyslexic students, some researchers have advocated a battery of tests to uncover the underlying processes, namely phonological processing skills, thought to be causally related to reading disability (Frith, 1995; Torgesen & Wagner, 1998). Inherent in this argument is the assumption of specificity within the dyslexic poor reader, which in turn promotes the need for the categorisation of subtypes of dyslexic and non-dyslexic poor readers.

There is no doubt that a test which enables the detection of reading disability prior to formal reading instruction would be useful in circumventing lifelong reading failure, but it is unclear whether such a test would have any great utility in determining reading disability at a later age and/or stage of reading development. The phonological assessment battery or PhAB (Frederickson, Frith, & Reason, 1997), discussed in full in Pogorzelski and Wheldall (2002), has been designed to detect those readers who are poor in phonological processing skills and provide remedial reading assistance on this basis. Although a test such as this has the potential to provide researchers with a great deal of diagnostic information, it does not necessarily inform practice in a useful way (Pogorzelski & Wheldall, 2002). In fact, a number of researchers (Siegel, 1999; Stanovich, 1991, 1994, 2000; Stanovich & Siegel, 1994; Torgesen & Wagner, 1998) agree that although the reading delay experienced by most poor readers will be due to a phonological processing deficit, there is no significant difference between poor readers on a range of phonological tasks, despite the fact that they present with differences in IQ (Gundersen & Siegel, 2001; Siegel, 1999; Stanovich, 1991, 1994, 2000; Stanovich & Siegel, 1994; Torgesen & Wagner, 1998).

To summarise, it is clear that a deficit in phonological processing skills coexists with poor or delayed reading. It is further substantiated that a small proportion of students will be considered to be dyslexic because such phonological processing deficits are severe and of an intrinsic or biological nature. This is in comparison to a larger number of non-dyslexic poor readers who present with similar difficulties to the dyslexic reader but for whom the cause is hypothesised to be of an environmental nature (see Pogorzelski & Wheldall, 2002 for a full discussion). Initially, it was thought that the dyslexic reader would be more treatment resistant (Frith, 1995; Stanovich, 1988) because of the severity and specificity of the phonological processing deficit.

Pogorzelski and Wheldall (2002) presented preliminary findings, based on results after just one term of intensive literacy intervention, that older low-progress readers identified by the PhAB as dyslexic made gains just as great as those made by non-dyslexic poor readers on tests of word recognition, reading fluency and spelling. They found no evidence to suggest that PhAB overall score or subscale scores were predictive of gains made following intervention. The present study follows up the same sample of students following a further term of intensive literacy instruction (two terms in total) when they were again retested. The retest included a re-assessment on the Neale analysis (accuracy and comprehension) and, importantly, the PhAB as originally administered prior to the intervention two terms before. The aim of this follow-up study was to determine whether the PhAB-identified dyslexic group, after two terms of intensive instruction, were still gaining to the same extent as the non-dyslexic group, as had been the case after one term of instruction, and also whether the intervention program had influenced performance on the PhAB.

Method

Participants

The sample of low-progress readers comprised 22 students (14 boys and 8 girls) attending the Schoolwise Program delivered at the Exodus Foundation Tutorial Centre in Ashfield, New South Wales. The mean age of the participants at initial testing was 11 years and 9 months

(141 months, SD 8.76 months) with 16 students in year 6 and six in year 7. Students were selected into the program on the basis of meeting specific criteria. They were required to be at least two years behind in reading accuracy, socially disadvantaged and at serious risk of disaffection from school. The mean reading age for the group as measured by the Neale analysis of reading (Neale, 1999) was 91.55 months (7 years 6 months) for reading accuracy and 91.14 months (7 years 5 months) for reading comprehension. The sample was thus, on average, four years behind their chronological age for both reading accuracy (range = 5 years 7 months to 2 years 9 months) and comprehension (range = 5 years 9 months to 2 years 1 month).

Measures

On program entry in February, the participants were given a battery of standardised tests, administered over five days by trained research assistants.

The standardised tests included a phonological processing battery, measures of reading accuracy and comprehension, single word recognition, oral reading fluency and spelling. Follow-up data were collected after one term of instruction (10 weeks) on the measures of single word recognition and oral reading fluency (the Burt word reading test and the WARP measures respectively – see below) and reported in Pogorzelski and Wheldall (2002). Following two terms of instruction, the students were retested on all of the initial measures. All measures were detailed by Pogorzelski and Wheldall (2002) and will only be summarised here.

The Phonological Assessment Battery (PhAB; Frederickson et al., 1997)

Phonological processing was measured using the PhAB. The PhAB is designed to assess phonological processing and includes: four phonological awareness tests of alliteration, rhyme, spoonerism and non-word reading; two phonological production speed tests of naming speed in pictures and digits; two phonological fluency tests of alliteration and rhyme; and a test of semantic fluency. Students who have three or more highlighted (that is, low) scores on the subtests are considered to have a severe phonological processing deficit. For the purposes of analysis, these students are referred to as the 'low P' group. Students with fewer than three highlighted scores are referred to as the 'high P' group. Highlighted scores are standardised scores that fall one standard deviation (15) below the mean (100); that is, scores below 85.

The Neale Analysis of Reading (3rd edition; Neale, 1999)

This test is used to provide information regarding a student's ability in reading accuracy and reading comprehension.

Burt Word Reading Test (Gilmore, Croft, & Reid, 1981)

This test is a measure of single word recognition skills. Students are required to read a series of words presented on a test card in order of difficulty.

South Australian Spelling Test (Westwood, 1999)

This test was used to determine spelling age. It can be used with children aged 6 to 15.5 and can be individually or group administered.

Wheldall Assessment of Reading Passages (Wheldall, 1996)

The WARP is a curriculum-based measure of oral reading fluency (Wheldall & Beaman, 2000). Students are required to read three 200-word text passages each for one minute and words read correctly per minute (WPM) rate is recorded.

Intervention

The Schoolwise Program at the Exodus Tutorial Centre comprises intensive MULTILIT literacy instruction (Wheldall & Beaman, 2000) during sessions from 9.00am to 1.00pm, five mornings per week. Students received two hours of independent work; one half hour group spelling lesson; group reading, comprehension and language lessons for about an hour; and serial reading. In addition to this, students received individual reading instruction for half an hour each day. The Schoolwise Program is a version of the MULTILIT intervention, developed by Wheldall and colleagues at Macquarie University Special Education Centre, Sydney (Wheldall & Beaman, 2000), featuring the MULTILIT reading tutor program. This program teaches phonic word attack skills, sight words and reinforced reading using pause, prompt and praise. See Wheldall and Beaman (2000) for a fuller discussion of the program.

Test of Auditory Analysis Skills (TAAS; Rosner, 1975, 1993)

As part of the intensive literacy intervention program, 12 of the 22 students, based on the outcomes of placement testing on the TAAS, received one to one training in the TAAS program to develop auditory analysis skill (Rosner, 1975, 1993). The main goal of TAAS is to teach students how to discriminate between and manipulate phonemes. Further detail was provided by Pogorzelski and Wheldall (2002).

Results

Literacy and phonological processing measures

After two full terms of intensive literacy instruction, large and significant outcomes were achieved across the whole sample for all literacy measures. Table 6.1 shows the means and standard deviations for all literacy measures for the whole sample at pre-test and subsequent post-test two terms (five months) later.

The 22 students in the Schoolwise sample had made significant gains with large effect sizes on all literacy measures over two terms (five months) of instruction. Students made mean gains of 13 months in reading accuracy and 11 months in reading comprehension, as measured by the Neale and 23 months on single word recognition as measured by the Burt. On average, students made gains of 18 months in spelling and they increased the number of words read correctly per minute by 46 words on the WARP (65%). The gains achieved by the Schoolwise sample of students, who at best would typically make 2.5 months' gain in this period of time (Wheldall & Beaman, 2000), are five times greater than their regular expected rate of progress for reading accuracy. These gains are evidenced in an average effect size of 1.57 for all the literacy measures (see Table 6.1).

Table 6.1   Means (and standard deviations) for reading accuracy, reading comprehension, word recognition, spelling and oral reading fluency for February and the resultant gains after two terms for the whole sample

Literacy variable	n	Reading level February (SD)	Retest June (SD)	Gain (SD)	t	P	ES*
Neale accuracy	22	91.55	104.55	13.00	8.07	< 0.0001	1.71
(months)		(7.62)	(11.27)	(7.03)			
Neale comprehension		91.14	101.73	10.59	3.96	< 0.001	1.01
(months)		(10.52)	(14.76)	(12.56)			
WARP (WPM)	22	69.86	115.45	45.59	16.07	< 0.0001	1.98
		(23.02)	(27.70)	(13.30)			
SA spelling	22	97.95	115.82	17.86	9.25	< 0.0001	1.59
(months)		(11.22)	(11.13)	(9.06)			
Burt (months)	22	99.14	121.77	22.64	9.65	< 0.0001	1.56
		(14.54)	(21.62)	(11.0)			

*Effect sizes are typically regarded as small (0.20), medium (0.50) or large (0.80). See, for example, Aron and Aron (1999).

In addition to achieving significant literacy outcomes, the Schoolwise sample also made highly significant gains on most of the PhAB subtests after two terms of instruction. Moderate and large effect sizes were yielded for the significant phonological awareness subtests rhyme (0.54), alliteration (0.69), non-word reading (1.39) and spoonerisms (0.79). Moderate effect sizes were found for the significant phonological production and fluency subtests naming speed digits (0.58) and fluency test alliteration (0.60). The fluency test rhyme and naming speed pictures were not significantly improved upon and both yielded small effect sizes of 0.31. Means and standard deviations for the subtests of the PhAB for the whole sample are shown in Table 6.2.

Table 6.2   Means (and standard deviations) of the raw scores for the PhAB subtests for February and June, and the resultant gains after two terms for the whole sample

Phonological variable	n	Mean score February (SD)	Mean score June (SD)	Gain (SD)	t	P	ES
Alliteration	22	8.73	9.41	0.66	3.07	< 0.05	0.69
		(0.99)	(0.80)	(1.04)			
Rhyme	22	12.18	15.000	2.82	2.54	< 0.05	0.54
		(5.24)	(4.34)	(5.20)			
Spoonerisms	22	12.00	16.50	4.50	4.69	< 0.001	0.79
		(5.67)	(5.05)	(4.50)			
Non-word reading	22	8.96	14.00	5.05	7.58	< 0.0001	1.39
		(3.63)	(3.28)	(3.12)			
Naming speed pictures	22	97.00	88.05	-8.95	1.48	> 0.05	0.31
		(29.01)	(19.87)	(28.35)			
Naming speed digits	22	57.91	44.82	-8.09	4.67	< 0.001	0.58
		(14.00)	(9.82)	(8.13)			
Fluency alliteration	22	12.23	14.09	1.86	2.16	< 0.05	0.60
		(3.09)	(4.01)	(4.04)			
Fluency rhyme	22	7.87	8.46	0.59	0.97	> 0.05	0.31
		(3.17)	(2.61)	(2.86)			
Fluency semantic	22	21.09	23.68	2.59	2.26	< 0.05	0.41
		(6.27)	(5.78)	(5.37)			

Table 6.3   Mean differences between low and high PhAB groups for gains on all literacy measures after two terms of instruction

Literacy variable	Mean gains for low P (n = 16)	Mean gains for high P (n = 6)	t	P	ES
Neale accuracy (months)	12.62 (5.84)	14.00 (10.18)	0.40	> 0.05	0.20
Neale comprehension (months)	10.88 (14.88)	9.83 (7.60)	0.17	> 0.05	−0.08
WARP (WPM)	43.81 (14.05)	50.33 (10.67)	1.03	> 0.05	0.49
SA spelling (months)	16.81 (8.45)	20.67 (10.84)	0.88	> 0.05	0.43
Burt (months)	21.25 (10.59)	26.33 (12.21)	0.96	> 0.05	0.46

Further analysis was undertaken of the differences in literacy gains for those students who were low in phonological processing skills (low P), as determined by their initial scores on the PhAB, and those who were high in phonological processing skills (high P). No significant differences were found between the high and low P groups, with the low P students (n = 16) gaining on average 13 months in reading accuracy and 11 months in comprehension after two terms of intensive instruction (see Table 6.3) The t-test analyses of gains reported in Table 6.3 were verified by analyses of covariance, which confirmed that there were no significant differences between the reading gains for the high and low P groups, taking into account any differences in pre-test scores.

The results in Table 6.3 suggest that the categorisation does not effectively predict reading gains after intensive remedial instruction. Results after two terms of instruction show that there was no difference on the Neale, but there is some evidence for differential improvements on the other literacy measures as indicated by moderate effect sizes for single word recognition, spelling and oral reading fluency (see Table 6.3). It should be noted that these effect sizes are not taking into account initial differences between the two groups, which showed differences in favour of the high P group. Table 6.4 shows that the high P group were higher on all of the initial pre-test literacy measures.

Phonological awareness training

There were no significant differences in gains made between the group who received TAAS (n = 12) and the group who did not receive such training in auditory analysis skills (n = 10). Table 6.5 shows the results for each group and their literacy outcomes; note that the t-test analyses of gains reported were confirmed by analyses of covariance.

Whilst some improvement in favour of the group who received TAAS was found for oral reading fluency and reading comprehension, which is supported by small and moderate effect sizes (see Table 6.5), there was no difference for single word recognition or spelling. The group who received TAAS achieved gains of 13 months in reading comprehension and increased their oral reading fluency by 47 words. The untrained group improved in comprehension by seven months and increased their words read per minute by 43 words. The group who did not receive TAAS achieved greater gains in reading accuracy (15 months) compared

Table 6.4   Mean differences between low (*n* = 16) and high (*n* = 6) PhAB groups pre-test (February) and after two terms (June) for the whole sample

Literacy variable		Pre-test (February)	Post-test (June)
Neale accuracy	High	95.67	109.07
		(8.15)	(14.77)
	Low	90	102.62
		(6.94)	(9.53)
Neale comprehension	High	94. 67	104.50
		(12.01)	(16.94)
	Low	89.81	100.69
		(10.00)	(14.31)
WARP	High	85.7	135.50
		(14.63)	(14.52)
	Low	64.13	107.94
		(23.28)	(27.98)
SA Spelling	High	104.56	125.17
		(10.71)	(13.17)
	Low	95.50	112.31
		(10.70)	(8.21)
BURT	High	111.17	137.50
		(22.60)	(31.0)
	Low	94.62	115.88
		(6.81)	(14.05)

Table 6.5   Mean gains (and standard deviations) for the whole sample on all literacy measures

Literacy variable	TAAS	*n*	Pre-test (February)	Post-test (June)	Gains	*t*	*P*	ES
Neale accuracy (months)	No	10	91.90	107.10	15.20	1.37	> 0.05	0.57
			(9.31)	(13.80)	(5.98)			
	Yes	12	91.25	104.42	11.17			
			(6.30)	(8.72)	(7.55)			
Neale comprehension (months)	No	10	91.60	93.70	7.10	1.20	> 0.05	0.51
			(12.25)	(15.54)	(10.40)			
	Yes	12	90.75	104.25	13.50			
			(9.39)	(14.24)	(13.87)			
Burt (months)	No	10	104.70	128.00	23.30	0.25	> 0.05	0.11
			(19.23)	(27.38)	(12.68)			
	Yes	12	94.50	116.58	22.08			
			(7.05)	(14.63)	(9.93)			
SA spelling (months)	No	10	100.2	118.80	18.60	0.34	> 0.05	0.15
			(13.64)	(15.10)	(10.49)			
	Yes	12	96.08	113.33	17.25			
			(8.94)	(5.91)	(8.10)			
WARP (WPM)	No	10	67.90	111.0	43.10	0.79	> 0.05	0.34
			(25.44)	(33.4)	(14.04)			
	Yes	12	71.50	119.17	47.67			
			(21.82)	(22.75)	(12.89)			

TABLE 6.6 **Means (and standard deviations) for low P students on initial, follow-up and resultant gain**

Literacy variable	TAAS	n	Pre-test (February)	Post-test (June)	Gains	t	P	ES
Neale accuracy	No	7	89.43	102.14	12.71	0.05	> 0.05	0.03
(months)			(7.81)	(9.65)	(4.39)			
	Yes	9	90.44	103.00	12.56			
			(6.64)	(10.00)	(7.04)			
Neale comprehension	No	7	83.57	93.29	4.72	1.61	> 0.05	0.77
(months)			(10.67)	(8.65)	(10.50)			
	Yes	9	90.78	106.44	15.66			
			(9.98)	(15.58)	(15.35)			
Burt (months)	No	7	94.43	114.43	20.00	0.40	> 0.05	0.21
			(6.13)	(12.51)	(10.80)			
	Yes	9	947.8	117.00	22.22			
			(7.66)	(15.80)	(10.97)			
SA spelling	No	7	95.57	112.29	16.72	0.04	> 0.05	0.02
(months)			(12.59)	(10.67)	(8.67)			
	Yes	9	95.44	112.33	16.89			
			(9.79)	(6.40)	(8.80)			
WARP (WPM)	No	7	57.43	97.1	39.67	1.03	> 0.05	0.52
			(21.85)	(30.3)	(14.80)			
	Yes	9	69.33	116.33	47.00			
			(24.25)	(24.44)	(13.42)			

to the group who received training (11 months). The results reveal no clear pattern in favour of either reading group: the TAAS trained group yielded higher (but not significant) gains in reading comprehension and oral reading fluency, whilst the untrained group achieved higher (but not significant) gains in reading accuracy, word recognition and spelling.

Analysis of the students categorised by the PhAB as dyslexic ($n = 16$) further revealed no significant differences between those who received TAAS training and those who did not receive training. Table 6.6 shows initial, follow-up and resultant gains on all literacy measures.

The results revealed no statistically significant differences between the two groups for reading accuracy, spelling or single word recognition. There was a moderate effect size (0.52) for oral reading fluency with the TAAS trained group. increasing their words read per minute by 47 compared to 40 for the untrained group. A large effect size (0.77) was found for reading comprehension, with the TAAS trained group making a gain of 16 months compared to five months by the untrained group. The t-test analyses of gains reported in Table 6.6 were confirmed by analyses of covariance.

As no significant differences were found between group (TASS or no TASS) on all literacy measures, the data were further analysed to determine whether the implementation of auditory analysis training influenced gains on the variable phonological processing (PhAB scores); that is, could this training be sufficient to improve phonological processing skills? Table 6.7 shows the mean gains and standard deviations for the low P groups after two terms of instruction in TASS.

The results in Table 6.7 show that there were no statistically significant or consistent differences for the group of dyslexia students (low P) who were trained in TAAS as compared to those students who did not receive training. The trained group ($n = 9$) showed greater

Table 6.7 Mean gains (and standard deviations) for the low P group after two terms of instruction

PhAB subtests	TAAS	n	Pre-test (February)	Post-test (June)	Gains	t	P	ES
Alliteration	No	7	9.14 (0.69)	9.43 (0.79	0.29 (0.76)	1.69	> 0.05	0.80
	Yes	9	8.00 (0.87)	9.22 (0.83)	1.22 (1.30)			
Rhyme	No	7	9.86 (6.09)	15.29 (4.54)	5.43 (6.02)	1.07	> 0.05	0.54
	Yes	9	10.67 (4.12)	13.11 (4.65)	2.44 (5.15)	1.43	> 0.05	0.70
Spoonerisms	No	7	12.57 (4.58)	15.00 (6.30)	2.43 (2.07)			
	Yes	9	8.67 (4.97)	14.67 (2.74)	6.00 (6.28)			
Non-word reading	No	7	9.29 (2.81)	13.00 (2.94)	3.71 (1.25)	1.51	> 0.05	0.7 3
	Yes	9	7.33 (2.83)	13.22 (3.11)	5.89 (3.62)			
Picture naming	No	7	112.29 (23.61)	94.86 (22.97)	−17.43 (12.51)	0.41	> 0.05	0.11
	Yes	9	106.78 (14.25)	91.67 (11.01)	−15.11 (10.02)			
Digit naming	No	7	62.43 (14.56)	52.00 (10.21)	−10.43 (11.46)	0.70	> 0.05	0.36
	Yes	9	59.11 (14.95)	51.89 (10.65)	−7.22 (6.69)			
Fluency alliteration	No	7	12.43 (1.72)	15.57 (5.13)	3.14 (5.43)	1.53	> 0.05	0.70
	Yes	9	11.67 (4.27)	11.56 (2.74)	−0.11 (2.98)			
Fluency rhyme	No	7	7.571 (2.23)	8.00 (2.89)	0.43 (098)	0.08	> 0.05	0.04
	Yes	9	7.67 (4.18)	8.222 (2.59)	0.56 (4.22)			
Fluency semantics	No	7	19.14 (5.81)	21.57 (5.56)	2.43 (7.98)	0.19	> 0.05	0.10
	Yes	9	19.78 (6.36)	22.78 (6.42)	3.00 (4.09)			

improvement in alliteration, spoonerisms, and non-word reading, which is supported by moderate to large effect sizes, but the untrained group performed better on the rhyme sub-test (ES 0.54) and fluency alliteration (ES 0.70).

Analysis of reading subtypes

At the initial February pre-test, there were six students categorised as non-dyslexic (high P) and 16 students categorised as dyslexic (low P), as determined by their performance on the PhAB. After two terms of instruction, only eight of the original 16 students remained in the low P (dyslexic) group; that is, eight students improved their phonological processing skills

Table 6.8   Mean gains (and standard deviations) for students diagnosed as low in phonological processing skills (low P)

Literacy variable	Mean gains for low P (n = 8)	Mean gains for low to high P (n = 8)	t	P	ES
Neale accuracy (months)	13.75 (7.36)	11.50 (4.00)	0.76	> 0.05	0.39
Neale comprehension (months)	7.37 (11.89)	14.38 (16.18)	0.99	> 0.05	0.49
Burt (months)	19.62 (10.80)	22.88 (10.86)	0.60	> 0.05	0.31
SA spelling (months)	16.75 (6.67)	16.88 (10.41)	0.03	> 0.05	0.02
WARP (WPM)	38.88 (14.91)	48.75 (12.04)	1.46	> 0.05	0.70

sufficiently to move into the high P group after two terms of literacy intervention. Table 6.8 shows the mean gains and standard deviations for the eight students who remained low in phonological processing skills compared to the eight who moved into the high P group.

The t-test analyses of gains reported in Table 6.8 were confirmed by analyses of covariance. There were no significant differences between the group of students who improved their phonological processing skills and those that remained in the dyslexic category, although moderate and large effect sizes were found for reading comprehension (0.49), word recognition (0.31) and oral reading fluency (0.70).

The final analysis concerned those students who made less than six months' gain in reading accuracy. The data of each individual student (see Table 6.9) were examined to determine whether or not PhAB categorisation assisted in predicting smaller literacy gains in those students selected as dyslexic. More specifically, does the categorisation by PhAB provide any more useful information than the literacy measures already utilised in the assessment battery? That is, do initial differences in reading performance reveal as much as the PhAB when it comes to predicting reading growth in a sample of low-progress readers such as the group presented in this study? Individual scores for all students for all literacy measures are presented in Table 6.9.

The data presented in Table 6.9 show that of the three students who made less than six months' gain in reading accuracy (according to the Neale), PhAB identified two as having a phonological processing deficit. The PhAB did not detect the third student. In fact, the PhAB (in addition to these two students) also identified 14 other students as being low in phonological processing skills, which would ordinarily indicate that they require additional training in phonological awareness. Of the 16 students identified by PhAB as low in phonological processing, seven did not receive TAAS. All these students (3, 4, 5, 6, 19, 20, 22) still made substantial gains (greater than six months) on reading accuracy. All but one (student 19) made greater than six months' gain in word recognition and all made greater than six months' gain in spelling. All had gains in oral reading fluency of more than 20 words per minute.

Of even greater significance is the fact that PhAB identified the two students (2 and 11) who gained less than six months in reading accuracy as being poor in phonological processing. These students, as a result of placement testing, received training in phonological awareness (TAAS). In addition to this, PhAB identified student 17 as low in phonological

Table 6.9 Literacy gains and pre- and post-test PhAB categorisation for the whole sample after two terms of instruction

	PhAB (April)	PhAB (June)	TAAS	Neale accuracy (months)	Neale comprehension (months)	Burt (months)	SA spelling (months)	WARP (months)
1	Low	Low	Yes	11	6	10	16	48
2	Low	Low	Yes	4	-3	21	7	45
3	Low	High	No	11	17	17	23	37
4	Low	Low	No	16	-3	10	28	33
5	Low	High	No	9	-8	14	6	36
6	Low	High	No	10	3	28	6	50
7	Low	High	Yes	13	22	16	25	46
8	High	High	Yes	16	6	13	11	56
9	High	High	Yes	7	13	28	25	59
10	High	High	No	16	16	20	21	62
11	Low	High	Yes	4	6	15	3	56
12	High	High	No	27	20	49	9	43
13	Low	Low	Yes	27	30	30	11	23
14	High	High	No	20	2	24	39	48
15	Low	Low	Yes	9	5	15	18	40
16	Low	High	Yes	15	43	19	20	73
17	High	High	Yes	-2	2	24	19	34
18	Low	High	Yes	17	27	46	21	41
19	Low	Low	No	8	-5	5	18	24
20	Low	Low	No	20	15	39	23	30
21	Low	High	Yes	13	5	28	31	51
22	Low	Low	No	15	14	18	13	68

processing. This student received TAAS and like the other two students made poor gains in reading accuracy. Note, however, that these students still made substantial gains in word recognition, spelling and oral reading fluency, although students 2 and 17 made poor gains in comprehension.

The final step was to examine the students who moved from being low in phonological processing to being high in phonological processing (see Table 6.9). Of the students who improved their phonological processing skills, three (3, 5, and 6) did not have TAAS and five (7, 11, 16, 18, 21) did. These data show that the deficits of three students were remediated without any assistance from a phonological processing program such as TAAS, suggesting that the reading program itself is impacting on the initial deficit revealed by PhAB categorisation. Moreover, these students all made gains greater than six months in reading accuracy.

Discussion

The main aim of the present research was to test the specificity hypothesis regarding readers with dyslexia. More specifically, it was expected that readers with dyslexia, due to a core cognitive deficit (Frith, 1995; Stanovich, 1988), would make smaller gains in reading outcomes compared to a group of non-dyslexic poor readers, following intensive remedial instruction in reading. The results after two terms of instruction confirm the findings after one term (reported in Pogorzelski and Wheldall, 2002), that the categorisation of reading subtypes (dyslexic or non-dyslexic) as determined by the PhAB (Frederickson et al., 1997) does not reliably predict outcomes in reading and related skills following intensive literacy instruction. Moreover, the results from this research study suggest that the reading difficulties of both dyslexic and non-dyslexic poor readers can be effectively addressed and that the phonological deficits of both groups may not be as enduring as has been indicated by some researchers (Bruck, 1992, 1993; Fawcett & Nicolson, 1995; Felton et al., 1991; Gottardo et al., 1997; Shankweiler et al., 1996; Torgesen et al., 1997).

The results of the present study clearly show that all the students in the Schoolwise sample made gains on the literacy measures. The results of the present study also reveal that, regardless of categorisation as either dyslexic (low P) or non-dyslexic (high P), there were no significant differences between groups for all literacy measures. After two terms of instruction, there was some evidence of larger gains in single word recognition, oral reading fluency and spelling in favour of the high P (non-dyslexic) group, which was supported by moderate effect sizes, but these gains are less convincing when one considers that there was a small effect size for reading accuracy in favour of the low P (dyslexic) group and no difference between the groups for reading comprehension. Further, the differential improvement in word recognition, oral reading fluency and spelling by the high P group should be treated with caution as the results showed that the high P group was higher than the low P group on the literacy measures tested before intervention. The results from this current sample suggest that the PhAB has little predictive value in determining which lower-progress readers will respond to an intensive remedial program such as the MULTILIT Program (Wheldall & Beaman, 2000). As such, the results provide further evidence for the non-categorical approach advocated by the MULTILIT research team (Wheldall, 1994; Wheldall & Beaman, 2000; Wheldall & Carter, 1996).

A secondary aim of the current research was to examine performance on the phonological processing subtests of the PhAB (Frederickson et al., 1997) following intensive literacy intervention. Significant gains were found for the whole sample on six of the eight phonological subtests after two terms of instruction. Significant gains were found for alliteration, rhyme, spoonerisms, non-word reading, naming speed digits and fluency alliteration. Only two of the gains in phonological skills failed to reach statistical significance: naming speed pictures and fluency rhyme. These results provide strong evidence for the reciprocal causation hypothesis and suggest that phonological processing skills can be significantly improved by intensive reading instruction alone. The results of this study are in contrast to those of Bruck (1992) who found that older dyslexic readers who had improved their word recognition skills and demonstrated mastery of onset-rime awareness, equal to that of college students, still demonstrated difficulties in phonemic awareness. Rather than dismissing the theory of a core deficit in reading disability, however, it is believed that the results of the current research point to the effectiveness of the remedial program employed. The evidence supports the assertion that the training provided was effective in remediating phonological difficulties despite these skills not being explicitly trained, in isolation, as part of the program. It is, of course, embedded necessarily within the phonic word attack skills component.

The results reported after one term (Pogorzelski & Wheldall, 2002) showed some evidence for an effect of phonological awareness training on literacy outcomes through the TAAS program (Rosner, 1975, 1993), providing tentative support for the phonological linkage hypothesis proposed by Hatcher et al. (1994). After two terms of instruction, no statistically significant differences between students who received training in TAAS and those who did not receive such training were found. Out of the five literacy measures, there were moderate and small effect sizes in favour of the TAAS trained group for reading comprehension (0.51) and oral reading fluency (0.34) but a moderate effect size (0.57) for reading accuracy in favour of the group who were not trained. The results suggest that phonological awareness training (in the form of TAAS) failed to enhance or provide any further benefits beyond those afforded by the remedial program alone. This is in contrast to those researchers who have reported positive effects for groups of readers trained with a combination of phonological awareness and sound–symbol activities when compared to groups trained in phonological awareness or sound–symbol relations alone (Hatcher et al., 1994; Lovett et al., 1994). It should be noted that had this been a purely experimental study, it would have been methodologically appropriate to include a randomly allocated experimental group who received TAAS only and a control group, but this study was conducted within the context of a program predicated on the MULTILIT principles and hence this was not possible. With that in mind, perhaps the argument provided by Solity et al. (1999) is best considered in light of these results. First, it is only oral blending and segmentation skills that achieve positive transfer effects to reading. Second, letter–sound correspondence does need to be directly taught. The instruction provided by TAAS was not limited to blending and segmentation and was, therefore, probably not intensive enough to add any further benefits to the instruction already being implemented.

The data for the dyslexic sample (low P) were also examined to determine the impact of TAAS training on literacy outcomes. As was the case after one term (Pogorzelski & Wheldall, 2002), following two terms of instruction, there were no significant differences between the TAAS trained and untrained low P groups, although again there was some evidence that training favoured the TAAS trained group for comprehension and reading fluency. Strong and moderate effect sizes for reading comprehension (0.77) and oral reading fluency (0.52) favoured the low P group trained in TAAS. The large gains made by the TAAS trained groups in comprehension are difficult to interpret and drawing any theoretical conclusions from this pattern of results would be speculative at best, especially given the small size of these subsamples.

After two terms of instruction, the PhAB subtest data were also analysed for the group initially categorised as dyslexic (low P), to determine whether training in auditory analysis skills had the effect of increasing phonological skills. No statistically significant differences were found on any of the phonological subtests between those who received TAAS and those who did not. The group who received training in TAAS performed better on the subtests alliteration, spoonerisms and non-word reading, which is supported by moderate to large effect sizes. (Note: Although the trained TAAS group yielded larger effect sizes for alliteration, both groups were very close to reaching the ceiling on initial testing, which would have had the effect of magnifying the effect sizes for this group by decreasing the size of the standard deviation.) The larger gains in spoonerisms for the trained group are no doubt an effect of the nature of the training of TAAS, which is largely made up of phoneme deletion and manipulation. Additionally, it should be noted that the untrained group had moderate to large effect sizes for three of the eight phonological subtests.

The final analysis after two terms of instruction involved the examination of those readers who were initially categorised as dyslexic (low P) by the PhAB. The results revealed that after two terms of instruction, eight students improved their phonological processing skills so that they no longer met the criteria for a severe phonological processing deficit. According to the authors of the PhAB (Frederickson et al., 1997), a standardised score of 85 or less (one standard deviation below a mean of 100) on three or more phonological sub-tests indicates a severe phonological processing deficit. The fact that eight of the original 16 dyslexics no longer met these criteria provides further support for the reciprocal causation theory, that the process of learning to read may actually induce phonological awareness.

The comprehensive nature of the battery of tests used in the assessment of the students in this sample allows for reliable and precise measures of growth in reading and related skills that would not have been evident had only one dependent variable been employed. For example, it was found that three students had performed poorly on the Neale for reading accuracy, making gains of less than six months. Closer examination of their other literacy scores, however, indicates substantial improvements on other measures. For example, one student, who only made three months' gain in reading accuracy on the Neale, gained 21 months in word recognition, seven months in spelling and improved in oral reading fluency by 45 words per minute. The results of the other two students who performed poorly on the Neale are comparable.

The evidence from this research suggests that effective instruction incorporating best practice methods may be all that is required to address enduring difficulties in reading for older low-progress readers. Although previous research provides strong support for providing explicit instruction in phonological awareness training for younger readers (Ball & Blachman, 1991; Bradley & Bryant, 1983; Hatcher et al., 1994) and in some cases older readers (Lovett et al., 1994), the findings presented here indicate that the evidence to date may be more equivocal. The results after two terms of instruction do not support the hypothesis that readers who are categorised as dyslexic because of severe deficits in phonological processing skills as determined by the PhAB (Frederickson et al., 1997) will be less responsive to an intensive literacy program than non-dyslexic poor readers. Rather, the evidence from this research suggests that the reading difficulties of both dyslexic and non-dyslexic students can be addressed if the intervention is one that incorporates both best practice methods and also acts as a facilitator in inducing the phonological skills required for competent and efficient reading. Finally, the evidence after two terms of instruction suggests that the phonological processing difficulties of students with dyslexia may not be as enduring as has been shown to be the case in previous studies (Bruck, 1992, 1993; Fawcett & Nicolson, 1995; Felton et al., 1991; Gottardo et al., 1997; Shankweiler et al., 1996; Torgesen et al., 1997).

Conclusions

Key components of the intervention employed in the present study are the teaching of letter–sound correspondences (word attack skills) and providing generalisation on these component skills through exposure to natural language texts. According to the research reviewed earlier, there is some evidence that along with letter–sound instruction, phonological awareness would also be a necessary component of an effective reading program, as it would promote the use of the self-teaching mechanism (Share, 1995). However, it appears from the results of this study that explicit instruction in generative decoding skills is sufficient for the activation of the self-teaching mechanism, and that in this sample of students, phonological processing skills (specifically phonemic awareness) are induced through the process of learning to read.

The results for this sample of low-progress readers indicate that older students, regardless of categorisation, still have the ability to improve upon their phonological deficit through explicit instruction in reading; that is, teaching reading and spelling may in fact induce phonological processing skills, as evidenced by the highly significant gains in six of the eight phonological subtests on the PhAB. It is instructive to note that students showed the greatest gain on the non-word and spoonerism subtests of the PhAB. The authors of the PhAB (Frederickson et al., 1997) contend that alliteration, rhyme, spoonerism knowledge and non-word reading are the phonological awareness tasks that are most 'influenced by grapheme-phoneme knowledge' (p. 60). Despite the fact that it is listed as a phonological awareness subtest in the PhAB manual, it should be noted that non-word reading is more a test of phonological recoding (matching letters to sounds) in short-term memory, and fails to meet the requirement of a phonological awareness task in that actual decoding is required to complete the test; it is not a purely oral skill. Pointedly, it was the gain on this test that was highly statistically significant and yielded an effect size of 1.39, providing further evidence for the assertion that it is more than a phonological awareness task; it is a measure of decoding per se. In fact, high correlations have consistently been found for reading accuracy and non-word reading (Martin & Pratt, 2001).

The fact that students showed significant improvement on the spoonerisms test should encourage researchers to examine whether or not phonological awareness training should be included in a remedial reading program. Spoonerisms require the ability to blend, segment and manipulate phonemes in words. As such, it is concluded that it is not necessary explicitly to train phonological awareness tasks in order to improve reading skills. Rather, the explicit teaching of blending and segmentation skills either orally or as part of reading instruction proper should be the key components of effective reading instruction. The fact that non-word reading and spoonerisms yielded the largest improvements suggests that it is the teaching of phonic word attack skills which improves overall word recognition and phonological skills, rather than instruction in phonological awareness (as provided by the TAAS program).

The evidence discussed thus far suggests that the intervention employed in this study is effective for all older low-progress readers, regardless of categorisation as dyslexic or non-dyslexic poor reader. Furthermore, the results after one and two terms provide strong support for the reciprocal causation hypothesis whereby effective reading instruction improves on the phonological deficit, which in turn acts as a facilitator for further reading acquisition. This has been shown to be the case for younger students (Ball, 1996; Ball & Blachman, 1991; Bruck, 1993; Share, 1995), where we know that phonological awareness is a 'necessary but not a sufficient condition for learning to read' (McGuinness et al., 1995, p. 830). The results of the current study suggest that explicit instruction in phonological awareness skills may not necessarily be required for either younger or older readers to achieve significant improvements in reading skills, whether they are dyslexic or non-dyslexic poor readers. In fact, the results suggest that even for younger students it may be that only oral blending and segmentation skills are required. This would support the earlier assertions made by Solity et al. (1999) and still concur with the reciprocal causation theory.

The results from this study revealed that the 22 low-progress readers who presented with relatively similar results on a battery of standardised literacy tests – they were all over two years behind in reading accuracy – nevertheless did have varying degrees of phonological ability. Consequently, it is not unlikely that many of the students apparently presenting as dyslexic (low P) may have demonstrated pervasive phonological difficulties because they had actually not been taught to read and, due to a lack of instruction, had never had the alphabetic principle made explicit to them. In a special study reported in the PhAB manual, it was reported that of a sample of 89 students with specific learning disabilities, 21% were identified as having no highlighted subtest scores (Frederickson et al., 1997). Additionally, only 51% presented with three or more highlighted scores, indicating that there might indeed be other factors contributing to reading failure. Despite this, the authors advocate the use of this test for informing remedial practice. The results of the present study clearly show that this is not necessary and it is likely that the PhAB may over-identify students as having dyslexia. In the same study, it was reported that of a comparison sample of 89 students randomly selected from the larger standardisation sample, 16% had three or more highlighted scores on the subtests, indicating that the PhAB may in fact over-identify students with a reading disability, given the incidence of true dyslexia is frequently reported to be 3–5% (Torgesen et al., 1997). The fact that in the present study the PhAB failed to predict which group of students would achieve greater literacy outcomes, however, indicates that the reading problems of such students can still be addressed. After effective instruction, the literacy outcomes for the whole sample were significant and large. It is apparent that once the students received instruction in the alphabetic principle, they showed significant improvement in both reading and in phonological processing skills.

According to Barker and Torgesen (1995, p. 90), the 'ultimate goal of phonemic awareness training is to impact the word recognition skills of students.' Considering the research regarding the reciprocal nature of phonemic awareness with reading and the training studies on younger readers, the reverse should also be true. The results of the current research support this and show how, through the explicit teaching of decoding/reading skills, phonological skills may be induced. There was evidence in this study that some students improved their phonological processing skills through reading alone without receiving any training in phonological awareness via the TAAS training program.

The results of this study also suggest that using a test such as the PhAB to determine the type of remedial intervention is unwarranted. While this or other similar tests might be useful for screening younger readers (Torgesen & Wagner, 1998) who initially compensate for weak decoding skills through the use of compensatory contextual or visual strategies, it appears that once a student is past the beginning stages of reading instruction, it has little benefit in informing remediation or instructional decisions. According to Hempenstall (1999), students who compensate for decoding difficulties will break down in their reading skills once they reach a level of reading where visual memory strategies become redundant. Although the PhAB might be useful in the detection of these students, it would no doubt be much quicker to test students' phonological recoding skills through the use of a non-word reading test (Martin & Pratt, 2001). For older low-progress readers, who will undoubtedly present with some degree of difficulty in phonological processing skill, either through a specific cognitive deficit or as a consequence of not having learnt to read, it would seem that testing a range of phonological skills is unwarranted. If students present with a delay in reading on a range of literacy and reading tests, similar to those employed in this study, then they should be considered to require instruction in reading, regardless of their categorisation as dyslexic or non-dyslexic.

In short, a strong case has been made for moving away not only from the traditional concepts of dyslexia in terms of IQ – reading discrepancy criteria – but also from investing too much energy in discerning the reasons for the underlying cause of the phonological processing difficulties with which older low-progress readers might present. In fact, the results of this study highlight the logic of working within a non-categorical approach to remediation, where regardless of the reasons for reading failure, effective reading instruction remains the focus for improving literacy outcomes.

References

Adams, M.J. (1990). *Beginning to read. Thinking and learning about print*. Cambridge, MA: The MIT Press.

Aron, A., & Aron, E.N. (1999). Statistics for psychology (2nd ed.). New Jersey: Prentice Hall.

Ball, E.W. (1996). Phonological awareness and learning disabilities: Using research to inform our practice. *Advances in Learning and Behavioural Disabilities*, 10, 77–100.

Ball, E.W., & Blachman, B.A. (1988). Phoneme segmentation training: Effect on reading readiness. *Annals of Dyslexia*, 38, 208–225.

Ball, E.W., & Blachman, B.A. (1991). Does phoneme awareness training in kindergarten make a difference in early word recognition and developmental spelling? *Reading Research Quarterly*, 26, 49–66.

Barker, T.A., & Torgesen, J.K. (1995). An evaluation of computer-assisted instruction in phonological awareness with below average readers. *Journal of Educational Computing Research*, 13, 89–103.

Bishop, D.V.M. (2001). Genetic influences on language impairment and literacy problems in children: Same or different? *Journal of Child Psychology and Psychiatry*, 42, 189–198.

Bradley, L., & Bryant, P.E. (1983). Categorising sounds and learning to read. A causal connection. *Nature*, 301, 419–421.

Bruck, M. (1992), Persistence of dyslexics' phonological deficits. *Developmental Psychology*, 28, 874–886.

Bruck, M. (1993). Word recognition and component phonological processing skills of adults with childhood dyslexia. *Developmental Review*, 13, 258–268.

Carnine, D.W., Silbert, J., & Kameenui, E.J. (1997). *Direct instruction reading* (3rd ed.). New Jersey: Prentice Hall.

Ehri, L.C., Nunes, S.R., Willows, D.M., Valeska Schuster, B., Yaghoub-Zadeh, Z., & Shanahan, T. (2001). Phonemic awareness instruction helps children learn to read: Evidence from the National Reading Panel's meta-analysis. *Reading Research Quarterly*, 36, 250–287.

Fawcett, A., & Nicolson, R.L. (1995). Persistence of phonological awareness deficits in older children with dyslexia. *Reading & Writing: An Interdisciplinary Journal*, 7, 361–376.

Felton, R.H., Naylor, C.E., & Wood, F.B. (1991). Neuropsychological profile of adult dyslexics. *Brain & Language*, 39, 485–497.

Frederickson, N., Frith, U., & Reason, R. (1997). *Phonological assessment battery: Manual and test materials*. Windsor, UK: NFER-NELSON Publishing Company Ltd.

Frith, U. (1995). Dyslexia: can we have a shared theoretical framework? *Educational and Child Psychology*, 12, 6–17.

Gallagher, A. (1995). The development of a phonological assessment battery: Research background. *Educational and Child Psychology*, 12, 18–24.

Gilmore, A., Croft, C., & Reid, N. (1981). *Burt word reading test: New Zealand revision*. Wellington: New Zealand Council for Educational Research.

Gottardo, A., Siegel, L.S. & Stanovich, K.E. (1997). The assessment of adults with reading disabilities: What can we learn from experimental tasks? *Journal of Research in Reading*, 20, 42–54.

Greenberg, D., Ehri, L.C., & Perin, D. (1997). Are word-reading processes the same or different in adult literacy students and third–fifth graders matched for reading level? *Journal of Educational Psychology*, 89, 262–275.

Gundersen, L., & Siegel, L.S. (2001). The evils of the use of IQ tests to define learning disabilities in first- and second-language learners. *The Reading Teacher*, 55, 48–55.

Hatcher, P.J., Hulme, C., & Ellis, A.W. (1994). Ameliorating early reading failure by integrating the teaching of reading and phonological skills: The phonological linkage hypothesis. *Child Development*, 65, 41–57.

Hempenstall, K. (1999). *Literacy and older children? What focus for instruction?* Feature address presented at the Australian Association of Special Education National Conference, September, Sydney, Australia.

Hulme, C., & Snowling, M. (1992). Phonological deficits in dyslexia: A 'sound' reappraisal of the verbal deficit hypothesis? In N. Singh & I. Beale (Eds.), *Learning disabilities: Nature, theory and treatment* (pp. 270–301). New York: Springer Verlag.

Lovett, M.W., Borden, S.L., De Luca, T., Lacerenza, L., Benson, N.J., & Brackstone, D. (1994). Treating the core deficits of developmental dyslexia: Evidence of transfer of learning after phonologically- and strategy-based reading training programs. *Developmental Psychology*, 30, 805–822.

Martin, F., & Pratt, C. (2001). *Martin and Pratt nonword reading test manual*. Camberwell: Australian Council for Educational Research Ltd.

McGuinness, D., McGuinness, C., & Donohue, J. (1995). Phonological training and the alphabet principle: Evidence for reciprocal causality. *Reading Research Quarterly*, 50, 830–852.

Neale, M.D. (1999). *Neale analysis of reading ability* (3rd ed.). Hawthorn: Australian Council for Educational Research.

Pogorzelski, S., & Wheldall, K. (2002). Do differences in phonological processing performance predict gains made by older low-progress readers following intensive literacy intervention? *Educational Psychology*, 22, 13–427.

Pratt, C., & Brady, S. (1988). Relation of phonological awareness to reading disability in children and adults. *Journal of Educational Psychology*, 80, 319–323.

Report of the National Reading Panel. (2000). *Teaching children to read: An evidence-based assessment of the scientific research literature on reading and its implications for reading instruction*. Report, National Institute of Child Health and Human Development. Retrieved June, 2000, from http:// www.nichd.nih.gov/publications

Reynolds, M. (2000). *What's new in reading research?* Sydney: Australian Association of Special Education (AASE) Inc.

Rosner, J. (1975). *Helping children overcome learning difficulties: A step by step guide for parents and teachers*. New York: Walker and Co.

Rosner, J. (1993). *Helping children overcome learning difficulties: A step by step guide for parents and teachers* (3rd ed.). New York: Walker and Co.

Shankweiler, D. (1999). Words to meanings. *Scientific Studies of Reading*, 3, 113–127.

Shankweiler, D., Lundquist, E., Dreyer, L.G., & Dickinson, C.C. (1996). Reading and spelling difficulties in high school students: Causes and consequences. *Reading & Writing: An Interdisciplinary Journal*, 8, 267–204.

Share, D.L. (1995). Phonological receding and self-teaching: Sin qua non of reading acquisition. *Cognition*, 55, 151–218.

Siegel, L.S. (1999). Learning disabilities: The roads we have travelled and the path to the future. In R.L. Sternberg & L. Spear-Swerling (Eds.), *Perspectives on learning disabilities: Biological, cognitive, contextual* (pp. 159–175). Boulder, CO: Westview Press.

Solity, J., Deavers, R., Kerfoot, S., Crane, G., & Cannon, K. (1999). Raising literacy attainments in the early years: The impact of instructional psychology. *Educational Psychology*, 19, 373–397.

Stanovich, K. E. (1986). Mathew effects in reading: Some consequences of individual differences in the acquisition of literacy. *Reading Research Quarterly*, 21, 360–391.

Stanovich, K.E. (1988). Explaining the differences between the dyslexic and the garden-variety poor reader: The phonological-core-variable-difference model. *Journal of Learning Disabilities*, 21, 590–604.

Stanovich, K.E. (1991). Discrepancy definitions of reading disability: Has intelligence led us astray? *Reading Research Quarterly*, 26, 7–23.

Stanovich, K.E. (1992). Speculations on the causes and consequences of individual differences in early reading acquisition. In P. B. Gough, L.C. Ehri, & R. Treiman (Eds.), *Reading Acquisition* (pp. 307–342). Hillsdale, NJ: Laurence Erlbaum Associates.

Stanovich, K.E. (1994), Romance and reality. *The Reading Teacher*, 47, 280–291.

Stanovich, K.E. (2000). *Progress in understanding reading. Scientific foundations and new frontiers.* New York: The Guilford Press.

Stanovich, K.E., & Siegel, L.S. (1994). Phenotypic performance profile of children with reading disabilities: A regression-based test of the phonological-core variable difference model. *Journal of Educational Psychology*, 86, 24–53.

Stuart, M., & Masterson, J. (1992). Patterns of reading and spelling in 10-year-old children related to prereading phonological abilities. *Journal of Experimental Child Psychology*, 54, 168–187.

Thomas, G. (2002) Are eggs the right size for egg cups because of good planning by hens? Where is reading research going? *Educational Psychology in Practice*, 18, 157–166.

Torgesen, J.K., & Wagner, R.K. (1998). Alternative diagnostic approaches for specific developmental reading disabilities. *Learning Disabilities Research & Practice*, 13, 220–232.

Torgesen, J.K., Wagner, R.K., & Rashotte, C.A. (1997). Prevention and remediation of severe reading disabilities: Keeping the end in mind. *Scientific Studies of Reading*, 1, 217–234.

Tunmer, W.E., Chapman, J.W., Ryan, H., & Prochnow, J.E. (1998). The importance of providing beginning readers with explicit training in phonological processing skills. *Australian Journal of Learning Disabilities*, 3, 4–14.

Westwood, P. (1999). *Spelling approaches to teaching and assessment.* Camberwell; Australian Council for Educational Research Ltd.

Wheldall, K. (1994). Why do contemporary special educators favour a non-categorical approach to teaching? *Special Education Perspectives*, 3, 45–47.

Wheldall, K. (1996). *The Wheldall assessment of reading passages: Experimental edition.* Sydney, Australia: Macquarie University Special Education Centre.

Wheldall, K., & Beaman, R. (2000). *An evaluation of MULTILIT 'Making up lost time in literacy'.* Canberra, Australia: Department of Education, Training and Youth Affairs.

Wheldall, K., & Carter, M. (1996). Reconstructing behaviour analysis in education: A revised behavioural intetactionist perspective for special education. *Educational Psychology*, 16, 121–140.

Yap, R., & Van Der Leij, A. (1993). Word processing in dyslexics. An automatic decoding deficit. *Reading and Writing: An Interdisciplinary Journal*, 5, 261–279.

7

Reception Class Predictors of Literacy Skills

Jennifer Simpson and John Everatt

[…]

The identification of reading and writing difficulties is vitally important for education, both in terms of the development of the individual, and the appropriate allocation of resources. In response, there has been an increase in the commercial availability of screening tests for kindergarten/preschool or reception class children, which measure a range of skills thought to be predictive of later achievement or failure. In addition to the Dyslexia Early Screening Test (DEST; Nicolson & Fawcett, 1996), in the UK these tests include the Cognitive Profiling System, the Phonological Abilities Test, the Phonological Assessment Battery, and in the USA, the Comprehensive Test of Phonological Processing (Frederickson, Frith, & Reason, 1997; Muter, Hulme, & Snowling 1996; Singleton, 1995; Wagner, Torgesen, & Rashotte, 1999). In the selection of any screening test, there needs to be confidence in its ability to accurately identify those in need of intervention. For those falsely identified as being at risk of literacy acquisition problems, the consequences may not be negative, as these individuals will receive intervention which we would expect to enhance their skills. However, those children that the screening battery fails to identify may go on to fail catastrophically. These children may be identified only through impoverished literacy skills following failure to learn 'accurate and fluent word reading and/or spelling' (Reason, Frederickson, Hefferman, Martin, & Woods, 1999). Therefore, screening tests need to show predictive validity in terms of the skills deemed to indicate failure to learn (reading and/or spelling, in this case). Additionally, such tests need to show that they present better levels of prediction than alternative methods used in schools and to indicate how applicable the findings are to different contexts (e.g. across age ranges and educational establishments).

The DEST is a UK-based commercially available initial screening tool that has been standardized on over 1,000 children from schools within the UK, with at least 100 children at age 4:6 to 4:11, 5:0 to 5:5, 5:6 to 5:11 and 6:0 to 6:5. The designers argue that the test's components are based on established findings in the literature, and use this as evidence of the test's validity (see also Nicolson & Fawcett, 1995). The manual presents test–retest (conducted one week apart) reliability estimates based on 26 children within the age group

From: *British Journal of Educational Psychology*, 75 (2), 2005, pp. 171–88.

of 5:5 to 6:5, but provides no evidence of the test's ability to predict future literacy difficulties. However, a subsequent paper (Fawcett, Singleton, & Peer, 1998) refers to data supporting the test's ability to predict future literacy deficits, although these data were obtained from children who, at 5 years of age and above, were approximately 1 year older than the lower end of the target population of the test. The DEST was designed to be used with very young children from approximately 4:6 to 6:5. The designers believe that they 'have found the practical catalyst for change in the form of diagnostic tests for all at school entry' (Fawcettt et al., 1998, p. 58). Further data that confirm the predictive validity of the test measures across different contexts and across the age ranges identified for the test's use are necessary. The longitudinal study reported in this [chapter] adds substantially to the assessment of the validity of the test and of its use with children at the lower end of the target population for the test.

The DEST comprises a series of subtests that the test authors argue are derived from evidence in the research literature on possible causes of dyslexia. Of particular note is that the measures were developed by drawing on three possible hypotheses of causation: that there exists a core phonological deficit; alternatively, that there is an impairment in the magnocellular auditory pathway, which causes difficulties in rapid processing of auditory stimuli; or, lastly, the theory that dyslexic children have difficulty in automatizing skills as a result of an impairment in the cerebellum. Each subtest score, as an important index of achievement in a particular skill area, is combined with other subtest scores to produce an 'at risk quotient' (ARQ). This index is used to predict the likelihood of future literacy deficits. However, the findings of Simpson and Everatt (2001) contrast with this view. They concluded that the ARQ offered limited insight into the variability in reading and spelling achievement in the national curriculum tests at 7 years of age. Instead, these authors argued that the individual subtest of rapid naming was a better predictor of later reading and spelling achievement than the other DEST subtest and the combined ARQ.

Research indicates that deficits in the rapid access to lexical information present a prevalent characteristic of the reading disabled (Bowers & Wolf, 1993; Denckla & Rudel, 1976; Spring & Capps, 1974). Tasks that measure skills in this area may offer a simple and effective predictor of children at risk of failure in literacy acquisition, although the precise reason why this might be the case is uncertain. For example, it may be that tests of rapid naming ability should be subsumed under phonological skills as they require verbal labelling of visual stimuli (Wagner & Torgesen, 1987). Alternatively, Wolf and Bowers (1999), for example, have proposed that rapid naming deficits should be regarded as separate from phonological skills, arguing instead for a double deficit perspective involving dissociated causes of literacy difficulties.

In their study, Simpson and Everatt (2001) included in-school assessments of reading and spelling, taken at the same time as the DEST. Such reading/spelling measures were found to account for a higher percentage of variability than any DEST subtest, including rapid naming. However, these measures can only be included in an assessment procedure when children are, at least, beginning readers. The children in the Simpson and Everatt study had a mean chronological age of 5:10 at the start of the study meaning that, with the inclusion of the reception year, they will have experienced some 2 years of formal education prior to the screening assessment. The present study focused on a younger group of children at the start of reception class (before formal literacy learning) to assess the efficacy of the DEST as an assessment tool amongst pre-readers. One of the practical attractions of a screening tool such as DEST is its potential for identifying problems before they lead to the experience of failure to learn. The present study, therefore, focused on the ability of the DEST to predict later literacy skills from the point at which formal learning had started. Reading and spelling skills were assessed after 2 years of learning, the point of initial testing in the Simpson and Everatt study.

The ability of the DEST to predict future literacy skills was also compared with measures already in use in the school where testing was performed. These measures were administered at the end of the reception year, and prior to the start of Year 1, as a check that essential literacy skills were developing as expected. The measures assessed the children's knowledge of letter sounds and letter names, their ability to read non-words and their ability to recognize that words rhyme. Their inclusion in the school's procedures was based on the wealth of evidence implicating a deficit in phonological processing as a major factor in the lack of progress in literacy and that poor performance on rhyming tasks is indicative of such deficits (Bryant & Bradley, 1983; Goswami & Bryant, 1990; Share, Jorm, Maclean, & Matthews, 1984; Vellutino et al., 1996; Wagner & Torgesen, 1987). Similarly, evidence indicates that letter knowledge is a good predictor of children's ability to deal with the alphabetic principle of linking graphemic to phonemic knowledge, an essential element in literacy achievement (see Adams, 1990; Badian, 1994; Muter & Snowling, 1998). Determining non-word reading ability provides a basis from which to assess the extent of the acquisition of letter–sound decoding skills (Snowling, 2000).

The DEST also includes tests of phonological awareness and letter knowledge. However, the test combines potentially different stages in the development of phonological skills and acquisition of letter knowledge. For example, the DEST subtest of letter knowledge allows a correct response to be the name or sound of the letter. This may mean that a lack of knowledge of letter sounds or names may be masked by knowledge of the alternative correct response. Similarly, the DEST subtest that most closely resembles measures of phonological awareness combines items that require an appreciation of rhyme with those that require the identification of the initial phoneme within a word. There is a huge variation in the developmental path of children across the formative years that span the 4–7 age range covered by the DEST. The selection of tests for any screening battery must take into account the fact that some skills evolve over time, have a hierarchical structure, become refined, and may, indeed, become obsolete as a means of providing indicators of future success or failure. The discovery that phonological skills are likely to be hierarchical (e.g. Goswami & Bryant, 1990) has led researchers to investigate which skills are likely to be present and measurable in very young children. Although rhyme detection seems to be evident in very young preschool children, other more complex phonological tasks that require the identification of phonemes as component parts of a word are not achievable until some 2 years after formal education has commenced (Liberman, Shankweiler, Liberman, Fowler, & Fischer, 1977). Combining such measures may reduce the ability of a test to predict variance in skills acquisition. Indeed, a comprehensive review of the research literature provides evidence that rhyming tasks may be poor predictors of later reading achievement (Macmillan, 2002). The present study, therefore, separately recorded response to rhyme items and initial sound items that comprise the rhyme detection subtest of the DEST. The inclusion of an additional rhyming test and of letter knowledge tasks that separate letter names from sounds also provided a means of assessing the variability in usefulness of potential predictors over this developmental period.

Method

Participants

Out of a total of 48 boys who were attending the reception class of an independent school in the south-east of England, 46 were selected to participate in the study. Two boys were omitted because they fell below the lower age limit of 4:6 as designated by the designers of the DEST. Attrition of one child after the initial stage of testing due to family reasons unrelated to the study reduced the number to 45. Results are reported for these 45 children only. At the start of the study, the boys were aged between 4:6 and 5:4 (mean age 4.87, $SD = 0.29$).

The group selected was relatively homogeneous in terms of socio-economic and educational background, with the majority from middle-class backgrounds with professional occupation parents. Therefore, neither socio-economic nor educational background factors would be likely to lead to literacy acquisition problems in this cohort. A single-sex cohort is also likely to be at a similar level of development in terms of language experience and some research suggests that boys are more likely than girls to be dyslexic (e.g. Miles, Haslum, & Wheeler, 1998). School records indicated that none of the boys tested had a known physical or neurological deficit that might interfere with educational achievement. The school's procedures provided an ideal opportunity to contrast its own tests with those of the DEST. Although the selected cohort means that caution needs to be taken before generalizing findings to all children, it provides an appropriate sample from which to assess the effectiveness of the DEST and its subtests for the target population proposed by the test's designers (i.e. all children at school entry). If the test fails in its predictive validity with the present cohort, then the envisaged target population needs to be redetermined.

Materials and procedures

Phase1 (Mean age 4.87, SD = 0.29, UK Reception Class)

The initial screening procedure consisted of administering nine of the 10 subtests of the DEST to all participants. The Postural Stability Test was excluded from the testing procedure due to problems with parental approval. Each subtest was scored, and results combined to give an ARQ.

Each child was individually assessed by one of two researchers who were fully trained in the administration of the DEST. Testing took place away from the classroom in a quiet room without any distractions. The nine subtests were administered in one session lasting approximately 20–25 minutes.

The DEST allows for practice of each subtest. Rapid naming and bead threading subtests are both timed. The order of the subtests followed that in the manual except that digit span was interposed between the test of phonological discrimination (Subtest 3), and that of rhyme/first sound detection (Subtest 5). This was based on the advice offered in the manual so as to avoid any confusion that may arise due to the similarity of the phonological discrimination and rhyme/first sound detection tasks.

The DEST comprises subtests of:

Rapid naming.   This test assessed the time taken by the child to name 40 simple but familiar outline pictures. The first half of the sheet of 20 different pictures was used for practice purposes and ensured knowledge of the object names. The main test comprised two sequences of the same 20 items used in the practice session. Time penalties were given to penalize errors.

Bead threading.   This task measured the number of beads that a child could thread in 30 seconds. Practice trials allowed the child to see what was required. This was followed by practice threading of two beads.

Phonological discrimination.   This was a test of auditory discrimination that required the child to detect subtle differences in spoken words (e.g. 'pat–bat' vs. 'dog–dog'). The child was asked to respond 'same' if they sounded exactly the same, or 'different', if not, according to the pairs of words presented. There were three practice items, plus two additional items for those who had not responded correctly. This was followed by the main test of nine two-word items.

Digit span.   This task used a prepared tape on which digits were spoken at intervals of 1 per second. The child was required to listen to sequences of digits and repeat these in order. Beeps indicated the start and end of each series of digits. Practice items allowed the administrator to pause the tape after presentation of each series to help explain the procedure. The first practice item comprised a one digit, followed by two and then three digits. Further practice items were offered if the child had not understood the requirements of the task. The main test followed this practice procedure, beginning with two strings of two digits and increasing incrementally by one digit every two sequences up to a maximum of eight digits. The test was discontinued following two incorrect responses at any length. The number of sequences correctly repeated was the measure used for this task.

Rhyme/first sound detection.   This task involved two parts. The first part assessed participants' ability to detect whether two spoken words rhyme, with simple 'yes' or 'no' responses required (e.g. 'cat–bat'; 'dig–hill'). Four practice items were used, with two additional pairs of words for a child who did not appear to grasp the idea. Eight pairs of words comprised the main test. The second part of the test required the child to identify the first sound in a word. In all cases, this was the initial phoneme, defined as the 'onset' by Nicolson and Fawcett (1996). The child is asked 'to listen to some words and see if you can pick the first sound. Like the 'big, bouncy bed' all start with a 'buh'. The child was then asked to indicate the first sound of a practice item, *cat,* and requested to give more words beginning with a /k/ sound. There followed a further three practice items where the instruction to the child was, 'Now can you tell me the first sound of this word?' At all times, corrective feedback was offered. The main test comprised five further items: 'dog', 'sack','hat', tap', and 'net'. Responses for correct initial sounds were recorded. Scores for the rhyme task and first letter task were combined to produce a total out of 13.

Digit naming.   This task assessed the ability of the child to name digits. Following practice at naming the digits one and two, the child was required to name the following sequence of digits: 4, 8, 3, 9, 5, 7, 6. The number of the seven digits correctly named was used as the measure for this task.

Letter naming.   This task tested the child's knowledge of letters. Correct responses permitted by the manual instruction comprised either the name of a letter or its associated sound. Practice was provided by a card with the letters *c* and *a* written on it. Three separate cards were then used for the main test. These contained the letters *t, s, d, e, w, o, b, q, n, y,* with the number of these letters correctly responded to being used as the measure of performance.

Sound order.   This test involved the presentation of two tones on a tape of a simulated 'quack' to represent a duck, and a simulated 'squeak' to represent a mouse, with the time between the sounds being reduced from 947 ms intervals for the first two items to 8 ms intervals for the last two items. Practice items consisted of three trials with corrections offered. The task required the child to indicate which of the two distinct sounds described above occurred first. The number of correct responses out of a possible 16 items was used as the measure of performance. The rationale offered for including this subtest as a measure was based on Tallal's (1980) theory that some children with dyslexia or language difficulties have an underlying deficit in the detection of 'rapid consonant changes' (Nicolson & Fawcett, 1996, p. 58).

Shape copying.   This task required the child to copy four simple geometrical shapes after the practice item of drawing an *X*. Scores are based on accuracy of drawings derived from a marking scheme provided in the test manual.

The raw score for each subtest was compared with the manual's age-appropriate norms and allocated an 'at risk index' in the form of indices which were recorded to measure participants' performance as follows: (– –) *well below average* (bottom 10%), (–) *below average* (bottom 10–25%), (0) *normal* (26–75%), (+) *above average* (76–90%), and (+ +) *well above average* (top 10%). These, in turn, were allocated a numerical score to indicate 'at risk'/'not at risk': (– –) = 2, (–) = 1, and (0). A score of 0 was given for (+) and (+ +) in order to work out the quantitative or combined subtest scores constituting the ARQ. When all the numerical scores had been added up, they were divided by the number of subtests used. 'An ARQ of 1 or greater is strong evidence of being at risk' (Nicolson & Fawcett, 1996, p. 18).

Phase 2 (Mean age 5.21, SD = 0.30, UK Reception Class)

Approximately 5 months after the initial screening, at the end of 1 year in the reception class, tests of letter names and sounds, using both upper and lower case letters, non-word reading, and a test of rhyme detection were administered. These were given individually to children by one of the school's specialist teachers who was trained in assessment techniques. Testing was performed away from the mainstream classroom, in a quiet room without distractions. All tests were performed consecutively and completed within approximately 15–20 minutes.

Letter knowledge.   This grapheme/phoneme correspondence test was taken from the Aston Index (Newton & Thomson, 1982). Lower case letters were presented on individual cards in the order designated by the test designers. The child was asked to state the letter–sound for each letter. The procedure was then repeated, this time with the child stating the letter name for each letter. The same procedure was followed for upper case letters, presented in a different random order as designated by the test designers. Raw scores were recorded separately for all four tests, providing four scores, each out of a maximum of 26.

Non-word reading.   A 12-item Non-word Reading Test was used as the middle task at this stage. This involved the child reading nine CVC letter strings (e.g. 'sab') and three CVCC or CCVC letter strings (e.g. 'dack') aloud. The number of readings that conformed to grapheme–phoneme correspondence rules was used as the measure for this task.

Rhyming Test.   The Rhyming Test used was Activity 2 of the Hatcher (1994) sound linkage programme. In this test, the administrator presents two words orally and the child is asked to say whether or not the words rhyme (e.g. 'night–light'; 'far–wide'). The child's verbal *yes/no* responses were recorded and the number correct out of 16 used as the test measure.

Phase 3 (Mean age 5.98, SD = 0.30; UK Year 1)

In March 2001, 14 months after the initial screening, tests of single-word reading and spelling were administered. The first of these tests was the Schonell Single Word Graded Reading Test (Schonell & Schonell, 1956). The second attainment test was the Vernon Graded Word Spelling Test (Vernon, 1997). Raw scores were used for both of these tests. Conversion to reading-age equivalents was not appropriate as some boys failed to produce enough correct words to allow norm tables to be used.

The reading test was administered by a specialist teacher to each child individually. This comprised a list of 100 individual words, graded in order of difficulty, without contextual cues. Each child was given a score based on the number of words read correctly. Class teachers administered the spelling test simultaneously to the three forms making up the year group. Each word was individually and orally presented, followed by presentation of the word in the context of a sentence and lastly individually presented again. The boys were instructed to write down the single words and not the sentences. The number of correctly spelt words was used as the score for this measure.

Phase 4 (Mean age 6.63, SD = 0.30; UK Year 2)

In October/November 2001, 20 months after the initial screening, tests of single-word reading, single-word spelling and text reading were administered. The first two tests were the same as those administered at Phase 3 (Schonell & Schonell, 1956; Vernon, 1997) and followed the same procedures. The text reading measure was the Primary Reading Test (France, 1981), which was administered simultaneously by the three form teachers to the whole year group. The first eight items of this test required the child to select one word from a list of five that matched a presented picture. Items 9–48 then required the child to read silently individual sentences, each of which was incomplete, and to select the most appropriate word from a selection of five that completed the sentence. Raw scores were obtained and used as attainment scores as in the previous tests.

Results

Means and standard deviations for each of the measures used in the study are presented in Table 7.1. These results suggest that some children in the age range 4.5–5.5 can produce maximum scores on the DEST and school attainment measures. Letter and digit naming tasks are particularly prone to ceiling *effects* in this cohort of children, although the effects seem to be confined to the sounds of letters rather than their names.

Table 7.2 presents Pearson product moment correlations and Spearman's rho correlation coefficients that indicate significant relationships between reception year screening measures and literacy ability following 2 years of formal instruction. Consistent with the aims of the DEST, there is good evidence that the AKQ is related to subsequent reading and spelling ability. However, some subtests of the DEST are only poorly related to literacy skills amongst these boys. The subtests of phonological discrimination and rhyme/first sound detection (see also the School Attainment Rhyming Test) are noteworthy here.

Table 7.1   Average scores and standard deviations (*SD*) produced by the 45 children tested for each of the variables measured

Variable	Mean	SD
Phase I measures (Mean age = 4.87, *SD* = 0.29, UK Reception Class)		
DEST at risk quotient	0.20	0.18
Rapid automatized naming time in seconds	60.91	12.47
Bead threading: number of beads threaded in 30 seconds	3.76	1.23
Phonological discrimination, maximum score 9	7.40	1.57
Rhyme/first sound task, maximum score: 13	9.60	2.75
*Rhyme (from rhyme/first sound detection)	5.36	2.08
*First sound (from rhyme/first sound detection)	4.58	1.12
Digit span: number of digit sequences out of 14	4.78	1.52
Digit naming, maximum score: 7	6.78	0.79
Letter naming, maximum score: 10	8.87	1.24
Sound order, maximum score: 16	12.82	2.84
Shape copying, maximum score: 21	10.44	3.09
Phase 2 measures (Mean age = 5.21, *SD* = 0.30, UK Reception Class)		
Letter-sounds lower case score out of 26	23.51	2.23
Letter names lower case score out of 26	8.76	9.61
Letter-sounds upper case score out of 26	21.47	6.76
Letter names upper case score out of 26	10.27	9.55
Non-words, maximum score: 12	5.73	4.03
Rhyming words, maximum score: 16	14.60	2.26
Phase 3 measures (Mean age 5.98 = .98, *SD* = 0.30, UK Year 1)		
Schonell single-word reading, Phase 3 raw score out of 100	24.04	11.87
Vernon graded word spelling, Phase 3 raw score out of 50	11.52	5.49
Phase 4 measures (Mean age = 6.63, *SD* = 0.30, UK Year 2)		
Schonell single-word reading, Phase 4 raw score out of 100	35.18	13.01
Vernon graded word spelling, Phase 4 raw score out of 50	13.04	6.11
Primary Reading Test reading, Phase 4 raw score out of 48	27.98	7.00

* These measures were derived from the DEST Rhyme/first sound task.

Although the level of correlation between these measures and the literacy measures increases with Spearman compared to Pearson, potentially suggesting a more monotonic than linear relationship, the majority are still non-significant. Additionally, the composite ARQ predicts less than 25% of the variability in reading or spelling, and other measures amongst those used seem to provide higher levels of prediction. In order to assess this possibility, a series of regression analyses were performed to determine the relative contribution of the ARQ, the subtests of the DEST, and the school attainment measures in predicting reading and spelling. In each of the analyses, the age of the child at the start of the study was controlled by entry into the regression equation before any other measure. ARQ scores were entered into the equation second for those analyses where they were included. Scores on the DEST subtests and the school attainment measures were included as a block, and were then analysed to provide an indication of how much variability in literacy attainment could be explained by the best predictor(s) amongst these test batteries. When DEST and school attainment measures were included in the same analysis, the latter were entered as a block after the DEST based on the order of the phases in the study in which measures were obtained (i.e. school attainment measures were closer in time to the literacy outcome measures).

Table 7.2   Pearson correlation coefficients, and Spearman's rho correlation coefficients in parenthesis, between literacy and potential predictor variables

Predictors	Reading single word Phase 3	Spelling single word Phase 3	Reading single word Phase 4	Spelling single word Phase 4	Reading prose Phase 4
At risk quotient	−.381** (−.272)	−.432** (−.377*)	−.480** (−.414**)	−.362* (−.332*)	−.376* (−.286)
Rapid automatized naming	−.406*** (−.396**)	−.290 (−.257)	−.382* (−.390**)	−.265 (−.299*)	−.499** (−.497**)
Beads	.241 (.237)	.183 (.113)	.228 (.279)	.217 (.269)	.073 (.092)
Phonological discrimination	.083 (.228)	.271 (.378*)	.143 (.263)	.166 (.266)	.081 (.222)
Rhyme/First sound detection	.183 (.179)	.248 (.324*)	.302* (.339*)	.255 (.300*)	.140 (.123)
Rhyme part of rhyme/first sound detection	.253 (.245)	.354* (.319*)	.305* (.325*)	.396** (.353*)	.133 (.184)
First sound part of rhyme/first sound detection	.274 (.137)	.270 (.315*)	.283 (.187)	.216 (.190)	.356* (.136)
Digit span	.374* (.349*)	.294* (.308*)	.333* (.309*)	.321* (.333*)	.356* (.361*)
Digit naming	.353* (.378*)	.314* (.4 16*)	.353* (.378*)	.325* (.390*)	.314* (.368*)
Letter naming	.293 (.291)	.169 (.168)	.297* (.354*)	.311* (.334*)	.115 (.200)
Sound order	.439** (.474**)	.464** (.502**)	.571** (.577**)	.488** (.526**)	.477** (.466**)
Shape	.343* (.298*)	.378* (.369*)	.397** (.395**)	.290 (.328*)	.261 (.256)
Letter-sounds – lower case	.418** (.567**)	.294* (.444**)	.395* (.537**)	.350* (.506**)	.459** (.583**)
Letter names – lower case	.557** (.571**)	.482** (.551**)	.505** (.504**)	.561** (.536**)	.494** (.521**)
Letter-sounds – upper case	.078 (.266)	.012 (.165)	.089 (.266)	−.006 (.202)	.099 (.186)
Letter names – upper case	.448** (.375*)	.437** (.383**)	.495** (.409**)	.527** (.455**)	.367* (.332*)
Non-word reading	.440** (.394**)	.429** (.314*)	.427** (.403**)	.509** (.439**)	.420** (.432**)
Rhyming words	.069 (.202)	.148 (.202)	.056 (.256)	.051 (.206)	.099 (.249)
Reading single word Phase 3		.835** (.854**)	.859™ (.868***)	.838** (.825**)	.865** (.861**)
Spelling single word Phase 3			.794** (.831**)	.821** (.807**)	.694** (.799**)
Reading single word Phase 4				.860** (.884**)	.722** (.793**)
Spelling single word Phase 4					.695** (.750**)

*Correlation significant at the .05 level (two-tailed)
**Correlations significant at the .01 level (two-tailed)

Reading

The initial regression analyses (Analyses 1 and 2 in Table 7.3) suggested that the subtests of the DEST provided a higher level of prediction of reading ability among these boys than the ARQ. In contrast to the 11–14 in variability in single-word reading at Phase 3 predicted by the ARQ score, after controlling for age, 30% of the variability in the same measure could be accounted for by two subtest measures. Sound order accounted for approximately 20–23% of the variance, with rapid naming adding a further 10% to the level of prediction. By Phase 4, the level of variability in single-word reading explained by these measures had increased to around 40%, compared to approximately 20% explained by the ARQ. The analysis indicated that sound order was entered into the regression equation first, explaining some 30–32%, with rapid naming adding 7–8% to the level of prediction when entered second. The analysis of text reading at Phase 4 showed a similar pattern, with the ARQ predicting some 11–14% of the variability compared to the 35–40% predicted by rapid naming and sound order. The order of entry varied in this analysis, with rapid naming accounting for 21–24% of the variability followed by sound order, which added a further 15% to the explained variability.

To assess whether the ARQ is a better predictor of reading than the school attainment measures, further regression analyses (Analysis 3 in Table 7.3) assessed the level of prediction provided by the best of the predictors amongst the letter names and sounds tasks, Non-word Reading Test and rhyming words measure of Phase 2. The analysis of single-word reading at Phase 3 indicated that 26–31% of variability could be accounted for by letter names lower case, again higher than that predicted by the ARQ in Analysis 1. By Phase 4, letter names lower case predicted 20–25% of variability in single-word reading and a similar amount of text reading, as much, if not more, than that predicted by the ARQ.

A final series of regression analyses (Analyses 4 in Table 7.3) combined the DEST subtests and the school-based measures. In each case, three measures, in combination, explained more variability than that accounted for by the ARQ. Sound order, rapid naming, and letter names lower case accounted for between 43% and 49% of the variability in single-word reading at Phase 3, as well as in single-word reading and text reading at Phase 4.

Spelling

For spelling, Analyses 1 and 2 in Table 7.3 indicated that a single subtest of the DEST could predict more variability in spelling ability at Phases 3 and 4 than the ARQ. Whereas the ARQ predicted 15–19% of variability in spelling at Phase 3, and 9–13% of variability in spelling at Phase 4, sound order accounted for 23–24% of the variability in spelling scores at Phase 3 and Phase 4, respectively.

Similarly, of the school-based measures, letter names lower case predicted 18–23% of variability in spelling at Phase 3, as much as that predicted by the ARQ. This same measure was much more predictive of spelling at Phase 4 than the ARQ. Letter names lower case contributed 26–31%, with the Non-word Reading Test adding an extra 8%, of the variability explained by the regression equation derived.

Combining the DEST subtests and school-based measures led to two measures predicting about 30–40% of the variability in spelling performance. For spelling at Phase 3, sound order accounted for between 19% and 23% of the variability, with letter names lower case adding approximately 11%. These same measures emerged from the analysis of spelling at Phase 4. Sound order predicting 21–24% and letter names lower case added a further 16–17%.

Table 7.3   Regression analyses for single-word reading, single-word spelling and text reading

Variable entered	Predictor	Phase 3					Phase 4				
		R^2	Adj. R^2	R^2 change	Sig. F change	Standardized β coefficients final model	R^2	Adj. R^2	R^2 change	Sig F change	Standardized β coefficient final model
Single-word reading											
Analysis 1											
Block 1. Age	Age	.005	−.018	.005	0.641	0.038	.006	−.017	.006	0.618	0.034
Block 2. ARQ	ARQ	.147	.106	.142	0.012	−0.378	.232	.195	.226	0.001	−0.477
Analysis 2											
Block 1. Age	Age	.005	−.018	.005	0.641	−0.071	.006	−.017	.006	0.618	−0.075
Block 2. DEST subtests	Sound order	.240	.203	.234	0.001	0.437	.327	.295	.321	< 0.001	0.528
	Rapid naming	.344	.296	.105	0.014	−0.334	.408	.365	.081	0.023	−0.293
Analysis 3											
Block 1. Age	Age	.005	−.018	.005	0.641	0.036	.006	−.017	.006	0.618	0.044
Block 2. School lower case attainment measures	Letter names	.311	.278	.306	< 0.001	0.554	.257	.221	.251	0.001	0.502
Analysis 4											
Block 1. Age	Age	.005	−.018	.005	0.641	−0.063	.006	−.017	.006	0.618	−0.069
Block 2. DEST subtests	Sound order	.240	.203	.234	0.001	0.298	.327	.295	.321	< 0.001	0.420
	Rapid naming	.344	.296	.105	0.014	−0.290	.408	.365	.081	0.023	−0.259
Block 3. School attainment measures	Letter names lower case	.484	.432	.139	0.002	0.403	.492	.441	.084	0.014	0.313

Table 7.3   (Continued)

Variable entered	Predictor	Phase 3					Phase 4				
		R^2	Adj. R^2	R^2 change	Sig. F change	Standardized β coefficients final model	R^2	Adj. R^2	R^2 change	Sig F change	Standardized β coefficient final model
Single-word spelling											
Analysis 1											
Block 1. Age	Age	.001	-.022	.001	0.847	-0.069	.001	-.022	.001	0.847	-0.003
Block 2. ARQ	ARQ	.191	.153	.191	0.003	-0.438	.131	.090	.130	0.016	-0.362
Analysis 2											
Block 1. Age	Age	.001	-.022	.001	0.847	-0.120	.001	-.022	.001	0.847	-0.063
Block 2. DEST subtests	Sound order	.229	.193	.228	0.001	0.486	.242	.206	.241	0.001	0.499
Analysis 3											
Block 1. Age	Age	.001	-.022	.001	0.847	-0.061	.001	-.022	.001	0.847	-0.088
Block 2 School attainment measures	Letter names lower case	.236	.200	.235	0.001	0.486	.315	.282	.314	< 0.001	0.405
	Non-words						.397	.353	.083	0.022	0.340
Analysis 4											
Block 1. Age	Age	.001	-.022	.001	0.847	-0.119	.001	-.022	.001	0.847	-0.062
Block 2. DEST subtests	Sound order	.229	.192	.228	0.001	0.355	.242	.206	.241	0.001	0.339
Block 3. School attainment measures	Letter names lower case	.342	.294	.113	0.011	0.361	.412	.369	.170	0.001	0.442

(Continued)

Table 7.3 (Continued)

Variable entered	Predictor	Phase 3					Phase 4				
		R^2	Adj. R^2	R^2 change	Sig. F change	Standardized β coefficients final model	R^2	Adj. R^2	R^2 change	Sig F change	Standardized β coefficient final model
Text reading											
Analysis 1											
Block 1. Age	Age						.013	−.009	.013	0.448	0.083
Block 2. ARQ	ARQ						.148	.108	.135	0.014	−0.368
Analysis 2											
Block 1. Age	Age						.013	−.009	.013	0.448	−0.037
Block 2. DEST subtests	Rapid naming						.249	.213	.236	0.001	−0.427
	Sound order						.399	.355	.150	0.003	0.400
Analysis 3											
Block 1. Age	Age						.013	−.009	.013	0.448	0.084
Block 2. School attainment measures	Letter names lower case						.251	.216	.238	0.001	0.489
Analysis 4											
Block 1. Age	Age						.013	−.009	.013	0.448	0.068
Block 2. DEST subtests	Rapid naming						.249	.213	.236	0.001	−0.419
	Sound order						.399	.355	.150	0.003	0.349
Block 3. School attainment measures	Letter names lower case						.490	.439	.090	.0011	0.731

Discussion

The results indicate that specific subtests within the DEST, specifically sound order and rapid naming, and school attainment measures of lower case letter names were better predictors of the reading and spelling skills of these young children in their initial years of formal schooling than was the global ARQ measure from the DEST. Specifically, the ability to process the order of rapidly presented auditory stimuli and name letters in the reception year were related to reading and spelling ability in the second half of Year 1. Additionally, the ability to name objects quickly was also predictive of reading ability in these children, particularly text reading at the end of Year 1. Other measures in the DEST, as well as school attainment measures, provided little evidence of predicting extra variability over these variables in these initial stages of learning literacy skills. These conclusions are consistent with those reported by Simpson and Everatt (2001) who also indicated that individual measures within the DEST were better predictors of reading and spelling ability some 18 months following screening than the accumulative ARQ. However, Simpson and Everatt argued that the rapid naming subtest was the best predictor amongst the DEST measures, whereas the sound order task was not related to subsequent literacy skills. These findings can be contrasted with the presented data where, with the exception of the text reading measure, sound order was usually entered into the regression equation before rapid naming. The main difference between these studies is the age range assessed. Simpson and Everatt tested an older cohort of boys, aged between 5:4 and 6:3 (mean age of 5.84), who, in contrast to those tested in the present study, had experienced at least 1 year of instruction in literacy-related skills. These disparate findings are consistent with the view that the level of prediction provided by a measure may vary with the age/development of the child, and argue against the use of single measure identifiers of deficits that might appear at an older age. In this respect, a range of different measures may be more appropriate to assess potential. Entry into a regression equation should be treated with caution as a means of determining importance of prediction, and the sample sizes of both studies mean that a lack of power may lead to an increase in Type II errors. However, the results are consistent in indicating that the ARQ predicts less variability in subsequent literacy ability than individual measures and, therefore, questions the use of single combined norms by which to determine future skills. This latter finding, however, is contrary to that presented by Fawcettt et al. (1998) and Nicolson, Fawcett, Moss, Nicolson and Reason (1999).

The Sound Order Test is of particular interest in terms of its ability to predict variance in reading and spelling at each assessment stage of this study. The designers of the DEST drew on the work of Tallal (1980) who hypothesized a causal link between temporal order judgments, or auditory processing deficits, and reading disability. However, in recent years, several independent researchers have failed to find evidence to support a causal link between an auditory processing deficit and reading disability in either adults or children, whilst others have been overtly critical of the concept (Bishop, Carlyon, Deeks, & Bishop, 1999; Mody, Studdert-Kennedy, & Brady, 1997; Marshall, Snowling, & Bailey, 2001; Nittrouer, 1999; Share, Jorm, Maclean, & Matthews, 2002; Studdert-Kennedy & Mody, 1995; Studdert-Kennedy, Mody, & Brady, 2000). Share et al. conclude that, at present, the evidence for an auditory processing deficit is characterized by the highly divergent nature of literature on temporal processing, which is in direct contrast to the convergent nature of research literature on phonological processing. One of the problems with ascribing poor performance on the DEST sound order subtest to underlying deficits in processing the temporal order of sounds is that the task requires the participant to attach a verbal label to each of the non-verbal sounds. If, as Wagner and Torgesen (1987) have suggested, the use of verbal labels is an aspect of phonological awareness and places demands on working memory, each of these areas could be the source of poor performance in the task.

In contrast to the sound order subtest, the DEST subtests of phonological discrimination and rhyme/first sound detection did not predict future reading or spelling ability. Similarly, the school-based rhyme measure also proved to be a poor indicator of future literacy skills. These findings support research which suggests that other phonological tasks, such as phoneme dele-tion tasks, may be much more predictive of later reading ability than rhyme tasks (Duncan, Seymour, & Hill, 1997; Muter, Hulme, Snowling, & Taylor, 1998). However, as with the rapid naming task discussion above, it could be that measures of phonological ability vary with devel-opment and that the rhyme-based tasks used in this study were simply not sensitive enough for use with the cohort tested. There is evidence that young preschool children have the ability to detect rhyme (Maclean, Bryant, & Bradley, 1987), which may lead to high performance levels that reduce the likelihood of rhyme-based measures predicting reading difficulties. Screening measures (such as to the DEST) may have to include further assessment measures that focus on similar phonological processes (the ability to perceive, store, and accurately produce phonolog-ical forms) in order to assess fully the children across the target age range.

A longitudinal study by Scarborough (1990) provides further support for the hypothesis that predictors of later literacy development change with age. Between 2 and 3 years of age, children who later developed reading disabilities were deficient in language skills related to pronunciation accuracy, receptive vocabulary, and object-naming abilities. By 5 years old, these same children exhibited weaknesses in object-naming, phonemic awareness, and letter–sound knowledge. Furthermore, Liberman, Shankweiler, Fischer, & Carter (1974) present evidence for the development of syllable-level to phoneme-level processing skills between nursery and the end of Grade 1. In this study, the youngest children were able to segment by syllables, but none could segment by phonemes until the end of the first grade when only about 46% could perform at the phoneme-level of analysis. The children tested in the present study showed a similar trend in improvement, with average scores on the rhyme task per-formed part way through the reception year (the first year of formal literacy instruction) approaching ceiling for the test, indicating that the majority of children had acquired these skills. Such results question the use of the same test items across the whole of this age range.

School-based attainment measures (in this case, that of letter knowledge) offered more insight into future literacy acquisition than any of the DEST subtests. The ability to recog-nize and name upper and lower case letters seems well documented in the research literature as being one of the best predictors of literacy skills amongst young children (see, for example, Adams, 1990; Badian, 1994). In fact, '[T]his single factor accounted for 25–36% of the vari-ation in reading ability at the end of the year, and it did so regardless of instructional approaches' (Adams, 1990, p. 43). Gallagher, Frith, and Snowling (2000) found evidence to support this premise in a longitudinal study that reported the precursors of literacy delay in young children at risk of dyslexia. They found that, as early as 45 months, the strongest pre-dictor of later literacy ability at 6 years was preschool letter knowledge. The findings of the present study are consistent with these conclusions, but point to the separation of letter names and letter sounds in assessment procedures in contrast to those used by the DEST.

In conclusion, any screening tool should be more effective than school-based attainment measures, otherwise there is little to be gained from financial investment in both its purchase and the time it takes to administrate it. Although the DEST may provide a basis on which to profile the strengths and weaknesses of each child, the findings suggest that its global index may not be an appropriate screening tool for all children at the lower end of the age range of the test, that of 4:6. Additionally, the best single predictor of later literacy achievement was the attainment measure of letter knowledge, a measure that can be used with very young pre-reading children, although care needs to be taken in deciding whether to assess letter names or sounds. This, in combination with the other measures such as those used in the DEST battery, may be used during the reception year to provide a basis for future strategies.

References

Adams, M.J. (1990). *Beginning to read: Thinking and learning about print.* Cambridge, MA: MIT Press.

Badian. N.A. (1994). Preschool prediction: Orthographic and phonological skills, and reading. *Annals of Dyslexia,* 44, 3–25.

Bishop, D.V.M., Carlyon, R.P., Deeks, J.M., & Bishop, S.J. (1999). Auditory temporal processing impairment: Neither necessary nor sufficient for causing language impairment in children. *Journal of Speech, Language, and Hearing Research,* 42, 1295–1310.

Bowers, P.G., & Wolf, M. (1993). Theoretical links among naming speed, precise timing mechanisms and orthographic skill in dyslexia. *Reading and Writing: An Interdisciplinary Journal,* 5, 69–85.

Bryant, P.D., & Bradley, L. (1983). Categorising sounds and learning to read: A causal connection. *Nature,* 301, 419–421.

Denckla, M.B., & Rudel, R.G. (1976) Naming of object-drawings by dyslexic and other learning disabled children. *Brain and Language,* 3, 1–l15.

Duncan, L., Seymour, P.H.K., & Hill, S. (1997). How important are rhyme and analogy in beginning reading? *Cognition,* 63, 171–208.

Fawcettt, A.J., Singleton, C.H., & Peer, L. (1998). Advances in early years screening for dyslexia in the United Kingdom. *Annals of Dyslexia,* 48, 57–88.

France, N. (1981). *The primary reading test (levels 1 & 2).* Windsor: NFER-Nelson.

Frederickson, N., Frith, U., & Reason, R. (1997). *The phonological assessment battery.* Windsor: NFER-Nelson.

Gallagher, A., Frith, U., & Snowling, M.J. (2000). Precursors of literacy delay among children at genetic risk of dyslexia. *Journal of Child Psychology and Psychiatry,* 41, 203–213.

Goswami, U., & Bryant, P.E. (1990). *Phonological skills and learning to read.* Hove: Psychology Press.

Hatcher, P. (1994). *Sound linkage: An integrated programme for overcoming reading difficulties.* London: Whurr.

Liberman, I.Y., Shankweiler. D., Fischer, F.W., & Carter, B. (1974). Explicit syllable and phoneme segmentation in the young child. *Journal of Experimental Child Psychology,* 18, 201–222.

Liberman, I.Y., Shankweiler, D., Liberman, A.M., Fowler, C., & Fischer, F.W. (1977). Phonetic segmentation and recoding in the beginning reader. In A.S. Reber & D.L Scarborough (Eds.), *Towards a psychology of reading* (pp. 207–226). Hillsdale, NJ: Erlbaum.

Maclean, M., Bryant, P., & Bradley, L. (1987). Rhymes, nursery rhymes and reading in early childhood. *Merrill-Palmer Quarterly,* 33, 255–281.

Macmillan, B.M. (2002). Rhyme and reading: A critical review of the research methodology. *Journal of Research in Reading,* 25, 4–42.

Marshall, C.M., Snowling, M.J., & Bailey, P.J. (2001). Rapid auditory processing and phonological ability in normal readers and leaders with dyslexia. *Journal of Speech, Language, and Hearing Research,* 44, 925–940.

Miles, T.R., Haslum, M.N., & Wheeler, T.J. (1998). Gender ratio in dyslexia. *Annals of Dyslexia,* 48, 27–55.

Mody, M., Studdert-Kennedy, M., & Brady, S. (1997). Speech perception deficits in poor readers: Auditory processing or phonological coding? *Journal of Experimental Child Psychology,* 58, 112–133.

Muter, V., Hulme, C., & Snowling, M. (1996). *Phonological abilities test*. Oxford: The Psychological Corporation.

Muter, V., Hulme, C., Snowling, M., & Taylor, S. (1998). Segmentation, not rhyming, predicts early progress in learning to read. *Journal of Experimental Child Psychology*, 71, 29–37.

Muter, V., & Snowling, M. (1998). Concurrent and longitudinal predictors of reading: The role of metalinguistic and short-term memory skills. *Reading Research Quarterly*, 33, 320–337.

Newton, M., & Thomson, M.E. (1982). *The aston index*. Wisbech: Learning Development Aids.

Nicolson, R.I., &. Fawcett, A.J. (1995). Dyslexia is more than a phonological disability. *Dyslexia: An International Journal of Research and Practice*, 1, 19–36.

Nicolson, R.I. & Fawcett, A.J. (1996). *The dyslexia early screening test (DEST)*. Oxford: The Psychological Corporation.

Nicolson, R.I., Fawcett, A.J., Moss, H., Nicolson, M.K., & Reason. R. (1999). Early reading intervention can be effective and cost-effective. *British Journal of Educational Psychology*, 69, 41–62.

Nittrouer, S. (1999). Do temporal processing deficits cause phonological processing problems? *Journal of Speech, Language, and Hearing Research*, 42, 925–942.

Reason, R., Frederickson, N., Hefferman, M., Martin, C., & Woods, K. (1999). *Dyslexia, literacy and psychological assessment. Report of a working party of the Division of Educational and Child Psychology of the British Psychological Society*. Leicester: British Psychological Society.

Scarborough, H.S. (1990). Very early language deficits in dyslexic children. *Child Development*, 61, 1728–1743.

Schonell, F.J., & Schonell, F.E. (1956). *Diagnostic and attainment testing: Including a manual of tests, their nature, use, recording and interpretation*. London: Oliver and Boyd.

Share, D.L., Jorm, A.F., Maclean, R., & Matthews, R. (1984). Sources of individual differences in reading acquisition. *Journal of Educational Psychology*, 76, 1309–1324.

Share, D.I., Jorm, A.F., Maclean, R., & Matthews, R. (2002). Temporal processing and reading disability. *Reading and Writing: An Interdisciplinary Journal*, 15, 151–178.

Simpson, J., & Everatt, J. (2001). Phonological skills and naming speed as predictors of future literacy deficits. In Johnson, M. (Ed.), *Proceedings of the British Dyslexia Association International Conference. Dyslexia: At the Dawn of the New Century, University of York*. Reading: British Dyslexia Association.

Singleton, C. (1995). *Cognitive profiling system*. Newark, Notts: Chameleon.

Snowling, M.J. (2000). *Dyslexia, second edition*. Oxford: Blackwell.

Spring, C., & Capps, C. (1974). Encoding speed, rehearsal, and probed recall of dyslexic boys. *Journal of Educational Psychology*, 66, 780–786.

Studdert-Kennedy, M., & Mody, M. (1995). Auditory temporal perception deficits in the reading-impaired: A critical review of the evidence. *Psychonomic Bulletin Review*, 2, 508–514.

Studdert-Kennedy, M., Mody, M., & Brady, S. (2000). Speech perception deficits in poor readers: A reply to Denenberg's critique. *Journal of Learning Disabilities*, 33, 317–321.

Tallal, P. (1980). Auditory temporal perception, phonics and reading disabilities in children. *Brain and Language*, 9, 182–198.

Vellutino, F.R., Scanlon. D.M., Sipay, E.R., Small, S.G., Pratt, A., Chen, R., & Denckta, M.B. (1996). Cognitive profiles of difficult-to-remediate and readily remediated poor readers: Early invention as a vehicle for distinguishing between cognitive and experiential deficits as basic causes of specific reading disability. *Journal of Educational Psychology*, 88, 601–638.

Vernon, P. (1997) *Graded word spelling test*. London: Hodder and Stoughton.

Wagner, R.K., & Torgesen, J.K. (1987) The nature of phonological processing and its causal role in the acquisition of reading skills. *Psychological Bulletin*, 101, 192–212.

Wagner, R.K., Torgesen, J.K., & Rashotte, C. (1999). *Comprehensive test of phonological processing*. Austin, TX: Pro-PEd.

Wolf, M., & Bowers, P. (1999). The double deficit hypothesis for the developmental dyslexias. *Journal of Educational Psychology*, 91, 415–438.

8

Principles for Literacy Assessment

Peter Johnston and Paula Costello

In a 'learning society' everyone will need to become, and remain, committed to learning. If assessment potentially represents the key to achieving this, it also currently represents the biggest single stumbling block. (Broadfoot, 2002, p. 6)

'What gets assessed is what gets taught' is a common assertion whose meaning is often underestimated. It is not just *what* gets assessed, but *how* it is assessed that has implications for what is learned. When a child who is asked the meaning of his report card grades responds, 'If I knew that I'd be the teacher,' he is saying something about the relationships of authority learned in the process of assessment. When a teacher wishes out loud that her faculty 'could discuss retention and realistic expectations for grade levels without the nastiness and accusations,' she is also reporting on the relational aspect of assessment practices (Johnston, 2003, p. 90). Our goal in this [chapter] is to offer a framework for understanding literacy assessment that incorporates these dimensions and reminds us of the broader picture of literacy assessment of which we often lose sight.

Literacy is a complex construct

Although we often think of literacy as a set of all-purpose skills and strategies to be learned, it is more complex, more local, more personal, and more social than that. Becoming literate involves developing identities, relationships, dispositions, and values as much as acquiring strategies for working with print (Brandt, 2001; Collins & Blot, 2003; Gee, 2000). Children becoming literate are being apprenticed into ways of living with people as much as with symbols. Consequently, literacy assessment must be grounded in current understandings of literacy and society (Johnson & Kress, 2003; Johnston, 1999). We have to consider what kind of literacy might benefit individuals, what kind of literate society we aspire to, and what assessment might best serve those ends.

For example, what kind of literacy assessment will enable children to live in and contribute to an increasingly democratic society? Democracy has to do with 'the way persons attend to one another, care for one another, and interact with one another ... [and] the

From: *Reading Research Quarterly*, 40 (2), 2005, pp. 256–67.

capacity to look at things as though they could be otherwise' (Greene, 1985, p. 3), and citizens who 'have the convictions and enthusiasms of their own responses, yet … are willing to keep an open mind about alternate points of view, and … to negotiate meanings and actions that respect both individual diversity and community needs' (Pradl, 1996, pp. 11–12). In other words, our literacy assessment practices must foster a literate disposition towards *reciprocity* (Carr & Claxton, 2002); that is, 'a willingness to engage in joint learning tasks, to express uncertainties and ask questions, to take a variety of roles in joint learning enterprises and to take others' purposes and perspectives into account' (p. 16).

What might such assessment look like? The National Educational Monitoring Project (NEMP) in New Zealand is charged with taking stock of the nation's progress in educating a literate society. To this end, the NEMP includes items such as providing a group of children with a set of books from which they, as a class library committee, must make their best selection. Students individually justify their choices to the group before the group negotiates and justifies the final selection. The negotiation has a time limit and is videotaped for analysis of reading and literate interactions (Flockton & Crooks, 1996). This item requires children to evaluate the qualities of texts, take a stance, make persuasive arguments, actively listen, and negotiate a collective position – all independent and interdependent literate practices central to a democratic classroom and society. The item reflects and encourages an individual and mutual disposition toward reciprocity, a foundation for a democratic literacy.

Literacy has complications that assessment must deal with. Not only is literacy complex and social but also the literate demands of the world keep changing with exponential acceleration. The apparent boundaries between spoken and written words and their conventions have been obliterated by instant messaging, book tapes, cell-phone text messaging, speech translation software, interactive hypertext, and the facility with which text and image (moving or still) are fused. Literate demands are changing so rapidly that we can't predict with certainty what kindergartners will face in adulthood. We do know, however, that they will need to be resilient learners (Carr & Claxton, 2002) to maintain their literate development in the face of the increasingly rapid transformations of literacy in their communities.

Because 'what is assessed is taught,' literacy assessment should reflect and encourage resilience – a disposition to focus on learning when the going gets tough, to quickly recover from setbacks, and to adapt. Its opposite is brittleness – the disposition to avoid challenging tasks and to shift into ego-defensive behaviors when learning is difficult. A brittle learner believes that having difficulty with a literate task reveals a lack of 'ability'. A brittle disposition in children prior to first grade negatively predicts word recognition in grades 1 and 2, and is a better predictor than assessments of phonological awareness (Niemi & Poskiparta, 2002). This negative effect on learning is amplified by the pressures of competitive and overly difficult situations, particularly where ability is the primary emphasis. These are exactly the contexts produced by current testing practices.

Resilience can be assessed. For example, teachers can collect specific examples of resilience with quotes and artifacts to produce documented narratives (Carr & Claxton, 2002) for later review with the student and other stakeholders (see also Himley & Carini, 2000). In fact, the process of generating such assessment narratives will foster a resilient literate disposition (Johnston, 2004).

We begin with these uncommon examples of literacy assessment to suggest that, although assessing literacy in its complexity can be challenging, it is possible. It is also important. Failure to keep our attention on the bigger picture might not be a problem except that, intended or not, literacy assessment instruments define literacy within the assessment activity and, particularly when the stakes are high, within instruction (Smith, 1991). The higher the stakes, the more necessary it is that assessments reflect the breadth of literacy. Alas, most assessment practices, particularly testing practices, oversample narrow aspects of literacy, such as sound-symbol knowledge (Stallman & Pearson, 1991), and undersample other aspects such as writing, any media beyond print on paper, and ways of framing texts and literacy, such as the critical literacies necessary for managing the coercive pressures of literacy.

The more an assessment focuses on a narrow sample of literate behavior, as happens in individual tests, the more undersampling occurs. Literacy assessments distorted in this way affect instruction in many subtle ways. For example, the extensive use of pencil-and-paper state tests has forced many teachers to decrease instructional use of computers, particularly for writing. This problem is most damaging in urban and poor-performing schools (Russell & Abrams, 2004). The tests simultaneously risk underestimating the writing competence of students used to writing on computers, while reducing the likelihood of students not familiar with computer writing to ever become so.

Assessment is a social practice

Assessment is a social practice that involves noticing, representing, and responding to children's literate behaviors, rendering them meaningful for particular purposes and audiences (Johnston & Rogers, 2001). Teacher feedback to students on their literate behavior is assessment just as much as is grading students' work, classifying students as handicapped, certifying students as being 'above grade level,' or establishing a school as 'in need of improvement' (Black & Wiliam, 1998a; Johnston, 1993). *Testing is* a subset of assessment practices in which children's literate behavior is elicited in more controlled conditions.

Although assessment often is viewed as a technical matter of developing accurate measuring instruments, it is more centrally a set of social practices in which various tools are used for various purposes. For example, leveled books can be used as part of reaching in order to monitor children's early reading growth without the use of tests. Some books can even be kept aside specifically for assessment. The same procedure could also be used as part of holding teachers accountable for children's progress (Paris, 2002). However, this is a very different social practice and would invite greater concern about the measurement precision of the 'levels' and different social action. For example, teachers would be more likely to use the assessment books for instruction and to focus the curriculum on the accuracy of word reading.

Although the instrument is the same, it has different meaning in different social practice. In the accountability context, we worry more about the measurement qualities of the instrument in order to be fair. Fairness in the teaching context is more about ensuring that children are developing adequately, focusing instruction, and ensuring that the discourse of 'levels' does not dominate the children's interactions and self-assessments. Paradoxically, though we worry more about the psychometric properties of an instrument in the accountability context, the social properties of the *use* of the instrument, such as the defensiveness it might induce, or the constriction of the curriculum, can be of far more significance.

With the realization that assessments are social practices has come the awareness that the validity of an assessment instrument cannot be established outside of its consequences in use (Messick, 1994; Moss, 1998). Literacy assessment practices affect the constructs used to organize teaching practice and to represent children (Johnston, 1997; Moss, 1998). This is especially powerful when tests are used for purposes that attach high stakes such as teacher salaries, student retention, graduation, or classification.

Although there are occasional studies claiming that high-stakes testing has no negative effects, or even some positive effects on children's learning, there are many more studies showing the opposite and with greater specificity. For example, high-stakes accountability testing has consistently been demonstrated to undermine teaching and learning (Allington & McGill-Franzen, 1995; Morrison & Joan, 2002; Rex & Nelson, 2004; Smith, 1991; Smith & Rottenberg, 1991) particularly for lower achieving students (Harlen & Crick, 2003). It restricts the literacy curriculum, thus defeating the original intention to improve literacy learning. Teachers under threat drop from the curriculum complex literacy practices involving, for example, multimedia, research, and role-play, and at the same time their learning community is disrupted (Rex & Nelson, 2004). Increasing accountability pressure on teachers is counterproductive, especially when teachers already have an internal accountability system. It results instead in 'escalating teacher outrage, diminishing moral [sic], and the exiting of committed teachers … from teaching' (Rex & Nelson, 2004, p. 1324).

The dictum 'first do no harm' has become part of validity in theory, though rarely in assessment practice. Indeed, although high-stakes testing has lately been supported by arguments that it will reduce literacy achievement differences associated with race and poverty, there is evidence that the long-term effect of such testing is to create a curriculum that extends stratification rather than reducing it (Darling-Hammond, 2004; McNeil, 2000).

Individual and institutional learning

Literacy assessment is part of a larger project to educate children both for their immediate and long-term benefit and for the evolution of society. The implication of this is that literacy assessment must be grounded in current understandings of individual and institutional learning. There are two general kinds of assessment – summative and formative. Summative assessments are the backward-looking assessments *of* learning, the tests we most commonly think of that summarize or judge performance as in educational monitoring, teacher and student accountability testing, and certification (Black & Wiliam, 1998a). These have not been overtly associated with current understandings of individual or institutional learning.

Indeed, the theories of learning underlying psychometric practices have largely been implicit, individualistic, and behavioristic (Shepard, 1991). For example, current accountability testing, driven by psychometries, is based on rewarding and punishing students, teachers, and school systems. The evidence so far is that, rather than accomplishing the intended learning, these practices shift participants' goals toward avoidance of punishment, which thwarts the goal of improving the quality of literacy learning for all students and particularly for historically low-achieving students (McNeil, 2000).

. Formative assessment, or assessment *for* learning, is the forward-looking assessment that occurs in the process of learning, the feedback the teacher provides to the student, and the nature of the feedback matters (Crooks, 1988). For example, rather than praise or grades, comments improve performance, though praise keeps students thinking they are doing well (Black & Wiliam, 1998a). Feedback that focuses attention on traits such as ability, smartness, or goodness, undermines resilience (Dweck, 1999).

But the *process* of formative assessment is also critical. For example, the most common assessment practices associated with comprehension involve asking for retellings or asking questions to which teachers already know the answers. These interactional patterns teach children about how literacy is done and how authority is organized (Johnston, Jiron, & Day, 2001; Nystrand, Gamoran, Kachur, & Prendergast, 1997). Arranging for children to ask the questions and selectively discuss them can provide more interesting information regarding children's understanding, while simultaneously socializing them into productive literacy practices and identities (Comeyras, 1995).

Formative assessment is specifically directed toward affecting learning. Its validity depends on its ability to do so (Crooks, 2001). This means that the validity of formative assessment rests on factors not normally considered in discussions of validity, such as trust and sensitivity, the social supports, and motivations of the classroom. Task factors will be important, such as the nature and difficulty of the task, its personal and external relevance, the articulation of task features, and performance criteria. Each of these will affect the development of self-assessment. The nature and timing of feedback will be important. But because human interactions are structured around who the participants think they are and what they think they are doing, teachers' understanding of such things as literate practice, how children learn, and cultural difference will also be important, as will their social imagination and insight on conceptual confusions.

While this is true of formative assessments, summative assessment practices affect learning too. Some, such as accountability testing, do so deliberately. Consequently, to be valid, *all* assessment practices should be grounded in current and consistent understandings of learning, including the above factors. Both summative and formative assessments participate in socializing children's and teachers' self-assessments, with implications for control of learning and the management of self-assessment to serve learning goals.

Basing assessment on current understandings about learning does not simply negate principles of psychometrics. For example, neo-Piagetian theories of learning view the process of confronting and resolving discrepancies as a primary vehicle for learning (Schaffer, 1996; Tudge & Rogoff, 1989). A self-extending literacy learning system requires children to attend to discrepancies between cue systems, for example (Clay, 1991). In a similar way, learning communities require disjunctures, such as between minority and mainstream performance, to stimulate learning. However, as with formative assessment, the independent sources of information providing the conflict must be trusted, and measurement principles can help provide the grounds for this. The context in which such discrepancies are presented affects what is learned. The assessment activity must enable productive *engagement* of the disjunctures and foster productive use of data.

Thinking about assessment in terms of individual and institutional learning can change the way we value technical characteristics of assessment. For example, consider the role of consistent agreement among examiners (reliability). Complex authentic assessment items such as those used in the NEMP often reduce reliability (Shavelson, Baxter, & Pine, 1992). Weighty assessment practices like sorting and certifying students demand practices that ensure agreement – the higher the stakes, the more important this agreement.

Disagreements in this context are viewed as 'measurement error,' which leads to a reduction of complex authentic items. By contrast, in low-stakes and more formative assessment, disagreement among teachers about the meaning of particular documentation, such as portfolios, can open an important learning space by inviting discussions that lead to improvements in instruction and assessment itself. Indeed, this negotiation of values, qualities, and purposes is the most productive part of standards-based or performance-based assessments (Falk, 2001; Johnston, 1989; Moss & Schutz, 2001; Sadler, 1987). Complex and problematic examples provoke the most productive teaching–learning conversations. In other words, when the stakes are low, the less reliable the assessment is – to a point – the more likely it is to produce new learning and innovation in teaching. Because the validity of an assessment rests partly upon its consequences, improving teaching increases the validity of the assessment. In this context, imperfect reliability, contrary to psychometric theory, can increase validity.

As a concrete example, consider the NEMP test item mentioned at the beginning of this [chapter] in which children evaluate books individually and collaboratively as a library committee. The item and instrument are possible because NEMP uses a light matrix sample. Different children take a different selection of items; nationally, only a sample of children takes any items at all. The sampling system is possible because the emphasis is on the performance of the system, not on individual schools, teachers, or children. The instrument provides system information without raising individual or organizational defenses (Argyris, 1990).

Aggregate performance is published and analyzed by kind and size of school, minority percentage, community size, socioeconomic status, ethnicity, and gender, but direct institutional comparisons cannot be made. Test items are also published to reduce emphasis on abstracted numerical comparisons. The four-year assessment cycle allows time for both the construction of complex assessments and productive institutional and societal responses. At the same time, each administration of the assessment requires training a group of teachers to reliably administer the assessment. Teachers involved in the training report that it is an exceptional form of professional development that influences their own assessment and teaching competence, and that they pass this competence on to others (Gilmore, 2002).

Minds in society

Children's thinking evolves from the discourses in which they are immersed. So, for example, the ways children assess themselves as literate individuals will reflect the discourse of classroom assessment practices. Consider Henry (all names are pseudonyms), for example, a fourth-grade student who describes himself as a writer (Johnston et al., 2001). Though he says writing takes him a little longer than some, he notes that he has a journal with lots of entries and can borrow ideas from other authors, among whom he includes peers whose feedback and suggestions he values. He talks about their writing in terms of the ways they can affect him as a reader. He enjoys reading, and if he wanted to learn about another person as a reader, he would ask about favorite and current books and authors.

Indeed, he describes peers first in terms of their reading interests (topic, author, genre, difficulty) and then, matter-of-factly, their reading speed. He is confident that he makes important contributions to book discussions, but he also feels he benefits from hearing other students' experiences and interpretations. He has learned to manage these discussions to maximize this learning. In his research efforts, he has encountered disagreements among authors, which he ascribes to one of them not 'doing his homework,' and he resolves them by consulting more sources (print, personal, and electronic). Henry has a strong sense of agency and uniqueness in his literate practice, which is an important part of who he feels he is. He recognizes a range of sources of authority and that none is beyond critique. When his teacher describes Henry's literate development, it is in terms of details of his interests and engagements, what he has accomplished, how he approaches literate activities, and what he is beginning to do collaboratively or with assistance.

Henry's self-assessment, his interpretation and representation of himself as a literate person, reflects the literate practices and values of his classroom. In a different discourse community, his and his teachers' assessments could have focused more centrally on his decoding skills, what he is unable to do, or on his normative standing. The test used by his school district does provide a numerical quantity to represent the amount of his literacy and places him in the lower quarter of his class. But this particular teacher in this particular school and district finds that representation of little significance, and it does not enter the discourse of the classroom. Another teacher in another discursive community in which the pressures and goals are different would likely represent the child's literacy development differently.

Indeed, teachers in districts more concerned with accountability pressures tend to describe children's literacy development with less detail, with less attention to the child's interests, and with more distancing language (Johnston, Afflerbach, & Weiss, 1993). In a similar manner, the pressures of standards assessment change not only the representations but also the relationships among teacher and students, making them more authoritarian (Deci, Siegel, Ryan, Koestner, & Kauffman, 1982), a relationship that is part of the literacy that is acquired.

A corollary of their 'mind in society' principle is that literate development is constructed. Mandy, for example, in the same grade in another school district, feels that she is a good writer because she 'writes fast' and feels that she will get an 'excellent' on her report card for writing with a comment that she 'has behaved and she is nice to other classmates.' She feels that the good readers are recognizable because they 'are quiet and they just listen … and they get chapter books.' However, she does not think that conversations between writers are good because they would result in other writers taking ideas and having the same stories and because feelings might get hurt.

Mandy's conception of literacy foregrounds convention, conformity, speed, and individualism (Johnston et al., 2001). Rather than acquiring similar amounts of literacy, as their test scores might suggest, Henry and Mandy have acquired different literacies. Literate development is not a matter of acquiring a series of stepping stones in a particular order. First graders are quite capable of acquiring knowledge of letters and sounds and other print conventions as part of developing a critical literacy. The conventions, however, will mean something different when acquired as part of different literacies. The fact that there are predictable sequences of development is as much a feature of our assessment and curricular imperatives as it is a feature of a natural sequence of literate subskills, or of biological or other potentials and limitations.

Representation and interpretation

Assessment practices are always representational and interpretive. A teacher, an administrator, and a parent are likely to make different sense of a child's literate behavior both because they bring different histories to the assessment and because they often have different goals as part of different, if overlapping, social practices. Even a test score (a particular choice of representation) will mean different things to them. Each assessment practice is associated with distinct ways of using language that influence the interpretarions made (Fairclough, 1992; Gee, 1996). A school psychologist or a speech therapist can tilt the representational language of a committee on the handicapped toward 'learning disabled' or 'language delayed' on the basis of the same evidence (Rueda & Mercer, 1985). A single teacher can bring different discourses to representing different children depending on the way the child has been categorized, and these representations have consequences for children's understandings of literacy, themselves, and one another as literate individuals (Arya, 2003; Johnston et al., 2001).

Representational practices in assessment perpetuate the wider cultural discourses. If our discourse offers a category called 'reading disabled,' then we will find assessment tools to identify members of the category and an appealing narrative of 'services' and 'support' (McDermott, 1993). The representational language of trait and deficit (Johnston, 1993; Mehan, 1993) within which learning narratives are set offers children, teachers, parents, and other community members problematic identities and dispositions. Once 'identified,' children remain caught in the problematic discursive web, partly because the problem is represented as a trait of the child rather than as in the instructional environment, partly because the identification process groups children together who share common identifications, and partly because the child is moved to a system that specializes in children's problems that often emphasizes different understandings about literacy learning (Allington & McGill-Franzen, 1989).

Although we might worry about the nature of the categories, which are surely important, the practice is about more than that. As Yalom (1989) pointed out, 'If we relate to people believing that we can categorize them, we will neither identify nor nurture … the vital parts of the other that transcend category' (cited in Greenberg & Williams, 2002, p. 107). This is evident in casual transformations such as 'He's a two, borderline three, right now and we hope that this enrichment program will put him over the edge' (Baudanza, 2001, p. 8).

Primacy of teachers' assessment practices

No instrument or assessment practice can overcome the fact that the the teacher is the primary agent of assessment (International Reading Association and National Council of Teachers of English Joint Task Force on Assessment, 1994). The bulk of literacy assessment occurs moment by moment as part of the activity of teaching (Black & Wiliam, 1998b; Crooks, 1988; Johnston, 1989). Consider an example. A teacher was observed introducing to a student a predictable book with the pattern 'Grandpa is [verb–e.g., sitting].' The last page was 'Grandpa is snoring,' at which the child laughed and said that his grandpa snores too. However, when he read the book, he read that page as 'Grandpa is so funny.' The teacher prompted the child to recall what his grandpa does and then prompted a rereading. The child reread, hesitated before *snoring,* and read it correctly.

But why *that* prompt or teaching strategy? Why not ask the child to read with his finger to emphasize the mismatch between the number of words spoken and in print? Because the teacher hypothesizes, based on her ongoing assessment of the child, that he thinks *so funny* is one word. Pointing would not prompt rethinking because he would still have a one-to-one match and an initial letter match. Why not simply provide accuracy feedback? Because, she hypothesizes, that the process through which the child solves the problem himself will help build a sense of literate agency. Her feedback is based on a theory of learning more than a notion of performance.

The essence of formative assessment is noticing details of literate behavior, imagining what they mean from the child's perspective, knowing what the child knows and can do, and knowing how to arrange for that knowledge and competence to be displayed, engaged, and extended. This requires a 'sensitive observer' (Clay, 1993) or 'kidwatcher' (Goodman, 1978), a teacher who is 'present' in the classroom – focused and receptive to noticing the children's literate behavior (Rodgers, 2002). A child's acquisition of a 'reading disabled' classification (and identity) begins with the teacher's assessment, and teachers who notice less about children's literacy development refer more children to be classified than do those who notice more (Broikou, 1992). The more detailed teachers' knowledge of children's literate development, the more agency they appear to feel with respect to solving literacy learning problems.

Formative assessment requires not only noticing and making productive sense of the literate behaviors that occur but also arranging classroom literacy practices that encourage children to act in literate ways and that make their literate learning visible and audible. A child explaining how she figured out a word is not only providing this information for the teacher but also spinning an agentive narrative of her own literate competence. She is building a productive self-assessment and literate identity (Johnston, 2004).

If a classroom is arranged so that children routinely engage in literate activities that provide manageable challenges and talk about the process and experience of their literate practice, assessment information is available to the teacher and, simultaneously, strategic information is available for the students. *Play* is a particularly rich context for the display of young children's understanding of how literate practices work (Roskos & Neuman, 1993; Teale, 1991). In a similar way, *collaboration* demands an externalization of shared thinking, which also provides an excellent source of information.

To the extent that formative assessment is a technical matter, the 'instrument' is the teacher and his or her mind and its social and textual supports. Improving performance on summative assessments requires improving formative assessment. There is research that suggests how to do this, but it also suggests that change will be slow because the practices assume active involvement on the part of students as well as changes in the ways teachers understand students, themselves, and what they are trying to accomplish (Black & Wiliam, 1998b). These changes are strongly resisted by societal assessment discourses and their sedimentation in teachers' own subjectivities, as we discuss presently.

Literacy assessment and context

Literacy is somewhat local in that people engage in literate practices differently in different contexts. Different tools and social contexts invoke different strategies and ways of thinking. Common assessment practices do not recognize this fact; instead they assume that performance on a particular task in a testing context is representative of all literate contexts. But children perform differently, for example, in more meaningful or authentic activities. The Primary Language Record (PLR) (Barrs, Ellis, Hester, & Thomas, 1989), an early literacy assessment instrument, requires the assessment community (teachers, families, administrators, and students) to recognize (and document) performance in different contexts including 'collaborative reading and writing activities,' 'play,' 'dramatic play,' and 'drama and storying' across different social groups that include 'pair,' 'small group,' and 'child with adult' (p. 38). It draws attention to what a child can do independently and with different kinds of support.

Assessing children's literate learning requires attending not only to what they know and do but also at least as much to the context in which they know and do. Indeed, as the PLR manual notes, 'progress or lack of progress should always be seen in relation to the adequacy of the context' (p. 18). When a child appears to be unsuccessful at literate endeavors, we want to know the circumstances in which this happens. Such circumstances include the extent to which literate practices and the logic of participation are made visible in the classroom and valued as purposeful social activities, the extent to which materials are relevant and accessible, and the extent to which classroom discourse is supportive, specific, reflective, nonjudgmental, and values problem solving (Allington & Johnston, 2002; Johnston & Rogers, 2001; Pressley, Allington, Wharton-MacDonald, Collins-Block, & Morrow, 2001).

Shifting the focus of assessment away from the isolated mind to the mind in a social context has begun to be recognized in the assessment of reading disabilities, For example, Clay (1987) proposed that labeling a child as reading disabled is premature without first eliminating the possibility that the child's progress is a result of poorly configured instruction. The assessment strategy of providing the best instructional intervention we can muster has proven effective in eliminating the need to classify most children (Scanlon, Vellutino, Small, & Fanuele, 2000).

However, because this strategy remains in a discourse that expects individual disabilities, the handful of children who remain unsuccessful become viewed as bona fide 'disabled,' or 'treatment resisters' (Torgeson, 2000). This need not happen. Indeed, Smith and her colleagues (Smith, 1997) rejected that discourse. Instead of locating the problem in the child, they entertained the possibility that their intervention might still be insufficiently responsive. Through collaborative self-assessment using videotapes, they refined their intervention and produced the desired acceleration in literate learning, removing the need to classify even these students. This concept of attending to the child in the learning context might be applied to large-scale assessments too. Teachers and schools do not operate in a vacuum.

Assessment discourses distribute power

Assessment discourses distribute and sustain power relationships. For example, formative assessments, while grounded in current understandings of learning, are not taken seriously as a form of assessment (Black & Wiliam, 1998a). They are referred to as 'informal,' as opposed to the more authoritative 'formal' assessments. There are probably many reasons for their lack of institutional power aside from the fact that they don't always involve a textual record or artifact such as running records, documented events, or writing samples. They are the purview of teachers, mostly women, and they are normally not in the language of mathematics. When brought to a Committee on Special Education meeting, these assessments are easily trumped by the tests of the school psychologist.

Rogers (2003) showed how a mother, vehemently committed to protecting her daughter from assignment to special education, is reduced to passive acceptance by an assessment discourse that invokes subjectivities from her own unsuccessful history in schooled literacy. Rogers also showed how the discursive context induces this passivity just as well in those with highly successful histories of schooled literacy. The normative discourse of testing provides a powerful tool for asserting symbolic domination and intimidation of students, teachers, and parents (Bourdieu, 1991; Fennimore, 2000; Rogers, 2002). When an adult basic education student at the end of a reading lesson asks timidly, 'Did I read this good?' (Rogers, 2002), she demonstrates the internalization of an oppressive assessment discourse.

It is possible to design assessment practices to alter these power arrangements. To return to the PLR, the manual describes specific ways for reducing power differences in assessment conferences with children and families. The form of the assessment also insists that members of the learning community focus attention on the child's assets and their instructional context. Because it directs attention toward differences in performance in a range of contexts and on a range of dimensions, it resists narrow and debilitating ability interpretations. At the same time, it provides a language that represents literacy as centrally involving identity and engagement in practice, describing a child's development as a reader and a language user and implying a dimension of agency.

However, breaking free of more limiting assessment discourses is increasingly difficult as these discourses saturate a wider array of media. Constant reminders in the newspaper and reports from school are now supplemented through the Internet. Parents going to the Web are encouraged to obtain reading tests that they can use with their child. Like any advertising, these tests create a need and then direct parents to purchase the remedial instruction *on the* basis of the normative assessment and the 'latest brain research' (Learning, 2002) to fulfill the need. At the same site, parents learn of the routinely massive company growth rate, its even better prospects following federal No Child Left Behind regulations (2002), and how they can profit through investment (Johnston & Rogers, 2001). By both reflecting and enforcing traditions of literate practice (including who gets to participate in what ways and in which media), assessment practices stabilize the literate society, limiting social change and adaptability.

Clashes in practices

Literacy assessment consumes resources, so there is a constant search for multipurpose assessments. However, each new function often has different demands, requiring difficult trade-offs and bringing different discourses. Recall the NEMP assessment described earlier. Many of the features of the NEMP were once part of the National Assessment of Educational Progress (NAEP in the United States). However, political pressures have changed the timing of the NAEP to a two-year cycle, increasing pressure for simpler computerized responses. The sampling structure has changed to enable state-by-state comparisons, and state performance has become pegged to federal funding through the No Child Left Behind legislation (2002), thus increasing the assessment stakes. These changes add up to a change in the nature of the assessment activity from educational monitoring for productive curricular conversations to instrumental control of literacy teaching and learning. This is a different assessment practice, grounded in different views of learning and literacy.

The clash of these different discourses is common in school systems as formative and summative functions are forced together, often catching teachers in the middle (Delandshere, 2001; Hill, 2004). As with the earlier example of using leveled books for accountability practices, the higher stakes assessment will generally subvert the lower stakes practice. However, it is possible to have consistency among school literacy curriculum and assessment practices.

The PLR, described earlier, was developed in London for literacy assessment in multicultural/multilingual inner-city communities. It represents a complex, contextual, and social view of literacy learning and assessment practice that involves teacher, student, and parent in collaboratively documenting the child's literacy development over time. It was deliberately designed to inform and support teaching, students, and family literacies through clear documentation and the *process* of that documentation – the assessment *activity*. Although it is a 'record,' its developers took seriously the educative, communicative, and relational dimensions of assessment practice. In systematic interviews, parents describe the child's home literacy and must agree on what is recorded. Because interview topics include 'opportunities that might be possible for writing at home and whether the child chooses to write' (Barrs, Ellis, Hester, & Thomas, 1989, p. 16), parents simultaneously learn about possible ways to expand family literacy practices.

The representation of the child is centrally focused on documentation of what the child does and how the child does it and understands it. In context, though, it also includes numerical ratings for aggregation at the institution level and to complement the descriptive detail. Serious professional development is required for a complex assessment system like the PLR. But that has not prevented its successful adoption (Falk, 1998; Falk & Darling-Hammond, 1993). Implementation is not expected to occur overnight, and it is recommended that teachers begin by selecting a small group of students to document, expanding the group as expertise develops.

However, much of the professional development is built into the process of the assessment. In order to obtain reliable ratings, participants in the assessment community (teachers, administrators, parent representatives) regularly gather to compare their analyses of one another's assessments. The discussion around cases of disagreement is productive in clarifying the need for recording detail and the bases for judgment. The public nature of these discussions keeps teachers responsible for their assessments and requires a measure of courage. Because the assessment requires a range of literacy learning contexts and particular kinds of evidence, it helps teachers to structure their classroom practice.

We provide this example to show that more common approaches to assessment should not be thought of as 'givens' that merely need tweaking. This assessment holds very different assumptions from the more standard views and has very different consequences. For example, the assumption behind current accountability testing is that schools as organizations, and the individuals within them, are not only unable to monitor their own performance but also are unlikely to provide the best instruction they can unless forced to do so annually through rewards and punishments. The successful use of the PLR suggests that this assumption, at least in some contexts, is not tenable. Instead, we might sensibly ask, 'Under what circumstances can organizations and individuals productively monitor their teaching and learning as part of improving literacy learning?'

Darling-Hammond (2004), examining successful examples of assessment-driven reforms, provided some answers, concluding that consistency in assessment and curricular imperatives across the institutional learning community is essential. Other critical properties that the system provides, in a timely way, included sophisticated information that is consistent with current understandings of learning and relevant for teaching individual students. Successful assessment systems also provide information about the qualities of students' learning opportunities (the context of learning), develop productive teacher–student relationships, and are able to 'leverage continuous change and improvement' through a focus on teacher quality and learning (p. 1078). She noted that relatively low stakes and consistency among the assessment and curricular imperatives are important and that institutional size is not trivial. Although Darling-Hammond focused on the testing context privileged in the United States, these emphases are exactly the design features of the PLR. This is a description of the PLR.

Final comment

Assessment always (a) is representational and interpretive; (b) is a dynamic part of ongoing, goal-directed social activities and societal discourses; (c) reflects and imposes particular values, beliefs, relationships, and ways of being literate; and thus (d) has consequences for individuals' and communities' understandings of themselves and one another, as well as for the kinds of individuals and communities they will become. If the accelerating shifts in society will require everyone 'to become, and remain, committed to learning,' (Broadfoot, 2002, p. 6) and to acquire literacies that are more flexible and open, more resilient and self-directed, and more collaborative in a culturally and linguistically diverse context (Kalantzis, Cope, & Harvey, 2003), they will need to be socialized into a literacy that makes this possible, and our assessment systems are part of that socialization.

This means that learning must form the basis of our assessment practice. Current understandings show that the ability to guide and monitor one's own learning is essential to this project (Crooks, 2001). Focusing on learning in this way might incidentally accomplish other shorter term goals. For example, creating classrooms in which assessment practices socialize children into self-regulated literacy learning not only serves students' development as learners but also develops their literate achievement (Harlen & Crick, 2003; McDonald & Boud, 2003). The same principles almost certainly apply to teachers as individuals and as institutional communities. Indeed, if we are to have consistency among assessment and curricular imperatives within schools, the consistency should apply to the processes as well as the content. If literacy assessment is to serve literacy learners and society, then it has to be grounded in processes that reflect current understandings of learning, literacy, and society. It also has to remain open to evolution in both literacy and assessment, which at the very least means encouraging some diversity in assessment practice.

Nearly a decade ago, Shepard and her colleagues interviewed officials from state departments across the United States and concluded that more complex and authentic forms of literacy assessment were developing and that the previous excesses and problems of assessing children, particularly young children, for high-stakes purposes like accountability and retention were largely gone (Shepard, Taylor, & Kagan, 1996). The opposite is now true, a development that has everything to do with politics and relatively little to do with research (Allington, 2002; Allington & Woodside-Jiron, 1999; Johnson & Kress, 2003; Wixson & Pearson, 1998).

Indeed, the United States has currently reached the highest volume of testing and the highest stakes testing in its history. We are reminded of a definition of fanaticism as the act of redoubling one's efforts while having forgotten what one is fighting for (de Toqueville, cited in Claxton, 1999, p. 281). Although this [chapter] is in the service of 'theory and research into practice,' we must not pretend that literacy assessment can be improved by simple application of either. At the very least, our theory in practice has to include the fact that changing assessment practices is about changing societal discourses regarding children, literacy, and education, with all the values, relationships, identities, and resources that entails.

[…]

References

Allington, R.L., (Ed.). (2002). *Big brother and the national reading curriculum: How ideology trumped evidence*. Portsmouth, NH: Heinemann.

Allington, R.L., & Johnston, P.H. (Eds.). (2002). *Reading to learn: Lessons from exemplary fourth-grade classrooms*. New York: Guilford.

Allington, R.L., & McGill-Franzen, A. (1989). Different programs, indifferent instruction. In A. Gartner & D. Lipsky (Eds.), *Beyond separate education* (pp. 75–98). Baltimore: Brookes.

Allington, R.L., & McGill-Franzen, A. (1995). Flunking: Throwing good money after the Bad. In R.L. Allington & S.A. Walmsley (Eds.), *No quick fix: Rethinking literacy programs in America's elementary schools* (pp. 45–60). New York: Teachers College Press.

Allington, R.L., & Woodside-Jiron, H. (1999). The politics of literacy teaching: How 'research' shaped educational policy. *Educational Researcher*, 28(8), 4–13.

Argyris, C. (1990). *Overcoming organizational defenses: Facilitating organisational learning*. Boston: Allyn & Bacon.

Arya, P. (2003). Influences of reading group experiences on second graders perceptions of themselves as readers. *Literacy Teaching and Learning*, 8(1), 1–18.

Barrs, M., Ellis, S., Hester, H., & Thomas. A. (1989). *The primary language record: Handbook for teachers*. London: Inner London Education Authority/Centre for Language in Primary Education.

Baudanza, L. (2001). *Disabilities of a child or disabilities of the system?* Unpublished manuscript, University at Albany, Albany, NY.

Black, P., & Wiliam, D. (1998a). Assessment and classroom learning. *Assessment in Education: Principles, Policy & Practice*, 5(1), 7–74.

Black, R., & Wiliam, D. (1998b, October). Inside the black box: Raising standards through classroom assessment. *Phi Delta Kappa International*, pp. 139–148.

Bourdieu, P. (1991). *Language and symbolic power* (J.B. Thompson, Ed.; G. Raymond & M. Adamson, Trans.). Cambridge, MA: Harvard University Press.

Brandt, D. (2001). *Literacy in American lives*. Cambridge, UK: Cambridge University Press.

Broadfoot, P. (2002). Editorial. Assessment for lifelong learning: Challenges and choices. *Assessment in Education*, 9(1), 5–7.

Broikou, K. (1992). *Understanding primary grade classroom teachers special education referral practices*. Unpublished doctoral dissertation, State University of New York at Albany, Albany, NY.

Carr, M., & Claxton, G. (2002). Tracking the development of learning dispositions. *Assessment in Education*, 9(1), 9–37.

Claxton, G. (1999). *Wise up: The challenge of lifelong learning.* New York: Bloomsbury.

Clay, M.M. (1987). Learning to be learning disabled. *New Zealand Journal of Educational Studies,* 22, 155–173.

Clay, M. (1991). *Becoming literate: The construction of inner control.* Portsmouth, NH: Heinemann.

Clay, M.M. (1993). An observation survey of early literacy achievement. Portsmouth, NH: Heinemann.

Collins, L., & Blot, R.K. (2003). *Literacy and literacies: Texts, power, and identity.* New York: Cambridge University Press.

Comeyras, M. (1995). What can we learn from students questions? *Theory Into Practice,* 34, 101–106.

Crooks, T. (2001, September). *The validity of formative assessments.* Paper presented at the annual meeting of the British Educational Research Association, Leeds, UK.

Crooks, T.J. (1988). The impact of classroom evaluation practices on students. *Review of Educational Research,* 58, 438–481.

Darling-Hammond, L. (2004). Standards, accountability, and school reform. *Teachers College Record,* 106, 1047–1085.

Deci, E.L., Siegel, N.H., Ryan, R.M., Koestner, R., & Kauffman, M. (1982). Effects of performance standards on teaching styles: Behavior of controlling teachers. *Journal of Educational Psychology,* 74, 852–859.

Delandshere, G. (2001). Implicit theories, unexamined assumptions and the status quo of educational assessment. *Assessment in Education,* 8, 113–133.

Dweck, C.S. (1999). *Self-theories: Their role in motivation, personality. and development.* Philadelphia: Psychology Press.

Fairclough, N. (1992). *Discourse and social change.* London: Longman.

Falk, B. (1998). Using direct evidence to assess student progress: How the Primary Language Record supports teaching and learning. In C. Harrison & T. Salinger (Eds.), *Assessing reading: Theory and practice: International perspectives on reading assessment* (pp. 152–165). London: Routledge.

Falk, B. (2001). Professional learning through assessment. In A. Lieherman & L. Miller (Eds.), *Teachers caught in the action: Professional development that matters* (pp. 118–140). New York: Teachers College Press.

Falk. B., & Darling-Hammond. L. (1993). *The Primary Language Record at P.S. 261: How assessment transforms teaching and learning.* New York: The National Center for Restructuring Education, Schools, and Teaching, Teachers College, Columbia University.

Fennimore, B.S. (2000). *Talk matters: Refocusing the language of public schooling.* New York: Teachers College Press.

Flockton, L., & Crooks, T. (1996). *National Education Monitoring Project: Reading and speaking: Assessment results: 1996* (No. 6). Dunedin, New Zealand: Educational Assessment Research Unit.

Gee, J.P. (1996). *Social linguistics and literacies: Ideology in discourses* (2nd ed.). London: Falmer.

Gee, J.P. (2000). Discourse and sociocultutal studies in reading. In M.L. Kamil, P.B. Mosenthal, P.D. Pearson, & R. Barr (Eds.), *Handbook of reading research* (Vol. III, pp. 195–207). Mahwah, NJ: Erlbaum.

Gilmore, A. (2002). Large-scale assessment and teachers' assessment capacity: Learning opportunities for teachers in the National Education Monitoring Project in New Zealand. *Assessment in Education,* 9, 343–361.

Goodman, Y. (1978). Kidwatching: Observing children in the classroom. In A. Jagger & M.T. Smith-Burke (Eds.), *Observing the language learner* (pp. 9–18). Newark, DE: International Reading Association.

Greenberg, K.H., & Williams, L. (2002). Reciprociry and mutuality in dynamic assessment: Asking uncomfortable questions. In G.M. v. d. Aalsvoort, W.C.M. Resing, & A.J.J.M. Ruijssenaars (Eds.), *Learning potential assessment and cognitive training* (Vol. 7, pp. 91–110). Amsterdam: JAI.

Greene, M. (1985). The role of education in democracy. *Educational Horizons*, 63, 3–9.

Harlen, W., & Crick, R.D. (2003). Testing and motivation for learning. *Assessment in Education: Principles, Policy & Practice,* 10(2), 169–207.

Hill, C. (2004). Failing to meet the standards: The English language arts test for fourth graders in New York State. *Teachers College Record,* 106, 1086–1123.

Himley, M., & Carini, P.F. (Eds.). (2000). *From another angle: Children's strengths and school standards: The Prospect Center's descriptive review of the child.* New York: Teachers College Press.

International Reading Association and National Council of Teachers of English Joint Task Force on Assessment. (1994). *Standards for the assessment of reading and writing.* Newark, DE: International Reading Association.

Johnson, D., & Kress, G. (2003). Globalisation, literacy and society: Redesigning pedagogy and assessment. *Assessment in Education*, 10(1), 5–14.

Johnston, P.H. (1989). Constructive evaluation and the improvement of teaching and learning. *Teachers College Record,* 90, 509–526.

Johnston, P.H. (1993). Assessment as social practice. In D. Leu & C. Kinzer (Eds.), *42nd yearbook of the National Reading Conference* (pp. 11–23). Chicago: National Reading Conference.

Johnston, P.H. (1997). *Knowing literacy: Constructive literacy assessment.* York, ME: Stenhouse.

Johnston, P.H. (1999). Unpacking literate achievement. In J. Gaffney & B. Askew (Eds.), *Stirring the waters: A tribute to Marie Clay* (pp. 17–25). Portsmouth, NH: Heinemann.

Johnston, P.H. (2003) Assessment conversations. *The Reading Teacher,* 57, 90–92.

Johnston, P.H. (2004). *Choice words: How our language affects children's learning.* York, ME: Stenhouse.

Johnston, P.H., Afflerbach, P., & Weiss, P. (1993). Teachers' evaluation of teaching and learning of literacy. *Educational Assessment,* 1(2), 91–117.

Johnston, P.H., Jiron, H.W., & Day, J.P. (2001). Teaching and learning literate epistemologies, *Journal of Educational Psychology,* 93(1), 223–233.

Johnston, P.H., & Rogers, R. (2001). Early literacy assessment. In S.B. Neuman & D.K. Dickenson (Eds.), *Handbook of early literacy research* (pp. 377–389). New York: Guilford.

Kalantzis, M., Cope. B., & Harvey, A. (2003). Assessing multliteracies and the new basics. *Assessment in Education: Principles, Policy & Practice,* 10, 15–26.

Learning, S. (2002). *Fast For Word.* Retrieved August 3, 2002, from http://www.scilearn.com

McDermott, R.P. (1993). The acquisition of a child by a learning disability. In S. Chaiklin & J. Lave (Eds.), *Understanding practice: Perspective on activity and context* (pp. 269–305). Cambridge, UK: Cambridge University Press.

McDonald, B., & Boud. D. (2003). The impact of self-assessment on achievement: The effects of self-assessment training on performance in external examinations. *Assessment in Education: Principles, Policy & Practice,* 10(2), 209–220.

McNeil, L.M. (2000). *Contradictions of school reform: Education costs of standardized tests.* New York: Routledge.

Mehan, H. (1993). Beneath the skin and between the ears: A case study in the policies of representation. In S. Chaiklin & J. Lave (Eds.), *Understanding practice: Perspectives on activity and context* (pp. 241–268). Cambridge, UK: Cambridge University Press.

Messick, S. (1994). The interplay of evidence and consequences in the validation of performance assessments. *Educational Researcher,* 23(2), 13–23.

Morrison, K., & Joan, T.F.H. (2002). Testing to destruction: A problem in a small state. *Assessment in Education,* 9, 289–317.

Moss, P., & Schutz, A. (2001). Educational standards, assessment and the search for consensus. *American Educational Research Journal,* 38(1), 37–70.

Moss, P.A. (1998). The role of consequences in validity theory. *Educational Measurement; Issues and Practice,* 17(2), 6–12.

Niemi, P., & Poskiparta, E. (2002). Shadows over phonological awareness training: Resistant learners and dissipating gains. In B. Hjelmquist & C.V. Euler (Eds.), *Dyslexia and literacy* (pp. 84–99). London, UK: Whurr.

No Child Left Behind Act of 2001, Pub. L. No. 107–110, 115 stat. 1425 (2002).

Nystrand, M., Gamoran, A., Kachur, R., & Prendergast, C. (1997). *Opening dialogue: Understanding the dynamics of language and learning in the English classroom.* New York: Teachers College Press.

Paris, S.G. (2002). Measuring children's reading development using leveled texts. *The Reading Teacher,* 55, 168–170.

Pradl, G.M. (1996). Reading and democracy: The enduring influence of Louise Rosenblatt. *The New Advocate,* 9(1), 9–22.

Pressley, M., Allington, R.L., Wharton-MacDonald, R., Collins-Block, C., & Morrow, L. (2001). *Learning to read: Lessons from exemplary first-grade classrooms.* New York: Guilford.

Rex, LA., & Nelson, M.C. (2004). How teachers' professional identities position high-stakes test preparation in their classrooms. *Teachers College Record,* 106, 1288–1331.

Rodgers, C. (2002). Defining reflection: Another look at John Dewey and reflective thinking. *Teacher College Record,* 104(A), 842–866.

Rogers, R. (2002). Between contexts: A critical analysis of family literacy, discursive practices, and literate subjectivities. *Reading Research Quarterly,* 37, 248–277.

Rogers, R, (2003). *A critical discourse analysis of family literacy practices: Power in and out of print.* Mahwah, NJ; Erlbaum.

Roskos, K., & Neuman, S.B. (1993). Descriptive observations of adults' facilitation of literacy in young children's play. *Early Childhood Research Quarterly,* 8, 77–97.

Rueda, R., & Mercer, J. (1985, June). *Predictive analysis of decision-making practices with limited English proficient handicapped students.* Paper presented at the Third Annual Symposium: Exceptional Hispanic Children and Youth. Monograph series, Denver, CO.

Russell, M., & Abrams, L. (2004). Instructional uses of computers for writing: The effect of state testing programs. *Teachers College Record,* 106, 1332–1357.

Sadler, R.R. (1987). Specifying and promulgating achievement standards. *Oxford Review of Education,* 13, 191–209.

Scanlon, D.M., Vellutino, F.R., Small, S.G., & Fanuele, D.P. (2000, April). *Severe reading difficulties – can they be prevented? A comparison of prevention and intervention approaches.* Paper presented at the American Educational Research Association, New Orleans, LA.

Schaffer, H.R. (1996). Joint involvement episodes as context for development. In H. Daniels (Ed.), *An introduction to Vygotsky* (pp. 251–280). London: Routledge.

Shavelson, R.J., Baxter, G.P., & Pine, J. (1992). Performance assessments: Political rhetoric and measurement reality. *Educational Researcher,* 21(4), 22–27.

Shepard, L.A. (1991). Psychometricians' beliefs about learning. *Educational Researcher,* 20(7), 2–16.

Shepard, L.A., Taylor, G.A., & Kagan, S.L. (1996). *Trends in early childhood assessment policies and practices,* Washington, DC: Office of Educational Research & Improvement.

Smith, M.L. (1991). Put to the test: The effects of external testing on teachers. *Educational Researcher,* 20(5), 8–11.

Smith, M.L., & Rottenberg, C. (1991). Unintended consequences of external testing in elementary schools. *Educational Measurement: Issues and Practice,* 10(4), 7–11.

Smith, P. (1997). *A third chance to learn: The development and evaluation of specialized interventions for young children experiencing difficulty with learning to read* (No. 13227). Wellington, New Zealand: National Council for Educational Research.

Stallman, A.C., & Pearson, P.D. (1991). Formal measures of early literacy. In L.M. Morrow & J.K. Smith (Eds.), *Assessment for instruction in early literacy* (pp. 7–44). Englewood Cliffs, NJ: Prentice Hall.

Teale, W. (1991). The promise and the challenge of informal assessment in early literacy. In L.M. Morrow & J.K. Smith (Eds.), *Assessment for instruction in early literacy* (pp. 45–61). Englewood Cliffs, NJ: Prentice Hall.

Torgeson, J.K. (2000). Individual differences in response to early interventions in reading: The lingering problem of treatment resisters. *Learning Disabilities Research and Practice,* 15(1), 55–64.

Tudge, J., & Rogoff, B. (1989). Peer influences on cognitive development: Piageuan-Vygotskian perspectives. In M.H. Bornstcin & J.S. Bruner (Eds.), *Interactions in human development* (pp. 17–40). Hillsdale, NJ: Erlbaum.

Wixson, K.K., & Pearson P.D. (1998). Policy and assessment strategies to support literacy instruction for a new century. *Peabody Journal of Education,* 74, 202–227.

Yalom, I.D. (1989). *Love's executioner and other tales of psychotherapy.* New York: Basic Books.

Part 3

Pedagogy and Planning

9

Dyslexia and Learning Style – a Note of Caution

Tilly Mortimore

[...]

Introduction

Like letters dispatched from a battlefield, action research undertaken in the workplace by practitioners should command respect, both for the authenticity and relevance of the practice and for the often demanding conditions under which it is undertaken. Practitioners are also frequently in the position to inform policy on a local scale and, through publication and discussion in journals, within a wider context. This requires them to ensure that their knowledge, methodology and reflection on the results meet criteria every bit as rigorous as those faced by researchers within an academic context before they can start to make recommendations based on a reflexive approach to their findings.

Exley's (2003) study is both interesting and informative and certainly meets Stenhouse's (1985) criterion of producing an ordered report of experience which invites judgement. It also builds bridges between research and practice. However, teachers encouraged to follow the learning styles route, and make changes in practice on the basis of this small-scale study, should exercise some caution. A number of questions still remain unanswered.

Before using Exley's (2003) findings to make policy recommendations, it would be advisable to take a closer look at the following areas: the learning style research context; her selection of research focus; and the effect of a type of methodology so often utilised in practitioner research upon her conclusions.

The learning style research context

Examination of the existing research into learning style and dyslexia reveals a complex picture. There is much theoretical and practical research into the constructs underlying learning style theory and its application, going back over 80 years and covering a wide

From: *British Journal of Special Education*, 32 (3), 2005, pp. 145–8.

range of contexts, both educational and within the work place. Riding and Rayner (1998), Babbage, Byers and Redding (1999), Mortimore (2003a) and Cassidy (2003) all provide reviews and useful suggestions for educational applications.

The field, however, is dogged with controversy over the appropriateness and number of the constructs used to describe learning style; the reliability of methods of diagnosis; and even over the usefulness of matching style to teaching approach, sometimes termed the 'matching hypothesis' (Riding & Rayner, 1998). Although my work in educational environments has led me to encourage the judicious application of learning style theory to practical teaching, my research has uncovered a number of reasons for exercising caution.

A recent review by Coffield, Moseley, Hall and Ecclestone (2004) revealed that learning style theorists have devised more than 70 constructs (or models), of learning style and ways of identifying them. Some models are related to areas of the brain; others are rooted in theories of personality or motivation. Some are developmental and follow Piaget in suggesting that style evolves from stage to stage throughout a learner's lifetime to achieve maturity. Each model is accompanied by its own assessment methodology and, frequently, with suggestions as to ways of implementing subsequent programmes. Currently, style can be assessed using questionnaires, interviews, behavioural observation, the creation of profiles or combinations of all four (see Babbage et al., 1999; Mortimore, 2003a). There are also a number of computer-administered instruments which measure cognitive behaviours, for example, Riding's (1991) *Cognitive Styles Analysis*, or analyse responses to questionnaires, for example, Zdzienski's (1997) *StudyScan*. Coffield et al.'s (2004) review staled that only one of all the assessment tools they investigated met adequate psychometric criteria for internal consistency, reliability and validity.

This plethora of models has given rise to at least five unresolved controversies related to learning style, centred upon the relationship between the environment and the individual (Mortimore, 2003a), and reservations are expressed by researchers such as Chinn and Ashcroft (1998) as to how far style may be situation-specific rather than an established trait. Coffield et al. (2004) are strongly critical of all but a couple of learning style assessment measures. They go so far as to suggest that to label a student with a particular learning style based upon what they would consider to be an unreliable measure can restrict rather than liberate a learner – and that emphasis upon learning style rather than other social and contextual factors in teaching and learning is, in itself, misplaced (Coffield et al., 2003). They would suggest that the restructuring of pedagogy and institutions to reflect a learning style approach maintains the power of the teacher at the expense of the empowerment of the student. Any researcher utilising cognitive or learning style theory needs to place the study firmly within the context of these unresolved controversies.

Selection of research focus

Laying aside such controversy, learning style research is complex and the term 'learning style' is applied to a myriad of constructs, from those rooted firmly in personality theory to approaches to learning and levels of processing (see Riding & Rayner, 1998, for a review). Exley (2003) has selected 'the narrower aspects of learning style preference, such as visual, auditory and kinaesthetic tendencies' as the focus for her study, but without providing a clear rationale for this particular focus.

The selection of what is, in essence, a verbal-visual-kinaesthetic construct could provide an opportunity to examine the claim, which seems to have become a 'given' within some dyslexia literature (see West, 1997), that there is some relationship between visuo-spatial strategies or strengths and dyslexia. This hypothetical relationship currently remains anecdotal, with no published empirical research to support it (Mortimore, 2003a). Exley states that five of her seven students preferred a visual learning style and suggests that this may be significant. A small-scale study (Mortimore, 1998) containing 15 students with dyslexia and 15 without, used the *Cognitive Styles Analysis* (Riding, 1991) to examine the extent to which those with dyslexia favour visual processing approaches over the verbal. This study did suggest some relationship between visual style labels and dyslexia but these findings were not replicated in a further study (Mortimore, 2003b) of 117 students. This study revealed no link between visuo-spatial learning styles and dyslexia, nor did it reveal that students with dyslexia, regardless of learning style, performed more successfully when encouraged to use visual reinforcements.

Another justification for Exley's (2003) focus upon visual versus verbal or kinaesthetic learning might be the opportunity to explore the evidence for a preference for right-hemisphere visuo-spatial processing, suggested in the research (Galaburda, 1993) that she cites. However, the hemispheric specialisation hypothesis has been strongly criticised (see Coren, 1993 and, for a review, Mortimore, 2003a). Goswami (2004) points out that the 2002 OECD report on understanding the brain not only coined the term 'neuromyth' to describe the way in which scientific research can be misrepresented when translated into lay terms, but also celebrated hemispheric specialisation theory as a leading neuromyth. Goswami (2004) emphasises that the evidence from neuro-imaging technology suggests that the two hemispheres work together in every cognitive process so far examined, including language and face recognition, giving no neuro-scientific credence to theories of left- or right-brained learning. Currently there is little evidence to support claims that learners with dyslexia favour visuo-spatial or 'right-brained' approaches to learning.

One practical reason for the selection of the verbal-visual-kinaesthetic focus might be to enable the teacher-researcher to try out alternative spelling methodologies, following Brooks and Weeks's research (1999). This is an interesting approach. However, Exley's (2003) spelling task, as is the case with many methods, is itself open to ambiguity both in terms of exactly what type of processing (visual, verbal or semantic) the students might be using during the task and of how the results might be interpreted.

Methodology

Practitioner researchers are frequently forced to rely upon small 'opportunity' samples and this inevitably raises questions as to the possibility of achieving quantitative rigour within what are likely to be essentially small-scale, descriptive studies. Exley's work has produced some interesting results and has evidently been of real help to her students. The close attention she has paid to these students' strengths and weaknesses and the way in which this provides them with the language in which to examine their own approaches to learning is likely to have equipped these learners with new practical and metacognitive skills and the confidence to apply them in other learning contexts. Exley (2003) reports that their self-esteem has been enhanced and that, for the students with behavioural difficulties, this has been a positive learning experience upon which to build. These are outcomes all practitioners would welcome.

Difficulties are likely to arise, however, in a number of aspects related to the interpretation and application of the results of small-scale studies like Exley's. These include attempts to extrapolate from the findings to other groups of learners; to attribute results to particular factors; and to avoid criticism, in intervention studies, over choice of instruments to set parameters and measure changes. There are, however, a number of strategies that can help to counter criticism and lend weight to the findings.

In situations where the small number of participants and absence of a control group makes it hard to apply any kind of statistical analysis and therefore renders the studies open to criticism, researchers could incorporate a range of strategies which would strengthen their cases. This could include attempting to run a parallel group, who are offered similar amounts of extra time and attention but an alternative intervention, or placing qualitative data, gathered from a range of sources during the study, alongside any quantitative analyses, enabling further triangulation and enrichment of the findings.

In situations where an attempt is made to use case-study narrative to attribute changes in the participants' performance to a particular factor, such as the application of learning style theory to practical classroom activities, extra rigour is required. The learning style research described earlier indicates the problematic nature of learning style assessment instruments. Although self-report questionnaires and observational analysis are valuable as tools to enable students and teachers to develop awareness of their approaches to learning, it is debatable whether they provide a sufficiently rigorous way of setting the parameters if a more quantitative outcome is also required and reliable attributions to the intervention are to be made. Any changes found could be attributable to a range of factors, such as motivation, self-esteem and teacher attention, and it is important to control for as many confounding elements as possible.

In small-scale studies which involve an intervention from which conclusions will be drawn, it is essential to undertake a meticulous analysis of the nature of the intervention task and to use a range of multiple and, ideally, standardised methods to establish baselines and to measure progress in the targeted skill.

Small-scale studies carried out by practitioners open a fascinating window into the real-life experience of working in education. However, the practical restrictions placed upon researchers by their working environment can undermine the significance of the results and therefore make it essential that close attention is paid to such elements of the study as establishing control groups; amassing the broadest possible range of data; analysing any intervention tasks; selecting multiple assessment and progress measures; and thoroughly discussing controversies that might arise from the research base at the outset of the study. If attention is paid to these elements, any case for using the results of such studies to influence policy will be considerably strengthened.

Conclusion

Exley's (2003) study has provided some insights of real use to educators. However, it could be argued that further investigation is warranted before general alterations are made to teaching approaches based upon her project's findings as to the effectiveness of the application of a learning style approach. There is currently little agreement in the world of learning style research as to the validity of the constructs or the outcomes of matching style and teaching methods. There is, however, evidence of some consensus as to the value of giving learners the awareness, respectful attention and language to recognise their own best strategies and the learners in Exley's study have gained much that was positive from this experience. Research to date may not have the power to offer unqualified support to the implementation of learning styles approaches for learners with dyslexia, but it should stimulate further investigation and provide encouragement to those tempted to engage in practitioner research on the topic.

References

Babbage, R., Byers, R. & Redding, H. (1999) *Approaches to Teaching and Learning – including pupils with learning difficulties.* London: David Fulton Publishers.

Brooks, P. & Weeks, S. (1999) *Individual Styles in Learning to Spell: improving spelling in children with literacy difficulties and all children in mainstream schools.* Nottingham: DfEE Publications.

Cassidy, S. (2003) 'Learning styles: an overview of theories, models and measures.' Paper published in *Bridging Theory & Practice*, the proceedings of the European Learning Style Information Network Eighth Annual Learning Styles Conference, University of Hull, 30 June to 2 July 2003.

Chinn, S.J. & Ashcroft, J.R. (1998) *Mathematics for Dyslexics: a teaching handbook.* London: Whurr.

Coffield, F., Moseley, D., Eccleston, K. & Hall, E. (2003) 'A systematic review of learning styles and pedagogy.' Paper published in *Bridging Theory & Practice*, the proceedings of the European Learning Style Information Network Eighth Annual Learning Styles Conference, University of Hull, 30 June to 2 July 2003.

Coffield, F., Moseley, D., Hall, E. & Ecclestone, K. (2004) *Should We Be Using Learning Styles? What research has to say to practitioners.* [Online at http://www.LSDA.oig.uk.]

Coren, S. (1993) *Left-hander: everything you need to know about left-handedness.* London: John Murray.

Exley, S. (2003) 'The effectiveness of teaching strategies for students with dyslexia based on their preferred learning styles', *British Journal of Special Education*, 30(4), 213–220.

Galaburda, A.M. (1993) *Dyslexia and Development: neurobiological aspects of extra-ordinary brains.* Cambridge, MA: Harvard University Press.

Goswami, U. (2004) 'Neuroscience, science and special education', *British Journal of Special Education*, 31(4), 173–183.

Mortimore, T. (1998) 'A comparison of learning style in dyslexic and non-dyslexic under-graduates.' MEd Dissertation, Cardiff, University of Cardiff.

Mortimore, T. (2003a) *Dyslexia and Learning Style: a practitioner's handbook.* London: Whurr.

Mortimore, T. (2003b) 'An examination of the relationship between learning style, dyslexia and the experience of students in Higher Education.' Paper published in *Bridging Theory & Practice*, the proceedings of the European Learning Style Information Network Eighth Annual Learning Styles Conference, University of Hull, 30 June to 2 July 2003.

Riding, R.J. (1991) *The Cognitive Styles Analysis.* Birmingham: Learning and Training Technology.

Riding, R. & Rayner, S. (1998) *Cognitive Styles and Learning Strategies.* London: David Fulton Publishers.

Stenhouse, L. (1985) 'Case study methods', in J.P. Reeves (ed.) *Educational Research, Methodology and Measurement: an international handbook.* Oxford: Pergamon Press.

West, T. (1997) *In the Mind's Eye.* Buffalo, NY: Prometheus Books.

Zdzienski, D. (1997) *StudyScan.* Limerick, Ireland: ISL.

10

Mapping a Pedagogy for Special Educational Needs

Brahm Norwich and Ann Lewis

[...]

Introduction

An assumption underlying recent government documents is that the effective curriculum is, broadly, a common curriculum for all pupils. This is well illustrated in broad terms in the Green Paper on special educational needs (SEN) (Department for Education and Employment [DfEE], 1997) and more specifically in the guidelines concerning the Literacy Strategy and pupils with SEN (DfEE, 1998). Similarly, the revised national SEN specialist standards reflect, in the eliding of some SEN groups, this shift towards stressing commonalities between them (Teacher Training Agency [TTA], 1998, 1999). These developments intensify the need for an in-depth review of evidence concerning the nature of curricular provision which will facilitate progress for pupils with difficulties in learning.

There is considerable evidence that teachers attempt to differentiate their teaching according to perceptions of broad pupil ability. Brown & McIntyre (1993) reported that general and specific ability were among the enduring characteristics which teachers perceived as important when planning teaching. Similarly, Cooper & McIntyre (1996), exploring teachers' 'craft knowledge' in relation to the teaching of 11–12 year-olds, found that response to pupils perceived as being of low ability included emphasising oral explanations, providing multiple examples, using pictorial stimuli and, for pupils with writing difficulties, providing highly structured written tasks. These strategies cannot be taken as necessarily representing either a common or a SEN-specific pedagogy. The starting point for this review is to take the pedagogic justification for such differentiation as problematic and uncertain.

Setting parameters for the review

The range of this review concerning effective pedagogy for pupils perceived as having SEN is potentially very wide indeed. Consequently, we have focused our review on the teaching of

From: *British Educational Research Journal*, 27 (3), 2001, pp. 313–29.

children with various degrees of learning difficulty and have taken pedagogy to mean the cluster of decisions and actions which aim to promote school learning. In asking whether pupils with SEN need a distinct kind of pedagogy, we are asking whether they need distinct kinds of teaching to learn the same content as others without SEN. We are interested in evidence about effective pedagogy across curricular subjects (not just literacy) and in so doing whether effective pedagogy for particular groups of pupils is the same across subjects or whether this is, at least in part, subject-specific. One problematic issue concerns terminology, as the labels Moderate Learning Difficulties (MLD), Severe Learning Difficulties (SLD), SpLD, Profound Learning Difficulties (PMLD) etc. are not used consistently by researchers or practitioners over time, place or context. Consequently, a lack of correlation between SEN grouping and pedagogic practice may be reflecting the involvement of different pupil groups. Thus, systematically different pedagogic needs may exist but be confounded by lack of consistency in how particular pupil subgroups are defined by the researchers.

We are also constrained by the foci of published research reports, which have tended to focus on literacy, numeracy and/or, occasionally, aspects of motivation/self-esteem. We have been open to evidence based on quantitative and/or qualitative research paradigms. The former has tended to be associated with quasi-experimental designs and the latter with idiographic studies. We regard both types of study as potentially illuminating our focus.

Research questions

Two questions are central to our review:

1. Can differences between learners (by particular SEN group) be identified *and* systematically linked with learners' needs for differential teaching? Many studies have addressed only the first part of this question.
2. What are the key criteria for identifying pedagogically useful learner groups? The conventional SEN groupings may (a) not be valid and/or (b) not useful when planning pedagogy. But even if this is so, there may still be valid groupings of learners to identify as the base for differential pedagogy.

At the start of the review, we formulated a conceptual framework, based on Norwich (1996), which focused on the commonality–differentiation of pedagogy. Three broad kinds of pedagogic need can be identified in this framework: pedagogic needs common to all learners; pedagogic needs specific, or distinct, to groups of learners; and pedagogic needs unique to individual learners. These are discussed further in Lewis & Norwich (1999).

Discussion of issues

Effective pedagogy in general

There is an extensive literature relating to pedagogy and 'effectiveness'. This encompasses work on 'effective teaching', 'effective learning' and 'effective/improving schooling'. These have a bearing on this review, but fall outside the parameters outlined in the introduction so we will deal with them briefly. The majority of these generic 'effectiveness' works do not address the crucial question of effective for whom (Slee et al., 1998). The assumption is that effective teaching is the same for all pupils, i.e. in effect, what works is taken as leading to effective learning for all pupils. Thus, in an idealised model, any differences between pupils in terms of learning outcomes would reflect random individual differences but not systematic, group-based pedagogic needs.

The correlates of effective teaching for all learners, and without reference to particular curricular areas, although usually referenced implicitly or explicitly to numeracy and/or literacy, have been widely reviewed (e.g. Scheerens, 1989; Yates & Yates, 1990; Cooper & McIntyre, 1996; Creemers, 1997; Gipps & MacGilchrist, 1999). Such reviews point to broad features of effective pedagogy, such as clarity about the purposes of a sequence of instruction, clear lesson presentations, teaching in small, explicit steps (some disagreement about when this is appropriate), teacher modelling of 'thinking aloud', careful monitoring of pupils' attention and maximising learning time. These features have face validity but are both broad and vague. Askew et al. (1997), in a UK-based review of effective teaching of numeracy, note that some features commonly cited as indicative of effective pedagogy (e.g. whole-class question and answer teaching styles, and a mix of individualised and small group forms of classroom organisation) were found across effective and less effective teachers, suggesting that some finer grained analysis is needed.

The failure of generic studies to support the concept of valid SEN-specific pedagogies may reflect various weaknesses in design, including problems in the designation of SEN (noted earlier) and the multiple needs of individual pupils. Pupils may be given a single administrative designation (such as MLD or SLD) for school placement or provision purposes, but the single label may not reflect the multiple nature of the pupil's difficulties (e.g. SpLD as well as SLD). Consequently, at least in theory, evidence for SEN-specific pedagogies would need to examine both, e.g. MLD × pedagogy interactions, as well as MLD + SpLD × pedagogy interactions. This issue reflects the broad and overlapping nature of currently used categories in this field. A further design problem in generic SEN studies is that they may demonstrate correlations but not necessarily causal connections between broad aspects of schools or teaching and pupil learning and the identification, in a crude way, of key features of pedagogy (such as the giving of feedback).

Some more focused studies of classroom practice (for example, concerning grouping/setting) have suggested differential effects for learners of differing attainments. There is, for example, evidence that lower attaining children, in particular, benefit cognitively and linguistically from mixed attainment workgroups in some literacy and problem-solving tasks (Bennett & Cass, 1988). (See Lou et al. [1996], Slavin [1987], Hallam & Toutounji [1997] for general reviews on ability grouping at school and class levels.)

A minority of writers has noted commonality of pedagogy works in both directions (Corbett & Norwich, 1999). That is, a corollary to ideas about the transfer of effectiveness from the mainstream to SEN is that effective pedagogy for the 'mainstream' may be derived from the SEN context. Examples of this transition of 'effective pedagogy' from special to mainstream contexts is reflected in, for example, the ideas developed by Montessori and by Feuerstein.

Effective instruction

Pedagogy encompasses a wide range of variables about teaching (including, for example, sequencing of lessons, grouping arrangements, promotion of particular attitudes, selection of content, etc.) Instruction is narrower and relates to teaching of a particular target skill or set of knowledge. This narrower focus may be illuminative in terms of clarifying whether particular subgroups of pupils require different instructional procedures from other learners. In summary, critical features (varying by theoretical perspective of the researchers) tend to be seen as applicable to all learners receiving instruction and are therefore reflective of a 'common pedagogy' position. (See Engelmann & Carnine [1982], A. Brown [1988], Anderson [1990], G. Brown [1998] for particular 'fine grained' perspectives.)

One might expect that studies stemming from a presumption of difference and taking a specific SEN focus would provide a clearer base for extrapolating a valid SEN-specific pedagogy. Baker & Zigmond (1995), reviewing five contrasting sites of 'inclusive' schooling, noted the tendency for group teaching decisions to dominate both mainstream and special educators. The former focused on the class group when planning teaching and the latter on the (stereotypical) SEN group.

Many studies examine the *identification* of different pupil subgroups and there is increasing evidence that various groups (e.g. pupils with dyslexia, pupils with Down's syndrome) have distinctive group characteristics. However, it does not follow that because a subgroup of pupils is identified as different from other learners (e.g. Pitta & Gray, 1997; Jordan & Oettinger Montani, 1997, both concerning mathematics; Gresham et al., 1996, more generally), even if in a generalisable group-specific way (e.g. problems with far transfer), that effective teaching for those pupils is different from teaching other pupils. Therefore, these studies will not be examined further because they do not illuminate our fundamental questions about SEN-specific pedagogy.

Some studies and reviews (e.g. Bulgren & Carta, 1992) focus on the *behaviours* of pupils with learning difficulties. These explicate what is happening in classrooms and have shown, for example, that pupils with learning difficulties (boys in particular) tended to be more off-task, received more teacher attention, particularly for off-task behaviour, and were given fewer academic questions, shorter response times and less extended feedback than were other pupils. Nor are these directly linked with issues about differential pedagogy.

Similarly, many 'integration' studies (reviewed by Hegarty, 1993; Wang & Baker, 1985–86) have analysed classroom behaviours in different class settings (placement × classroom behaviours) or learner outcomes in different placements (placement × learner outcomes [Carlberg & Kavale, 1980]), but do not make explicit learner × pedagogy relationships. Such work does not clarify questions about effective pedagogy beyond the level of inference.

Other studies do not provide evidence about SEN-specific strategies *contrasted with* non-SEN strategies. For example, the meta-analyses discussed by Lloyd et al. (1998) examine effect sizes for various aspects of SEN-based teaching approaches (e.g. perceptual training, peer tutoring, direct instruction, mnemonic training) and discuss the relative efficacy of the various features. They start from an assumption that a SEN-specific approach is needed and are, in effect, asking, 'which of these SEN-oriented approaches is most effective?' The basis for the assumption that some sort of SEN-specific approach is needed is invariably unclear, if stated at all. Such analyses provide inferences about, but not systematic evidence for, SEN-specific pedagogy.

The following sections examine evidence about SEN group-specific learner × teaching interactions.

Low attainment

The literature search confirmed our focus on teaching studies which relate to low attainment in literacy or mathematics irrespective of IQ levels (Gresham et al., 1996). We deal in the next section, on specific learning difficulties, with whether there is a distinction between low attainment and specific learning difficulties. Research into Reading Recovery represents one of few larger-scale studies of pedagogy focused on low attainment in literacy (Clay, 1987). Reading Recovery as an early teaching intervention for literacy difficulties does not depend on discriminating between different groups of poor readers, such as specific learning difficulties (learning disability) and low reading attainers. It is a sophisticated intervention which has been used in several countries for the lowest 20% of early readers. Its aim is the correction of inadequate strategies so that the children become independent readers through individual tutoring by highly trained teachers. (See review of research on Reading Recovery by Demtre [1993] in Sylva & Hurry [1995].) One of the assumptions made by reading recovery proponents is that this programme will help those with environmentally induced difficulties and some of those with milder, organically produced difficulties (Clay, 1987). Clay's position is that those not reaching independent reading after an intervention like this need additional specialist examination and help, and that this is a more useful way to identify children with specific learning difficulties (learning disabilities). She quotes a figure of between 1 and 9 in 1000 children being referred on from Reading Recovery.

There have been a large number of interventions designed to prevent or counter low attainment and learning difficulties in specific programmes, e.g. Milwaukee Project, Head Start, Direct Instruction, or within wider approaches, e.g. adaptive instruction. (See reviews by Wang et al., 1995; Lloyd et al., 1998.) Most evaluation studies do not explore the assiduity with which such programmes have been implemented, and consequently, the key pedagogic elements, as claimed by their constructors, may be diminished or lost in translation to the classroom context. Thus, the validity of the intervention variable may be questionable. Brooks et al. (1998), in a review of UK-based schemes to raise literacy levels, concluded that 'normal schooling [i.e.] "no treatment" does not enable slow readers to catch up'. However the features of effective schemes were those one might characterise as good 'normal' pedagogy, such as embedding work on phonological skills within a broad approach, involving reading partners, and using precisely targeted information technology programs. One reading of the Brooks review is that 'normal' teaching needs to be improved, rather than radically different approaches developed for 'slow learners'.

In general, research studies involving SEN groups have reached strikingly similar conclusions to the work summarised here concerning effective pedagogy. For example, core features of adaptive instruction (Wang, 1990) are described as including:

- instruction based on assessed capabilities of each learner;
- each learner able to progress at own pace;
- periodic evaluation of learner's progress by the teacher;
- learner acquires increasing responsibility for own learning;
- alternative learning activities available;

- learners have opportunities for choice/decision-making;
- learners assist one another.

So, it is unsurprising that special educators have concluded that the efficacy of differential programmes for pupils with SEN remains without evidence. Thus, the move is towards advocacy of an amalgam of common teaching strategies informed by 'effective practice' across SEN and non-SEN contexts.

In the area of teaching literacy, there has been growing evidence that approaches which emphasise phonics have generally better outcomes for word reading and spelling than meaning and context-based approaches (Snowling, 1996). Snowling includes poor readers in this general conclusion based on studies which compare different interventions, such as Hatcher et al. (1994). Though Reading Recovery does not include explicit reference to phonology in its original design, it has been used with the inclusion of explicit phonology in its teaching approach. For example, Iverson & Tunmer (1993) compared Reading Recovery with and without phonology in a US trial and found that though both reading recovery groups made more progress than controls, those receiving phonology training learned more quickly. More recently, Sylva & Hurry (1995) conducted an English study of Reading Recovery compared to phonology training. They found that children receiving both interventions made better progress than control children in reading and writing. These outcomes were evident 1 year after the end of the interventions. However, Reading Recovery was the more powerful intervention over a wider range of skills and with greater gains than the phonology intervention. It was also more effective with more socially disadvantaged pupils.

It has been commented that the effects of Reading Recovery after 1 year were less striking, with the advantage over within-school controls no longer being significant. The phonology intervention also did not run for as long as the Reading Recovery one (Snowling, 1996). However, in a subsequent 2-year follow-up, it was found that neither Reading Recovery nor phonological training were significantly better than controls. Both interventions were ahead of controls on average, but the effects were of the order of 3–4 months (reading age) (Hurry & Sylva, 1998). It was also found that while only phonological training had a significant effect on spelling, Reading Recovery was especially effective with pupils who were non-readers at the start. The implications of this longer follow-up were taken to be that early intervention could be effective but that it needed continued relevant support in the longer term.

Recent UK research into the class teaching of early reading (ER) has examined a framework and approach which integrates children's learning of phonological skills with other aspects of teaching reading to establish transfer to everyday class contexts (Solity et al., 1999). What is distinctive about this approach is that teaching is distributed across the day and emphasis is on skill fluency and generalisation. It teaches phonological skills, phonic skills and sight vocabulary skills based on the same instructional principles for all learners and not on individual differences. Compared to conventional teaching over a 2-year intervention period, the ER reception year groups were on average well above chronological age (CA) while the conventional groups were below. The lowest 25% of pupils receiving ER were 5 months below CA compared to 15 months for the conventional teaching group. Comparisons with pupils receiving the National Literacy Project (NLP) also showed advantages to the ER groups. In a further research phase, an additional intervention was introduced for lower achieving pupils (5 months below CA) in two ER classes. In addition to their three sessions per day as part of the ER framework, they received further distributed group teaching which made goals and principles of teaching explicit, used a wide range of books to promote generalisation, and teaching was done in-class by the class teacher. After 6 months of this, they had made enough progress on average to bring them within 4 months of their CA level.

What distinguishes the ER framework from the NLP, and now the National Literacy Strategy (NLS), is the use of distributed training rather than the literacy hour. In addition, ER focuses on phonemes at the word level and does not mix its strategies by including larger units, such as onsets-rimes. It also teaches synthesis and segmentation in a way that enables generalisation to unfamiliar words. The ER approach does recognise lower attainers in literacy, even if they achieve at higher levels than low attainers in conventional teaching. These low attainers seem to benefit from additional ER-type teaching, though there is no evidence whether some of these reach CA level. These pupils may be amongst those who are conventionally thought to have persistent specific difficulties in literacy.

Specific learning difficulties (Dyslexia)

There are continuing differences of position about the nature of specific learning difficulties and their distinction from lower attainment and general difficulties in learning, such as moderate learning difficulties. Much more research work has also been done on defining and explaining specific difficulties than on the effectiveness of different teaching approaches (Connor, 1994). It has also been noted that studies of differences between groups experiencing difficulties and typical learners do not necessarily identify factors which are causal of the difficulties and therefore relevant to teaching objectives (Reason et al., 1988). Clay (1987) expresses a commonly held position that given the difficulties in discriminating specific learning difficulties as a discrete kind of learning difficulty, it would be useful to focus on intervention studies. (See Reason et al. [1999] for a current review of issues and assessment options.)

The relevance of phonological interventions for pupils with specific learning difficulties has been demonstrated in various recent US studies (Torgeson et al., 1994; Herrara et al., 1997), though there have been few in the UK (Brooks, 1995). Boyle & Walker-Seibert (1997) have noted that there have been until recently few systematic studies with specific identified kinds of difficulties that examine the impact on wider word reading and not just the specific skills under training. These authors showed in a small-scale US study that pupils designated as having learning disabilities (LD) can make progress in their phonological and word reading skills through an intensive programme (12 weeks). These researchers advise that such interventions need to be continued over these pupils' school career. Brooks (1995), through using a single case study, has shown that structure in teaching in itself was not enough for a boy described as having 'phonological dyslexia'. A visual and semantic teaching approach was shown to be effective, illustrating the importance of gearing interventions to the individual and not just relying on approaches from group-based studies.

Most of the aforementioned interventions involve individual teaching outside mainstream classes. By contrast, there has been one large-scale US experimental study which has included pupils with LD in mainstream class study of a cooperative approach to reading and writing (Stevens & Slavin, 1995). This was the 2-year study of the impact of the cooperative integrated reading and comprehension programme (CIRC) on 7–12 year-olds. CIRC pupils work in mixed ability cooperative groups, using group goals and individual accountability, on reading and writing related to stories which they are reading. Teachers give the pupils explicit instruction on comprehension strategies and use a writing process approach to teach writing. Results for all pupils showed that CIRC pupils had a higher vocabulary, comprehension and language expression, with greater meta-cognitive aware-ness and a positive impact on attitudes to reading and writing. About 10% of pupils were considered to have LD in both CIRC and control schools overall. In the control schools, they had withdrawal specialist teaching for 30 minutes a day, spending the rest of their time in mainstream lessons. In the CIRC class, the special education teachers team taught with the mainstream class teachers and the pupils were included in the cooperative groups. The CIRC pupils with LD showed better reading, vocabulary, comprehension and language expression scores than comparison pupils with LD. A further US study using the CIRC approach (Jenkins et al., 1994) produced similar positive outcomes. The impact was greater on pupils identified as needing special education, most designated as having LD.

There has been continuing interest by special educators in interventions which focus on presumed underlying processing difficulties, what have been called process interventions. Considerable time and effort has been expended over the decades in attempting to resolve questions about the effectiveness of these approaches. The process intervention areas, especially in the USA, cover the fields of psycho-linguistic and perceptual-motor training and modality testing and teaching. One response to the continuing equivocation about these approaches has been the use of quantitative meta-analyses (Kavale, 1981). In a summary of meta-analyses, Kavale & Dobbins (1993) show that although psycho-linguistic training has a small impact overall, there is a more significant impact for the verbal expression area. By contrast, the meta-analyses show that perceptual-motor interventions are not bene-ficial. Nor is there meta-analytic evidence that the longstanding interest in modality testing and teaching (aptitude × treatment interactions) can be supported as beneficial. These analyses show considerable variation in the effect sizes between different studies, with many mean effect sizes being less than the variation between the highest and lowest effect sizes.

In a recent review of interventions in the specific learning difficulties field, Connor (1994) expresses a commonly held perspective that step-by-step approaches to reading involving skills in a bottom-up approach can be reconciled with meaning or apprenticeship (top-down approaches). This emphasis on a range of approaches is seen to be particularly important for pupils with literacy difficulties as too much attention can be focused on skills and not meaningful reading and writing. Connor also stresses the role of self-esteem, confidence and parental support, though there are few comparative well-designed studies relating interventions and affective outcomes. Connor agrees with Veluntino (1987) that specialist approaches have much in common with teaching literacy to any pupil, though there is a tendency towards the bottom-up approaches (phonics, phonological awareness). Other differences, according to Veluntino, involve the degree of structure, detail, continuous assessment, record-keeping and overlearning. Snowling (1996), in her review, also argues for the compatibility between literacy teaching which combines phonic and whole-language approaches. She concludes that pupils with reading difficulties, including those with specific learning difficulties (dyslexia), benefit most from teaching which combines a focus on reading and phonological skills and the links between them. Reason et al. (1988), in another review, concluded that there was nothing specific about the teaching of pupils with specific learning difficulties. All pupils required suitable 'cocktails' that reflected individual strengths, weaknesses and needs. In a more recent review, Reason et al. (1999) note that there is less of a gap between what is 'done for all and what is done for children with specific learning difficulties':

> In principle, those learning more slowly need more time to learn and more deliberate planning to ensure progress. (1999, p. 79)

This convergence is evident in the recent national development in the teaching of literacy (NLS) to all pupils to include elements of phonological skills. The growing consensus is that there are common approaches to teaching literacy for the diversity, including those with specific learning difficulties. However, the focus on more explicit and intense interventions (Torgeson et al., 1994) for those at risk or with literacy difficulties can mean differences in actual programmes and something additional that is not needed by most pupils.

There is little systematic research into teaching pupils with low mathematics attainment and specific mathematics learning difficulties by comparison with the teaching of literacy. General issues in relation to mathematics teaching and SEN have been addressed in [the UK] through projects and in texts (Denvir et al., 1982; Anghileri & Daniels, 1995). Jones et al. (1997), in a recent US review of mathematics teaching to secondary aged pupils with LD, argue that current research can, nevertheless, indicate what the issues are and indicate procedures associated with effective teaching. Studies show that pupils with LD have difficulties with basic operations and the language of mathematics. As pupils experience increasing failures, they also develop negative expectations about learning mathematics and develop motivational orientations which undermine their future mathematics learning. Jones et al. draw on the work of Carnine and colleagues on instructional design (Carnine, 1997) as relevant here. Examples used in teaching concepts are considered critical as pupils with learning difficulties frequently receive insufficient examples to attain mastery. The range of examples selected is also often inadequate. Explicitness is another crucial feature in Carnine's scheme for the effective teaching of pupils with learning difficulties. Without explicit instructional priorities, as Jones contends, pupils with low attainment and specific learning difficulties are less likely to master fractions, decimals, percentages, ratios or proportions.

Though open to different interpretations, direct instruction can be understood to involve an approach which is teacher-led, has explicit outcome expectations, systematic prompting, structured practice, monitoring of attainments and corrective feedback and reinforcement (Jones et al., 1997). Pupils with specific learning difficulties (related to LD in US terms) also generally require more practice, and practice that is well designed, than other pupils. Like other pupils, they need to be actively engaged in managing their learning, though they tend to have difficulties in applying learning and performance strategies. However, evidence from various US studies has shown that such pupils can be taught to use and apply such strategies (Pressley et al., 1989).

Pupils with Moderate Learning Difficulties (MLD)

Many pupils labelled as MLD have no known organic cause for their learning difficulties. There have been relatively few systematic studies of the characteristics of these pupils and problems in defining this pupil group have been widely acknowledged. It was not possible to come to MLD-specific conclusions in relation to our three main foci of literacy, numeracy and self-esteem. Our findings concurred with Dyson (1999) that 'There is little evidence of a systematic attempt to develop a MLD pedagogy, but lots of evidence of multiple local initiatives'. There is no 'MLD curriculum' as such except as a nebulous and/or narrow variant of the 'mainstream curriculum' or a nebulous and broader version of the 'developmental curriculum'.

Very few experimental studies were found in which pupils with MLD were identified and given selective teaching approaches. However, there was a suggestion from one such study (Mastropieri et al., 1997) that, in science, pupils with Mild Mental Retardation (MMR) may need to be told the general rule initially and then coached on the application of the rule (whereas other pupils could learn the rule inductively from the outset).

One group of pupils within the MLD/SLD groups are children with Down's syndrome. Children with Down's syndrome are characterised by bio behavioural homogeneity, although reflecting a wide spectrum of capability. A range of carefully designed studies by Wishart and her co-workers (e.g. Wishart, 1990, 1993) is pointing to systematic differences between the learning of children with Down's syndrome and other children. In summary, a number of researchers in this field have argued that the developmental differences in children with Down's syndrome indicate the need for different teaching strategies. These include: error-free (not trial and error) learning and the use of novelty to counter a tendency to perseverate. Such work is suggestive of but does not examine directly the validity of a group-specific pedagogy for these pupils.

Fuchs & Fuchs (1995, 1998) make a case for a special educational pedagogy. They argue, having reviewed a wide range of interventions, that there are two distinctive features of a SEN-specific pedagogy. These are 'the use of empirically validated procedures' and 'an intensive, data-based focus on individual students' which they group under the term 'curriculum based measurement' (CBM). They do not distinguish between learning difficulties subgroups. Fuchs & Fuchs conclude that general educators' teaching skills could be enhanced through training in CBM techniques but some pupils (with learning disabilities, possibly overlapping the 'MLD'/SpLD groups), being unresponsive to such an adapted classroom, need 'specifically individualised instruction, the small size instructional groups, and the more highly trained teachers available through special education' (1998, p. 31). One might characterise Fuchs & Fuchs's pedagogical position as one of a common pedagogy underpinned by this individual-oriented approach.

Pupils with Severe or Profound and Multiple Learning Difficulties (SLD/PMLD)

Ware (1997) discusses the problematic notion of progress concerning these pupils and in what terms it is to be defined. Her review of evidence concerning a SEN-specific pedagogy for pupils with SLD or PMLD (Ware, 1999) highlights the multiplicity of impairments which these children may experience, the commonality of children's underlying needs and the considerable impact of personality factors (e.g. perseverance and motivation) on the learning of pupils with PMLD. These pupils may also, unlike the other groups reviewed here, be likely to be receiving one or more forms of regular medication which may interfere with their learning.

The importance of establishing these pupils' readiness for learning is a strong theme in work by practitioners in this field (e.g. Longhorn, 1993; Ouvry & Saunders, 1996). Sensory approaches have been presented by a number of writers as valuable mechanisms at this and initial stages of learning. Physical or sensory 'readiness' for learning is an aspect of the teaching/learning process which is rarely considered for other pupils. (In the EBD field, a similar issue of readiness to learn tends to be approached from a motivational angle.)

Behavioural approaches to the teaching of pupils with SLD/PMLD have been popular and while they remain so with some writers (e.g. Ouvry & Saunders, 1996; Farrell, 1997), others (e.g. Hewett & Nind, 1992) have argued for more interactive approaches to be developed. These latter approaches may be seen as different from effective pedagogy with other pupils in terms of, for example, provision of a continuous running commentary (Hewett & Nind, 1992). However, many interactive approaches are strongly reminiscent of work with non-disabled pupils (e.g. Grove, 1998).

Intervention studies for pupils with SLD/PMLD constitute a highly specialised and fragmented collection. Particular conditions (e.g. pupils with autistic spectrum disorders, spina bifida) have been associated with various programmes, often contrasting in their underlying rationale. Evaluations of interventions with these pupils tend to be small scale ($n < 15$), but intensive. They often involve children with highly individualised patterns of functioning, compounding behavioural and cognitive difficulties. We found no studies in which explicit and systematic comparisons were made between different types of pedagogic intervention for these pupils or in which some other form of systematic experimental control enabled reliable judgements to be made about SEN-specific compared with other pedagogy.

Bray et al. (1988), in reviewing the education of children with profound and multiple learning difficulties, concluded that work in this field was increasingly approximating to what was recognised as good mainstream teaching. A contrasting view was taken by Hodapp (1998) in a review of work on organic causes of learning difficulties. Hodapp noted that children with severe abnormalities, as shown by EEG traces, appeared not to show similar developmental sequences in cognitive development to those of other children. However, the considerable problems in conducting valid and reliable assessments of these children necessitates caution about this conclusion.

A middle position is reflected in a comprehensive review (Jordan et al., 1998) into educational interventions for children with autism. Their summaries of others' meta-analyses of features of successful intervention programmes point to a combination of 'common pedagogy' and SEN-specific features. The former, common features, includes reference to the involvement of parents and the importance of social interaction. More specialised features include the need for routine, the use of visual cueing and explicit teaching of specific generalisation strategies. The inference from this review is that pupils with autism do need some pedagogical strategies which differ from those used routinely with other children. It is not clear how specific to the autistic group such strategies may be.

Similarly Ware's (1999) article, connected with this review, noted areas of commonality between PMLD and other learners but also cited various studies showing differences between the groups in terms of learning strategy. For example, she cited work by Barber & Goldbart showing that learners with PMLD did not, except in very limited situations, learn to modify attention-getting strategies which were ineffective. She also made the broader point that in general, pupils with PMLD, compared with developmentally or chronologically matched peers, spend a larger proportion of their time in states which are not conducive to learning. Thus, checking and ensuring preparedness for learning is particularly important for teachers of these pupils.

Overall, the literature on teaching interventions for pupils with severe, profound or multiple learning difficulties provides some support for differences in emphases in pedagogical practice; for example, towards a greater need to check that the pupil is in a 'ready' state for learning. Arguably, this is different in degree, but not in kind, from checking, with a mainstream class, that all the pupils are paying attention when instructions are being given to the whole class. Linked with this, Bray et al. (1988) cite work suggesting that instructional strategies are less important determinants of children's learning than are some qualitative aspects of teacher–child interaction (e.g. expectations). These may be particularly important for pupils who are very dependant on adult interaction (for example, for basic care). Further, if pupil–pupil interactions are as significant in fostering cognitive gains as much recent constructivist work suggests, then pupils with profound or multiple learning difficulties may be considerably disadvantaged through their limited communication with other children. Teaching of these pupils may need to address this directly as otherwise they may be missing a multitude of serendipitous and beneficial interactions with other pupils.

Discussion and conclusions

In our review, we have found a trend away from SEN-specific pedagogies which emerged in various ways. This took the form of generic teaching effectiveness studies which assumed that what works *with most pupils* would also work for *all pupils*. The outcomes of these studies are general teaching principles which might apply to all pupils. However, little direct evidence for this has been presented in the areas of learning difficulties which we have covered in this review. Even if these principles, such as the teacher provides the learner with feedback, are general enough to be applicable to all learners, a general principle like this is too imprecise. Even when a more specific principle is applicable to all learners, it may need to be applied in practice in different ways for those with learning difficulties. This distinction between common teaching principles and strategies and different practical ways of applying and implementing them for pupils with difficulties in learning is a crucial one.

The trend away from SEN-specific pedagogies was also evident in some position papers and chapters by SEN specialists. Though mostly unsubstantiated by empirical evidence, these expressed what we have called the *unique differences* position. This rejects distinctive SEN teaching strategies and accepts that there are common pedagogic principles which are relevant to the unique differences between all pupils, including those considered to be designated as having SEN. However, this position is qualified by some recognition of the need for more intense and focused teaching for those with SEN. This qualification relates to the aforementioned distinction between pedagogic principles and practical ways of applying them in particular cases and situations.

The trend away from SEN-specific pedagogies is also evident in studies which look retrospectively for learner differences in generic studies as well as studies which take a specific SEN group focus. However, many studies examine the learning characteristics of various subgroups (such as Down's syndrome) and show general differences between the SEN and non-SEN groups. Though these differences may suggest differences in teaching, they do not show that distinctive teaching is optimal for these subgroups. Other studies either focus on classroom learning behaviours or learning outcomes in terms of different placements (special versus mainstream schools and classes). They also do not show SEN-specific learner × teaching interactions.

The lack of evidence in our review to support SEN-specific pedagogies might be surprising as there is a persistent sense that special education means special pedagogy to many teachers and researchers. In not finding these distinctive pedagogies, we can [...] hold on to the hunch that such special pedagogies do exist and that the research is failing to identify them but will do so in time. One option is to consider that teaching decisions may, in theory, still come to be based on distinctive pedagogies, but that the bases of the general groups to which they apply have not yet been identified. More pedagogically relevant groups may be identified in terms of learning process, such as learning styles (Read, 1998), than in terms of general patterns of attainment and current cognitive abilities (e.g. MLD, SpLD). If what we have called the *general differences* position to teaching pupils with SEN is to be maintained, then it is likely to be along these lines.

Alternatively, we may reject a distinctive SEN pedagogy perspective and accept the commonality of pedagogy because SEN subgroups (MLD, SpLD and so on) are not associated with specific pedagogies. As Skrtic (1999) argues, all pupils have unique learning needs which call for decisions about teaching to be informed through individual assessment. This is an expression of what we have called the *unique differences* position. However, the unique differences position, expressed in this way, is not the end of the matter. Our review indicates that although common teaching principles and strategies are relevant to the subgroups we have considered, more intensive and explicit teaching is also relevant to pupils with different patterns and degrees of difficulties in learning. At this point in the conclusion, we need to recall that the subgroups we have considered do not represent categorically distinct groupings, but a range of pupils along continua of attainment and current cognitive abilities. There are many pupils whose difficulties in learning make it hard to place them clearly in one or other subgroup as this depends on where cut-offs between the subgroups are drawn. This is what has been called the continuum of SEN, which has usually been matched with a continuum of special provision. The continuum of special provision refers to the different kinds of settings, organisational and staffing arrangements, from the most integrated (mainstream classes without any additional support) to the most segregated (residential special schooling). What has been missing in talk about continua of special needs and special provision has been the notion of *continua of teaching or pedagogic approaches*. The concept of a continuum implies that there are differences of degree, so by teaching continua we mean that the various strategies and procedures which make up teaching can be considered in terms of whether they are used more or less in practice. It is also important at this stage in the discussion to remember that some pupils with SEN might need more of common teaching approaches at some times, but some distinct kinds of teaching at other times. This could be relevant to other areas of SEN which we have not considered in this review.

The position we have developed is also consistent with other research which shows how pupils with different kinds of learning difficulties are not provided for adequately in general class teaching. For example, teachers have been shown to move on before low attainers have reached mastery (Silbert et al., 1990). Such research indicates the need for more practice time. This would be one of the strands of teaching which can be considered to lie along a continuum. From this review, we suggest that there are other facets of teaching where additional emphasis on common teaching approaches is required, depending on the individual learning needs of those with learning difficulties covered here – for example, more practice to achieve mastery, more examples to learn concepts, more experience of transfer, and more careful checking for preparedness for the next stage of learning. In proposing the notion of continua of teaching approaches, we are not suggesting that practical instances of teaching at distant points on the continua do not look distinct or different. However, teaching which emphasises high levels of practice to mastery, more examples of a concept, more error-free learning, more bottom-up phonological approaches to literacy, for instance, is not qualitatively different from teaching which involves less emphasis on these approaches.

[…]

References

Anderson, J.R. (1990) *The Adaptive Character of Thought* (Hove, Lawrence Earlbaum).

Anghileri, J. & Daniels, H. (1995) *Secondary School Mathematics and Special Educational Needs* (London, Cassell).

Askew, M., Brown, M., Johnson, D., Rhodes, V. & William, D. (1997) *Effective Teachers of Numeracy* (London, Teacher Training Agency).

Baker, J. & Zigmond, N. (1995) The meaning and practice of inclusion for students with learning disabilities: themes and implications from the five cases, *Journal of Special Education,* 29, pp. 163–180.

Bennett, N. & Cass, A. (1988) The effects of group composition on group interactive processes and pupil understanding, *British Educational Research Journal,* 15, pp. 19–32.

Boyle, J.R. & Walker-Seibert, T. (1997) The effects of phonological awareness strategy on the reading skills of children with mild difficulties, *Learning Disability,* 8, pp. 143–153.

Bray, A., McArthur, J. & Ballard, K.D. (1988) Education for pupils with profound disabilities: issues of policy, curriculum, teaching methods and evaluation, *European Journal of Special Needs Education,* 3, pp. 207–223.

Brooks, G., Flanagan, N., Henkhuzens, Z. & Hutchison, D. (1998) *What Works for Slow Readers? The Effectiveness of Early Intervention Schemes* (Slough, National Foundation for Educational Research).

Brooks, P. (1995) A comparison of the effectiveness of different teaching strategies in teaching spelling to a student with severe specific learning difficulties/dyslexia, *Educational and Child Psychology,* 12, pp. 80–88.

Brown, A.L. (1988) Motivation to learn and understand: on taking charge of one's own learning, *Cognition and Instruction,* 5, pp. 311–321.

Brown, G. (1998) The endpoint of reading instruction: the ROAR model, in: J.L. Metsala & L.C. Ehri (Eds) *Word Recognition in Beginning Literacy* (Mahwah, NJ, LEA).

Brown, S. & McIntyre, D. (1993) *Making Sense of Teaching* (Buckingham, Open University Press).

Bulgren, J.A. & Carta, J.L. (1992) Examining the instructional contexts of students with learning disabilities, *Exceptional Children,* 59, pp. 182–191.

Carlberg, C. & Kavale, K. (1980) The efficacy of special versus regular class placement for exceptional children: a meta-analysis. *Journal of Special Education,* 14, pp. 295–309.

Carnine, D. (1997) Instructional design in mathematics for students with disabilities, *Journal of Learning Disabilities.* 2, pp. 130–141.

Clay, M. (1987) Learning to be learning disabled, *New Zealand Journal of Educational Studies,* 22, pp. 155–165.

Connor, M. (1994) Specific learning difficulty (dyslexia) and interventions, *Support for Learning,* pp. 114–119.

Cooper, P. & McIntyre, D. (1996) *Effective Teaching and Learning* (Buckingham, Open University Press).

Corbett, J. & Norwich, B. (1999) Learners with special educational needs, in: P. Mortimore (Ed.) *Understanding Pedagogy and its Impact on Learning* (London, Sage).

Creemers, B. (1997) *Effective Schools and Effective Teachers: an International Perspective* (Coventry, University of Warwick, CREPE Occasional Paper).

Denvir, B., Stolz, C. & Brown, M. (1982) *Low Attainers in Mathematics 5–16: Problems and Practices in School* (London, Methuen).

Department for Education (DfEE) (1997) *Excellence for All Children* (London, The Stationery Office).

Department for Education (DfEE) (1998) *National Literacy Strategy: Additional Guidance. Children with Special Educational Needs* (London, DfEE).

Dyson, A. (1999) Children with moderate learning difficulties, presentation to *Mapping a SEN Pedagogy, invited seminar, British Educational Research Association, National Events Programme,* University of London, April.

Engelmann, S. & Carnine, D. (1982) *Theory of Instruction: Principles and Applications* (New York, Irvington).

Farrell, P. (1997) *Teaching Pupils with Learning Difficulties: Strategies and Solutions* (London, Cassell).

Fuchs, D. & Fuchs, L. (1995) What's 'special' about special education? *Phi Delta Kappan,* March, pp. 522–530.

Fuchs, L.S. & Fuchs, D. (1998) General educators' instructional adaptations for students with learning disabilities, *Learning Disability Quarterly,* 21, pp. 23–33.

Gipps, C. & MacGilchrist, B. (1999) Primary school learners in understanding, in: P. Mortimore (Ed.) *Understanding Pedagogy and its Impact on Learning* (London, Sage).

Gresham, F.M., Macmillan, D.L. & Bocian, K.M. (1996) Learning disabilities, low achievement, and mild mental retardation: more alike than different? *Journal of Learning Disabilities,* pp. 570–581.

Grove, N. (1998) *Literature for All* (London, David Fulton).

Hallam, S. & Toutounji, L. (1997) *What Do We Know about the Grouping of Pupils by Ability?* (London, University of London, Institute of Education).

Hatcher, P.J., Hulme, C. & Ellis, A.W. (1994) Ameliorating early reading failure by integrating the teaching of reading and phonological skills: the phonological linkage hypothesis. *Child Development,* 65, pp. 41–57.

Hegarty, S. (1993) Reviewing the literature on integration, *European Journal of Special Needs Education,* 8, pp. 194–200.

Herrara, J.A., Logan, C.H., Cooker, P.G., Morris, D.P. & Lyman, D.E. (1997) Phonological awareness and phonetic-graphic conversion: a study of the effects on two interventions paradigms with learning disability children. Learning disability or learning difference? *Reading Improvement,* 32, pp. 71–89.

Hewett, D. & Nind, M. (1992) Returning to the basics: a curriculum at Harpenbury Hospital School, in: T. Booth, W. Swann, M. Masterton & P. Potts (Eds) *Learning for All I: Curricula for Diversity in Education,* pp. 200–210 (Buckingham, Open University Press).

Hodapp, R. (1998) *Development and Disabilities – Intellectual, Sensory and Motor Impairments* (Cambridge, Cambridge University Press).

Hurry, J. & Sylva, K. (1998) *Long Term Effects of Early Intervention for Children with Reading Difficulties* (London, Qualifications and Curriculum Authority).

Iversen, S. & Tunmer, W.E. (1993) Phonological skills and the reading recovery programme, *Journal of Educational Psychology,* 85, pp. 112–126.

Jenkins, J., Lewell, M., Leicester, N., O'Connor, R., Jenkins, L. & Troutner, N. (1994) Accommodations for individual differences without classroom ability groups: an experiment in school restructuring, *Exceptional Children,* 60, pp. 344–358.

Jones, E.D., Wilson, R. & Bhojwani, S. (1997) Mathematics instruction for secondary students with learning disabilities, *Journal of Learning Disabilities,* 30, pp. 151–163.

Jordan, N.C. & Oettinger Montani, T. (1997) Cognitive arithmetic and problem solving: a comparison of children with specific and general mathematics difficulties, *Journal of Learning Disabilities,* 30, pp. 624–634.

Jordan, R., Jones, G. & Murray, D. (1998) *Educational Interventions for Children with Autism: a literature review of recent and current research,* DfEE Research Report RR 77 (London, Department for Education and Employment).

Kavale, K.A. (1981) The potential advantages of meta-analyses techniques for research in special education, *Journal of Special Education,* 18, pp. 61–72.

Kavale, K.A. & Dobbins, D.A. (1993) The equivocal nature of special education interventions, *Early Child Development and Care,* 86, pp. 23–37.

Lewis, A. & Norwich, B. (1999) Mapping a pedagogy for special educational needs, *Research Intelligence,* 69, pp. 6–8.

Lloyd, J.W., Forness, S.R. & Kavale, K.A. (1998) Some methods are more effective than others, *Intervention in School and Clinic,* 33, pp. 195–200.

Longhorn, F. (1993) *Prerequisites for Learning for Very Special People* (Woking, Catalyst).

Lou, Y., Abrami, P.C., Spence, J.C., Poulsen, C., Chambers, B. & D'Apollonia, S. (1996) Within class grouping: a meta analysis, *Review of Educational Research,* 66, pp. 423–458.

Mastropieri, M.A., Scruggs, T.E. & Butcher, K. (1997) How effective is inquiry learning for students with mild disabilities? *Journal of Special Education,* 31, pp. 199–211.

Norwich, B. (1996) *Special Needs Education, Inclusive Education or Just Education for All.* Inaugural Talk, London University, Institute of Education.

Ouvry, C. & Saunders, S. (1996) Pupils with profound and multiple learning difficulties, in: B. Carpenter, R. Ashdown & K. Bovair (Eds) *Enabling Access: Effective Teaching and Learning for Pupils with Learning Difficulties,* pp. 201–217 (London, David Fulton).

Pitta, D. & Gray, E. (1997) In the mind … what can imagery tell us about success and failure in arithmetic? in: G.A. Makrides (Ed.) *Proceedings of the First Mediterranean Conference on Mathematics,* Nicosia, Cyprus, pp. 29–41 (Cyprus, University of Nicosia Press).

Pressley, M., Symons, S., Snyder, B.L. & Cariglia-Bull, T. (1989) Strategy instruction has come of age, *Learning Disability Quarterly,* 12, pp. 16–30.

Read, G. (1998) Promoting inclusion through learning styles, in: C. Tilstone, L. Florian & R. Rose (Eds) *Promoting Inclusive Practice,* pp. 128–137 (London, Routledge).

Reason, R., Brown, B., Cole, M. & Gregory, M. (1988) Does the specific in specific learning difficulties make a difference in the way we teach? *Support for Learning,* 3, pp. 230–236.

Reason, R., Frederickson, N., Heffernan, M., Martin, C. & Woods, K. (1999) *Dyslexia, Literacy and Psychological Assessment,* Draft Report by a Working Party of the Division of Educational and Child Psychology (Leicester, British Psychological Society).

Scheerens, J. (1989) *Effective Schooling: Research, Theory and Practice* (London, Cassell).

Silbert, J., Carnine, D. & Stein, M. (1990) *Direct Instruction Mathematics,* 2nd edn (Columbus, OH, Merrill).

Skrtic, T.M. (1999) Learning disabilities as organisational pathologies, in: R.J. Sternberg & L. Spear-Swirling (Eds) *Perspectives on Learning Disabilities,* pp. 193–226 (New York, Westview Press).

Slavin, R.L. (1987) Ability grouping in elementary schools: do we really know nothing until we know everything? *Review of Educational Research,* 57, pp. 347–350.

Slee, R., Weiner, G. & Tomlinson, S. (Eds) (1998) *School Effectiveness for Whom?* (London, Falmer Press).

Snowling, M.J. (1996) Contemporary approaches to the teaching of reading, *Journal of Child Psychology and Psychiatry,* 37, pp. 139–148.

Solity, J., Deavers, R. & Kerfoot, S. (1999) The early reading research: implications for word level work within the National Literacy Strategy, paper for *Office for Standards in Education seminar, The importance of phonics in learning to read and write,* 29 April.

Stevens, R.J. & Slavin, R.E. (1995) Effects of co-operative learning approaches in reading and writing on academically handicapped and nonhandicapped students, *Elementary School Journal,* 95, pp. 241–262.

Sylva, K. & Hurry, J. (1995) *Early Intervention in Children with Reading Difficulties: an Evaluation of Reading Recovery and a Phonological Training,* Thomas Coram Research Unit Report. London, School Curriculum and Assessment Authority.

TTA (1998) *National Standards for Special Educational Needs Coordination* (London, TTA).

TTA (1999) *National Special Educational Needs Specialist Standards* (London, TTA).

Torgeson, J.K., Wagner, R.K. & Rashotte, C.A. (1994) Longitudinal studies of phonological processing and reading, *Journal of Learning Disabilities,* 27, pp. 276–286.

Veluntino, F. (1987) Dyslexia, *Scientific American,* 256, pp. 34–41.

Wang, M.C. (1990) Learning characteristics of students with special needs and the provision of effective schooling, in: M.C. Wang, M.C. Reynolds & H.J. Walberg (Eds) *Special Education Research and Practice: Synthesis of Findings,* pp. 1–34 (Oxford, Pergamon).

Wang, M. & Baker, E. (1985–86) Mainstreaming programs: design features and effects, *Journal of Special Education,* 19, pp. 503–521.

Wang, M.C., Reynolds, M.C. & Walberg, H.J. (1995) *Handbook of Special and Remedial Education: research and practice* (Oxford, Elsevier).

Ware, J. (1997) Education, progress and pupils with profound and multiple learning difficulties, *Curriculum,* 18, pp. 28–36.

Ware, J. (1999) Children with severe and profound learning difficulties, presentation to *Mapping a SEN pedagogy, invited seminar, British Educational Research Association National Events Programme,* University of London, Institute of Education, April.

Wishart, J.G. (1990) Learning to learn: the difficulties faced by children and young people with Down's syndrome, in: W.I. Fraser (Ed.) *Key Issues in Research in Mental Retardation,* pp. 249–261 (London, Routledge).

Wishart, J.G. (1993) The development of learning difficulties in children with Down's syndrome, *Journal of Intellectual Disability Research,* 37, pp. 389–403.

Yates, G.C.R. & Yates, S.M. (1990) Teacher effectiveness research: towards describing user-friendly classroom instruction, *Educational Psychology,* 10, pp. 225–238.

11

Shaping Literacy in the Secondary School: Policy, Practice and Agency in the Age of the National Literacy Strategy

Andy Goodwyn and Kate Findlay

[...]

Introduction

That literacy is one of the key issues in almost all education systems is now axiomatic. What is especially striking is that those English speaking educational systems[1] that have the longest established tradition of teaching literacy to their populations seem to have developed an almost obsessive concern with literacy over the last decade of the twentieth century. We have discussed elsewhere (Goodwyn and Findlay, 1998) how the term's rise to dominance is somewhat paradoxical. For most of the twentieth century, it was almost exclusively discussed in relation to *illiteracy,* especially amongst adults; currently its use as *literacy* is prevalent, implying an entitlement and level of competence required by all post-industrial economies. This emergent definition is in itself much contested and we shall return to this point.

Our ongoing research (for a summary, see Goodwyn, 2002) has coincided with official policy initiatives which have promoted a particular version of literacy in schools. In 1997, a National Literacy Strategy (NLS) was introduced in England, its principal initial focus being primary schools. However, it was always clear that the strategy would influence secondary schools and later it became apparent that the strategy itself would be continued into the secondary phase. The historical context for these recent developments may be summarised, focusing chiefly on key documents, as a timeline (see Fig. 11.1).

We begin the timeline in 1975 because the Language Across the Curriculum movement has some parallels with the current strategy, but more fundamentally makes an interesting contrast with the NLS. It evolved from the educational research of the 'London' school (for an account, see Ball *et al.,* 1992), chiefly represented by Britton, Barnes, Martin, Rosen *et al.* who argued for a review of schooling *in line with a new focus on language and learning across the curriculum* and for a national initiative to reform the way language was used by

From: *British Journal of Educational Studies*, 51 (1), 2003, pp. 20–35.

1973	Bullock Committee established to investigate falling reading standards
1975	The Bullock Report: A Language for Life
1975–1985	Language Across the Curriculum movement
1984	HMI – English 5–16
1986	HMI – Responses to English 5–16
1988	The Kingman Report
1989	The Cox Report/National Curriculum
1993	Revision to the National Curriculum
1995	Further revisions to the National Curriculum
1995	National Literacy Project
1997	The Labour Party National Literacy Task Force
1997	National Literacy Strategy pilot projects
1998	NLS full implementation Key Stages 1 and 2 Framework for teaching introduced
1998–9	The National Year of Reading
1999	NLS review of research. Literacy conferences for secondary schools and training packs sent to LEAs and schools
2000	First Evaluation report of Ontario Institute for the Study of Education (OISE)
2000	Pilot of secondary 'framework' (all schools encouraged to be pro-active)
2001	Framework for English/whole school literacy
2001	Second report of OISE evaluation
2002–3	Full implementation of Framework in KS3

Figure 11.1

teachers and understood by students *in all subject areas*. For our purposes, the key issue is that the government inquiry into falling standards of reading was completely overtaken by the work of the London school and became a very different project called 'Language Across the Curriculum' (LAC), around the slogan 'every teacher is a teacher of language'. The official publication, The Bullock Report, subtitled 'A Language for Life' (DES, 1975), was essentially a manifesto of the London group. The project was never 'official' government policy but was taken up enthusiastically by Local Education Authorities, their schools and by teachers. As LEAs in particular were then[2] the most powerful agents in education, their channelling of resources and expertise into this initiative was highly effective. Over time, the momentum was lost and also new initiatives such as the Technical and Vocational Education Initiative (which was government policy) and the reform of the examination system took over as the 'big issues'. However, the influence of LAC was very far reaching and its penetration into practice was very real. The introduction of coursework and speaking and listening into the curriculum in the 1980s can be seen as a direct result of LAC. Although the Report did not conceptualise literacy as such – its key term was always 'language' – what is implicit throughout the LAC movement is a recognition that school language, that is, teacher discourse, the terminologies of 'subjects' etc. need to be taught, but also that the language of the home/community must be brought into school and used to connect the two domains – hence a 'Language for Life'. The latter concern, we argue, is missing from the current strategy.

By the mid-1980s, a right-wing government was once more concerned about 'standards' in schools, especially in the subject 'English' and commissioned studies by Her Majesty's Inspectors of schools, focusing particularly on perceived falling standards in grammar. The two HMI documents (DES, 1984, 1986) about English were the first official attempts to define a curriculum area in national terms. The eventual outcome of this approach was the decision to set up a highly centralised national curriculum, the intention being to control content and assessment and to wrest power from the LEAs. However, one may initially continue to trace the influence of LAC in the original NC for English (DES, 1989a) in its emphatic influence on speaking and listening and multiculturalism. Later revisions have consistently reduced the influence of LAC (see Goodwyn and Findlay, 1999a).

One effect of the National Curriculum was a profound change to primary practice. The child-centred model of the 1970s and 1980s was gradually replaced by a much more subject-driven approach to pedagogy. For example, the 1990s saw subject names like Science and English appearing on the primary curriculum and primary teachers adopting a 'subject lesson' approach to teaching rather than a more holistic, topic-led style. By the mid-1990s, there was some evidence that primary teachers were paying much less attention to reading and writing per se. The right-wing government still in power initiated yet another review of reading and writing and entitled it the National Literacy Project. This small-scale project involved 250 schools in a pilot study. However, the Labour Party, sensing imminent political victory, set up its own Literacy Task Force and, on gaining power in 1997, operationalised this Task Force into the National Literacy Strategy by 1997. The 'New' Labour government was absolute about occupying the central political ground and thus drawing on what would previously have been perceived as right-wing thinking – the NLS made a perfect educational vehicle for this ideological repositioning.[3] The NLS was always conceived as a top-down strategy (in direct contrast to LAC) and so would require a hierarchy and to employ staff, 'agents' at every level. *The NLS expectations bear directly on all schools in the state-funded sector.*

In simple, descriptive terms, these agents include the architects of the National Literacy Strategy, a governmental 'organisation'. At this, national, level the agents may be divided into the political and the educational policy makers. These 'national' agents devise strategies, appoint other agents, create documents and thus, they hope, change practice and 'raise standards'. At the regional level are similar agents charged with ensuring that this process is working. Within each region, there continue to be Local Education Authority level agents who come in various guises with differing titles and job descriptions. Broadly, however, they are concerned with groups of schools and with ensuring the impact of all the above on actual schools, usually on key staff. Essentially, they are direct implements of policy and contracted as such. Schools have various key staff, chiefly with management and co-ordination roles, meant to link with the LEA level. Teachers themselves experience all of this and are expected to mediate it to their pupils, the ultimate 'beneficiaries' of the whole process. Ofsted[4] provides another set of key agents whose role is very visibly to inspect individual schools and local authorities and to check up on them. Although the status of the NLS has always been 'recommended', it has been perceived by primary schools as essentially mandatory.

Other very 'interested' parties are involved. For example, there are two other governmental bodies. One is the Qualifications and Curriculum Authority, which designs all the assessments and specifically all Standard Assessment Tests (SATs) that produce the Literacy 'levels' by which schools and teachers are judged. The other body, the Teacher Training Agency, oversees all initial (and other) teacher training. There are charitable organisations – for example the National Literacy Trust. The Ontario Institute of Education (see above) has been commissioned to evaluate the primary strategy, although its findings and recommendations seem to have had little impact and very little effort has been made to disseminate their recommendations. Other independent research has been small scale and relatively critical of aspects of the policy and its developing practice. Publishers clearly have a huge interest in the provision of endless resources for such a vast scheme. This list is indicative not exhaustive.

Theoretical framework

There are two key elements in our framework. The first is what constitutes literacy, i.e. how it is defined and, frequently, how it is carefully undefined and so what it ignores. The second is the relationship between policy and practice and more particularly the role of the teacher charged with enacting the policy into practice.

School-centric literacy

The National Literacy Strategy operates an implicit definition of literacy which has implications for the agents responsible for its implementation. This increasingly consensual definition is what we have characterised as a *school-centric* literacy which constructs a very particular version of literate pupils and the kinds of literacy practices they must develop in order to meet the demands of schooling.

Our use of the term school-centric follows on partly from work done by Street (Street, 1984) and others who use the term 'school literacy'; we have added the centric to emphasise and clarify how absolutely and exclusively this literacy belongs to school. However, the conceptualisation of that form of literacy is essentially vocationalised with an economic imperative. The rationale is that the school model of literacy is the one that will ensure 'our' economic survival and competitiveness.

We are also adapting here Lankshear's analysis of the meanings of literacy in educational reforms (Lankshear, 1998). He argues that his analysis of key reform texts[5] suggests four different constructions of literacy as follows: lingering basics, new basics, élite literacies and foreign language literacy *(ibid.,* p. 355). Lingering basics refer to survival level decoding competences, principally print with some reference to numbers. The new basics are premised on the idea that much higher order skills are now needed by all workers; critical thinking, Lankshear argues, is a kind of 'grab bag' *(ibid.,* p. 356) for a whole range of capacities seen as desirable in the new work order. A strong link occurs here with Street's work. He has focused on how literacy is seen as autonomous and the new basics are very focused on making individuals self-reliant, problem solving etc. One might argue that workers once needed literacy to be told what to do; now they need it to know what to do without being told. Elite literacies relate to domains of knowledge and disciplines and stress the capacity for improvement and innovation within those fields; they seem to offer a limited criticality. We feel that these three elements are strongly present in the NLS conceptualisation of literacy. Interestingly, the 'foreign language' construction is completely missing from the National Literacy Strategy, perhaps unusually clear evidence of England's linguistic complacency?

We argue that this school-centric definition informs the thinking of both the agents of the strategy and of the increasingly important school agents. It is essentially a skills deficit model, and 'at risk' pupils are subjected to a curriculum framed within the 'lingering basics', on the assumption that this will provide access to élite subject literacies and the higher order thinking skills associated with the 'new basics'. Whilst this may not be the definition of all teachers, the agents see resistance as essentially ignorance rather than knowledgeable subversion: their mission is therefore to enlighten teachers who will then comply with the consensual definition.

However, this view is not that of much of the research community, which has increasingly adopted the concept of 'literacies' sometimes, 'multi-literacies' (e.g. Buckingham, 1993; Lankshear, 1997). There the debate has often centred on how many literacies we might identify, e.g. visual, print, computer, media etc. and on the extent to which these literacies overlap or compete with each other. There has also been much work on the value positions and status of these various literacies with the general suggestion that the former dominance of print literacy is now under threat and that the 'new' literacies, especially those associated with technology, will soon supplant print literacy in every sense including status. A point often made there, and relevant to this discussion, is that schools in England remain technologically primitive whilst the real world and the domestic space are often sophisticated omnitech environments; the recent Children, Young People and the Changing Media Environment project provides overwhelming evidence of this trend (see Livingstone, 2002). There is no doubt that the new basics model in some education systems, especially in Australasia (see Lankshear, 1998), does include a technological dimension. However, we feel that our research suggests that Information and Communications Technology (ICT) not only remains outside the English school-centric definition but, as we analyse it, actually reinforces the essentially lingering basics notion specified in the NLS.

Policy into practice

Our research has been informed by the work of Ball *et al.* (1992) who propose a model of the policy cycle to avoid the idea that 'policy is simply something done to people'. They specify three policy contexts: *initial influence,* when policies are initiated and key concepts established; *policy text production,* when the policy document is publicly represented; and of *practice* where the policy text may be subject to reinterpretation and recreation as it is recontextualised. Each context involves 'struggle and compromise and ad hocery'.

Our research has followed the principles of a 'policy trajectory study', which '… employ a cross-sectional rather than a single level analysis by tracing policy formulation, struggles and response from within the state itself through to the various recipients of policy' (Bowe and Ball, 1992).

A nationally representative survey of secondary schools, interviews with regional directors and LEA literacy consultants, together with teacher interviews and classroom observation, provide valuable data and insights into the various strands of the policy cycle (for details, see Goodwyn and Findlay, 1999a, 2002).

The policy text: NLS definition

Where is the explicit definition of literacy in the NLS that secondary schools should at least consider? In the 'Rationale' section of the Framework document (DfEE, 2001b, pp. 9–10), we have these two paragraphs:

The notion of literacy embedded in the objectives is much more than simply the acquisition of basic skills, which is sometimes, implied by the word: it encompasses the ability to recognise, understand and manipulate the conventions of language, and develop pupils' ability to use language imaginatively and flexibly. The Framework also encompasses speaking and listening to support English teachers in planning to meet the full demands of the National Curriculum, and to tie in the development of oral skills with parallel demands in written text.

English teachers have the leading role in providing pupils with the knowledge, skills and understanding they need to read, write, speak and listen effectively, but this document also addresses other subject staff. Language is the prime medium through which pupils learn and express themselves across the curriculum, and all teachers have a stake in effective literacy. A set of cross-curricular Language for Learning objectives has been identified to support the co-ordination of departments working together on literacy.

In order to reinforce the idea that these skills are not basic, the next section outlining the 'overall aim of the framework' *(ibid.,* p. 10) states it 'is to enable all pupils to develop sophisticated literacy skills' and as a result at the end of Year 9 (age about 14), each pupil is expected to be:

A shrewd and fluent independent reader:

- orchestrating a range of strategies to get at meaning in text, including inferential and evaluative skills;
- sensitive to the way meanings are made;
- reading in different ways for different purposes, including skimming to quickly pick up the gist of a text, scanning to locate specific information, close reading to follow complex passages and re-reading to uncover layers of meaning; reflective, critical and discriminating in response to a wide range of printed and visual texts.

A confident writer:

- able to write for a variety of purposes and audiences, knowing the conventions and beginning to adapt and develop them;
- able to write imaginatively, effectively and correctly;
- able to shape, express, experiment with and manipulate sentences;
- able to organise, develop, spell and punctuate writing accurately.

An effective speaker and listener:

- with the clarity and confidence to convey a point of view or information;
- using talk to explore, create, question and revise ideas, recognising language as a tool for learning;
- able to work effectively with others in a range of roles; having a varied repertoire of styles, which are used appropriately.

Clearly, the emphasis is on what a pupil can do, and with the recently introduced (September 2002) policy emphasis on Citizenship[6], it is not surprising there are some interesting words to highlight. Readers should be shrewd, independent, reflective, critical and discriminating– this sounds rather like critical literacy of the Freirian variety. However, the emphasis is also on the singular pupil, the autonomous individual. Each reader will be displaying these critical capacities on the narrow cultural heritage model of the English National Curriculum and will be assessed on their literary powers at the end of Key Stage Three, for example, on two scenes from a Shakespeare play. An examination of the content to be covered in Key Stage Three reveals a very heavy emphasis on linguistic terminology and language rules (see the Framework for English, DfEE, 2001b). It might be argued that language is portrayed as for analysis in a sense distancing the pupil from language in use. This reveals yet another step away from the attempt by the Language in the National Curriculum project of the early 1990s, to place language study firmly in a Hallidayean socio-linguistic model (Carter, 1990).

In this respect, the content certainly displays continuity with the well established Key Stage Two Literacy Hour. We are suggesting, therefore, that the critical element implied in the definition is severely blunted by the conservative content of the curriculum and forms of assessment. The emphasis of that curriculum, including the revised Curriculum 2000 (DfEE, 2000) in place from September 2000, is still far more on fairly traditional models of reading and writing and far less on speaking and listening. On balance, there is a new element in the National Curriculum, the core skills, where one strand is clearly intended to highlight working with others. This can rightly be seen as potentially significant but the lesson of the original NC cross-curricular themes, the supposed cement of the NC, is that vague shared responsibilities do not produce results in subject-divided secondary schools. Some of our previous work, investigating the views of English teachers (Goodwyn and Findlay, 1999a, 2001; Goodwyn, 2001), has revealed how frustrated they are by the extremely narrow and conservative nature of the various versions of the English curriculum.

Our essential point is that this school-centric definition of literacy remains just that, a means of succeeding within a traditional/élite academic curriculum. In one clear way, this is an honest acknowledgement that schools, secondary ones especially, place enormous demands on children and the literacy they require is a very particular one; here may be seen a positive link with the LAC movement. Students are thus being trained in school-centric literacy and one would expect standards that test this literacy to rise quite dramatically and rapidly. In the primary phase, there have been rises in test scores although their validity on the one hand and their usefulness on the other have been constantly questioned (Goodwyn, 2002).

Implicit in the focus on language is a critical potential to shift the traditional emphasis on curriculum content to a new focus on the literacy practices through which that content is given meaning and status. Knowing about a subject could give way to knowing in the subject which is thus demystified and made transparent. This would require a very different stance on pedagogy for many subject specialists. For example, the QCA, following from the now defunct SCAA (1997), is revisiting the Language Across the Curriculum model by offering guidance about literacy across the curriculum and reinforcing this with statutory requirements that teachers of all subjects should demonstrate their awareness in their planning and teaching. Ofsted are empowered to check that schools are 'compliant'. Essentially, this emphasis *on literacy as a concern of all subject teachers,* if not the process adopted to create it, mirrors what Barnes (1976) and Britton (1970) were asking for in the 1970s.

The element missing from this current definition is a simple one. As the curriculum remains what we have called elsewhere a 'preservative one' (Goodwyn and Findlay, 1999b), this school-centric literacy remains singularly divorced from the social experience of children. Literacy is, in the Freirean (Freire, 1972) sense, a means of individual and group empowerment, a vehicle for cultural and economic participation in the discourses that shape our lives, including those in the evolving electronic media. It is also never ahistorical or apolitical, insisting that literacy is always 'problematic' and will be contested by the powerful. But the school model pays very little attention to the historical and political nature of literacy and even less to the whole area of media and electronic text, especially to the multi-modal world of the internet and interactive technologies (for a more developed discussion of these points, see Goodwyn, 2002 and Livingstone, 2002). We also recognise that schools in England are still rather more nineteenth- than even twentieth-century structures. The irony remains then that the school-centric model genuinely suits the demands of schooling.

The asocial model of literacy also promotes – and tests – individual ability and achieve- ment, at the expense of an alternative perspective which recognises the cultural nature of literacy practices, and the differences in language use which relate to class, ethnicity and gender. It rarely acknowledges the social experiences of pupils who operate infor- mal literacies in their homes and communities, glossing over differences in the name of standards. Yet if teachers are concerned to attend to the diversity of pupils' experiences and needs, they may resist the imposition of a 'one for all' policy and instead veer towards Street's model of ideological literacy which emphasises the social and cultural specificity of literacy practices. Alternatively, they may engage in what Street describes as the 'pedagogisation' of autonomous literacy whereby the literacy practices not valued in school 'come to be seen as inferior attempts at the real thing, to be compensated for by enhanced schooling' (Street, 1991). The move to provide extra literacy lessons for pupils with low literacy levels reported by many respondents suggests that this may be the course schools are taking; it is also evident in the introduction of the 'Progress units' in 2001 (DfEE, 2001a), aimed at Year 7 pupils with level 3s from their primary tests in Year 6. It also has implications for teachers developing supportive dynamics in inclu- sive classrooms and denies equal access to the higher order skills associated with the 'new basics' (Lankshear, 1998).

Teachers: agents or recipients? The context of practice

We are concerned in this research with the complex and inevitably contradictory nature of a huge national project that is clearly 'working' and simultaneously being transformed and interpreted by its workers. Stephen Ball has summarised this complexity very effectively, explaining how policy discourses may shape individual agency but also emphasising the possibility of individuals claiming agency within these discourses. The effect of policy is, he explains, primarily discursive, since it changes the possibilities for thinking things 'other- wise' and so limits our responses to change. Yet this totalising effect is tempered by the policy text which is just that, an encoded representation which must be decoded and enacted on a number of levels.

> Given constraints, circumstances and practicalities, the translation of the crude, abstract simplicities of policy texts into interactive and sustainable practices of some sort involves thought, invention and adaptation. And the more ideologically abstract any policy is, the more distant in conception from practice, the less likely it is to be accommodated in unmediated form into the context of practice. ... (Ball, 1994)

This helps us both to conceptualise the national project and therefore discuss it as a kind of actuality whilst also treating individuals as encompassed by this actuality and yet not engulfed by it.

We also draw on another helpful perspective, that of Croll *et al.* (1994) who have articulated various ways of defining the agency, or lack of it, of teachers caught up in some large-scale policy initiative. They discuss four models: teacher as either partner, implementer, resister or, their preferred description, as 'policy maker in practice'.

> If, either because of similar structural or situational constraints, or because of similar attitudes and ideologies (or because of an interaction of these), teachers interpret and prioritise policy changes in consistent ways, then the outcomes of these individual actions will have a systematic effect on the practical outcomes of policy ... [which] ... may effectively re-direct educational activities in a way that makes teachers policy makers. *(ibid.)*

This latter definition fits well with our research, which reveals the ways in which individual teachers are accommodating policy in broadly similar ways and the cumulative effect may be that they are working as both policy makers at the level of practice but also as 'implementers'; the interesting question for the future lies in the tension between these roles. We see both teachers and others as having agency whilst acknowledging that policy shapes their thoughts and actions sufficiently to lead to what we call 'semi-systematic outcomes'. The interview data reveal the sensitivity of LEA personnel in particular as they make subtle judgements about how to interact with individual schools and teachers, to make the NLS meaningful to them. Teacher comments and interview data provide clearer evidence of where the policy may be seen to be only 'semi-systematic' in its effects. Overall, however, there is evidence of the 'fundamentalist tendency' (see below) of the NLS and the limitations placed on individual agents caught up in the policy cycle.

Discussion

It might be argued that this form of centralist, national strategy is now a well-established and well-understood process and we acknowledge this to a degree. However, before analysing our theoretical framework in relation to such policies and their relationship to actual practices, it is worth stressing some distinctive features of the NLS that we find make it especially interesting. The most fundamental of these is that, in a profound sense, it cannot be opposed. In simple terms, how could any educational professional or politician stand against raising standards in literacy? Indeed, one of the factors we shall explore below is what we have called the 'fundamentalist tendency' in the strategy. By this, we mean its ubiquitous ability to make criticism almost unthinkable; the only question is how to implement this great good and to convert unbelievers. In relation to many individuals we have spoken to, this is to do them and their critical powers an injustice; they do frequently express certain kinds of reservation. As we have suggested above, individuals certainly have agency and use it. However, even in these moments of criticality, there is no real deep-seated opposition; indeed there are far more moments of evangelical enthusiasm and even occasional awe. This seems true even in the secondary sector – traditionally the point of real resistance to imposed policy – but we need more research to substantiate this point. Ongoing work has been providing data from September 2002.[7]

Another factor that we feel distinguishes the NLS, particularly at present and for the next few years, is its unplanned benefit in creating 'phase related role reversal'. It has broken the implicit belief that primary and secondary schools are actually different planets in an age when interplanetary travel for teachers themselves is just possible but not really very desirable. Even more iconoclastically, secondary schools certainly saw themselves in the past as a very important planet around which smaller moons, called primary schools, orbited and annually they received parties of young aliens who had to be taught the ways of the real world by the real, expert teachers. Our research shows very clearly that these big secondary planets are in a state of considerable shock. They find the young aliens alarmingly knowledgeable and their teachers challengingly expert. As a result, secondary teachers are discovering how to travel and are returning mightily impressed and not a little daunted at the task they face; most secondary schools now expect their English staff to observe literacy teaching in primary settings. So the NLS is fostering meaningful exchanges between primaries and secondaries with the genuinely different element in the 'upward' flow of expertise, hence our term 'role reversal'.

In the quite near future, we believe, this strategy will have had significant impact on every teacher in every school in the mainstream 5–16 age range. It is worth noting that the Language Across the Curriculum (LAC) movement of the 1970s (DES, 1975), that was greeted with real enthusiasm by the teaching profession (Marland, 1977), is generally seen to have petered out with little long-lasting impact (we feel this vastly underestimates its impact but we are aware that the perception is that it faded away); in other words, the evangelicals did not convert the masses. LAC was also never 'statutory' and existed in the 'pre-inspection' age. We have discussed the relationship between LAC and the NLS above and in previous papers (e.g. Goodwyn and Findlay, 2002) and will not elaborate further here, except for a simple and revealing finding in our current research that LAC was not mentioned by any respondent (questionnaire and interviews) at any point.

Another factor concerns the point that the original National Curriculum was *concerned to provide a 'broad and balanced curriculum' and its chief focus was on curriculum* content *but* was generally accompanied by strong messages that schools and teachers had control over pedagogy (DES, 1989b). The NLS is emphatically about both and its documentation, videos and relentless training sessions are a form of explicit insistence that teachers change their teaching. The NLS, therefore, through a variety of means, appears to be 'reaching' all teachers and all their pupils. No other educational policy can be said to have had such a powerful impact. Its drive is clearly to make teachers implementers and not policy makers in any meaningful sense.

Conclusion

We have attempted to highlight the very powerful ongoing impact of the National Literacy Strategy and to focus particularly on its ambitions to 'transform' literacy teaching in the primary and secondary school. In many ways, we suggest, it is likely to succeed in its own somewhat narrow and prescriptive terms. Whilst welcoming its aim to demystify subject teaching and to involve all subject specialists, not just English teachers, in helping pupils become literate within each subject, we maintain that there are serious weaknesses in the 'school-centric' definition of literacy involved. The most glaring of these are, first, its pronounced emphasis on the 'autonomous individual' and, second, its failure to acknowledge the ever changing nature of literacy and specifically current developments in the electronic media. For example, ICT is still seen as a distinct curriculum element in school rather than an integral part of literacy needed to participate in ordinary life.

Whilst we are able to report (Goodwyn and Findlay, 2002) that schools are working hard to prepare to accommodate the NLS with the intention of benefiting all their pupils, we are also concerned about their lack of resources and also the 'fundamentalist' tendency of the discourse of the policy which may straitjacket all schools but especially those with challenging and diverse contexts. An interesting side-effect of secondary schools 'gearing up' for the NLS is that they are experiencing 'role reversals', looking towards primary schools for advice and expertise. We are therefore able to illustrate from our data that individuals exercise interpretation and agency and can act as 'policy makers' as this role reversal substantiates. However, the influence of the NLS is such that teacher agency is decidedly modest and that the dominance of school-centric literacy is clear, a very strong contrast to the egalitarian principles and practices of LAC. We anticipate increasing tension between the roles of 'implementer' and 'policy maker in practice' and forecast a very significant test of teacher agency in the next three years as the Key Stage Three Strategy attempts to 'transform' secondary schools.

Notes

1   The USA, Canada, UK, Australia, New Zealand – we accept that other countries might easily be added. However, these education systems appear most directly to compare themselves to each other.
2   LEAs have had their power and their resources diminished progressively for about 15 years, radically reducing their degree of agency.
3   The most striking and symbolic example of this 'move' was New Labour's retention of Chris Woodhead (a ferocious critic of all things left/progressive) as Head of Ofsted.
4   The Office for Standards in Education – this body is charged with the inspection of the education system at all levels (except all aspects of Universities apart from teacher training which is within their remit) and for the production of public domain reports reporting their judgements on each institution. Perhaps the most telling phrase in their inspection instruments is that they can find an institution 'not compliant', i.e. not fitting in with a directive – such institutions can be closed down.
5   Lankshear draws mostly on North America and Australasia.
6   All English secondary schools had to teach Citizenship from September 2002.
7   The provisional title is 'English versus Literacy', a paper given at BERA 2002.

References

Ball, S.J. (1994) *Education Reform: A Critical and Post-structuralist Approach* (Buckingham, Open University Press).

Ball, S., Kenny, A. and Gardiner, D. (1992) Literacy politics and the teaching of English. In I. Goodson and P. Medway *Bringing English to Order: the History and Politics of a School Subject* (London, The Falmer Press).

Barnes, D. (1976) *From Communication to Curriculum* (Harmondsworth, Penguin).

Bowe, R. and Ball, S.J. with Gold, A. (1992) *Reforming Education and Changing Schools* (London, Routledge).

Britton, J. (1970) *Language and Learning* (Harmondsworth, Penguin).

Buckingham, D. (1993) *Children Talking Television: The Making of Television Literacy* (London, The Falmer Press).

Carter, R. (1990) *Knowledge about Language and the Curriculum* (London, Hodder and Stoughton).

Croll, P. *et al.* (1994) Teachers and education policy: roles and models, *British Journal of Education Studies,* 42(4).

DES (1975) *A Language for Life* (London, HMSO).

DES (1984) *English from 5 to 16* (London, HMSO).

DES (1986) *English from 5 to 16: The Responses* (London, HMSO).

DES (1989a) *National Curriculum from Policy to Practice* (London, DES).

DES (1989b) *The Cox Report* (London, HMSO).

DfEE (2000) *Transforming Key Stage Three: National Pilot, Briefing Pack for Pilot Schools* (London, DfEE).

DfEE (2001a) *NLS KS3 Literacy Progress Units, 1–6* (London, DfEE).

DfEE (2001b) *Framework for Teaching English: Years 7, 8 and 9* (London, DfEE).

Freire, P. (1972) *Pedagogy of the Oppressed* (Harmondsworth, Penguin).

Goodwyn, A. (2001) Second tier professionals: English teachers in England, *L1-Educational Studies in Language and Literature,* 1(2), 149–161.

Goodwyn, A. (Ed.) (2002) *Improving Literacy at KS2 and KS3* (London, Paul Chapman Publishing).

Goodwyn, A. and Findlay, K. (1998) English Teachers' Theories of Good English Teaching and their Theories in Action. Paper given at the BERA conference, York 1998.

Goodwyn, A. and Findlay, K. (1999a) The Cox Models revisited: English teachers' views of their subject and the National Curriculum, *English in Education,* 33(2), Summer.

Goodwyn, A. and Findlay, K. (1999b) Versions of Literacy in English Teaching. Paper given at the BERA conference, Cardiff 1999.

Goodwyn, A. and Findlay, K. (2001) Literacy at Key Stage Three. Paper presented at the Creativity, Continuity and ICT conference, Becta, March.

Goodwyn, A. and Findlay, K. (2002) Shaping Literacy in the Secondary School, Policy, Practice and Agency. Paper given at the American Educational Research Association conference, New Orleans, April.

Lankshear, C. (1997) *Changing Literacies* (Buckingham, Open University Press).

Lankshear, C. (1998) Meaning of literacy in contemporary educational reform proposals, *Educational Theory,* 48(3), 351–372.

Livingstone, S. (2002) *Young People and New Media* (London, Sage).

Marland, M. (1977) *Language across the Curriculum* (London, Heinemann Educational).

SCAA (1997) *Use of Language: A Common Approach* (London, SCAA).

Street, B.V. (1984) *Literacy in Theory and Practice* (Cambridge, Cambridge University Press).

Street, B.V. (1991) The schooling of literacy. In D. Barton and R. Ivanic (eds) *Writing in the Community* (London, Sage).

12

Headwoman's Blues: Small Group Reading and the Interactions of Culture, Gender, and Ability

Shuaib J. Meacham

The grouping of students in literacy instruction has been a topic of much study and debate within educational research and practice. Ability grouping, heterogeneous grouping, and more recently, literature discussion groups and book clubs have become prominent practices in literacy research and instruction. These issues have also been examined from cultural diversity and second-language perspectives. This chapter, taken from a larger study of cultural diversity and literacy instruction, examines interactions among these grouping factors. Specifically, this chapter demonstrates how factors of ability, culture, and gender interact dynamically to effect an impact on student literacy experiences in small group instruction. The following sections briefly review the literature, describe research methods, and present the findings and conclusion.

Themes in the literature on grouping and literacy

This brief literature review examines three primary areas of emphasis in the research on grouping and literacy instruction. This research includes studies that have examined the comparative achievement resulting from different grouping practices, studies that have looked at student and teacher conduct and group productivity, and studies that have focused on practices conducive to literacy acquisition. Studies examining the effectiveness of different grouping practices have looked at whole class, small group, and ability grouping, as well as heterogeneous grouping practices.

Lou, Abrami, Spence, Pulsen, Chambers, and d'Apollonia (1996) described a recent comprehensive review of this literature. Their review focused on the comparative effectiveness of different grouping practices. The effectiveness of whole group literacy instruction was compared with that of small group instruction, whereas the effectiveness of homogeneous

From: Willis, A.I., Garcia, G.E., Barrera, R. and Harris, V.J. (eds) *Multicultural Issues in Literacy Research and Practice,* pp. 49–67 (Mahwah, NJ: Lawrence Erlbaum, 2003).

ability grouping was compared with that of heterogeneous grouping. Although no grouping practice was found to be uniformally superior, small group learning was more effective than whole group learning, and homogeneous ability grouping was slightly more effective than heterogeneous grouping. The authors emphasized, however, that maximum effectiveness, regardless of grouping, was achieved when instructional materials and teaching practices were adapted to instructional objectives. Berghoff and Egawa (1991) performed a comparative analysis of student learning in the variety of grouping contexts they used in their classrooms. The authors found that each grouping practice, whether whole group, small group, pairs, or independent, provided instructional advantages for the teacher and learning advantages for the students depending on why, when, and how the practices were implemented.

Several studies have examined student and teacher conduct in small group learning (Barnes, Barnes, & Clarke, 1984; Berghoff & Egawa, 1991; Cazden, 1986; MacGillivray & Hawes, 1994; McMahon & Goatley, 1995). These studies investigated the practices in which teachers and students engaged during small group instruction and evaluated their impact on the achievement of instructional objectives. MacGillivray and Hawes (1994) examined the different 'roles' that students adopted in the context of 'partner reading' (p. 213). They found that students adopted four types of relationships or 'role sets' in peer literacy interactions: pleasure, assistance, teacher–student, and boss–employee relationships. Two of the roles, teacher–student and boss–employee, implied the presence of hierarchical relationships in student practice. This prominence of hierarchy led the researchers to suggest that even in the absence of ability grouping, students still carried out reading tasks in terms of power relationships.

Other studies have examined instructional approaches in cooperative groupings that maximize reading comprehension, meaning-making, and collaboratively negotiated understanding of text (Leal, 1993; Meloth & Deering, 1992; Tinalli & Drake, 1993). Meloth and Deering (1992) discussed the quality and frequency of various kinds of talk in cooperative learning groups as well as the level of literacy comprehension associated with various instructional strategies. In particular, they found that activity sheets used to guide interactions lead to less off-task talk and higher gains in student reading comprehension. Tinalli and Drake (1993) looked at literature groups and the manner in which children collectively negotiated the meaning of texts. In contrast to the assumption that there is a 'natural' quality of child interaction with literature, they found that 'think aloud' strategies, in which children are encouraged to be aware of their thought processes, enhanced the abilities of peers to negotiate the meaning and understanding of texts collectively.

Issues of race, culture, and gender diversity also have been integrated into the study of grouping and literacy instruction. Research such as that of Braddock and Dawkins (1993) and Troyna (1992) has emphasized the negative impact of ability grouping on the learning outcomes of students from nonmainstream backgrounds. In contrast, Lee and Slaughter-Defoe (1994), Garcia (1994), and Lomawaima (1994) have discussed the cultural appropriateness of cooperative learning frameworks for the literacy achievement and overall learning of African American, Latino, and Native American students. Cherland (1992) and Evans (1996) have discussed the differing qualities of literature responses between boys and girls in literature discussion groups. In another recent study, Kreuger and Townsend (1997) found that practices in the 'reading club' improved the literacy acquisition of second-language learners. Specifically, the authors found that through a recurring sequence of instructional practices, all of the children were able to read the weekly story independently by the end of the week.

Collectively, the studies cited have provided considerable insight into factors that impede or promote literacy achievement and productive student interactions in reading groups. Over time, these studies gradually have integrated more variables into the analysis of small group practices in literacy instruction. Kreuger and Townsend (1997), in particular, were able to look simultaneously at issues of grouping, literacy acquisition, and second-language acquisition. This is an important trend because most studies in this literature do not examine the interactions among multiple variables. Thus, the manner in which diversity, grouping, and student and teacher conduct as well as the ways that they may influence one another are not evident. This limitation is of considerable importance because the small group literacy instruction in an increasing number of classrooms, particularly those in major urban settings, must contend with multiple influences simultaneously. This chapter attempts to expand on recent trends and supplement traditional limitations by looking at interactions among the factors of culture, gender, and teacher practice, and their impact on small group literacy instruction.

Theoretical Framework

The blues idiom and the crossroads

This chapter adopts cultural theorist Albert Murray's (1970) concept of the 'blues idiom' as a theoretical lense through which to make sense of literacy instruction in a multiply diverse classroom context. The blues idiom, not to be confused or equated with 'twelve-bar' blues music, is a theoretical synthesis of rituals, dispositions, and attitudinal patterns implicit in African American music, art, style, language, and social interactions. Western European-based conceptions of knowledge and culture emphasize hierarchy, division, and categorization (Foucault, 1975 in Rabinow, 1984; West, 1982). The blues idiom was selected because it embodies a worldview that more closely approximates the relations between knowledge and culture found in a culturally diverse classroom. Specifically, the blues idiom implies an ethos in which intersections, connections, and interactions across categories are considered the norm (Gates, 1988). However, before describing the specific features of the blues idiom, it is necessary to discuss a larger process undergirding the blues cosmology, specifically that of the 'crossroads.'

Described as a foundational concept in many African cosmological systems (Gates, 1988; Thompson, 1984), the crossroads represents a definitive personal and cultural moment during which a sense of norm is disrupted. Gates (1988) also suggested that the crossroads is that point at which one's previous level of conceptual understanding is no longer sufficient to meet current challenges. Specific to the contingencies of cultural diversity, the crossroads also is represented in spatial terms. Thompson (1984) described the crossroads according to the following spatial parameters:

A fork in the road (or even a forked branch), ... [a] crucially important symbol of passage and communication between worlds, ... the point of intersection between the ancestors and the living. (p. 109)

As Thompson (1984) suggested, the crossroads is a place where worlds come together, the point at which differences intersect. Often, it is this intersection of different worlds that precipitates the disruption of norms.

Break, improvisation, and affirmation

Murray (1970) suggested that many aspects of African American culture, particularly the music of jazz, constitutes a ritualization of the crossroads experience. According to Murray (1970), jazz ritualizes an experiential norm (p. 70) for African American people, the disruption and improvisational response of which has been a definitive cultural experience.

The blues idiom ritualizes the crossroads experience in three interconnected phases. The first phase is that of 'the break.' The break is the ritualization of the crisis, that point of intersection at which a singular sense of norm is disrupted. The break corresponds to that moment in a jazz composition when the rhythmic and melodic structures are disrupted, leaving the soloist with a comparatively empty sonic landscape. This is the moment at which improvisation, the second phase of the blues idiom, begins. Improvisation, however, is not to be confused with an 'anything goes' or a 'winging it' mentality. Improvisation, in fact, requires the soloist to call on her or his already known repertoire of skills and knowledge and adapt it to the current challenge. Because the context of improvisation is the intersection of multiple worlds, improvisation frequently includes the integration of multiple cultural norms.

The final phase in the blues idiom process is that of affirmation. Within affirmation, the break has been confronted, the improvisation conducted, and a new yet connected set of understandings regarding both self and circumstance is put in place. Affirmation primarily amounts to a new level of understanding from which 'higher and richer levels of improvisation' (Murray, 1970, p. 59) may be conducted in the future.

With respect to the blues idiom, literacy and literacy instruction becomes constructed as a cultural practice that invariably confronts readers with disruptions of normative assumptions. In general, Vygotsky (1986) identifies this disruption of children's 'spontaneous' conceptual understanding learned at home as a basic component of the school learning experience. Tharp and Gallimore (1991) suggested that literacy comprehension is a process through which children 'weave' school knowledge with the home-based understandings that they bring to school. These disruptive processes are only magnified in a context of cultural diversity, particularly in the reading of multicultural literature and expository texts. Multicultural literature and expository texts necessarily confront readers with material that disrupts personal and cultural normative assumptions. However, to understand the concepts in this kind of literacy instruction, these disruptions must somehow be improvisationally woven into children's prior knowledge.

Method

The setting

To study the interactions among multiple variables in literacy instruction with a focus on cultural diversity, a highly diverse classroom population was selected. Classroom data were taken from a combined second- and third-grade classroom wherein 11 different cultures were represented. Many of the students were in their first 4 years of residence in the United States. Thus, there literally existed an international network of influences in the classroom.

Framework for data collection and analysis

In an attempt to methodologically capture the crossroads dynamics of the blues idiom, I adopted Baker's (1984) literary conception of 'matrix' (p. 3) as a structural framework for data collection and analysis. In his study, *Blues, Ideology and Afro-American Literature,* Baker defined a matrix as 'a network … a web of intersecting, crisscrossing impulses always in productive transit' (p. 3). Thus, methods of data collection and analysis were perceived as constructing a 'network' of interconnected information sources. Therefore, the data collection drew information from multiple contexts in terms of student and teacher life experiences. Data analysis attempted to map out the contextual sources and trajectories of information while identifying when these contexts overlapped. The specifics of this process are outlined in the following sections.

Data collection and analysis

The foundation of data collection involved audiotaped participant observations of classroom literacy instruction supplemented by field notes. These observations were conducted 3 days a week for 3 and 5 hours each day throughout the school year. Classroom data were supplemented by data from a variety of interconnected sources: parent interviews with 24 of the 28 student families, teacher interviews, student interviews, document collections, and observations of community cultural events in which students and their families participated.

Family interviews focused on issues such as home literacy practices and expectations, parent education experiences, and if applicable, literacy and schooling practices and expectations from the students' non-United States countries of origin. Four 90- to 120-min teacher interviews also were conducted over the course of the study. The interviews were, in fact, conversations wherein the teacher and the researcher collaboratively discussed the literacy and cultural issues examined by the study. The teacher, with more than 25 years of experience, acted as what I refer to as a cotheorist, coconstructing meaning of observed classroom activities through informal data analysis. Formal audiotaped interviews were supplemented by ongoing, informal conversations in which impressions were exchanged immediately after significant instructional events.

Document collections consisted of four document sources: student writing and classroom literacy documents, teacher–family correspondence, international documents, and cotemporaneous articles. Student writing and classroom literacy collections were composed of daily journal entries, creative and expository writing assignments, and classroom literacy worksheets. Family correspondence documents consisted of teacher newsletters and notices, which elicited parental responses regarding information related to instruction. Document collection gathered education documents via the Internet originating from the countries of origin of students not born in the United States. These sources, mainly educational policy documents from departments of education, were used to verify and elaborate on statements made in interviews regarding literacy and educational expectations in international contexts. Cotemporaneous articles were taken from local, national, and regional newspapers and periodicals collected during the period of classroom data collection. These articles were used to add depth and richness to classroom overlaps as they dealt with issues that corresponded to classroom events.

Data analysis

The data analysis aimed to identify 'intertextual overlaps' across the variety of data collection sources. Data analysis used the constant comparative method described by Strauss (1987), with an emphasis not only on categorical distinctions, but also on contexts wherein categories crossed. Through the analysis, I initially identified distinct domains based on cultural categories such as African American, Nepalese, Indian, and Chinese, but subsequently examined instances in which these domains crossed or overlapped experiences, practices, and conceptual understandings regarding the literacy of other cultural domains. This analysis occurred in five stages.

The first stage of analysis was that of 'open coding.' Through open coding, I identified student–teacher, student–student, and student–researcher discussions of texts, both literary and expository, that related to the topic of culture. The coding identified the students involved, the nationalities of the students, and the text or curricular context that promoted the discussion. The open coding results were filed according to the nationality of the student or students making the statement.

Open coding was followed by a second stage of analysis, 'overlap identification,' which analyzed the cultural discussions found through open coding, identifying explicit and implicit relations between literacy text or instructional topic and the student's cultural background. In an explicit relation, the student verbally identified the relation. In an implicit relation, the content of the discussion was informed by the relation between the cultural content of the text or instructional topic and the student's background, but not verbally identified. These overlaps were coded in terms of the students, their nationalities, and the cultures involved in the overlap.

After the identification of overlaps, 'selective coding' was conducted to identify contextual factors such as 'conditions [and] consequences' (Strauss, 1987, p. 33) that may have been conducive to the emergence of cross-cultural connections. At this stage, the particular instructional context of the overlap was identified. For example, the instructional context such as reading group (ability), whole-class story reading and discussion, independent reading, or unit instruction group (mixed ability) was determined. In addition to details about the instructional context, specific characteristics of the overlap were identified. Many overlaps, for example, involved commonalities or tensions related to students' religious traditions and those overlaps represented in the text or curricular topic. Other overlaps involved issues related to gender roles, classroom rituals, and corporate influences on literacy and culture.

The fourth level of classroom data analysis examined the relations among categories and factors. This level of analysis documented the way that instructional components in various domains worked together to produce the overlapping connections and tensions.

The fifth and final stage of analysis was conducted to enhance the conceptual richness of the overlaps identified in classroom literacy instruction. This analysis involved identifying connections between overlaps identified in [the] classroom and issues discussed in parent–teacher interviews, the running article collection, participant observation in nonschool settings, and document collections via the Internet. Data from these domains then were superimposed over the literacy instruction overlaps to which they most closely related. This enabled me to identify family practices, teacher cultural dispositions, educational experiences outside the United States, and global cultural trends that may have played a part in literacy discussions observed in the classroom.

The headwoman and cultural weaving

Unit instruction

The small group interactions of mixed ability level examined in this chapter were taken from data collected in an instructional unit focused specifically on the Iroquois nation. Within the classroom, unit instruction is that context in which students normally worked in small groups representing mixed levels of literacy competency. This heterogeneous grouping contrasted with morning reading groups, which were formed according to literacy competency. An attempt was made to conceal the hierarchy by naming the groups according to the text they were reading. Therefore, not only did the names not designate hierarchy, but they were changed regularly throughout the year. At this point in the year, however, the reading groups consisted of Fried Worms as highest in literacy competency, Freckle Juice as the next group, and Garden Gates as the third in reading level. *Blue-Tailed Horse* was the book read by the name assigned to the students who spoke English as a second language. However, as Berghoff and Egawa (1991) suggested, students frequently are able to gauge the hierarchy despite attempts to conceal it.

Unit instruction begins with a whole-class 5- to 10-min presentation, followed by small group interaction for the remainder of the 40-min period. Depending on the activity, the 40-min period was regularly extended so group work could be completed.

Curricular weaving

'Curricular weaving' denotes the regular instructional practice by which the classroom teacher takes topical issues and integrates them into classroom rituals, themes, and organizational or instructional practices. An apprentice weaver in her spare time, Gloria frequently used weaving as a metaphor to describe her classroom practice. She regularly conceived of curricula and cultural variables as 'threads' in a woven fabric of instruction. When the threads were resonant or compatible, Gloria would weave curricular content, instructional practices, and cultural themes together as she constructed educational experiences for her students.

In the Iroquois unit, Gloria identified resonant threads between the clan structure of the Iroquois and the small group instruction of the unit class period. She wove the two threads together by having the heterogeneous literacy groups identify themselves as clans. In keeping with the Iroquois tradition, each of the clans was required to have a 'headwoman' act as the leader of the group. Thus, each of the unit instructional groups or clans would have a girl as leader of the group. This headwoman was charged with supervising the proper conduct of all clan activities, which included allocating shared reading responsibilities and turn taking toward the completion of clan assignments.

The primary outcome from the weaving of instructional and cultural variables is that the learning becomes multifaceted. Gloria used the instructional objectives not only to increase literacy competency and students' store of cultural knowledge, but also to complement the values of equity, service, and respect that she ritually promoted in her classroom. The Iroquois role of headwoman therefore was replicated not only to provide the children with an abstract experience of Iroquois leadership, but also to reinforce primary classroom values through an experience guided by Iroquois principles of gendered leadership. Thus, within the unit framework, the students engaged in literacy practices, learned cultural information, and reinforced values conducive to a diverse classroom environment.

'Crossing' and the interaction of multiple variables

Gloria's weaving of the Iroquois clan structure with the mixed reading group instructional format created a crossing of instructional and diversity variables. Iroquois content related to culture and gender crossed literacy pedagogical variables related to mixed ability grouping. The initial outcome of the crossing was that reading group leadership became gendered, in that a girl led each group. Another outcome of Gloria's instructional weaving was that the experience of female leadership crossed the diversity of cultural dispositions related to female leadership represented by the students. Specifically, the provision for female leadership interacted with the range of student cultural backgrounds, which may or may not have been compatible with the concept of female leadership. Interviews with parents and community informants from a variety of backgrounds suggested that among certain cultures, significant tensions would emerge from the idea of female leadership. The remainder of this chapter investigates the outcomes of these crossings.

Headwoman's blues

Headwoman: an introduction

Weaving conceptual connections

The concept of the headwoman in the Iroquois unit was introduced, not as an abstract, isolated concept peculiar to Indian traditions, but as one that embodied qualities with which the students were already familiar. The remainder of this chapter examines small group interactions involving literacy texts and preparatory activities for reading texts during the Iroquois instructional unit. This discussion focuses on the practices of one group consisting of four students: Daniel, a third-grade high-performing boy from the Philippines; Mei, a second-grade Chinese girl from Hong Kong just above the level of limited English proficiency; Mikelle, a second-grade girl from the United States in a lower reading group; and Ravi, a Nepalese second grader in a midlevel morning reading group.

As suggested earlier, not only was there a diversity of culture, reading level, English language proficiency, and grade level, but there also was a diversity of cultural assumptions regarding the concept of 'female leadership.' Mei, in particular, was shy, rarely speaking above a whisper during classroom activities. Outwardly, she seemed to embody in her behavior traditional Chinese assumptions regarding the role of women and girls. Mikelle, by contrast, had a mother who was a gender activist. In fact, Mikelle missed the first 2 days of school to attend the Women's March on Washington that August. Ravi and

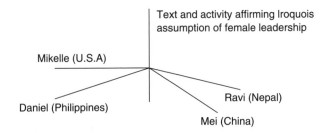

Figure 12.1   Crossroads of text and culture

Daniel both came from households in which their mothers were responsible for child care while their fathers studied in the university.

Choosing a headwoman

In the first activity of the unit, the students were divided into 'clans' and instructed to select a 'headwoman' for their clan. In keeping with Iroquois tradition, the headwoman would then select the 'chief' of the clan. This activity was implemented to impress on the students the fact that in the Iroquois nation, the chief, a more familiar male model of Indian leadership, was actually selected by a woman.

After selecting the headwoman and the chief, the students were to choose a name for their clan and begin reading an expository text that described the details of Iroquois clan leadership. Figure 12.1 illustrates the cultural crossing of Iroquois gendered leadership assumptions in activity and text with the cultures represented by the children in the reading group.

The crossing of Iroquois cultural assumptions in the text and the prereading activity of leadership selection passed through four cultural domains embodied by the children in the group. This crossing, not only in this group, but also in every group in the class, fostered a disruption of cultural norms, making it difficult for many of the students to select female leaders and engage in a productive reading of the text. This corresponded to the 'break' phase of the blues idiom process described earlier. This break and disruption becomes evident in the following student discussion just after groups have been formed and the group is trying to decide who the headwoman is going to be:

Mikelle:	I want to be the headwoman.
Daniel:	You can be headwoman, and we can get rid of the headwoman.
Shuaib:	Can I tape your conversation?
Daniel:	Can I say something?
Shuaib:	Go ahead, say whatever you want.
Daniel:	We've got to get rid of the headwoman. We've got to get rid of the headwoman. Okay? That's what it means. Get rid of the headwoman. Get rid of the headwoman? (in a chanting refrain-like rhythm)
Daniel:	Okay guys, you have to pick; okay you choose the chief. (to Mei) You're the head woman. You have to choose the chief. Between the guys.
Mei:	No you …
Ravi (to Mei):	I'm the medium, and he's in the aqua spelling group. He's in the 'Fried Worms.'

Daniel: Okay hurry up. This tape doesn't last that long. Pick the one, pick the uh uh uh uh or whatever, just take one.

Mikelle: Me!

Daniel: Nooooo!! You're (Mei) the Headwoman and you have to pick. If you don't pick anything, then nobody's going to be the chief. Then we can't start up [reading] there.

In the passage, Daniel openly resisted the idea of a headwoman. In opposition to the instructions of cooperatively selecting a headwoman, Daniel imposes the role of head-woman on Mei, although Mikelle sought to be named headwoman. It is safe to assume that Mei's shyness, and perhaps Daniel's implicit understanding of her cultural norms, led him to perceive Mei as a more pliable headwoman, in contrast to Mikelle. Thus, the primary decision involved the selection of 'chief,' the more traditional symbol of Indian leadership. In enacting a criterion for the chief, Ravi suggested Daniel because of his status in the highest reading and spelling groups. Consequently, hierarchies associated with reading became a means of reenacting more traditional gender norms. Because of his reading group status, Daniel, an aggressive, higher-performing third-grade boy, was made 'chief' in tandem with Mei, a shy, passive Chinese girl. It is safe to assume that Daniel perceived in Mei's shyness the potential for a more pliable headwoman, in contrast to Mikelle, who aggressively sought the role.

This disruptive and resistant behavior had implications for the proper enactment of read-ing activities. Not only did Daniel's reading level factor into the decision of his being named chief, but he used his higher reading ability to subvert Mei's authority as a head-woman. Gloria instructed the headwoman to collect and distribute reading materials, designate turn taking with respect to group reading, and monitor the completion of clan lit-eracy work. Clans were instructed to complete assignments cooperatively. The following examples depict the manner in which Daniel subverted this cooperative process as a gesture resistant to female leadership:

Daniel: Since you are the headwoman, you've got to know everything. And since you are not much of a headwoman, you've got to think and figure it out. And I'm not going to be part of this, 'cause I know what to write already?

In another example three days later, Daniel confused Mei by criticizing her written work:

Daniel: We have to write in complete sentences.

(A look of confusion comes over Mei's face, because she has written complete sentences and does not know what the comment refers to. She eventually begins to erase her previously written answers. Daniel has almost completed his work sheet and is far ahead of the others.)

Resistance to the headwoman was not peculiar to the boys in this group. The pervasive nature of the resistance on the part of the boys in the class influenced Gloria to modify the headwoman identity. Ten days after the clan groups were initiated, Gloria changed the name of the female clan leader from 'headwoman' to 'clanmother.' Clanmother is an implicit domestication of female leadership because it moves the leadership to the more domestic and therefore 'normal' domain of 'mother.' Mother is a more acceptable designation of leader than woman because of the domestic associations. Gloria also replaced Mikelle with Gina because Mikelle, silenced in her desire to be the headwoman, eventually refused to participate in clan activities.

Mei: improvising into a headwoman

As suggested earlier, Mei was selected by Daniel to be the headwoman because of her overt shyness and apparent conformity to more traditional Chinese expectations regarding female behavior. However, interviews with Mei's mother revealed that Mei's background has familiarized her with resistance to the imposition of traditional gender roles and behavior. Mei's mother had to resist traditional norms associated with female roles and behavior to pursue an education. Her parents had sent her to be raised by her grandmother, who discouraged her from pursuing an education. Later, however, as she became older, her mother supported not only her own desire for an education, but that of her children as well:

> Mei's mother: My Mom is different [in] my grandmother's opinion. Because she also prefers that me and also my children to study. She has a different opinion. She prefer us to study so she came to live with us to help us so that I can study. So I respect my mom a lot.

The statement of Mei's mother reflects a state of tension and change in Mei's family with respect to gender expectations and education. In addition to a familiarity with cultural tension with respect to gender, Mei also was the product of an extremely rigorous education system in Hong Kong. There, even as a second grader, she had to practise considerable discipline and dedication to education:

> Mei's mother: Yeah, she always crying in Hong Kong, because she has to study until midnight in Hong Kong. And I have to ask an English tutor to help her to study, because she could not keep her grades up in Hong Kong. She was very upset … No social life. So lots of pressure when you go to school in Hong Kong.

Mei, in contrast to more surface appearances, brought considerable discipline to the reading group and to the task of becoming a headwoman. Mei, in her responses to Daniel's aggressive gestures, seemed to draw from these aspects of her background to improvise more assertiveness in her reading group participation. Over time, Mei became far more vocal, moving from silent resistance to vocal defiance of Daniel in the context of reading instruction.

In contrast to her ostensible shyness, at no time did Mei accept the imposition of [the] headwoman role on herself. As the following passage suggests, she resisted until Gloria, not knowing the struggles in the group, told her that she was to be the headwoman:

> (Mei and the other headwomen go up to the front of the room to collect the readings from Gloria, which are to be passed out to the other members of each clan. Mei returns to the table and passes out the papers.)

Daniel: Okay, I'm going to read the first paragraph.

Mei: Stop!! (looks at Daniel with an angry look, then turns to Mikelle) Mikelle, would you read the paragraph?

Mei's resistance to Daniel is constructed as an improvisation because it represents a level of assertiveness that Mei had rarely if ever displayed before in class. This assertiveness enabled Mei to orchestrate a properly conducted reading group session, although she was at a lower reading level than Daniel.

Affirmation and new understanding

Throughout the clan unit, despite the turmoil surrounding the headwoman concept, Gloria systematically reinforced the authority of the headwoman. Each time the groups assembled, Gloria called on the headwomen to organize and take control of clan activities. Thus, in the midst of cultural and political uncertainty, Gloria continued to affirm the concept of female leadership. This affirmation began with the first clan meeting, when the status of each headwoman was most precarious, and continued throughout the unit. Gloria's affirmation occasioned Mei's acceptance of the role, which she would not take on from the boys. [...] Mei's initial resistance involved resisting Daniel's behavior by following through on a threat to tell Gloria about his failure to follow directions. Gloria used the occasion to affirm Mei's improvisation by sanctioning her particular authority over the clan:

Mei: He's not cooperating.

Gloria: Well then you. He's not cooperating. Alright, so Mei, as headwoman, what are you going to say to him?

Mei: Please cooperate.

Gloria performed such affirmations throughout the unit. On one occasion, when two boys from one of the other clans approached Gloria about a problem in the clan, Gloria returned them to the authority of the headwoman for her to decide. Gloria's affirmations conveyed the message to the entire class that female leadership was an acceptable classroom practice and norm.

In addition to Gloria's affirmations, classroom peers, male and female, began to support the authority of the headwoman. Twelve days after the initial clan meeting, Deron and Murphy, two boys from different clans, acknowledged the hard work and quality leadership of their headwomen. Within Mei's bear clan, affirmation began to emerge slightly more than two weeks after the clans began. On a day when Mei was absent, progress on a longhouse construction activity slowed down considerably. At one point, Daniel threw down his scissors and said, 'I give up.' Gina, Mikelle's replacement, verbalized the impact of Mei's absence, and affirmed her leadership when she said, 'We'd be done with this thing if Mei was here.' Eventually, Mei took on a legitimate headwoman role, settling disputes, as when Ravi turned to her to settle a disagreement with Daniel, assuming nearly total authority over all clan decisions.

This general affirmation of the new female leadership norm contributed directly to more productive reading group conduct by all the members of the group. Daniel, who eventually adopted a more cooperative disposition during group reading, provided the most profound affirmation. Instead of using his high literacy competency to exert male authority, he became supportive, even helping Mei to decode text. The following passage reflects Daniel's new disposition:

Mei: (reading from the text) Nuts and berries were also part of the Iroquois meals. (faster than her normal pace). The wild … (tries to decode strawberries)
Daniel: Where are we? 'The wild strawberries, the earliest …'
Mei: The earliest fruit of the year was a special favorite. The Iroquois held a feast …
Daniel: Festival.
Mei: Festival to celebrate the feast of the rip …
Daniel: Ripe.
Mei: Ripe berries.
Daniel: Okay, we're done.

Through affirmation, Daniel moved into a helpful, nonhierarchical literacy, which was occasioned by Mei's leadership.

Discussion

Before this Iroquois unit, Daniel was capable of cognitively comprehending the concept of female leadership. However, his cultural and personal biases precluded an acceptance of the term, leading to both cognitive and behavioral resistance. Gloria's weaving of the textual Iroquois leadership theme with classroom practices confronted each student not only with disruptive cultural information, bur also with experiences through which they could improvise responses. Mei, usually shy and reticent, dealing with her family's own ambivalent relation to changing female roles, was able not only to read about female leadership, but also to improvise her own leadership practice. Daniel, overtly hostile to the concept of female leadership, also was able to improvise his own acceptance, conveyed not only through verbal recall, but also through his active cooperation with a female peer.

Conclusion

This chapter attempts to convey the idea that a reading group, particularly one of culturally diverse students, really is a crossroads of educational and cultural influences and implications. Educators who regard such learning contexts merely in the singular terms of comprehension and coconstructed meaning are missing important variables with respect to the learning experiences that children actually have in these groups. For example, the term 'cooperative' in 'cooperative learning' is a culturally loaded term. The accounts in this chapter suggest that cooperation is achieved, in some contexts, only as long as certain cultural assumptions are in place. These assumptions place girls at a disadvantage with respect to leading literacy group activities. When these assumptions are disrupted, resistance can result.

As previous studies have demonstrated, cooperative grouping alone does not necessarily lead to cooperative reading practice. Unless certain assumptions are disrupted, culturally diverse reading groups can be a setting in which gender discrimination can be carried out in the name of literacy. Higher-achieving boys can dominate lower-achieving girls, using their literacy competency as an instrument of power.

Culturally diverse contexts and concepts encountered often in literacy instruction confront students with unfamiliar norms that may disrupt cultural and educational assumptions. Disruption in the hands of a skilled teacher need not be negative, however. Disruption actually can be looked on as a necessary stage through which children grow as they confront diverse norms, improvise accepting responses in a supportive environment, and affirm the validity of these alternatives. At a 'postmodern' moment (Jameson, 1984), during a time when the norms in many societies are increasingly uncertain, children need opportunities to read about, experience, and perform new possibilities. Reading groups can be an important place for such performances.

References

Baker, H.A. (1984). *Blues, ideology and Afro-American literature. A vemacular theory.* Chicago: University of Chicago Press.

Barnes, D., Barnes, D., & Clarke, S. (1984). *Versions of English.* London: Heinemann.

Berghoff, B., & Egawa, K. (1991). No more 'rocks': Grouping to give students control of their learning. *The Reading Teacher,* 44(8), 536–541.

Braddock, J.H., & Dawkins, M.P. (1993). Ability grouping and attainments: Evidence from the national longitudinal study of 1988. *Journal of Negro Education,* 62(3), 324–336.

Cazden, C. (1986). Classroom discourse. In M. Willrock (Ed.), *Handbook of research on teaching* (3rd ed., pp. 432–463). New York: MacMillan.

Cherland, M.R. (1992). Gendered readings: Cultural restraints upon response to literature. *The New Advocate,* 5(3), 187–198.

Evans, K.S. (1996). A closer look at literature discussion groups: The influence of gender on student response and discourse. *The New Advocate,* 9(3), 185–196.

Garcia, E.E. (1994). Educating Mexican American students. In J.A. Banks & C.A.M. Banks (Eds.), *Handbook on multicultural education* (pp. 372–387). New York: Simon & Schuster.

Gates, H.L. (1988). *The Signifying Monkey: A theory of African-American literacy criticism.* New York: Oxford University Press.

Jameson, F. (1984). Postmodernism, or the cultural logic of late capitalism. *New Left Review,* 53–92.

Kreuger, E., & Townsend, N. (1997). Reading clubs boost second-language first graders' reading achievement. *The Reading Teacher,* 51(2), 122–127.

Leal, D. (1993). The power of literary peer-group discussions: How children collaboratively negotiate meaning. *The Reading Teacher,* 47(2), 114.

Lee, C.D., & Slaughter-Defoe, D.T. (1994). Historical and sociocultural influences on African American education. In J.A. Banks & C.A.M. Banks (Eds.), *Handbook on multicultural education* (pp. 348–365). New York: Simon & Schuster.

Lomawaima, K.T. (1994). Educating Native Americans. In J.A. Banks & C.A.M. Banks (Eds.), *Handbook on multicultural education* (pp. 331–342). New York: Simon & Schuster.

Lou, Y., Abrami, P.C., Spence, J.C., Pulsen, C., Chambers, B., & d'Apollonia, S. (1996). Within class grouping: A meta-analysis. *Review of Educational Research,* 66(40), 423–458.

MacGillivray, L., & Hawes, S. (1994). 'I don't know what I'm doing – they all start with "B"': First graders negotiate peer reading interactions. *The Reading Teacher,* 48(3), 210–216.

McMahon, S.I., & Goatley, V.J. (1995). Fifth graders helping peers discuss texts in student-led groups. *The Journal of Educational Research*, 89(1), 23–35.

Meloth, M., & Deering, M. (1992). Effect of two cooperative conditions on peer-group discussions, reading comprehension, and metacognition. *Contemporary Educational Psychology*, 17, 175–193.

Murray, A. (1970). *The omni-Americans: Some alternatives to the folklore of White supremacy.* New York: Vintage Books.

Rabinow, P. (1984). Introduction. In P. Rabinow (Ed.), *The Foucault reader* (pp. 3–30). New York: Pantheon Books.

Strauss, A.L. (1987). *Qualitative analysis for social scientists.* New York: Cambridge University Press.

Tharp, R.G., & Gallimore, R.G. (1991). *Rousing minds to life: Teaching, learning, and schooling in social context.* New York: Cambridge University Press.

Thompson, R.F. (1984). *Flash of the spirit: African and Afro-American art and philosophy.* New York: Random House.

Tinalli, B., & Drake, L (1993). Literature groups: A model of the transactional process. *Childhood Education*, 5, 221–224.

Troyna, B. (1992). Ethnicity and the organization of learning groups: A case study. *Educational Rrsearch*, 34(1), 45–55.

Vygotsky, L.S. (1986). *Thought and language.* Boston: MIT Press.

West, C. (1982). *Prophesy and deliverance: An Afro-American revolutionary Christianity.* Philadelphia: The Westminister Press.

Part 4

Interventions in Different Contexts

13

Excluded Voices: Class, Culture, and Family Literacy in Scotland

Lyn Tett

In this [chapter], I focus on family literacy programs in order to examine the ways in which the literacies of working-class Scottish communities can be marginalised by a system that privileges middle-class, English, school-based literacies. I examine the relationships between literacy and language to find out why people feel that their own ways of speaking and writing are 'wrong' and what action might be taken by family literacy practitioners to help challenge this view. I use a case study of a program, based in a disadvantaged area of Scotland, to show how deficit views of children and their parents might be overcome so that real learning can take place. First, however, I look at the relationship between family literacy programs and the literacies of the home, community, and school.

Literacy in the home, community, and school

Family literacy programs date from the mid-1980s and represent a different response to the challenges of literacy education. Unlike previous approaches that focused on either children or adults, these programs identify the whole family as the site for educational intervention. The classification of these programs as 'family literacy' arises from this wider focus, and the central element that they have in common is consideration of the family as a 'learning unit.' Their central assumption is that the high correlation between the literacy difficulties of the child (e.g., in school) and those of the parent means that these two areas of literacy difficulty should be tackled together. One issue that such programs are designed to address is the situation whereby teachers make assumptions about building upon home literacy experiences but have little idea of what actually happens in the local culture. This means that the literacy history of parents or the differences between home and community practices and those of the school are unexamined: what follows, as Gregory (1996) showed, is that

> [A] deficit model is easily adopted by teachers if parents are asked to perform school-like activities they are incapable of. Parents' lack of cooperation may be interpreted as lack of interest or even hostility. If, on the other hand, work starts by building upon the families' strengths and literacy activities the families are already familiar with, then the picture looks very different. (p. 99)

From: *Journal of Adolescent & Adult Literacy*, 44 (2), 2000, pp. 122–8.

If families are to be real partners in their children's education, then they must be able to share power, responsibility, and ownership with schools in ways that show a high degree of mutuality (see Bastiani, 1993). This becomes problematic not only for the reasons outlined above but also when parents' knowledge about schools and schools' knowledge about parents are characterized by a lack of understanding. Tomlinson (1993) provided one example of this problem: '[T]here is evidence that teachers are still not well-informed about the lives, backgrounds, expectations and desires of ethnic minority parents and are still willing to stereotype such families as "problems"' (p. 144).

The idea that adults whose background is different from that of their children's teachers suffer from an educational deficit that the school has the responsibility to fill is neither accurate nor helpful. Barton (1995), amongst many others, has pointed out that 'Parents may have difficulty reading and writing; nevertheless, they engage in a wide range of literacy activities' (p. 4), and it is these activities that a school-centered approach does not recognize. Research projects in the United States have reached the same conclusion, suggesting that although the form of literacy activity may vary from family to family and from class to class, the amount of activity is often far greater than is assumed by a school-centered analysis (cf. Purcell-Gates, 1993). If the range of literacy activities that people already engage in and feel comfortable about can be built on, then some of these deficit views can be challenged and parents can be helped to see that they are competent first teachers of their children. This will involve family literacy educators, teachers, and parents working in partnership to challenge these deficit views.

Challenging deficit views through a family literacy program

Challenging deficit views of so-called disadvantaged families is, in practice, one way in which the culture of the home can be valued rather than seen as an inadequate environment for the child's literacy development. How this might be done can be illustrated by a family literacy project based in an outer-city housing estate in a poor working-class area of Edinburgh, Scotland. By taking a responsive approach to curriculum building – while at the same time valuing the participants' home and community life – the project seeks to include the literacy practices of everyday life in the curriculum and build on them. The participants in the project are parents of children who attend one of the three primary schools in the area, and they have identified themselves as having literacy problems they would like to work on to help themselves and their children. Groups of up to 12, of whom 90% are mothers, engage in an educational program lasting about 12 weeks. Each group has two tutors who work directly with the participants for about six hours per week.

When they begin the program, participants are asked to identify the literacy practices that they use in the home and community. This reveals a significant range of reading and writing practices that they regularly engage in but that are easily neglected or considered insignificant. These involve, for example, scanning the TV pages to find out what is on that day, checking on their horoscopes, understanding a range of signs and symbols in the local environment, writing brief notes for family members, making shopping lists, labeling family photographs, keeping a note of family birthdays and anniversaries, and sending greeting cards. Recognizing and working on these literacy practices provides an appropriate starting point for the curriculum. Such an approach bases education in everyday literacy concerns and builds on what people already know and do, rather than emphasizing what they can't do. It is coupled with a curriculum based on students' own concerns and aspirations about their own and their children's learning and relationships with their teachers. This combination of approaches leads to a concentration on what really matters to the participants that provides a real motivation for their learning.

Negotiating work in this way is not, however, simply a matter of passing responsibility for developing the curriculum from the tutor to the student, which would be an abdication of tutors' critical interpretative role. The project staff members are committed to a particular understanding of the nature and purpose of their work that informs their practice. Valuing home and community literacies is one example. So is the way they approach the inherently ambivalent nature of family literacy, with its potential to be used as a convenient way of attributing educational failure to 'deficit families.'

Through the curriculum, this type of ideological agenda is challenged. For example, the project explicitly encourages adults to think critically about their own school experiences and works to avoid simplistic, pathological explanations of failure at school. In order to help participants do this, they were asked to talk about their most positive and negative learning episodes, which enabled the wide range of experience in the group to be discussed. This discussion was coupled with student-led presentations that included reflecting upon their own experiences of school in ways that problematised their earlier internalized understandings of failure. In addition, they were asked to discuss the differences between their own school experiences and those of their children in order to identify changing pedagogical practices. Similarly, participants were encouraged to identify and value their own educative role with their children. The emphasis was on the positive ways in which parents already successfully educate their children through different ways of knowing the world (see Heath, 1983; Taylor & Dorsey-Gaines, 1988) instead of assuming that parents lack knowledge and skills that the teacher has to impart.

Using the literacy practices of everyday life

The project studied also sought to include the literacy practices of everyday life in the curriculum so that the home and community life of participants was valued. Students kept a log of their own reading and writing practices and also interviewed others about their role as readers in the family. This revealed a significant range of communication, reading, and writing practices that people regularly engaged in but were easily neglected or considered insignificant – outside as well as within the school. These included adult–child conversations that, as Tizard and Hughes (1984) have pointed out, are rich learning experiences. Recognizing and working on actual literacy practices provided an appropriate starting point for the curriculum because it grounded the educational intervention in real literacy concerns and everyday life. This included challenging assumptions about the homogeneity of reading practices when the wide variation in the group's experiences and the influence of gender, ethnicity, and class on what was considered 'normal' was revealed in discussion. This then led on to a critical examination of the presumptions about family life that were contained in their children's reading books, which revealed assumptions about nuclear family roles that were at odds with many of the participants' own experiences. The next stage of this part of the project was for the participants to create, with the help of computers, stories for their children that reflected their own lives. Access to good word-processing and drawing packages enabled attractive texts to be produced that were authentic reflections of the issues in participants' own families and communities.

The project staff also focused on developing critical language awareness through enabling learners to see language and the reading of texts as problematic (see Wallace, 1992). This involved, for example, collecting texts that the participants came across in everyday use from a range of genres (advertisements, newspapers, letters from school, bills, cereal packets, 'junk mail,' and family photograph albums) to work on as a group. They were asked to identify to whom the text was primarily addressed, who produced it, why it was interesting, and what message the producer was trying to get across so that they could see that all writing is created for a particular purpose. Such decoding challenged the participants' taken-for-granted assumptions that there is just one form of writing and helped them to see that the writing that they create can vary in form too. Student-led investigations, which involved taking photographs of a range of public writing including graffiti, public notices, shop signs, and posters and then coming together to decode these pictures, enabled discussion to take place about the concerns in the community and the messages that were presented to them. Both these approaches let the participants see the ways in which literacy is constructed in different contexts and for different purposes and led to lively discussions about, for example, racism in the community as revealed through graffiti and how particular family lifestyles were assumed by the manufacturers of breakfast cereals. Sometimes the materials produced by the students were used to create a group poem around the theme of the discussion. On other occasions the theme generated letters of complaint to the appropriate authorities, for example, in relation to the removal of racist graffiti. The general approach of the project has been to link reading with writing and talking so that these three important facets of literacy can be brought together into a seamless web.

Another important aspect of the project was the use of 'authentic assessment' (see Fingaret & Drennon, 1997), rather than standardized tests, to assess the adults' progress. This involved developing a portfolio of examples of their literacy work including the titles of books that they read with their children; copies of stories that they had created with their children about their own family life; copies of letters written to friends and families; diaries; examples of reading and writing done in church, neighborhood meetings, or on the job; and photographs of writing that had interested them. This type of assessment helped the students to reflect both on what they had learned and how they learned. This reflection was enhanced when the portfolio was brought along to the group and formed part of a 'show and tell' session that could also be shared with the children. This approach to assessment enabled the extent to which students were able to change their literacy practices to be assessed and also included changes in relationships, particularly with their children and the school, to be recorded.

It appears that by taking a problematising approach to reading and writing practices, the participants in this project were enabled to see that there are a variety of literacies rather than just the one used by the school. This approach, in turn, helped to challenge deficit views of the culture of the home and the community as parents gained confidence. A particular effect was that parents felt able to discuss their own literacy practices on a more equal basis with the school's staff so that they were involved more directly in their children's education. This required the development of a greater understanding by teachers of what parents needed to know about school practices. Understanding was achieved through joint training sessions with the family literacy project and school staff and also through helping parents be in a better position to know what to ask the school in ways that took account of the culture of the local community. Parents learnt by sharing and valuing experiences as well as through suggestions and ideas introduced by the tutor. In this low-key way, the project subtly aided the process of generating new knowledge based on the local culture and context by a process of making the implicit pedagogical activities of the parents explicit.

Literacy, language, and power

One important issue that the project did not address was the ways in which the form of the language through which written literacy is accomplished reflects the values and interests of the dominant groups and classes in society. If this issue is not addressed, then oral traditions and speech patterns are presented as somehow separate from literacy. This means, for example, no connection is made between spoken Scots and written English. What is more, negative views about language are internalized, and this has consequences for how people see themselves and thus functions to undermine their own self-esteem.

This project, despite being based in an area where working-class Scots was the language of the home and the community, appeared to develop language and literacy that conformed to the form of standard, middle-class English. Such English has a powerful ideological stranglehold on what we understand literacy to mean. It downgrades other forms of written and verbal communication as second rate. Language is, therefore, closely interconnected with power. As one of the participants interviewed stated, 'I don't like the way I speak.' This shows how difficult it is for the culture that people express through their language to really have an impact on the literacies of family literacy projects. So improving confidence and self-esteem must also include addressing the issue of language and its relationship to power. In discussions with adults participating in this project, the subject of language stimulated the most animated exchange. Not surprisingly, many considered the use of Scots words in their speech as inferior and a hindrance, as the following remarks from a parent suggest.

> [Referring to her child saying *'trussers.'*] 'Can I say *trussers?'* I say 'No, it's trousers,' but my friend says 'No, she's Scottish, let her speak as she wants.' But I try to teach her to speak property. She'll learn more that way.

Also, the relationship between language and power is clearly grasped in the following parent's comment:

> When they grow up they need to know there is a right time and place to speak. When my girl goes for an interview I'd like to think she'd speak the way the person expects her to speak. That she doesn't go in and speak all slang. But if she comes back and speaks slang that's fine.

The assumption that there is a correct way to speak and that the speech of their children is inherently inferior and inadequate is evident in both comments. Yet there is also a recognition in both that the child's speech patterns are natural (Scottish) and acceptable in a variety of contexts (at home, with friends). Both parents quoted also recognize the way in which language and power work in education ('she'll learn more') and in the material context of work (an interview for a job). This situation also illustrates how difficult it is to avoid dominant forms of language and literacy even in a project concerned to develop a model of practice appropriate to a Scottish context and culture (Lothian Regional Council, undated).

As the Scottish Consultative Council on the Curriculum (1996) has pointed out, because Scots is the language of the home for many people, it provides speakers with their first awareness of themselves and their relationships. Use of the language also helps people to:

> [E]stablish their own sense of values, and [is] closely involved in the development of thinking skills, and those related, equally important, worlds of feeling and social consciousness. Neglecting Scots has, therefore, unwelcome social and personal consequences. (p. 15)

Clearly, one of these unwelcome consequences is a message internalized by the participants in this family literacy program that the language of their home and community is of value only within a very limited range of social contexts. I am not arguing, however, that people should be denied access to dominant literacies or that their own vernacular literacy is somehow privileged. School literacy embodies the language of power, a language that disadvantages working-class and other excluded communities. Some people are able to develop multiliteracy skills that enable them to move freely between vernacular and dominant literacies without disadvantage, but I think that these individuals are unusual and should not be treated as if they were the norm. What is being suggested for family literacy projects is shifting the way the literacy 'problem' has been defined. This shift would involve the recognition that some people are at a disadvantage because of the ways in which a particular literacy is used in dominant institutions. 'The culture children learn as they grow up is, in fact, "ways of taking" meaning from the environment around them' (Heath, 1983, p. 49) and not a 'natural' way of behaving. The social practices of institutions, and the language and literacy they reinforce, have to be made visible to show that they represent a selection from a wider range of possibilities – none of which are neutral. These practices then become a critical resource for learning and literacy.

It should also be remembered, as Hannon (1995) argued, that 'reflecting back and facilitating the family's existing uses for literacy may simply reinforce children's exclusion from school and whatever benefits school success confers' (p. 150). The parent quoted earlier clearly recognized the importance of being able to use different registers and vocabularies in the appropriate contexts, and the same is true for the wider aspects of literacy. Family literacy projects therefore need to promote the literacies of the home and the community to the school in ways that alert both parents and schools to the range of cultures available, of which vernacular literacies are one important example. Schools, for their part, need to be aware that when they involve parents in teaching literacy and promote school literacy in families that do not habitually use it they are 'subtly imposing new uses for written language without changing the cultural context that supports the existing ones' (Hannon, 1995, p. 150). Of course, familiarity with the dominant form of spoken and written English is a vital part of adults' and children's communication, but it should not be the only objective of education.

Emphasizing strengths

bell hooks (1989) argued that:

> [M]oving from silence into speech is, for the oppressed, the colonized, the exploited, and those who stand and struggle side by side, a gesture of defiance that heals, that makes new life and new growth possible. (p. 70)

If the language and literacy of the home and community is unacknowledged or actively suppressed, then coming to voice is particularly difficult. How people feel about their spoken and written literacy shows how community literacies are marginalised in relation to dominant forms of literacy. Asserting the relevance and value of the literacies of the home and community helps to make clear the role of power in shaping our understanding of literacy. Family literacy projects that make explicit such issues in relation to literacy and language and their use can show that they are not working with disadvantaged deficit communities but, on the contrary, communities that are at a disadvantage in relation to a monolingual culture. As Delpit (1995) pointed out:

> [T]hose who have acquired additional codes because their local language differs significantly from the language of the national culture may actually be in a better position to gain access to the global culture than 'mainstream' Americans. Rather than think of these diverse students as problems, we can view them instead as resources who can help all of us learn what it feels like to move between cultures and language varieties, and thus perhaps learn how to become citizens of the global community. (p. 69)

As long as people remain voiceless with their experience interpreted on their behalf by others, then their own meanings are rendered illegitimate and disqualified. Giroux (1992) argued that people need to be able 'to reclaim their own memories, stories and histories as part of an on-going collective struggle to challenge those power structures that attempt to silence them' (p. 170). Family literacy programs could play a part in this struggle through a clear and proactive commitment to starting from people's strengths rather than emphasizing their deficits. This commitment involves valuing difference and starting from people's everyday uses, meanings and purposes for reading and writing and developing authentic texts that reflect the reality of their lives. It also requires access to, and use of, the resources available in the home and the community to support these practices.

Family literacy educators also need to recognise that 'personal troubles' are 'public issues' (Mills, 1959) and so ensure that all taken-for-granted assumptions are subjected to critical questioning in ways that challenge the prevailing 'common sense.' The dominant culture is not monolithic, and this means that there are opportunities for resisting and contesting so the vernacular literacies of the home and the community are also valued. This, in turn, leads to the development of literacies that are about subordinated cultures writing their own stories, rather than just reading other people's books to their children at bedtime. [...]

References

Barton, D. (1995). *Literacy. An introduction to the ecology of written language.* Oxford, England: Blackwell.

Bastiani, J. (1993). Parents as partners: Genuine progress or empty rhetoric? In P. Munn (Ed.), *Parents and schools: Customers, managers or partners* (pp. 101–116). London: Routledge.

Delpit, L. (1995). *Other people's children.* New York: The New Press.

Fingaret, H.A., & Drennon, C. (1997). *Literacy for life.* New York: Teachers College Press.

Giroux, H. (1992). *Border crossings: Cultural workers and the politics of education.* London: Routledge.

Gregory, E. (1996). Learning from the community. In S. Wolfendale & K. Topping (Eds.), *Family involvement in literacy* (pp. 89–102). London: Cassell.

Hannon, P. (1995). *Literacy, home and school.* London: Falmer.

Heath, S.B. (1983). *Ways with words: Language, life and work in communities and classrooms.* Cambridge, England: Cambridge University Press.

hooks, B. (1989). *Talking back: Thinking feminist – thinking black.* Boston: South End Press.

Lothian Regional Council (undated). *Pilton 'Family Literacy' Project: Aims and objectives statement.* Edinburgh, Scotland: Author.

Mills, C.W. (1959). *The sociological imagination.* London: Oxford University Press.

Purcell-Gates, V. (1993). Issues for family literacy research: Voices from the trenches. *Language Arts, 70,* 65–73.

Scottish Consultative Council on the Curriculum. (1996). *The Kist: Teacher's handbook.* Glasgow, Scotland: Nelson Blackie.

Taylor, D., & Dorsey-Gaines, C. (1988). *Growing up literate: Learning from inner-city families.* Portsmouth, NH: Heinemann.

Tizard, B., & Hughes, M. (1984). *Young children learning, talking and thinking at home and in school.* London; Fontana.

Tomlinson, S. (1993). Ethnic minorities: Involved partners or problem parents? In P. Munn (Ed.), *Parents and schools: Customers, managers or partners* (pp. 131–147). London: Routledge.

Wallace, C. (1992). Critical language awareness in the EFL classroom. In N. Fairclough (Ed.), *Critical language awareness* (pp. 59–92). Harlow, England: Longman.

14

Trust Your Own Observations: Assessment of Reader and Tutor Behaviour in Learning to Read in English and Māori

Ted Glynn and Stuart McNaughton

[...]

Introduction

Twenty-seven years ago, we reported on some simple procedures for observing and analysing reading behaviour. These were developed as part of a two-year project aimed at improving attending, reading, and writing behaviour of nine special class children whose reading and writing achievement was minimal (Glynn & McNaughton, 1975). Setting up observation procedures to monitor changes in children's day-to-day attending behaviour was straightforward. However, it was not so easy to set up appropriate day-to-day measures of their reading behaviour.

Standardised measures of reading progress, with their emphasis on long-term outcomes, could not provide us with the precise and continuous information about changes over time in reading behaviour. This information was needed to inform and assist the teacher to change her teaching strategies with respect to individual children. Nor could they inform us about which particular instructional or reader behaviours were the appropriate ones to target. Based on the work of Clay (1972) and Smith (1971), we found that one context highly suited for gathering such information was children's regular classroom reading activity and, in particular, the context of the one-to-one oral interactions that occur between a child and a teacher around a specific text.

We drew extensively on Clay's (1972) theoretical and empirical analyses of reading behaviour in this context, and targeted first the specific directional behaviours identified in her work as prerequisite to early reading, namely, orienting the book correctly, locating the correct place to start on the page, left to right progression, returning from the end of one line to the beginning of the next, and correspondence between each spoken word and printed word. We drew next on Clay's analyses of reading errors and self-corrections for the information they provided about strategies children may be learning to use to make sense of written text. In some of their errors, children preserved correct sematic and/or

From: *International Journal of Disability, Development and Education*, 49 (2), 2002, pp. 161–73.

syntactic information, while their self-corrections suggested a degree of independent monitoring of the match or mis-match between the word they have spoken and the word in print. In our reading program, we targeted children's use of sematic, syntactic, and letter–sound information and self-corrections for explicit prompting and social reinforcement by the teacher.

The 1975 article describes how we attempted operational definitions of these theoretically important reading and tutoring behaviours, and devised simple strategies for coding and recording their occurrence from transcribed tapes of children's regular reading with their teacher. The article also demonstrated how these observational data were used to monitor change in both child and teacher behaviour during oral reading on an ongoing basis across a one-year time span. These data enabled us to generate consistent and objective performance criteria for advancing or not advancing a reader to a more difficult reading text. The criteria took into account whether a text was novel or familiar, the rate of errors occurring, the rate of reader self-corrections occurring, and the rate of prompting provided by the teacher, about letters or sounds or word meanings. The criteria were designed to ensure that teacher decision-making would be based on direct observation of reader performance, so that advancement of children from one reading level to the next would represent the same or similar performance gains across different readers. In the 1975 article, we described how we used this information to depict reading gains by nine special class children participating in our classroom behaviour management and reading and writing program over a 12-month period, between April 1973 and April 1974. We noted also that our observational data identified inconsistencies in teacher response to the performance of different readers.

Reflecting on this study after 27 years, we believe four operational strategies were guiding our use of direct observation to assess reading performance. These strategies have continued to guide our approach to data gathering and assessment in much subsequent work in the area of literacy, particularly reading.

The four operational strategies are summarised as:

1. *Taking continuous observation measures of reading performance in children's regular classroom contexts.* This allowed for the assessment of quite small changes over time and generated information sensitive enough to provide the teacher with detailed feedback on changes in individual children's reading. This type of information was not available from standardised tests of reading achievement.

2. *Combining the technology of systematic observation and recording with appropriate theoretical understandings of how children learn to read.* This required careful operationalising of theoretical constructs such as reader self-corrections and responses to semantic and syntactic information within meaningful texts. What needed to be observed were specific oral and orienting responses consistent with a coherent theoretical position on how children utilise various sources of information within texts.

3. *Taking multiple measures of reading performance.* One-off summative assessments of word knowledge or reading age we found were too gross and lacked the detailed information needed to assist individual children. We realised how important it was not just to observe and record errors, but also to obtain information on specific characteristics of children's responses to those errors, such as whether children were responding to semantic or syntactic features of the words and texts they were reading.

It was also important to observe and record children's rates of self-correction, and how this varied according to text difficulty. We came to appreciate the need for a range of measures covering both accuracy (e.g., percentage of words read incorrectly) and rate (e.g., the percentage of words read correctly in a 3 min sample, or the advancement through text levels of increasing difficulty within a given time, such as a school term). Our data on text level gains plotted against time indicated that although our prime concern was to improve reading performance within individual students, it was also possible to compare changes in performance over time between children.

4. *Measuring the interactions between the reader and the teacher, and not first the reader's responses alone.* This recognised that many reading behaviours occur in specific interactive contexts, which incorporate teacher prompts (likely antecedents of reader behaviours) and teacher responses to errors, as well as teacher social reinforcement (likely consequences of reader behaviours). It also recognised that such teacher behaviours are likely to vary between different children and according to the difficulty and other characteristics of the text being read. In some ways, this approach anticipated the concept of ecological assessment (Brown et al., 2000; Ysseldyke & Christenson, 1987, 1993). Ecological assessment is a major dimension of inclusive education, which locates learning difficulties not just within the child, but also within the interaction between children and the learning contexts available to them. Assessment in an inclusive education paradigm involves finding out what modifications need to be made to tasks, settings, or teacher behaviour in order to more fully include children with special difficulties or learning needs. The fine-grained continuous measures we employed in the 1975 study were pointing us in this direction. We realised that the same teacher, using her intuitive judgement, was advancing some children through texts of increasing difficulty more readily than others, despite the similarity in reading performance of some of these children. Feedback on specific dimensions of teacher behaviour such as differential attention to children's errors and differential reinforcement of reader behaviour, we believed, might be useful in facilitating change in the effectiveness of teacher behaviour.

Over the next few years, these four observation strategies informed and guided the development of the continuous assessment procedures that form part of a widely used reading tutoring program formerly known as the *Mangere Home and School Reading Procedures,* developed in South Auckland in 1977. A team of researchers worked intensively with parents of a group of 10- to 12-year-old low-progress readers to produce a training booklet and video published by the New Zealand Council for Educational Research (Glynn, McNaughton, Robinson, & Quinn, 1979; McNaughton, Glynn, Robinson, & Quinn, 1981). Subsequent research with the program led to its being republished in the UK under the title *Pause Prompt Praise* (McNaughton, Glynn, & Robinson, 1987).

Pause Prompt Praise aimed to break into the cycle of reader dependence, in which low-progress readers encountering unknown words may have learned to cue the teacher to tell them the correct word immediately. *Pause Prompt Praise* tutor behaviours prompt the readers instead to draw on all available information to solve unknown words. Tutor prompts might focus on the reader's background knowledge of the story, familiarity with the language structure of the text, the meaning contained within the context of each sentence or paragraph, and the letter–sound information within words.

Tutors give priority to prompts that focus the reader on understanding word and text meaning. Only after reader responses indicate that the reader has some understanding of the meaning of what is being read does the tutor focus reader attention onto letter and sound information. Tutors may ignore minor errors that do not greatly alter the meaning of the text. Tutors tell the reader the correct word only as a last resort and only after two prompts have been tried.

There has been considerable evidence reporting on the effectiveness of *Pause Prompt Praise* in improving children's reading performance when used by either parent or peer tutors (Glynn, 1995; Glynn & McNaughton, 1985; Houghton & Bain, 1993; Houghton & Glynn, 1993; Wheldall & Glynn, 1989; Wheldall & Mettem, 1985). We believe that one of the reasons for the positive reading gains usually reported in studies implementing *Pause Prompt Praise* is the quality of the information generated on tutor implementation of the program strategies as well as on students' reading performance. This information is gathered using an observation and recording strategy, usually along the lines shown in Figure 14.1.

Figure 14.1 illustrates the four observational strategies in use in the context of the *Pause Prompt Praise* program. The behaviours to be observed and recorded are consistent with theoretical perspectives that depict independent reading as learning to use all sources of information (both contextual and letter–sound) to 'make sense' from written text. They are also consistent with applied behaviour analysis perspectives that utilise the power of both antecedents and consequences in changing behaviour (Wheldall & Glynn, 1989). Further, multiple measures are taken of both reader and tutor behaviour, enabling detailed analysis of the interaction between the two. For example, children's errors may provide differential antecedents for teacher responses, while certain teacher behaviours (e.g., pausing) may act as a powerful antecedent for children to engage with the text. Multiple measures are also able to provide a more detailed framework for feedback on tutor implementation of the procedures.

Figure 14.1 illustrates how the reader–tutor interaction in *Pause Prompt Praise* can be completed from a brief tape-recording of a few minutes' reading on the run. Reader–tutor input can be observed and recorded as frequently and continuously as required.

In Figure 14.1, column (1) is for recording the text word that was read incorrectly, and column (2) is for recording the reader's actual response (either the incorrect word, or a blank if no attempt was made at the word). Analysis of the responses in column (2) enable the tutor to assess whether the error: (a) is close in meaning to the correct word, (b) follows the appropriate syntax required by the sentence, (c) matches the letter–sound information in the word, or (d) whether error is simply a 'non-attempt.'

When an error occurs, the tutor's first task is to pause. The pause prevents the tutor from interrupting too soon. This may allow readers to notice for themselves that what they have read may not quite make sense and, possibly, to self-correct. Tutors should pause either for up to 5 s, during which a self-correction may occur or, alternatively, until the reader has reached the end of the phrase or sentence containing the error. If an appropriate pause has occurred after each error, a tick is entered in column (3) (tutor behaviour). When a self-correction occurs, a tick is placed in column 11 (child correction). When the tutor provides specific praise for this (self-correction), a tick is placed in column (8) (tutor praise).

The pause also allows the tutor time to decide which of three kinds of error has occurred, whether it is a non-attempt, a substitution that does not make sense, or a substitution that does make sense. After the tutor has paused, and if the reader has not self-corrected, the tutor offers a prompt to help the reader with the word (see Prompt columns (4), (5), and (6) in Figure 14.1). Tutors are required to select one of three kinds of prompt,

PAUSE PROMPT PRAISE RECORD SHEET

READER ERRORS		PAUSE	PROMPT			PRAISE				READER CORRECTIONS		
						TUTOR						
(1) correct word from the test	(2) word read by mistake or word omitted	(3) wait up to 5 secs unless self-corrects before then	(4) to read on or read again	(5) about the meaning of the word	(6) about the look or sound of the word	(7) if reader's word is word is correct	(8) if reader self-corrects NO tutor help	(9) if reader uses tutor prompt to correct	(10) if reader tries hard or works well	(11) reader self-corrects error without help from tutor	(12) reader corrects error after tutor prompts	(13) reader is told the word by tutor

1
2
3
4
5
6

Figure 14.1   *Pause Prompt Praise* record sheet, for recording reader–tutor interactions during *Pause Prompt Praise* tutoring

according to the type of error the reader has made. Moving from left to right, these three kinds of prompt correspond to three types of error.

When the reader's error is a non-attempt (which is not self-corrected after a tutor pause), the tutor prompts the reader either to 'read on' or 'read again.' 'Read on' prompts are used if the error is at the beginning or middle of a sentence or clause, and 'read again' prompts are used if the error is near the end. Sometimes this kind of prompt is sufficient for the reader to 'pick up' the meaning of the word from the context of the sentence or story. When this happens, a tick is placed in column (4) (tutor prompts), and in column (12) because the reader has made a 'prompted correction.' If the tutor provides specific praise for this (prompted correction), a tick is placed in column (9) (tutor praise).

When the reader's error is a word that does *not* make sense, the tutor uses a 'meaning prompt' directing the reader's attention to what the word means (e.g., a question referring to the picture, the context of the sentence, the page, the whole story, or to the reader's prior knowledge and experience). When this happens, a tick is placed in column (5) (tutor prompts) and in column (12) because the reader has made a prompted correction. If the tutor provides specific praise for this (prompted correction), a tick is placed in column (9) (tutor praise).

When the error is a word that *does* make sense, the tutor may then use a 'letter or sound prompt,' directing the reader's attention to what the word looks or sounds like. Note that this kind of prompt is offered only when the error suggests that the reader has already understood something of the meaning of the word. When this happens, a tick is placed in column (6) (tutor prompts) and in column (12) because the reader has made a prompted correction. If the tutor provides specific praise for this (prompted correction), a tick is placed in column (9) (tutor praise).

When readers do not read the correct word following two tutor prompts, the tutor should supply the correct word. When this happens, a tick should be placed in column (13). This is the 'bottom line' which tutors try to avoid. Lengthy reader–tutor interactions can distract the child from attending to the text. Instead, tutors should focus on making their first two prompts as effective as possible.

Table 14.1 provides an example of how these same direct observation strategies have contributed to the reporting of data on reading progress of students in a home and school literacy program in nine urban primary schools (Glynn, Berryman, & Glynn, 2000). Data in Table 14.1 represent pre- and post-measures of reading performance in two groups of 8- to 9-year-old Māori students learning to read in English medium. Group 1 had participated in a 20-week home and school literacy program in addition to the literacy program implemented at school. Group 2 had participated only in the school's literacy program over the same period. Table 14.1 shows that students in the home and school program had advanced four book levels, while those participating only in the school's program advanced two book levels. Further, students in the home and school group increased their scores on a cloze comprehension measure from 53% to 65% (while reading texts four levels in advance of their pre-program levels). In contrast, students in the school-only group showed a decrease on this measure from 65% to 52% (while reading texts two levels in advance of their pre-program levels). Table 14.1 shows there were only minor changes in correct and incorrect reading rates, with no appreciable differences between groups. Students were not increasing their reading rate at the expense of accuracy.

These data on students' reading show the usefulness of observing and recording multiple measures of reading performance, in this case, fluency (correct rate), accuracy (incorrect rate),

Table 14.1   Pre- and post-program reading data from students in the home and school and school groups

	Group 1 (n = 15) Home and School		Group 2 (n = 11) School	
	Pre-program	Post-program	Pre-program	Post-program
Book level (difficulty)	17	21	18	20
Comprehension (cloze measures %)	53	65	65	52
Correct rate (words per min)	40	43	44	47
Incorrect rate (words per min)	6	5	5	6

and comprehension (cloze), as well as reading progress through texts of increasing difficulty (book level). It is the combination of outcomes across all four measures that provides
a balanced assessment of the reading gains made by the two groups of students, and allows
one to conclude that there were additional gains accruing to the home and school program
group.

In more recent years, the observation strategies from the 1975 article have also been able
to contribute in quite a different arena, that of the revitalisation of indigenous, language
and culture. *Pause Prompt Praise* has been evaluated in the context of assisting learning to
read Māori as a second language in primary and intermediate school settings (Glynn et al.,
1996; Glynn et al., 1998).

The historical relationship between indigenous and European people in New Zealand
education has been characterised by political and social control by the European majority.
Government educational policies have ranged through assimilation, integration, multiculturalism, and biculturalism. The cumulative effects of these policies have been to require
Māori to sacrifice more and more of their language, their culture, and their own indigenous educational aspirations to the needs and goals of the nation, as determined largely by
the European majority. Participation in mainstream education in New Zealand has come
for Māori at a cost of their own language and culture (Glynn, 1998).

In recent years, Māori have made major initiatives to take control of their own education and to ensure the survival of the language and culture. They have strived to establish
state-funded preschools (kōhanga reo), primary schools (kura kaupapa Māori), and secondary schools (whare kura) that deliver the national curriculum through immersion in the
indigenous language. However, the large majority of Māori students are in mainstream
schools and are likely to be there for the foreseeable future. Hence, it is increasingly
important for mainstream educators to address the learning needs of Māori students, a
great many of whom are seriously underachieving in the mainstream. However, it is
equally important to do this in ways that affirm and legitimate the language and cultural
differences indigenous students bring with them into mainstream classrooms. Educators
need to recognise that in terms of success at school, affirmation of language and cultural
identity count just as much for indigenous students as for refugee and migrant students
(Bishop & Glynn, 1999).

At Poho-o-Rawiri marae (meeting place, including house and grounds, sited on tribal
land) at Gisborne in 1991, the *Pause Prompt Praise* program was offered as a resource to
Māori staff members of the New Zealand Specialist Education Service (now part of the
Ministry of Education). Following acceptance by Māori staff from the Tauranga region,

the program was explored and trialed in a Māori cultural context (Māori language immersion classes at an urban primary school) and redeveloped in Māori language. It is known as *Tatari Tautoko Tauawhi* (Berryman, Bidois, Furlong, Atvars, & Glynn, 1995; Harawira, Glynn, & Durning, 1993).

Critical research issues arise in situations when methodologies from non-indigenous knowledge bases and researchers who are non-indigenous people become involved in assessing and interpreting the achievement of indigenous students and their families. These issues can involve questions of *initiation, benefits, legitimation, representation,* and *accountability* for research procedures and information generated (Bishop, 1996; Bishop & Glynn, 1999). Careful planning and attention to these issues may avoid data from indigenous students being understood by non-indigenous researchers as indicators of cultural deficits rather than as reflecting cultural differences and preferences. In the following two studies, these questions were managed through ensuring that ownership and control over the entire research process remained with Māori, even though the observation strategies based on those from the 1975 study clearly had come from a positivist Western research paradigm. It is not the selection of paradigm and methodology that provides the key distinction between indigenous and non-indigenous research. Rather, the distinction lies in who is asking the research questions, who is in control of the research process and interpreting what the findings mean, and to whom the researchers are accountable.

Management of these critical questions in the two studies reported below was achieved through having the research carried out by the Poutama Pounamu research whanau (a group of researchers working together in the manner of an extended family but not necessarily formed along kinship lines) (Glynn et al., 1997; Harawira et al., 1996). This research whanau operates according to Māori tikanga (protocol), works under the guidance of kaumatua and kuia (elders) and follows decision-making processes that are culturally safe and effective for Māori. In undertaking this trial of *Tatari Tautoko Tauawhi*, the whanau decided to adopt the observation and recording procedures that were developed with *Pause Prompt Praise,* and to assess their usefulness in providing feedback to tutors working within a Māori language-learning context.

The program was trialed over 10 weeks in a peer-tutoring context with seven tuākana (tutor)–teina (tutee) pairs in the Māori medium classes at one urban primary school (Glynn et al., 1993). Tutoring sessions lasted 15 min and occurred three times a week. Within a Māori worldview, the tuākana–teina relationship carries with it more than just the connotation of peer tutoring or buddy support. It also carries cultural meanings to do with the caring relationship of an elder sibling towards a younger sibling, including the rights and responsibilities that each has towards the other within a kinship whanau (extended family).

In the first study, tutors readily learned to implement the *Tatari Tautoko Tauawhi* strategies. Following training, tutors showed that they greatly increased their rate of pausing following reader errors and increased their use of specific praise, although this was already considerable. Tuākana also increased their use of prompting and reduced their rate of simply telling readers the correct word. The observation and recording and tutor feedback procedures developed from the earlier *Pause Prompt Praise* proved effective in this context of students learning Māori as a second language.

At the end of 10 weeks, the data showed that readers increased their correct reading rate (from 38 to 43 words per min) and decreased their incorrect reading rate (from 2.4 to 1.8 words per min). Readers also self-corrected more of their errors following the training of their tuākana in *Tatari Tautoko Tauawhi*. Tutors, who in their own independent reading were already displaying higher correct rates than readers, did not further increase this. However, like the readers, the tutors reduced their incorrect reading rate. Data indicated that this decreased from 1.6 to 0.6 words per min. These results, indicating benefits for tutors, are consistent with those from other research studies reporting gains for tutors as well as tutees in English language peer-tutored reading contexts (Glynn & Glynn, 1986; Houghton & Bain, 1993; Houghton & Glynn, 1993; Limbrick, McNaughton, & Glynn, 1985; Medcalf & Glynn, 1987; Tang & Moore, 1992; Tavener & Glynn, 1989; Wheldall & Mettem, 1985).

While these results from the observational measures were encouraging, two issues emerged that were not addressed in the trial. First, a number of parents and several teachers were concerned about the possible negative impact of these gains on children's learning to read in English. Second, while assessing reading accuracy, self-correction, and correct and incorrect reading rates, the trial did not include measures of reading comprehension.

Accordingly, the Poutama Pounamu research whanau undertook a second study at an urban intermediate school. This study monitored the reading progress in both Māori and English, of the 26 reader–tutor pairs, as well as eight control students from several Māori medium classes (Glynn et al., 1996). This study also included measures of reading comprehension in both languages. Tutor training and feedback were undertaken by the students' classroom teachers.

After 10 weeks of tutoring, readers gained between 1.5 and 2.0 years in reading level, increased their correct reading rate by 15 words per min, and lowered their incorrect rate by almost 2 words per min. They also increased their comprehension scores by between 20 and 46%.

As in the first study, tutors also benefited from participating in the tutoring role. They gained between 0.5 and 1.3 years in reading level, increased their correct reading rate by 7 words per min, and lowered their incorrect rate by 0.8 words per min. They also increased their comprehension scores by between 19 and 41%.

In this study, all students read exclusively Māori language texts and the *Tatari Tautoko Tauawhi* program was implemented predominantly in Māori, yet gains were made by both readers and tutors on measures of reading in English. Readers gained 1 year in English reading level and 20% in English comprehension. Tutors gained 0.5 years in English reading level and 25% in English comprehension. Clearly, gains made in learning to read in a second language did not occur at the expense of reading in the first. Important cultural learning also took place in this study. Students learned to understand and value the tuākana–teina relationship and its two-way responsibilities, thus highlighting the inseparable linkages between language learning and cultural learning.

Positive outcomes from research studies with children learning to read in both English and Māori attest to the effectiveness of the *Pause Prompt Praise* and *Tatari Tautoko Tauawhi* programs, whether implemented by peer tutors (Glynn et al., 1998) or by parent and family tutors (Glynn, Berryman, & Glynn, 2000). These outcomes, in turn, attest to the continued usefulness of the simple observational strategies, and of the one-to-one oral reading context as helpful tools for assessing students' reading progress. Over the 27 years since our study of nine students in a special class, we have refined the 1975 observation assessment procedure to provide measures of rate, accuracy, comprehension, and analyses of patterns of students' errors, which are sensitive enough to assess short-term changes in reading behaviour. We have combined these measures to develop consistent criteria for advancing readers to more difficult texts, and for assessing longer-term changes in reading achievement, in terms of rate of progress through texts of increasing difficulty.

In our experience, data collected and presented in the research format shown in Figure 14.1 and Table 14.1 can be readily understood by teachers and by peer and adult tutors. These data on reader–tutor interaction have proved invaluable in helping tutors or teachers to change their teaching behaviour. Presenting teachers and tutors with such specific and focused information on their own teaching behaviour is a powerful component for self-managed behaviour change. The Poutama Pounamu research whanau have consistently incorporated guided discussions of reader and tutor interaction around a small number of reader errors as a part of many training workshops on *Pause Prompt Praise* or *Tatari Tautoko Tauawhi*. Guided discussions typically take the form of 'talking through' with a tutor their own responses to four or five specific reader errors, from information recorded on the data sheet (Figure 14.1). Tutors are invited to reflect on their tutoring behaviour as they follow the line from left to right for each error and, with the benefit of the recorded information, to suggest alternative responses to try on a further occasion.

The recent *Report of the Literacy Task Force* (Ministry of Education, 1999) recommended to the New Zealand Ministry of Education that: 'monitoring and assessment of individual children is an on-going and integral part of teaching practice' (p. 26); 'the Ministry of Education develop a comprehensive professional development package to assist teachers to implement best practice in their teaching of reading and writing' (p. 19); and 'research be undertaken to support the development of diagnostic tools for use in Māori medium education' (p. 26).

We believe that the observational strategies that underpinned the reading intervention in the Glynn and McNaughton (1975) study, which have guided the development of continuous reading assessment strategies in a range of studies involving *Pause Prompt Praise* and *Tatari Tautoko Tauawhi* have a distinct role to play in the implementation of these key recommendations. The strategies may be 'close to the ground' in their focus on continuous observation of fine-grained detail, but their scope for contributing to professional development in literacy is wide-ranging:

Iti rearea, teitei kahikatea, ka taea.
(The smallest bird can reach the top of the tallest tree.)

References

Berryman, M., Bidois, P., Furlong, M., Atvars, K. & Glynn, T. (1995). Tatari Tautoko Tauawhi: A Maori language reading tutoring programme. Item 6. *S.E.T. Research Information for Teachers*, 1, 1–6.

Bishop, R. (1996). Addressing issues of self determination and legitimation in Kura Kaupapa Maori research. In B. Webber (Ed.), *He Paepae Korero: Research perspectives in Maori education* (pp. 143–160). Wellington, NZ: New Zealand Council for Educational Research.

Bishop, R. & Glynn, T. (1999). *Culture counts: Changing power relations in education.* Palmerston North, NZ: Dunmore Press.

Brown, D., Moore, D., Thomson, C., Anderson, A., Walker, J., Glynn,T., Macfarlane, A., Medcalf, J. & Ysseldyke, J. (2000). Resource teachers learning and behaviour: An ecological approach to special education. *Australian Journal of Special Education,* 24(1), 15–20.

Clay, M. (1972). *Reading: The patterning of complex behaviour.* Auckland: Heinemann Educational.

Glynn, E.L. & McNaughton, S.S. (1975). Trust your own observations: Criterion referenced assessment of reading progress. *The Slow Learning Child,* 22, 91–108.

Glynn, E.L., McNaughton, S.S., Robinson, V.R. & Quinn, M. (1979). *Remedial reading at home: Helping you to help your child.* Wellington, NZ: New Zealand Council for Educational Research.

Glynn, T. (1995). Pause Prompt Praise: Reading tutoring procedures for home and school partnership. In S. Wolfendale & K. Topping (Eds.), *Family involvement in literacy: Effective partnerships in education* (pp. 33–44). London: Cassell.

Glynn, T. (1998). Bicultural challenges for educational professionals in Aotearoa. Inaugural Lecture, University of Waikato. *Waikato Journal of Education,* 4, 3–16.

Glynn, T., Atvars, K., Furlong, M., Davies, M., Rogers, S. & Teddy, N. (1993). *Tatari Tautoko Tauawhi: Hei awhina tamariki ki le panui pukapuka. Some preliminary findings.* Paper presented at the New Zealand Psychological Society Annual Conference, Wellington, New Zealand.

Glynn, T., Berryman, M., Atvaks, K., Harawira, W., Walker, R. & Kaiwai, H. (1998). Bicultural research and support programmes for Maori students, teachers and communities. In I. Livingstone (Ed.), *New Zealand annual review of education* (Vol. 8, pp. 43–64). Wellington, NZ: Victoria University, School of Education.

Glynn, T., Berryman, M., Atvars, K., Harawira, W., Walker, R. & Tarj, R. (1997). *Research, training and indigenous rights to self-determination: Challenges arising from a New Zealand bicultural journey.* Paper presented at the International School Psychology XXth Annual Colloquium – School Psychology, Making Links: Making the Difference, Melbourne.

Glynn, T., Berryman, M., Bidois, P., Furlong, M., Thatcher, J., Walker, R. & Atvars, K. (1996). Bilingual reading gains for tutors and tutees in a Maori language immersion programme. In B. Webber (Ed.), *He Paepae Korero: Research issues in Maori education* (pp. 35–58). Wellington, NZ: New Zealand Council for Educational Research.

Glynn, T., Berryman, M. & Glynn, V. (2000). *Reading and writing gains for Maori students in mainstream schools: Effective partnerships in the Rotorua Home and School Literacy Project.* Paper presented at the 18th World Congress on Reading, Auckland.

Glynn, T. & Glynn,V. (1986). Shared reading by Cambodian mothers and children learning English as a second language. *The Exceptional Child,* 33, 159–172.

Glynn, T. & McNaughton, S. (1985). The Mangere Home and School Remedial Reading Procedures: Continuing research on their effectiveness. *New Zealand Journal of Psychology,* 15(2), 66–77.

Harawira, W., Glynn, T. & Durning, C. (1993). *Tatari Tautoko Tauawhi: Hei awhina tamariki ki te panut pukapuka.* Tauranga, NZ: New Zealand Special Education Service.

Harawira, W., Walker, R., Atvars, K., Berryman, M., Glynn, T. & Duffull, T. (1996, June). *A bicultural research journey: The Poutama Pounamu Education Research Centre.* Paper presented at The Fourth Indigenous Peoples' Conference, Albuquerque, NM.

Houghton, S. & Bain, A. (1993). Peer tutoring with ESL and below-average readers. *Journal of Behavioral Education,* 3, 125–142.

Houghton, S. & Glynn, T. (1993). Peer tutoring of below average secondary school readers with Pause Prompt and Praise: Successive introduction of tutoring components. *Behaviour Change,* 10, 75–85.

Limbrick, E., McNaughton, S. & Glynn, T. (1985). Reading gains for underachieving tutors and tutees in a cross age peer tutoring programme. *Journal of Child Psychology and Psychiatry,* 26, 939–953.

McNaughton, S., Glynn, T. & Robinson, V. (1987). *Pause, Prompt and Praise: Effective tutoring of remedial reading.* Birmingham, UK: Positive Products.

McNaughton, S., Glynn, T., Robinson, V. & Quinn, M. (1981). *Parents as remedial reading tutors: Issues for home and school.* Wellington, NZ: New Zealand Council for Educational Research.

Medcalf, J. & Glynn, T. (1987). Assisting teachers to implement peer-tutored remedial reading using pause prompt and praise procedures. *Queensland Journal of Guidance and Counselling,* 1(1), 11–23.

Ministry of Education (1999). *Report of the Literacy Task Force.* Wellington, NZ: Author.

Smith, F. (1971). *Understanding reading: A psycholinguistic analysis of reading and learning to read.* New York: Holt, Rinehart and Winston.

Tang, H. & Moore, D. (1992). Effect of cognitive and metacognitive pre-reading activities on the reading comprehension of ESL learners. *Educational Psychology,* 12, 315–331.

Tavener, J. & Glynn, T. (1989). Peer tutoring of reading as a context for learning English as a second language. *Language and Reading: An International Journal,* 3(1), 1–111.

Wheldall, K. & Glynn, T. (1989). *Effective classroom learning.* Oxford: Blackwell.

Wheldall, K. & Mettem, P. (1985). Behavioural peer tutoring: Training 16 year old tutors to employ the Pause Prompt and Praise method with 12 year old remedial readers. *Educational Psychology,* 5(1), 27–44.

Ysseldyke, J., & Christenson, S. (1987). Evaluating students' instructional environments. *Remedial and Special Education,* 8(8), 17–24.

Ysseldyke, J. & Christenson, S. (1993). *TIES II: The Instructional Environment System II* (4th ed.). Longmont, CO: Sopris West.

15

Long-term Outcomes of Early Reading Intervention

Jane Hurry and Kathy Sylva

[…]

Early reading intervention: who does it help and for how long?

Increasingly, children with reading difficulties are being offered early intervention, and based on the evidence of its short-term effectiveness (e.g. National Reading Panel, 2000; Torgesen, 2000; Wasik & Slavin, 1993), this is to be welcomed. Early intervention is also promoted as a way of preventing 'Matthew effects' (Chall, 1983; Stanovich, 1986) whereby the gap between poor readers and their peers widens as they move through school, because poor readers read less than their peers (Allington, 1984; Biemiller, 1977–1978; Clay, 1967; Juel, 1988), which in turn holds back their language development, their general knowledge and even their IQ. It is therefore important to know just how durable are the gains made during early interventions, in order to plan effective later provision, if necessary, for children who have received early intervention. The present [chapter] examines whether or not early reading intervention is indeed effective in the long term, at the end of primary or elementary schooling. Two programmes are evaluated, both with a proven track record, but with very different approaches, broadly representative of the two dominant contemporary intervention strategies. The first, a phonological intervention closely based on that of Bradley and Bryant (1985), is a successful intervention with a specifically phonological focus. The second, Reading Recovery (Clay, 1985), is one of the most successful early interventions with a broad model of reading (Pinnell, Lyons, DeFord, Bryk & Seltzer, 1994). In this type of intervention, reading for meaning is foregrounded.

Both intervention programmes are underpinned by a view of reading development that would predict sustained gains following early intervention.

Phonological intervention

Decoding is one of the central tasks of reading (Gough, 1996) and current theories identify phonological processing as fundamental to decoding (Bishop & Snowling, 2004; Harm &

From: *Journal of Research in Reading*, 30 (3), 2007, pp. 227–48.

Seidenberg, 2004; Jackson & Coltheart, 2001; Stuart, 2002). 'Phase' models of reading development suggest that understanding the alphabetic principle is the critical early hurdle for the child, underpinning further development of fluent reading and reading comprehension (Byrne, 1998; Ehri, 1991, 1992, 1998, 1999, 2005; Ehri & Wilce, 1985; Frith, 1985; Juel, 1991; Stanovich, 1986) and recent interpretations of dual route models of reading also propose that the development of a lexical route relies too on insight into the alphabetic principle (Stuart, 2002). Research has consistently identified deficits in phonological processing as one of the most common causes of literacy difficulties (Frith, 1995; Goswami & Bryant, 1990; Hulme & Snowling, 1992; Jackson & Coltheart, 2001; Rack, Snowling & Olson, 1992; Siegel, 1989; Stanovich & Siegel, 1994). If mastery of the alphabetic principle is critical to reading development, then children who have responded well to phonological intervention should experience fewer problems as they mature as readers. Theories which address phonological skills describe development in terms of word-level skills, such as a 'full alphabetic phase', where the reader is not only able to form alphabetic connections but can also map phonemes and graphemes on to sight words, and a 'consolidated alphabetic phase' where recurring letter patterns become consolidated (Ehri, 1999).

Reading Recovery

Clay (1991) proposes that there is a critical 'acquisition period', corresponding approximately to the first two years of formal schooling (p. 318). During this period, children form a basic network of strategies 'conducive to literacy learning' which include searching, selecting and checking understanding of print. She writes that 'during the reading acquisition phase the novice reader is not only learning words or letter–sound relationships but is also learning how to use each of the sources of information in texts, how to link these to stored knowledge and which strategic activities make "reading" successful' (p. 321). Children who successfully negotiate this stage become relatively independent readers aware of whether or not they understand what they read and able to draw on a range of key strategies to correct their own mistakes. The critical stage implied is one of an explicit orientation towards the reading process, that it is something that should make sense. The importance of specific skills, such as a good grasp of letter–sound correspondences, is recognised, but only as part of a range of strategies being actively employed to draw meaning from print. Thus, Clay's view of the early developmental stage of reading is much broader than that of theorists reviewed above who foreground phonological processing. Clay argues that children experiencing problems during this stage run the risk of developing bad habits and a negative approach to reading. In Reading Recovery lessons, children are shown how to self-monitor, to check their understandings using all the strategies available to them, to predict and to confirm. In other words, they are shown how to develop and make use of meta-cognitive strategies in their reading. According to Clay, this allows them to become self-sustaining, independent readers, still requiring adequate classroom instruction, but no longer in need of additional help except in a few cases where there are more deep-seated problems.

An alternative view: the need for ongoing intervention

If the early developmental stages of literacy acquisition are critical in determining later success, then it can justifiably be argued that early intervention to accelerate and improve children's passage through these early developmental stages should produce lasting long-term effects. However, the more weight one gives to other aspects inherent in children (e.g. their cognitive and linguistic abilities) and the more weight one gives to environmental factors (e.g. the input of home and school), the more likely it is that the effectiveness of targeted early intervention will not be sustained in the long term. If reading development is seen as ongoing, underlying causal factors not addressed by early intervention, such as impoverished literacy experience outside school, inappropriate classroom provision and children's more general learning problems, are likely to re-exert their influence with the passage of time. What is the existing evidence concerning long-term effects of early intervention?

Long-term effects of early intervention

Bus and van Ijzendoorn (1999) in a meta-analysis of studies measuring the effects of phonological intervention found large short-term effects on phonological awareness (effect size [es] = 1.04) and medium effects on reading (es = .70). This is consistent with a large body of evidence of the effectiveness of explicit phonics instruction but this evidence does not address the durability of early gains (Hurry, 2004; National Reading Panel, 2000). In the eight studies reported by Bus and van Ijzendoorn (1999) which examined long-term effects (maximum 29 months), these were much weaker. After an average of about a year and a half, there were no significant effects on reading (es = .16) but small but significant effects on spelling (es = .25) and reading comprehension (es = .26).

Byrne, Fielding-Barnsley and Ashley (2000) did find significant long-term effects for their preschool phonological training. Six years after children had received the 12-week intervention (30 minutes per week), they did significantly better than controls on both word and non-word reading. Although the long-term effect of such a limited intervention is impressive, es were small (ranging from .33 to .39) and Byrne, Fielding-Barnsley and Ashley conclude that 'children who are slow to grasp ideas early in reading development ... are liable to remain slow to acquire other principles' (p. 666) and may continue to need support. Overall, the evidence suggests that early, time-limited phonological intervention alone may not be enough to ensure long-term reading success.

Reading Recovery is one of the most fully evaluated broadly based early interventions, and several studies have examined its effectiveness a year or two post-intervention. In the most methodologically rigorous study, Pinnell et al. (1994) found a substantial immediate effect of Reading Recovery, and Reading Recovery children were still performing significantly better than controls eight months after intervention but there was a reduction in the effect compared with immediate post-test. DeFord, Pinnell, Lyons and Young (1988) followed up two cohorts of Reading Recovery and comparison children to the end of third grade. After two years, the Reading Recovery children had maintained their gains in terms of months of reading age advantage; however, this advantage ceased to be statistically significant and the intervention effect diminished. The lack of significant long-term effects of Reading Recovery in Ohio is confirmed in the report of the Battelle study group to the Ohio Department of Education (1995) which concludes that short-term reading gains are not maintained in Grades 3 and 4.

In Australia and New Zealand, four studies have examined the medium/long-term effects of Reading Recovery. One found only very small differences between Reading Recovery children and a comparison group one year after intervention (Glynn, Crooks, Bethune, Ballard & Smith, 1989). Center, Wheldall, Freeman, Outhred and McNaughton (1995) present a mixed picture one year post-intervention, with Reading Recovery children significantly ahead of their controls on Book Level (a measure using graded texts) but not on the range of other measures used (words in context, text comprehension and metalinguistic processes. Two further Australian studies of Reading Recovery (Rowe, 1989; Wade & Moore, 1997) report more powerful long-term effects, with advantages persisting for Reading Recovery children to the end of Years 5 and 6. However, Wade and Moore followed up only children who had successfully completed the programme. Such comparisons tell us little about the overall long-term effectiveness of Reading Recovery because they fail to follow up children who participated in the programme but were not successful on it.

In summary, the international evidence of longer-term effects of Reading Recovery, with one exception (Rowe, 1989), does not support the hypothesis that Reading Recovery can alter children's 'learning curve' beyond the period of intervention, though gains made during the intervention tend to be maintained (Shanahan & Barr, 1995). Similarly, for the other major broad-based intervention, Success for All (SFA), Venezky (1998) reports that after the early primary grades, SFA students begin to fall behind the national average until by the end of Grade 5 they are almost 2.4 years behind.

The evidence base for long-term effects of early intervention is small, particularly for children with early reading difficulties and for the United Kingdom. The present study adds to the existing evidence and explores interactions between two models of intervention (Reading Recovery and Phonological Training) and children's initial reading levels to inform us about the fit between child and intervention.

Methods

Research design

Children receiving Reading Recovery (provided by their schools) and children receiving Phonological Training (provided by the research team) were compared with similar (control) children receiving their school's standard provision.

As shown in Figure 15.1, children were pre-tested on a battery of reading tests in September/October 1992, before the start of intervention (pre-test). Short-term gains were assessed in June/July 1993 after the interventions were completed (post-test 1). Medium-term gains were assessed one year later, in May/July (post-test 2). Long-term effects were assessed in September/December 1996, when children were in Year 6 (final year of primary school, post-test 3).

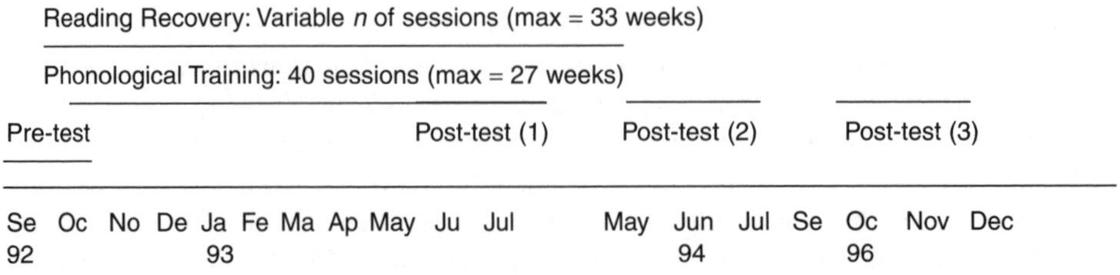

Reading Recovery: Variable n of sessions (max = 33 weeks)

Phonological Training: 40 sessions (max = 27 weeks)

| Pre-test | | Post-test (1) | Post-test (2) | Post-test (3) |

| Se Oc No De Ja Fe Ma Ap May Ju Jul | May Jun Jul Se Oc Nov Dec |
| 92   93 | 94   96 |

Figure 15.1   Timetable of the research

Sampling

Schools
At the start of the study in 1992, all 24 English schools which had chosen to provide Reading Recovery with a trained teacher were initially included in the evaluation. During the intervention year, two schools which had to abandon Reading Recovery were dropped from the study, leaving 22 self-selected Reading Recovery schools. For each Reading Recovery school, the LEA primary schools adviser identified two schools with similar intake, which were then randomly assigned to be 'Control' (18) or 'Phonological Training' (23) schools.

Children
In each of these 63 schools, the six poorest Year 2 readers in the age range 6 to 6 years 6 months (approximately the bottom 20% of readers) were selected on the basis of their performance on the Diagnostic Survey (Clay, 1985). In the 22 Reading Recovery schools, the poorest scorers among selected children (usually the bottom four) were offered intervention, the remainder being assigned to a within-school control condition. In each of the 23 Phonological Training schools, the six poorest readers were randomly assigned to Phonological Training ($n = 4$) or to within-school control condition ($n = 2$). In the remaining 18 Control schools, all the selected children became part of the control group.

On the basis of these groups, four comparisons are reported:

1. Reading Recovery children with their within-school Controls, a quasi-experiment.
2. Reading Recovery children with between-school Controls (children in Control and Phonological Training schools), a quasi-experiment.
3. Phonological children with their within-school Controls, a randomised controlled trial.
4. Phonological children with between-school Controls (children in Control schools), a quasi-experiment. (Control children in Reading Recovery schools were not included in this Phonological between-school control group as Reading Recovery schools explicitly share the principles of Reading Recovery with classroom teachers, thus compromising their 'control' status).

Table 15.1 shows numbers of children in each group at the four measurement points. Boys were overrepresented at 61% of the sample (class average = 52% boys); 42% of the sample were receiving free school meals (class average 32%, national average 16%); 16% spoke English as a second language (class average 17%). The groups were well matched on these demographic factors, with no significant differences.

Measures

Pre-test and post-test 1
Children were assessed on standardised reading tests, tests sensitive to the skills addressed by Reading Recovery and tests sensitive to the focus of Phonological Training:

(1) The British Ability Scale (BAS) Word Reading test (Elliott, Murray & Pearson, 1984).
(2) Neale Analysis of Reading (Neale, 1988).
(3) Book Level. This entails establishing which of a series of texts, graded from 1–26 according to the Reading Recovery levels, children can read with 90% accuracy or above. Level 1 texts are the simplest caption books suitable for children with very

Table 15.1   Children tested at each measurement point

	Reading Recovery	Reading Recovery within-school control	Phonological Training	Phonological Training within-school control	Control schools
Pre-test (September/ October 1992)	95	41	96	46	111
Post-test (1) (June/ July 1993)	89	40	92	43	109
Post-test (2) (May/ July 1994)	92[1]	36	88	43	107
Post-test (3) (September/ December 1996)	89	35	81	38	99

Note: [1]At post-test 2, four children changed condition in the Reading Recovery schools, from Control to Reading Recovery. These children all received Reading Recovery late in the school year 92/93 and for a small part of the Autumn term 93/94. They were also classified as Reading Recovery at post-test 3.

limited reading skills. Level 26 equates to a reading age of between 8 and 9 years (Glynn et al., 1989, p. 11). At post-test 1, Book Level correlated .85 with both BAS Word Reading and the Neale.

(4) The Diagnostic Survey (Clay, 1985) which includes: Letter Identification, Concepts about Print, a word test, Written Vocabulary and Dictation. Raw scores from each subtest were transformed to z scores and summed. At first post-test, summed z scores correlated significantly with the BAS Word Reading test ($r = .78$), the Neale ($r = .76$) and with Book Level ($r = .80$).

(5) The Oddities Test (Kirtley, Bryant, Maclean & Bradley, 1989), which measures awareness of rhyme and of initial and final phonemes. Bryant, MacLean, Bradley and Crossland (1990) report a Spearman-Brown reliability coefficient of 0.78 in their sample of 64 children aged 5 years 7 months; in the present study, internal consistency of the Oddities Test was 0.83 (Cronbach's α). However, scores on the Oddities Test were only modestly correlated with the Dictation task at first post-test (Spearman's $\rho = .44$) and with the Non-word Reading test at second post-test (Spearman's $\rho = .46$), suggesting that these tests measure different subskills.

An overall measure of reading and spelling was calculated by summing z scores for the Diagnostic Survey, Book Level, BAS Word Reading and the Neale and transforming again into a z score.

Background information was also collected on age, sex, IQ (BAS Short Form, Elliott et al., 1984), whether the children spoke English as a first or additional language and free school meals status.

Post-test 2

Children were reassessed on the standardised reading tests (BAS Word Reading, Neale), and on the Oddities Test, but not on the Diagnostic Survey or Book Level, which were no longer appropriate for the age group. Children were also assessed on a standardised spelling test (BAS Spelling test, Elliott, Murray & Pearson, 1983) and on the Graded Non-word

Reading test (Snowling, Stothard & McLean, 1996), which measures children's phonological decoding ability.

An overall measure of reading and spelling was calculated by summing the z scores for BAS Word Reading, the Neale and BAS Spelling and transforming again into a z score.

Information was again collected on free school meals status.

Post-test 3

At the final follow-up, children were assessed on:

(1) The NFER-Nelson Group Reading Test 6–12, (NFER-Nelson, 1985), a standard-ised test of reading comprehension at the sentence level, using cloze procedures.
(2) The Parallel Spelling Test (Young, 1983).

An overall measure of reading and spelling was calculated by summing the z scores for reading and spelling and transforming again into a z score.

Information was again collected on free school meals status.

Procedures

All participating children were pre-tested by a member of the research team trained over several days to administer the tests, including pilot sessions. At each of the three post-tests, members of the research team tested the children 'blind', i.e. without knowing to which group children belonged.

Interventions

Reading recovery

All Reading Recovery teachers were fully trained in Reading Recovery by an accredited trainer. The intervention, which includes reading of graded tests, word-level phonics work and writing, was delivered in standard form. The rigorous training, support and monitoring of the Reading Recovery programme results in high programme fidelity (Hurry, 1996). Children are withdrawn from class for individual tuition daily for half an hour, until they reach the average reading band for their class when they are 'discontinued' (for full programme details, see Clay, 1993). In the present study, children received on average 21 weeks' intervention, with an average of 77 sessions. Eighty-nine percent of the children made sufficient progress to be 'discontinued'. All children receiving Reading Recovery were included in the analyses reported below, irrespective of their discontinued status.

Phonological training

Following Bradley and Bryant (1985), this involved sound awareness training plus word building with plastic letters. The training focused initially on alliteration and rhyme but also included work on boundary sounds and vowels and digraphs in response to the child's progress. Children also matched sounds with plastic letters and constructed words. Each child was given 40, 10-minute, individual sessions, spread over seven months.

The five teachers who delivered the Phonological Training were all highly experienced primary teachers, but, unlike the Reading Recovery teachers, they were part of the research team and did not share details of the intervention with classroom teachers. They were given a one-day training session in the required techniques by Kirtley and MacLean, researchers who had taught the phonological programme in the original Bryant and Bradley studies (Bradley & Bryant, 1985; Bryant & Bradley, 1985; Kirtley et al., 1989), together with a training manual and one week's practice delivering the programme to nonparticipating children. Problems encountered were discussed with Kirtley and MacLean, who also gave feedback. Further training sessions were held monthly for the duration of the intervention period. Programme fidelity was monitored by the senior research officer who observed each member of the team teaching and listened to audiotapes of five sessions. The researchers recorded the content of every lesson, for every child, to facilitate monitoring. At the end of the intervention, the performances of children by phonological tutor were compared. Regression analysis (controlling for pre-test scores on the Diagnostic Survey and the BAS Word Reading Test) established that there were no significant differences on any of the first post-test measures which were due to the tutor delivering the Phonological Training.

Provision for the control group

Children in both within and between-school control groups received the standard provision available in their school. As weak readers, they often received extra, specialised help with reading – on average, 21 minutes weekly. Classroom teachers of all participating children in the intervention year were asked to complete a questionnaire describing their practice (closely based on one devised by Ireson, Blatchford & Joscelyne, 1995). One hundred and ten of the 127 teachers involved returned the questionnaire (86% response rate). There were no statistically significant differences between teachers from the different types of school (Reading Recovery, Phonological Training and Control) on the basis of average years' teaching experience or the frequency with which they used most types of reading activities in class (for fuller details, see Sylva and Hurry, 1995).

Results

Children's reading and spelling at the beginning of the study

At pre-test in 1992, many of the original cohort of children could barely read, but, as shown in overall reading/spelling z scores in Table 15.2, the children selected for intervention were doing slightly worse than the control groups – significantly so in both Reading Recovery comparisons and in the between-schools Phonological Training comparison. This can be clearly observed by looking at the overall reading/spelling score (Table 15.2). Both intervention groups have minus scores, i.e. are below the mean for the entire sample.

Table 15.2   Pre-intervention reading skills, autumn 1992

Experimental groups (mean chronological age = 6 years 3 months)	Mean Raw Scores (SD)						
	(BAS) Word Reading[1]	(Neale) Prose Reading	Book Level	Diagnostic Survey	Overall reading/spelling	(Oddities Test) Phonological Awareness	IQ
Reading Recovery Intervention children	2 (4) reading age, below 5 years	0 (1) reading age, below 5 years	1 (1)	−0.3 (0.8)	−0.32 (0.5)	2 (3)	92 (13)
Within-school controls	4 (4) reading age, 5 years 3 months	2 (3) reading age, below 5 years	2 (2)	0.4 (0.9)	0.10 (0.8)	4 (4)	96 (12)
Between-school controls	6 (8) reading age, 5 years 6 months	2 (3) reading age, below 5 years	2 (3)	0.2 (1.1)	0.26 (1.1)	3 (3)	96 (13)
Phonological Training Intervention children	3.5 (5) reading age, 5 years 1 month	1 (3) reading age, below 5 years	1 (2)	−0.2 (0.9)	−0.17 (0.9)	3 (3)	93 (13)
Within-school controls	4.5 (7) reading age, below 5 years	1.5 (3) reading age, below 5 years	1 (2)	0 (1)	0.01 (1.0)	3 (3)	94 (14)
Between-school controls	6 (8) reading age, 5 years 6 months	2 (3) reading age, below 5 years	2 (3)	0.35 (1.1)	0.34 (1.3)	3 (3)	96 (13)
Total	4 (6) reading age, 5 years 3 months	1 (3) reading age, below 5 years	1.5 (2)	0 (1)	0 (1)	3 (3)	94 (13)

Notes: [1]Reading ages are very approximate as many children scored nothing on this test at this time.
Neale, Neale Analysis of Reading; BAS, British Ability Scale.

Children's reading and spelling over the follow-up period, descriptive statistics

Table 15.3 shows the progress children in the various groups made during the intervention. Since the intervention children had slightly poorer literacy skills levels than controls at pre-test, intervention effects are calculated with account taken of initial reading ability as measured by the Diagnostic Survey and BAS Word Reading test. These variables are always entered first into fixed-order regression analyses, followed by child's experimental group status in the second block of the regression analysis. Response variables are the range of reading/spelling outcomes, transformed where necessary to reduce skewness and all the response variables satisfy the assumptions for regression. The β coefficients and es are reported for all the regression analysis. The es reported here is Cohen's d (Cohen, 1988), i.e. the mean of the experimental group minus the mean of the control group, divided by the

Table 15.3a   First (short-term) follow-up (summer 1993) (mean chronological age = 7 years)

Experimental group	(BAS) Word Reading		(Neale) Prose Reading raw score	Diagnostic Survey	Overall reading/ spelling
	Raw score	Reading age			
Reading Recovery					
Intervention children	19.4 (10.5)	6 years 4 month	11.3 (6.6)	0.45 (0.62)	0.39 (0.74)
Within-school controls	15.7 (12.4)	6 years 1 month	10.7 (9.7)	0.00 (1.07)	0.05 (1.01)
Between-school controls	15.8 (14.1)	6 years 1 month	9.2 (7.9)	−0.12 (1.13)	−0.06 (1.08)
Phonological Training					
Intervention children	13.0 (11.8)	5 years 11 month	7.2 (8.5)	−0.27 (1.13)	−0.31 (0.98)
Within-school controls	14.5 (12.5)	6 years 0 month	8.1 (7.5)	−0.07 (1.00)	−0.15 (1.01)
Between-school controls	16.4 (14.7)	6 years 1 month	9.7 (8.1)	−0.12 (1.03)	0 (1.06)

Note: Neale, Neale Analysis of Reading; BAS, British Ability Scale.

Table 15.3b   Second (medium-term) follow-up (summer 1994) (mean chronological age = 8 years)

Experimental group	(BAS) Word Reading		(Neale) Prose Reading raw score	(BAS) Spelling	Overall reading/ spelling
	Raw score	Reading age			
Residing Recovery					
Intervention children	33.4 (17.0)	6 years 11 months	19.5 (11.3)	17.8 (7.0)	0.04 (0.84)
Within-school controls	34.1 (19.4)	7 years 0 months	20.1 (I4.8)	18.9 (9.0)	0.10 (1.05)
Between-school controls	32.5 (19.2)	6 years 11 months	18.9 (13.2)	18.2 (9.2)	0.04 (1.02)
Phonological Training					
Intervention children	30.0 (19.4)	6 years 10 months	17.1 (13.3)	17.1 (9.2)	−0.10 (1.02)
Within-school controls	32.3 (17.9)	6 years 11 months	18.8 (12.7)	18.0 (8.2)	0.02 (1.00)
Between-school controls	32.6 (19.8)	6 years 11 months	19.0 (13.5)	18.2 (9.6)	0.04 (1.00)

Note: Neale, Neale Analysis of Reading; BAS, British Ability Scale.

Table 15.3c   Third (long-term) follow-up (autumn 1996) (mean chronological age = 10 years 3 months)

	Reading		Spelling		
	Raw score	Reading age	Raw score	Spelling age	
Reading Recovery Intervention children	30.5 (9.1)	8 years 4 months	12.7 (6.5)	8 years 7 months	–0.08 (0.87)
Within-school controls	31.8 (8.1)	8 years 7 months	14.8 (9.0)	8 years 11 months	0.13 (0.01)
Between-school controls	31.4 (9.7)	8 years 8 months	14.5 (8.4)	8 years 10 months	0.09 (1.01)
Phonological Training Intervention children	29.8 (10.2)	8 years 3 months	13.8 (9.7)	8 years 8 months	–0.05 (1.06)
Within-school controls	31.9 (9.7)	8 years 7 months	14.8 (6.9)	8 years 9 months	0.13 (0.95)
Between-school controls	31.2 (9.7)	8 years 7 months	14.4 (8.9)	8 years 9 months	0.07 (1.04)

standard deviation of the groups. Effect sizes help to interpret magnitude of an experimental effect. According to Cohen's classificatory scheme (Cohen, 1988), es of .2–.5 are small, of .5–.8 are medium and > .8 are large. The results reported here do not use multi-level modelling as the sample size in each school is insufficient to identify anything but very large school-level effects; a previous report of multi-level modelling analysis (Sylva & Hurry, 1995) found between-school variation to be very small after controlling for pre-test.

Children's reading and spelling at first (short-term) follow-up

Reading Recovery

At first post-test on completion of intervention, Reading Recovery children had made substantially more progress than both their within and between-school controls on all the measures of reading and spelling and on the overall measure. The es on these measures were found to be medium to large (.63–.87, Table 15.4). They had an approximately eight-month reading age advantage over controls. Even without controlling for their significantly poorer scores at pre-test, the Reading Recovery group had significantly higher mean scores across all reading and spelling measures than their between-school controls and on the Diagnostic Survey and Book Level for the within-school comparison. However, Reading Recovery children were only significantly better than the between- (not the within) school controls on the Phonological Awareness measure.

Phonological Training

The short-term effects of Phonological Training were much more specific than those of Reading Recovery, and not as secure. Phonological Training children were

Table 15.4   The effect of Reading Recovery on reading, spelling and phonological skill at first (short-term) follow-up (summer 1993)

	Reading Recovery comparison			
	Within-school[1] (sample size = 72 vs 40)		Between-school (89 vs 153)	
Measures	B	Effect size	B	Effect size
(BAS) Word Reading	1.2	.81***	1.4	.84***
(Neale) Prose Reading	0.79	.63**	1.4	.85***
Book Level	5.2	.78***	7.2	.96***
Diagnostic Survey	0.75	.87***	0.94	.99***
(Oddities Test) Phonological Awareness	0.74	.14	1.3	.26*
Overall read/spell	0.68	.77***	0.88	.88***

Notes: The results of a regression analysis controlling for initial scores on the Diagnostic Survey and BAS Word Reading.
*$p < .05$, **$p < .01$, ***$p < .001$.
[1]The Reading Recovery children in five schools were excluded from the within-school analyses as there were no control children available in these schools.
Neale, Neale Analysis of Reading; BAS, British Ability Scale.

Tables 15.5   The effect of the Phonological Training on reading, spelling and phonological skills at first (short-term) follow-up (summer 1993)

	Phonological Training comparison			
	Within-school (92 vs 43)		Between-school[1] (92 vs 109)	
Measures	B	Effect size	B	Effect size
(BAS) Word Reading	0.12	.08	0.30	.16
(Neale) Prose Reading	1.1	.13	0.9	.09
Book Level	0	0	0	0
Diagnostic Survey	0.1	.10	0.3	.30**
(Oddities Test) Phonological Awareness	1.7	.34*	3.6	.72***
Overall read/spell	0.08	.08	0.18	.16

Notes: The results of a regression analysis controlling for initial scores on the Diagnostic Survey and BAS Word Reading.
*$p < .05$, **$p < .01$, ***$p < .001$.
[1]Control children from Reading Recovery schools were not included in the between-school analysis because of the ambiguity of their status (see Methods section). Therefore, numbers in the control group differ between Reading Recovery and Phonological Training throughout all analyses.
Neale, Neale Analysis of Reading; BAS, British Ability Scale.

only consistently ahead of their controls on phonological awareness, and the effect size was small in the within-school comparison (Table 15.5). In the between-school comparison, the Phonological children also performed significantly better than controls on the Diagnostic Survey, which contains measures sensitive to phonological skills and spelling, but there was no significant effect on reading, nor on the overall measure.

Children's reading and spelling at second (medium-term) post-test

Reading Recovery

As shown in Table 15.6, one year after children had graduated from Reading Recovery, they were still significantly ahead of their between-school controls in reading (both Word and Prose Reading, es = .41 and .42, respectively) and to a lesser extent in spelling (es = .32) and on the overall reading/spelling measure (es = .39). However, these es of between .32 and .42 are small. The gap between the Reading Recovery and the control children had narrowed. Also, Reading Recovery only predicted statistically significantly higher scores on Non-word Reading and not on the Oddities test, the other measure of phonological skill.

Reading Recovery children were no longer reading and spelling significantly better than their within-school controls, possibly because the control children in Reading Recovery schools had benefited from the presence of Reading Recovery in their school.

Phonological Training

As shown in Table 15.7, in the between-school comparison, children who had received Phonological Training one year previously had now made significantly more progress overall, in reading (both word and prose) and spelling, as well as phonological skills, but the overall reading/spelling es was small (.24). There were no significant differences between the Phonological children and their within-school controls even on the Oddities test, which directly assesses the intervention focus (Table15.7).

Children's reading and spelling at third (long-term) post-test

When the children were tested in the autumn of 1996, their average age was 10 years 3 months. In the fixed-order regression analyses carried out at this point, it was necessary to enter free school meals status into the regression, alongside initial reading, as this was now a significant predictor of reading/spelling progress. Both reading and spelling response variables were transformed to reduce skewness. Once initial reading skills and free school meals status had been entered in the analysis, neither of the interventions predicted significantly raised reading scores (Table 15.8). Although both intervention groups were somewhat ahead of their between-school controls, the sizes of the intervention effects were negligible or small (.15 for Reading Recovery and .21 for Phonological Training), and not statistically significant. The between-school effects represent a reading age advantage of around three months. Reading Recovery did not predict better spelling progress. However, in the between-school comparison, where intervention children had shown substantially greater phonological skills than control children in the first two post-tests, there was a significant effect of Phonological Training on spelling (es = .27). Also, Phonological Training was significantly associated with better progress in the between-school but not the within-school comparison of the overall measure of reading/spelling (es = .25). Reading Recovery did not predict a significant effect in either comparison.

Overall, on average, those children who had made a poor start in their reading at 6 were quite noticeably behind national norms on both the reading and spelling tests at 10.

Table 15.6   The effect of Reading Recovery on reading, spelling and phonological skills at second (medium-term) follow-up (summer 1994)

	Reading Recovery comparison			
	Within-school[1] (68 vs 34)		Between-school (91 vs 150)	
Measures	B	Effect size	B	Effect size
(BAS) Word Reading[2]	5.1	.25	7.6	.41***
(Neale) Prose Reading	3.2	.26	5.3	.42***
(BAS) Spelling	1.3	.18	2.7	.32**
(Oddities) Phonological Awareness	0.3	.01	0.1	.03
Non-word Reading	2.6	.29	3.2	.38**
Overall read/spell	0.23	.25	0.37	.39***

Notes: The results of a regression analysis controlling for initial scores on the Diagnostic Survey and the BAS Word Reading test.
$**p < .01$, $***p < .001$.
[1]The Reading Recovery children in five schools were excluded from the within-school analyses as there were no control children available in these schools.
[2] Word Reading was transformed using a square root transformation to improve the normality of the distribution.
Neale, Neale Analysis of Reading; BAS, British Ability Scale.

Table 15.7   The effect of the Phonological Training on reading, spelling and phonological skills at second (medium-term) follow-up (summer 1994)

	Phonological Training comparison			
	Within-school (88 vs 43)		Between-school (87 vs 107)	
Measures	B	Effect size	B	Effect size
(BAS) Word Reading	2.5	.13	5.2	.27**
(Neale) Prose Reading	1.3	.10	2.9	.22*
(BAS) Spelling	1.4	.16	2.5	.27*
(Oddities) Phonological Awareness	0.1	.02	2.4	.49***
Non-Word Reading	1.5	.18	2.8	.33**
Overall read/spell	0.13	.13	0.27	.24*

Notes: The results of a regression analysis controlling for initial scores on the Diagnostic Survey and the BAS Word Reading test.
$*p < .05$, $**p < .01$, $***p < .001$.
Neale, Neale Analysis of Reading: BAS, British Ability Scale.

Their average chronological age was 10 years 3 months but their average reading and spelling ages were 8 years 6 months and 8 years 9 months, respectively. This was in part due to the fact that many of them attended schools in socially disadvantaged areas, where the average reading age for children in their classes at 10 years old was 6 months below national norms (Hurry & Sylva, 1998). However, it would appear that, in the long term, neither of the interventions had allowed the children to overcome their poor start with reading.

Table 15.8   The effects of Reading Recovery and Phonological Training on reading and spelling skills at the third (long-term) follow-up, autumn 1996

| Experimental groups | Results of a regression analysis, controlling for pre-test score on the Word Reading test and the Diagnostic Survey | | | | | |
| | Reading/comprehension[1] | | Spelling[2] | | Overall read/spell | |
	B	Effect size	*B*	Effect size	*B*	Effect size
Reading Recovery						
Within-school						
comparison (*n* = 98)	10.8	.17	.04	.04	.02	.03
Between-school						
comparison (*n* = 223)	11.6	.15	.12	.11	.12	.12
Phonological Training						
Within-school						
comparison (*n* =119)	26	.03	.08	.07	.10	.09
Between-school						
comparison (*n* = 179)	16.6	.21	.34	.27*	.27	.26*

Notes: Controlling for initial reading attainment.
*$p < 0.05$.
[1]In all subsequent regression analyses, the cube of raw scores on the reading test were squared to reduce skewness.
[2]In all subsequent regression analyses, square root transformation was used on the raw scores on the spelling test.

Initial reading skills and responsiveness to intervention

Children were dichotomised into two groups on the basis of their performance at pre-test: non-readers (scoring < 3 on the Word Reading test, 0 on the Prose Reading test and 0 or 1 on Book Level), and those with some word reading skills. Just under a half were non-readers at 6. A Matthew effect was evident even in this truncated sample, with the initial non-readers making significantly less progress than those with some word reading at 6 years old ($B = .24$, $p < .05$ on the combined reading/spelling measure at final long-term post-test). This might suggest that the poorest readers, who were roughly the bottom 10% of readers in their class, may be less responsive to intervention.

Tables 15.9 and 15.10 show that this was not the case for either intervention and that Reading Recovery was actually more powerful for non-readers. In the short term, in the Reading Recovery comparisons, es for non-readers were at least twice those for children with some word reading at 6 years old. The interaction effect between reading status at pre-test and Reading Recovery was significant on overall reading/spelling in the between-school comparison ($B = .55$, $p < .01$). In the medium term, one year post-intervention, the effect of Reading Recovery for children with some word reading at 6 was reduced, with small and insignificant es of .11 and .07. However, for those who started as complete non-readers, medium es of .54 and .59 were still evident in both within and between-school conditions. Again, the interaction effect between initial reading status and Reading Recovery was significant in the between-school comparison ($B = .46$, $p < .05$).

Table 15.9   The differing effect of the two interventions on reading and spelling by children's reading level at pre-test

	Baseline	Short-term	Medium-term		Long-term	
Experimental groups	Reading	Reading	Reading	Spelling	Reading	Spelling
Subsample: starting to read at 6 years old						
Reading Recovery						
Intervention children	5.2 (4.4) 5 years 5 months	22.9 (11.1) 6 years 6 months	37.7 (15.0) 7 years 2 months	20.0 (5.9) 7 years 4 months	33 (6) 8 years 8 months	14 (6) 8 years 10 months
Between-school controls	9.2 (8.5) 5 years 10 months	21.9 (14.3) 6 years 5 months	41.0 (17.3) 7 years 3 months	22.5 (8.3) 7 years 7 months	35 (7) 9 years 3 months	17 (9) 9 years 5 months
Phonological Training						
Intervention children	7.6 (5.9) 5 years 9 months	21.6 (11.7) 6 years 5 months	41.9 (17.7) 7 years 4 months	22.8 (8.7) 7 years 7 months	37 (5) 9 years 4 months	19 (3) 9 years 7 months
Between-school controls	9.6 (9.0) 5 years 8 months	22.7 (14.7) 6 years 6 months	44.2 (16.0) 7 years 4.5 months	22.6 (8.2) 7 years 7 months	36 (7) 9 years 4 months	18 (9) 9 years 6 months
Subsample: non-readers at 6 years old						
Reading Recovery						
Intervention children	0.4 (0.6) Below 5 years	17.2 (9.6) 6 years 3 months	30.6 (18.0) 6 years 10 months	16.4 (7.4) 7 years 1 months	28 (10) 8 years 2 months	11 (7) 8 years 4 months
Between-school controls	0.6 (0.8) Below 5 years	6.5 (7.2) 5 years 5 months	19.8 (14.5) 6 years 5 months	11.7 (6.4) 6 years 9 months	25 (10) 7 years 8 months	10 (6) 8 years 0 months
Phonological Training						
Intervention children	0.4 (0.7) Below 5 years	6.7 (6.9) 5 years 6 months	19.6 (14.4) 6 years 5 months	13.2 (7.8) 6 years 9 months	25 (10) 7 years 7 months	10 (8) 8 years 2 months
Between-school controls	0.6 (0.8) Below 5 years	6.3 (7.4) 5 years 5 months	18.4 (13.4) 6 years 4 months	11.1 (6.0) 6 years 8 months	24 (9) 7 years 6 months	9 (5) 7 years 11 months

Raw score, mean (*SD*) Reading/Spelling age

Note: Descriptive statistics for between-school comparison.

Table 15.10   The differing effect of the two interventions on overall reading/spelling by children's reading level at pre-test

	Reading Recovery comparison				Phonological Training comparison			
	Within-school		Between-school		Within-school		Between-school	
	B	Effect size	B	Effect size	B	Effect size	B	Effect size
Short-term follow-up								
Some word reading	.3	0.34	0.52	0.56***	.16	.16	.12	.13
Non-readers	.95	1.15***	1.1	1.22***	−.01	.01	.17	.25
Interaction between reading level at pre-test and intervention	.53		0.55**		−.17		−.03	
Medium-term follow-up								
Some word reading	.09	0.11	0.07	0.07	.32	.34	.4	.42*
Non-readers	.43	0.54	0.48	0.59***	−.05	−.06	.19	.26
Interaction between reading level at pre-test and intervention	.44		0.46*		−.33		−.16	
Long-term follow-up								
Some word reading	−.09	−0.06	−0.07	0.1	.24	.37	.22	.3
Non-readers	.15	0.19	0.3	0.34 (p < 0.07)	.07	.07	.32	.38*
Interaction between reading level at pre-test and intervention	.24		0.36 (p < 0.07)		−.26		−.004	

Note: Results of regression analyses, controlling for free school meals status and scores on the Diagnostic Survey and BAS Word Reading.
*p < .05, **p < .01, ***p < 0.001.
BAS, British Ability Scale.

In the long term, on the combined reading/spelling score, Reading Recovery was still more effective for the initial non-readers, though not quite significantly so, even in the between-school comparison ($p = .07$, es = .34) and the interaction between initial reading status and intervention also just failed to reach statistical significance ($p = .07$). When the combined measure was separated into reading and spelling scores, for reading, in the between-school comparison, there was a significant effect of having received Reading Recovery on the bottom 10% of readers ($p < .05$, es = .39) and the interaction between initial reading status and intervention was significant ($p < .05$). No significant main effects or interactions were found for spelling.

No significant interaction effects were found between the Phonological intervention and initial reading level. It would appear that Phonological Training is equally effective for all children with reading difficulties, whether or not they can read any words when first offered the intervention, though there is a non-significant tendency for it to be more effective for the slightly better readers.

Discussion

We report here on the effect of two early interventions on reading progress over four years, of children who were in the bottom 20% of readers in their class at 6 years old. In the short term, both interventions worked. Consistent with other research, in both within and between-school comparisons, Reading Recovery was found to be a powerful method of improving children's reading and spelling over a broad spectrum, doubling reading children's progress (Pinnell et al., 1994; Shanahan & Barr, 1995; Wasik & Slavin, 1993). However, Reading Recovery did not have a consistent effect on children's phonological awareness. The Phonological Training on the contrary was effective at improving phonological awareness in both within and between-school comparisons, consistent with research on phonological intervention (Bryant & Bradley, 1985; Bus & van Ijzendoorn, 1999; Hurry, 2004; National Reading Panel, 2000), but had little short-term impact on children's reading. This tendency for phonological intervention not to generalise to word reading and comprehension in the short term has been observed by others (Bus & van Ijzendoorn, 1999; National Reading Panel, 2000).

Based on the large impact that Reading Recovery had on children's reading during the intervention, when they made about twice as much progress as controls, a Matthew effect would predict that the gap between Reading Recovery and control children should have widened further with the passage of time. The better readers should have been reading more books, building their vocabulary and world knowledge and feeling better about reading. However, 3½ years on, for most of the comparisons made, children who had received Reading Recovery were no longer significantly ahead of their peers. Only those Reading Recovery children who were non-readers at 6 (the bottom 10% in their class) had made significantly more progress than similar between-school controls by the time they were 10 years old, and only in reading, not spelling.

Despite the fact that, overall, those who were better readers at 6 made significantly greater progress over the follow-up period than initial non-readers, it was the weakest readers who benefited most from Reading Recovery. For the children who were not reading at all at 6 years old, Reading Recovery was more effective at every follow-up point than for slightly better readers. However, even this group of Reading Recovery children did not increase their lead over their controls; they fell back slightly. Immediately on completing the intervention programme, Reading Recovery children who started as non-readers had an average reading age of 6 years 3 months on the BAS Word Reading test, compared with an average of 5 years 5 months for their between-school controls. Three years four months on, the Reading Recovery children had made (roughly) 1 year 11 months' progress, compared with 2 years 3 months of the between-school control group. For those who were slightly better readers at 6, the children who had received Reading Recovery had made (roughly) 3 years 5 months' progress in their reading over the course of the 4 years 2 months of the study. Their between-school controls had made 3 years 7 months progress. Clay's (1991) proposition that children can be taught reading strategies early on which will protect them from later reading problems receives only limited support and only for the weakest readers.

Phonological Training did not improve reading immediately post-intervention and, in fact, the between-school control group had a significantly higher mean on the overall reading measure at first follow-up than the intervention group. However, one year and three years later, the Phonological group was doing significantly better on the overall reading/spelling measure than their between-school controls. The sustained effect of the Phonological Training in this comparison is consistent with the theory that phonological awareness is an essential early building block for decoding, which is itself a critical component of reading. This is all the more impressive since children only received 40 10-minute sessions in Phonological Training, as compared to an average of 77 30-minute sessions for those on the Reading Recovery programme.

The delay in the impact of Phonological Training on reading is surprising, but a similar effect is reported by Bond and Dykstra (1967, 1997). In their comparisons of a range of methods of teaching initial reading, they found that whole-word techniques produced the largest immediate results, but that phonics programmes outstripped basal programmes in Grades 2 and 3. In our study, the only reading measure that showed a significant effect from the Phonological Training in the short term was the Diagnostic Survey. This was largely due to the superior performance of the phonological group on Writing Vocabulary, a measure of spelling appropriate for young children, and on the Dictation task. Frith (1985) has argued that children first use phonic strategies to spell, and that their reading is initially heavily reliant on whole-word recognition. She suggests that as children's understanding of the link between the alphabet and sounds in words develops through spelling, it subsequently helps them in their reading. This offers an explanation for our finding that Phonological Training had a significant long-term effect on spelling rather than reading and is consistent with other studies which have found larger effects on spelling than reading (Bradley & Bryant, 1985; Byrne et al., 2000; Lundberg, Frost & Petersen, 1988). The act of word construction in spelling would seem to be a natural medium to practise and develop phonological skills.

The fact that intervention effects that went beyond phonological awareness were not evident in the within-school Phonological Training comparison must temper the confidence with which these results can be interpreted. This within-school comparison was the strongest design of all as it was a randomised controlled trial, with children being randomly assigned within their schools to intervention or control conditions. Immediately post-intervention, there was a much more substantial difference in phonological awareness between Phonological Training children and between-school controls than within-school controls. It is plausible that the control children in the Phonological schools were exposed to some elements of the Phonological Training in their classes, undermining the within-school experiment. However, class teachers were not supposed to be introduced to the intervention. The research team who delivered the training were explicitly told not to show class teachers their methods and class teachers reported that having the intervention in their school had not changed their teaching methods.

Conclusion

The present study finds that children who are poor readers after the first year in school will tend to fall further behind as they move through school, with reading and spelling ages on average one and a half to two years behind their chronological age in the last year of primary school. Sadly, early intervention of either a broad or phonics-based nature, even though effective at the time of delivery, does not appear to inoculate children from later problems. The partial long-term success of Phonological Training supports the proposition that early phonological skills are critical but it only explains around 1% of the variance on the reading/spelling measure when the children were 10 years old. Even in the short term, Bus and van Ijzendoorn (1999) report that phonological awareness training only accounts for about 12% of the variance in reading skills. It could be argued that another form of phonics intervention would have been more effective. McGuinness (2004), for example, argues that the teaching of rimes, which is a part of Phonological Training, is ineffective, and that it is best to teach from sound to letter using the 40+ phonemes of English and their main spellings. However, even the studies of phonics training reviewed by the National Reading Panel (2000) leave a lot of variance unexplained. The long-term success of Reading Recovery for the weakest readers supports Clay's proposition of the critical nature of the early stages of reading acquisition for this group, but again, most of the variance remains unexplained. Hatcher and colleagues (Hatcher, Hulme & Ellis, 1994; Hatcher, Hulme & Snowling, 2004) suggest that combining the elements of a phonics programme with the broader focus of Reading Recovery produces enhanced results and perhaps such a programme would have sustained effects. However, our study suggests that children who find reading difficult at 6 have problems in developing and making use of strategies in reading that may persist. This may be due to child-related factors or to the home or school environment. Early intervention helps by explicitly teaching some of the early skills such as phonological awareness and the techniques of self-monitoring appropriate to the level of reading. Further progress is likely to be impeded by the underlying difficulties responsible for the children's early problems. In terms of cognitive skills, research clearly demonstrates the continuing nature of reading development, involving blending and segmenting, orthographic strategies and higher-order comprehension skills (e.g. Byrne et al., 2000; Frith, 1985; Oka & Paris, 1986; Palinscar & Brown, 1984). The areas of concern in reading for 10-year-olds are different from those of 6-year-olds. Venezky's (1998) review of the evidence on Success for All concludes that it also becomes less effective by Grade 5. He remarks that it is better designed and more intensive in the lower grades, giving too little attention to higher-level reading and thinking skills further up the school. There has been an impressive body of work on the importance of explicitly teaching phonological skills to beginning readers and our own results tend to confirm the value of this element of instruction, but there is a tendency to disregard the continuing nature of reading development beyond the first stages of decoding.

Other non-cognitive factors are likely to have an impact on children's reading progress: their enjoyment of reading, their teachers' expectations or skill, encouragement at home or from their peers. For example, it has been consistently reported that teachers tend to restrict poorer readers' choice in the reading curriculum (e.g. Ofsted, 2004). Student choice has a strong effect on reading engagement, comprehension and achievement (Guthrie & Humenick, 2004). Although early interventions may impact on children's reading skill, teachers may still expect too little, the home environment may fail to nurture the child's learning, [and] the social context may remain unaffected by intervention which solely targets the child.

The findings reported here do not support the proposition that early and effective cognitive intervention is sufficient to prevent later reading problems. Rather, the evidence presented here is consistent with Shanahan and Barr's (1995) proposition that cognitive support must be ongoing. Also, cognitive instruction does not address social and affective issues, which may exert a continuing influence. [...]

References

Allington, R.L. (1984). Content coverage and contextual reading in reading groups. *Journal of Reading Behavior,* 16, 85–96.

Biemiller, A. (1977–1978). Relationships between oral reading rates for letters, words, and simple text in the development of reading achievement. *Reading Research Quarterly,* 13, 223–253.

Bishop, D.V.M. & Snowling, M.J. (2004). Developmental dyslexia and specific language impairment: Same or different? *Psychological Bulletin,* 130, 858–886.

Bond, G.L. & Dykstra, R. (1967). The cooperative research program in first-grade reading instruction. *Reading Research Quarterly, 2,* 5–141.

Bond, G.L. & Dykstra, R. (1997). The cooperative research program in first-grade reading instruction. *Reading Research Quarterly,* 13, 348–427.

Bradley, L. & Bryant, P. (1985). *Rhyme and reason in reading and spelling.* Ann Arbor, MI: University of Michigan Press.

Bryant, P. & Bradley, L. (1985). *Children's reading problems.* Oxford: Blackwell.

Bryant, P., MacLean, M., Bradley, L. & Crossland, J. (1990). Rhyme and alliteration, phonemic detection, and learning to read. *Developmental Psychology,* 26, 429–438.

Bus, A. & van Ijzendoorn, M. (1999). Phonological awareness and early reading: A meta-analysis of experimental training studies. *Journal of Educational Psychology,* 91, 403–414.

Byrne, B. (1998). *The foundation of literacy. The child's acquisition of the alphabetic principle.* East Sussex: Psychology Press Ltd.

Byrne, B., Fielding-Barnsley, R. & Ashley, L. (2000). Effects of preschool phoneme identity training after six years: Outcome level distinguished from rate of response. *Journal of Educational Psychology,* 92(4), 659–667.

Center, Y., Wheldall, K., Freeman, L., Outhred, L. & McNaughton, M. (1995). An evaluation of Reading Recovery. *Reading Research Quarterly,* 30, 240–263.

Chall, J.S. (1983). *Stages of reading development.* New York: McGraw-Hill.

Clarke, A.M. & Clarke, A.D.B. (1976). *Early experience: Myth and evidence.* London: Open Books.

Clay, M.M. (1967). The reading behaviour of five year old children: A research report. *New Zealand Journal of Educational Studies, 2,* 237–248.

Clay, M.M. (1985). *The early detection of reading difficulties: A diagnostic survey with recovery procedures.* (3rd edn). Auckland, New Zealand: Heinemann.

Clay, M.M. (1991). *Becoming literate: The construction of inner control.* Auckland, New Zealand: Heinemann.

Clay, M.M. (1993). *Reading recovery: A guidebook for teachers in training.* Auckland, New Zealand: Heinemann Education.

Cohen, J. (1988). *Statistical power analysis for behaviour sciences.* New York: Academic Press.

DeFord, D.E., Pinnell, G.S., Lyons, C. & Young, P. (1988). *Reading recovery: Vol. IX. Report of the follow-up studies.* Columbus, OH: The Ohio State University.

Ehri, L. (1991). Development of the ability to read words. In R. Barr, M. Kamil, P. Mosenthal & P. Pearson (Eds.), *Handbook of reading research.* (Vol. II, pp. 383–417). New York: Longman.

Ehri, L. (1992). Reconceptualizing the development of sight word reading and its relationship to recoding. In P. Gough, L. Ehri & R. Treiman (Eds.), *Reading acquisition.* (pp. 107–143). Hillsdale, NJ: Lawrence Erlbaum.

Ehri, L. (1998). Grapheme–phoneme knowledge is essential for learning to read words in English. In J. Metsala & L. Ehri (Eds.), *Word recognition in beginning literacy.* (pp. 3–40). Mahwah, NJ: Lawrence Erlbaum Associates.

Ehri, L. (1999). Phases of development in learning to read words. In J. Oakhill & R. Beard (Eds.), *Reading development and the teaching of reading.* (pp. 79–108). Oxford: Blackwell.

Ehri, L. (2005). Learning to read words: Theory, findings and issues. *Scientific Studies of Reading,* 9(2), 167–188.

Ehri, L. & Wilce, L. (1985). Movement into reading: Is the first stage of printed word reading visual or phonetic? *Reading Research Quarterly*, 20, 163–179.

Elliott, C., Murray, D. & Pearson, L. (1983). *British ability scales spelling test.* Slough: NFER-Nelson.

Elliott, C., Murray, D. & Pearson, L. (1984). *British ability scales.* Slough: NFER-Nelson.

Frith, U. (1985). Beneath the surface of developmental dyslexia. In K. Patterson, M. Coltheart & J. Marshall (Eds.), *Surface dyslexia.* (pp. 301–330). London: Lawrence Erlbaum Associates Ltd.

Frith, U. (1995). Dyslexia: Can we have a shared theoretical framework? *Educational and Child Psychology*, 12, 6–17.

Glynn, T., Crooks, T., Bethune, N., Ballard, K. & Smith, J. (1989). *Reading Recovery in context.* Wellington, New Zealand: Department of Education.

Goswami, U. & Bryant, P. (1990). *Phonological skills and learning to read.* London: Lawrence Erlbaum Associates Ltd.

Gough, P. (1996). How children learn to read and why they fail. *Annals of Dyslexia*, 46, 3–20.

Guthrie, J. & Humenick, N. (2004). Motivating students to read. In P. McCardle & V. Chhabra (Eds.), *The voice of evidence in reading research.* (pp. 329–354). Baltimore: Paul Brookes Publishing.

Harm, M. & Seidenberg, M.S. (2004). Computing the meanings of words in reading: Cooperative division of labor between visual and phonological processes. *Psychological Review*, 111(3), 662–720.

Hatcher, P., Hulme, C. & Ellis, A.W. (1994). Ameliorating early reading failure by integrating the teaching of reading and phonological skills: The phonological linkage hypothesis. *Child Development*, 65, 41–57.

Hatcher, P., Hulme, C. & Snowling, M. (2004). Explicit phoneme training combined with phonic reading instruction helps young children at risk of reading failure. *Journal of Child Psychology and Psychiatry*, 45, 338–358.

Hulme, C. & Snowling, M. (1992). Phonological deficits in dyslexia: A 'Sound' reappraisal of the verbal deficit hypothesis? In N. Singh & I. Beale (Eds.), *Learning disabilities: Nature, theory and treatment.* (pp. 270–301). New York: Springer Verlag.

Hurry, J. (1996). What's so special about Reading Recovery? *The Curriculum Journal*, 7(1), 93–108.

Hurry, J. (2004). Comparative studies of instructional methods. In P. Bryant & T. Nunes (Eds.), *Handbook of children's literacy.* (pp. 557–598). Dordrecht: Kluwer.

Hurry, J. & Sylva, K. (1998). *The long-term effects of two interventions for children with reading difficulties.* London: Qualifications and Curriculum Authority.

Ireson, J., Blatchford, P. & Joscelyne, T. (1995). What do teachers do? Classroom activities in the initial teaching of reading. *Educational Psychology*, 15(3), 245–256.

Jackson, N.W. & Coltheart, M. (2001). *Routes to reading success and failure.* New York: Psychology Press.

Juel, C. (1988). Learning to read and write: A longitudinal study of fifty-four children from first through fourth grade. *Journal of Educational Psychology*, 80, 437–447.

Juel, C. (1991). Beginning reading. In R. Barr et al. (Eds.), *Handbook of reading research.* (Vol. 2, pp. 759–788). New York: Longman.

Kirtley, C., Bryant, P., Maclean, M. & Bradley, L. (1989). Rhyme, rime and the onset of reading. *Journal of Experimental Child Psychology*, 48, 224–245.

Lundberg, I., Frost, J. & Petersen, O. (1988). Effects of an extensive program for stimulating phonological awareness in pre-school children. *Reading Research Quarterly*, 23(3), 263–284.

McGuinness, D. (2004). *Early Reading Instruction.* Cambridge, MA: MIT Press.

National Reading Panel (2000). *Teaching children to read: An evidence-based assessment of the scientific research literature on reading and its implications for reading instruction.* Washington, DC: National Institute of Child Health and Human Development/National Institutes of Health.

Neale, M.D. (1988). *Neale analysis of reading ability,* revised. Windsor: NFER-Nelson.

NFER-Nelson (1985). *NFER-Nelson group reading test 6–12.* Windsor: NFER-Nelson.

Ofsted (2004). *Reading for enjoyment.* London: HMSO.

Ohio Department of Education (1995). *Longitudinal study of reading recovery 1990–91 through 1993–94.* Battelle, OH: Final Report.

Oka, E. & Paris, S. (1986). Patterns of motivation and reading skills in underachieving children. In S. Ceci (Ed.), *Handbook of cognitive, social and neuropsychological aspects of learning disabilities.* (Vol. 2, pp. 115–145). Hillsdale, NJ: Erlbaum.

Palinscar, A. & Brown, A. (1984). Reciprocal teaching of comprehension-fostering and comprehension-monitoring activities. *Cognition and Instruction, 1,* 117–175.

Pinnell, G.S., Lyons, C.A., DeFord, D.E., Bryk, A.S. & Seltzer, M. (1994). Comparing instructional models for the literacy education of high-risk first graders. *Reading Research Quarterly, 20*(1), 9–39.

Rack, J.P., Snowling, M.J. & Olson, R.K. (1992). The nonword reading deficit in developmental dyslexia: A review. *Reading Research Quarterly, 27*(1), 28–53.

Rowe, K.J. (1989). *100 schools project – summary report of second stage results.* Melbourne, Australia: School Programs Division, Ministry of Education.

Shanahan, T. & Barr, R. (1995). Reading Recovery: An independent evaluation of the effects of an early intervention for at risk learners. *Reading Research Quarterly, 30,* 958–997.

Siegel, L.S. (1989). IQ is irrelevant to the definition of learning disabilities. *Journal of Learning Disabilities, 22,* 469–479.

Snowling, M.J., Stothard, S.E. & McLean, J.M. (1996). *Graded non-word reading test.* Bury St. Edmunds: Thames Valley Test Company.

Stanovich, K.E. (1986). Matthew effects in reading: Some consequences of individual differences in the acquisition of literacy. *Reading Research Quarterly, 21*(4), 360–406.

Stanovich, K.E. & Siegel, L.S. (1994). Phenotypic performance profile of children with reading disabilities: A regression-based test of the phonological-core variable-difference model. *Journal of Educational Psychology, 86,* 24–53.

Stuart, M. (2002). Using the dual-route cascade model as a framework for considering reading development. In R. Stainthorp & P. Tomlinson (Eds.), *Learning and teaching reading.* (pp. 45–60). Leicester: The British Psychological Society.

Sylva, K. & Hurry, J. (1995). *Early interventions in children with reading difficulties.* No. 2. Schools Curriculum and Assessment Authority.

Torgesen, J.K. (2000). Individual differences in response to early interventions in reading: The lingering problem of treatment resisters. *Learning Disabilities Research and Practice, 15,* 55–64.

Young, D. (1983). *Parallel spelling tests.* London: Hodder & Stoughton.

Venezky, R. (1998). An alternative perspective on Success for All. In K. Wong (Ed.), *Advances in educational policy.* (Vol. 4, pp. 145–165). New York: JAI Press.

Wade, B. & Moore, M. (1997). *Longitudinal case studies of Reading Recovery: New Zealand and Australia.* (unpublished).

Wasik, B.A. & Slavin, R.E. (1993). Preventing early reading failure with one-to-one tutoring: A review of five programs. *Reading Research Quarterly, 28*(2), 179–200.

16

Student Writing in Higher Education: An Academic Literacies Approach

Mary R. Lea and Brian V. Street

[...]

Introduction

The opinion is often expressed that standards of student 'literacy' are falling, whether at school or in higher education: many academic staff claim that students can no longer write. 'Back to basics' ideas are now fast taking hold in today's higher education. Recently, we received an award from the Economic and Social Research Council to conduct a research project entitled 'Perspectives on Academic Literacies: an institutional approach' that attempted to look at these issues in more depth. The research looked at perceptions and practices of student writing in higher education, taking as case studies one new and [one] old university in southern England. Set against the background of numerous changes in higher education in the UK and increasing numbers of non-traditional entrants, this research has been concerned with a wider institutional approach to student writing, rather than merely locating 'problems' with individual students. One of the main purposes of the research has been to move away from a skills-based, deficit model of student writing and to consider the complexity of writing practices that are taking place at degree level in universities. As a starting point, the research adopts the concept of academic literacies as a framework for understanding university writing practices.

Academic literacies

Learning in higher education involves adapting to new ways of knowing: new ways of understanding, interpreting and organising knowledge. Academic literacy practices – reading and writing within disciplines – constitute central processes through which students learn new subjects and develop their knowledge about new areas of study. A practices approach to literacy takes account of the cultural and contextual component of writing and reading practices,

From: *Studies in Higher Education*, 23 (2), 1998, pp. 157–72.

and this in turn has important implications for an understanding of student learning. Educational research into student learning in higher education has tended to concentrate on ways in which students can be helped to adapt their practices to those of the university (Gibbs, 1994); from this perspective, the codes and conventions of academia can be taken as given. In contrast, our research is founded on the premise that in order to understand the nature of academic learning, it is important to investigate the understandings of both academic staff and students about their own literacy practices, without making prior assumptions as to which practices are either appropriate or effective. This is particularly important in trying to develop a more complex analysis of what it means to become academically literate. We believe that it is important to realise that meanings are contested amongst the different parties involved: institutions, staff and students. Viewing literacy from a cultural and social practice approach (rather than in terms of educational judgements about good and bad writing) and approaching meanings as contested can give us insights into the nature of academic literacy in particular and academic learning in general: through researching these differing expectations and interpretations of university writing, we hope to throw light on failure or non-completion, as well as success and progression.

The notion of academic literacies has been developed from the area of 'new literacy studies' (Street, 1984; Barton, 1994; Baynham, 1995) and is an attempt to draw out the implications of this approach for our understanding of issues of student learning. We have argued elsewhere (Lea & Street, 1997a) that educational research into student writing in higher education has fallen into three main perspectives or models: 'study skills'; 'academic socialisation'; and 'academic literacies' (see appendix). The models are not mutually exclusive, and we would not want to view them in a simple linear time dimension, whereby one model supersedes or replaces the insights provided by the other. Rather, we would like to think that each model successively encapsulates the other, so that the academic socialisation perspective takes account of study skills but includes them in the broader context of the acculturation processes we describe later, and likewise the academic literacies approach encapsulates the academic socialisation model, building on the insights developed there as well as the study skills view. The academic literacies model, then, incorporates both of the other models into a more encompassing understanding of the nature of student writing within institutional practices, power relations and identities, as we explain later. We take a hierarchical view of the relationship between the three models, privileging the 'academic literacies' approach. We believe that, in teaching as well as in research, addressing specific skills issues around student writing (such as how to open or close an essay or whether to use the first person) takes on entirely different meanings if the context is solely that of study skills, if the process is seen as part of academic socialisation, or if it is viewed more broadly as an aspect of the whole institutional and epistemological context. We explicate each model in turn as both a summary of our major findings in the research project and as a set of lenses through which to view the account we give of this research.

The study skills approach has assumed that literacy is a set of atomised skills which students have to learn and which are then transferable to other contexts. The focus is on attempts to 'fix' problems with student learning, which are treated as a kind of pathology. The theory of language on which it is based emphasises surface features, grammar and spelling. Its sources lie in behavioural psychology and training programmes and it conceptualises student writing as technical and instrumental. In recent years, the crudity and insensitivity of this approach have led to refinement of the meaning of the 'skills' involved and attention to broader issues of learning and social context, and have led us to what we (Lea & Street, 1997a) have termed the 'academic socialisation' approach.

From the academic socialisation perspective, the task of the tutor/adviser is to induct students into a new 'culture', that of the academy. The focus is on student orientation to learning and interpretation of learning tasks, through conceptualisation, for instance, of a distinction between 'deep', 'surface' and 'strategic' approaches to learning (Marton et al., 1997). The sources of this perspective lie in social psychology, in anthropology and in constructivist education. Although more sensitive both to the student as learner and to the cultural context, the approach could nevertheless be criticised on a number of grounds. It appears to assume that the academy is a relatively homogeneous culture, whose norms and practices have simply to be learnt to provide access to the whole institution. Even though at some level, disciplinary and departmental difference may be acknowledged, institutional practices, including processes of change and the exercise of power, do not seem to be sufficiently theorised. Similarly, despite the fact that contextual factors in student writing are recognised as important (Hounsell, 1988; Taylor et al., 1988), this approach tends to treat writing as a transparent medium of representation and so fails to address the deep language, literacy and discourse issues involved in the institutional production and representation of meaning.

The third approach, the one most closely allied to the New Literacy Studies, we refer to as academic literacies. This approach sees literacies as social practices, in the way we have suggested. It views student writing and learning as issues at the level of epistemology and identities rather than skill or socialisation. An academic literacies approach views, the institutions in which academic practices take place as constituted in, and as sites of, discourse and power. It sees the literacy demands of the curriculum as involving a variety of communicative practices, including genres, fields and disciplines. From the student point of view, a dominant feature of academic literacy practices is the requirement to switch practices between one setting and another, to deploy a repertoire of linguistic practices appropriate to each setting, and to handle the social meanings and identities that each evokes. This emphasis on identities and social meanings draws attention to deep affective and ideological conflicts in such switching and use of the linguistic repertoire. A student's personal identity – who am 'I'? – may be challenged by the forms of writing required in different disciplines, notably prescriptions about the use of impersonal and passive forms as opposed to first person and active forms, and students may feel threatened and resistant – 'this isn't me' (Lea, 1994; Ivanic, 1998). The recognition of this level of engagement with student writing, as opposed to the more straightforward study skills and academic socialisation approaches, comes from the social and ideological orientation of the 'New Literacy Studies'. Allied to this is work in critical discourse analysis, systemic functional linguistics and cultural anthropology, which has come to see student writing as being concerned with the processes of meaning-making and contestation around meaning rather than as skills or deficits. There is a growing body of literature based upon this approach, which suggests that one explanation for problems in student writing might be the gaps between academic staff expectations and student interpretations of what is involved in student writing (Cohen, 1993; Lea, 1994; Street, 1995; Lea & Street, 1997b; Stierer, 1997).

The research

During 1995–96, we carried out research at two universities, one new and one traditional, in the south-east of England. Ten interviews were conducted with staff in the older university and 21 students were interviewed, either individually or in small groups. At the new university, 13 members of academic staff and 26 students were interviewed in the same way. The interviews at both institutions included the Directors of Quality Assurance Units and 'learning support' staff.

One of our initial research objectives was to explore the contribution of ethnographic-based research to educational development in higher education. The short length of the project limited the in-depth ethnographic approach which such research could warrant. However, we did adopt an 'ethnographic style' approach (Green & Bloome, 1997) to the research which included conducting in-depth, semi-structured interviews with staff and students, participant observation of group sessions and attention to samples of students' writing, written feedback on students' work and handouts on 'essay' writing. A major part of the research has included a linguistically based analysis of this textual material. As the research progressed, we realised that this was an equally important source of data which we needed to consider in relation to the interview data. As researchers, we were able to benefit from our own situated knowledge of the institutional settings within which we were researching. Adopting an ethnographic style approach to the research, within settings of which we already had prior knowledge, enabled us to move away from the focus on transcribed interview material to a more eclectic approach, merging the importance of understanding both texts and practices in the light of staff and student interpretations of university writing.

Our research, then, was not based on a representative sample from which generalisations could be drawn but rather was conceived as providing case studies that enabled us to explore theoretical issues and generate questions for further systematic study. Our approach, therefore, was in the ethnographic tradition described by Mitchell (1984). Rather than applying 'enumerative induction' (as in much scientific and statistical research) as a means to generalising, and for establishing the 'representativeness' of social data, Mitchell advocates what he terms 'analytical induction':

> What the anthropologist using a case study to support an argument does is to show how general principles deriving from some theoretical orientation manifest themselves in some given set of particular circumstances. A good case study, therefore, enables the analyst to establish theoretically valid connections between events and phenomena which previously were ineluctable. (Mitchell, 1984, p. 239)

In the present context, the tutors and students whom we interviewed and the documents we collected can be taken as case studies of different perspectives on academic literacies. Whilst not representing a sample from which generalisations can be drawn regarding the whole of English higher education, these case studies can point to important theoretical questions and connections that might not otherwise be raised. The data, for instance, enable us to explore the hypothesis that, viewed as 'academic literacies', the beliefs and practices of tutors and students constitute a different kind of evidence than if this same data were viewed in terms of skills or academic socialisation. These accounts can, for instance, provide evidence for differences between staff and students' understanding of the writing process at levels of epistemology, authority and contestation over knowledge rather than at the level of technical skill, surface linguistic competence or cultural assimilation. We have therefore approached our research data in order to acquire insights and conceptual elaboration on our three models of student writing and to generate from it analytic induction rather than 'enumerative induction'.

The unstructured, in-depth interviews examined how students understand the different literacy practices which they experience in their studies and in what ways academic staff understand the literacy requirements of their own subject area and make these explicit to their students. We gave participants the opportunity to reflect upon the writing practices of the university, at different levels and in different courses, subject areas and disciplines, and to consider not only the influences that were being brought to bear upon them from within the university but also those from other writing contexts. We asked staff to outline, as they saw them, the writing requirements of their own disciplines and subject areas and to describe the kinds and quantities of writing that were involved for their students. We also asked them to talk about their perceptions of problems with student writing and the ways in which these were addressed at both an individual and departmental level. Students explained the problems that they experienced with writing at the university and their perceptions of the writing requirements of different courses and subject areas. We also collected copious amounts of documentation from both staff and students: handouts on essay writing; examples of students' written work; course handbooks; assignment guidelines.

A further objective of our research was to contribute towards an institutional understanding of academic literacy practices in higher education and we therefore began the project with a focus upon three traditional academic categories: humanities, social sciences, and natural sciences. In both universities, we began by carrying out interviews with academic staff within each category and then went on to interview students. Early in the research, it became clear from the interview data we were collecting that the traditional boundaries that we had identified to frame the research were in many senses irrelevant, particularly for students. Our interviews with students alerted us to the fact that old disciplinary divides were often not appropriate as research categories.

The diverse nature of the degree programmes at preliminary level resulted in students undertaking what we term 'course switching' which, we suggest, can be paralleled with linguistic code switching (Gumperz, 1982). In the case of 'course switching', students are having to interpret the writing requirements of different levels of academic activity. Such switching may range from academic disciplines in a traditional sense (such as physics and anthropology) to what we see as 'fields of study', such as modular programmes that incorporate elements of different disciplines and of interdisciplinary courses (such as Asian studies and business studies) and to specific modules or course units within programmes (such as twentieth-century women's literature and operations management). This switching may also encompass the different demands of individual subject tutors and their personal interpretations of writing requirements. As students switch between such disciplines, course units, modules and tutors, different assumptions about the nature of writing, related to different epistemological presuppositions about the nature of academic knowledge and learning, are being brought to bear, often implicitly, on the specific writing requirements of their assignments. Evidence from interviews with tutors and students and from handouts prepared for students on aspects of 'good' writing suggests that it is frequently very difficult for students to 'read off' from any such context what might be the specific academic writing requirements of that context. Nor, as we shall see below, did the provision of general statements about the nature of academic writing help students with the specificity of demands in each context.

We also interviewed learning support staff in both institutions. The data collected from these interviews reinforced the views expressed by students that many of the difficulties they experienced with writing arose from the conflicting and contrasting requirements for writing on different courses and from the fact that these requirements were frequently left implicit. Learning support staff also questioned whether academic staff were aware that they were asking for specific ways of writing knowledge from their students.

Requirements of student writing: staff interpretations

The interviews with staff suggest that academic staff have their own fairly well-defined views regarding what constitutes the elements of a good piece of student writing in the areas in which they teach. These tend to refer to form in a more generic sense, including attention to syntax, punctuation and layout, and to such apparently evident components of rational essay writing as 'structure', 'argument' and 'clarity'. Their own disciplinary history had a clear influence on staff conceptualisations and representations of what were the most important elements to look for in students' writing at both levels, although the epistemological and methodological issues that underlay them were often expressed through the surface features and components of 'writing' in itself – as we detail below. It was this confusion, we argue, that led to difficulties for students not yet acquainted with the disciplinary underpinnings of faculty feedback. This confusion was compounded by the move towards multidisciplinary courses at degree level and the modular system that was fully in place at one of the universities. As a result, although faculty understanding of student writing was often described in disciplinary terms (for example, 'In history the use of evidence is particularly important', or 'In English we are looking for clarity of expression'), in practice staff were often teaching within programmes which integrated a number of disciplinary approaches and for which the writing requirements consequently varied.

Additionally, some academic staff were teaching in courses where even the traditional disciplines were looking at new ways of communicating that discipline outside of the academic community, developing what we term 'empathy' writing: in physics, for instance, students were asked to write texts for non-specialist audiences, such as Select Committees of MPs, or commercial groups, to 'empathise' with their reader's lack of disciplinary knowledge and at the same time take account of their desire or need to know. In management science, mathematical principles were used to address commercial problems, and writing reports for putative clients was an essential part of student writing for assessment. The writing requirements of these exercises differed from those of more standard 'essay text' kinds of writing but the same students may encounter both in their progress through a degree programme.

Despite this variation in modes of writing across disciplines and fields of study, many staff we interviewed were still mainly influenced by specific conceptualisations of their own disciplines or subject areas in their assessments of students' writing. The twin concepts of 'structure' and 'argument' came to the fore in most interviews as being key elements in student writing, terms which we examine more closely below. Even though staff generally had a clear belief in these concepts as crucial to their understanding of what constituted a successful piece of writing, there was less certainty when it came to describing what underlay a well-argued or well-structured piece of student work. More commonly, staff were able to identify when a student had been successful, but could not describe how a particular piece of writing 'lacked' structure. We suggest that, in practice, what makes a piece of student writing 'appropriate' has more to do with issues of epistemology than with the surface features of form to which staff often have recourse when describing their students' writing. That is to say, underlying, often disciplinary, assumptions about the nature of knowledge affected the meaning given to the terms 'structure' and 'argument'. Since these assumptions varied with context, it is not valid to suggest that such concepts are generic and transferable, or represent 'common sense ways of knowing' (Fairclough, 1992), as the reference to 'writing problems' frequently implied. We believe that this finding has considerable implications for current attempts to define generic skills.

The research data, then, suggests that, whilst academic staff can describe what constitutes successful writing, difficulties arose when they attempted to make explicit what a well-developed argument looks like in a written assignment. At the level of form, one tutor is able to explain what he wants clearly:

> I need my students to have an introduction which sets the scene and a main body which covers a number of issues highlighted in the introduction and introduces economic theory, application and analysis. Students need to be critical, to evaluate, to try and reach some sort of synthesis and then to simply summarise and conclude. You need a good solid introduction leading into your main body and each part of your main body will be crafted and it will link with the next. It will have a professional feel about it and will not describe but will critically analyse and then it will lead into a summary and conclusion.

However, the descriptive tools he employs – 'critically analyse', 'evaluate', 'reach a synthesis' – could not be explicated further. As another lecturer put it: 'I know a good essay when I see it but I cannot describe how to write it'. This lends credence to the idea that elements of successful student writing are in essence related to particular ways of constructing the world and not to a set of generic writing skills as the study skills model would suggest. Successful university lecturers are likely to have spent many years developing acceptable ways of constructing their own knowledge through their own writing practices in a variety of disciplinary contexts. Other writers have explicated in some detail how writing practices construct rather than merely reflect academic knowledge (Bazerman, 1988; Berkenkotter & Huckin, 1995). These practices, then, are integrally related to the ways in which staff constitute their own academic world-view and their own academic knowledge. Faced with writing which does not appear to make sense within their own academic framework, they are most likely to have recourse to what feel like familiar descriptive categories such as 'structure and argument', 'clarity' and 'analysis', in order to give feedback on their students' writing. In reality, their own understandings of these categories may be bound by their own individual, disciplinary perspective, but the categories may be less meaningful outside of this framework and therefore not readily understood by students unversed in that particular orientation of the discipline. Our later analysis of a student essay illustrates this in some detail.

Writing requirements: student interpretations

The research interviews with students revealed a number of different interpretations and understandings of what students thought that they were meant to be doing in their writing. Students described taking 'ways of knowing' (Baker et al., 1995) and of writing from one course into another, only to find that their attempt to do this was unsuccessful and met with negative feedback. They were consciously aware of switching between diverse writing requirements and knew that their task was to unpack what kind of writing any particular assignment might require. This was at a more complex level than genre, such as the 'essay' or 'report', but lay more deeply at the level of writing particular knowledge in a specific academic setting. Students knew that variations of form existed, but admitted that their real writing difficulties lay in trying to gauge the deeper levels of variation in knowledge and how to set about writing them. It was much more than using the correct terminology or just learning to do 'academic writing – as what we term the academic socialisation model would suggest – and more about adapting previous knowledge of writing practices, academic and other, to varied university settings:

> The thing I'm finding most difficult in my first term here is moving from subject to subject and knowing how you're meant to write in each one. I'm really aware of writing for a particular tutor as well as for a particular subject. Everybody seems to want something different. It's very different to A levels where we used dictated notes for essay writing.

Such common descriptions in interviews with students did not appear to support the notion of generic and transferable writing skills across the university.

Students themselves often internalised the language of feedback. They knew that it was important to present an argument and they knew that structure played an important part, but had difficulties in understanding when they had achieved this successfully in a piece of writing. Students would frequently describe how they had completed a piece of work that they believed was well constructed and appropriate to the subject area, only to discover that they had received a very low grade and fairly negative feedback. They often felt unsure and confused about what they had done wrong. What seemed to be an appropriate piece of writing in one field, or indeed for one individual tutor, was often found to be quite inappropriate for another. Although students frequently had guidelines, either from individual tutors or as departmental documents on essay writing, they found that these often did not help them very much with this level of writing. They felt that such guidelines dealt with matters that they knew from A level or Access courses. The guidelines involved issues broadly defined as structure, such as those concerned with the formal organisation of a piece of writing (introduction, main body, conclusion) or as argument, involving advice on the necessity of developing a position rather than providing 'just' a description or narrative. Students could assimilate this general advice on writing 'techniques' and 'skills' but found it difficult to move from the general to using this advice in a particular text in a particular disciplinary context. In both universities, the majority of the documents offering guidelines of this nature that we analysed took a rather technical approach to writing, concentrating on issues of surface form: grammar, punctuation and spelling. They also dealt fully with referencing, bibliographies and footnotes, and supplied warnings about plagiarism. They rarely dealt with the issues that students reported they had most difficulty grasping – for example, how to write specific, course-based knowledge for a particular tutor or field of study.

The conflicting advice received from academic teaching staff in different courses added to the confusion. For example, in some areas, students were specifically directed to outline what would follow in the main body of a traditional essay, whilst other tutors would comment, 'I do not want to know what you are going to say'. Many different conventions were to be found around the use of the first person pronoun in student writing. Even within the same courses, individual tutors had different opinions about when or if it was appropriate to use this. Such conventions were often presented as self-evidently the correct way in which things should be done. Student perceptions were influenced by their own experiences of writing within and outside higher education. An example of this was the A level entrant who came unstuck when she wrote a history essay drawing on just one textual source as she regularly and successfully had done in English. Similarly, another entrant to the traditional university who had worked in industry for five years and was used to extensive, succinct report writing, had no idea how to go about writing a traditional essay text in politics, as part of a course in public administration and management.

Students took different approaches to the course switching that they experienced. Some saw it as a kind of game, trying to work out the rules, not only for a field of study, a particular course or particular assignment, but frequently for an individual tutor. They adopted writing strategies that masked their own opinions, in a sense mimicking some implicit or even explicit convention. There were, for instance, the first-year history students who had learnt to hide what they thought behind 'it can be said' rather than using the first person in their writing, and had also learnt how to balance one recognised author against another as a way to present their own personal viewpoint in their writing. On the other hand, a mature student writing social policy felt severely constrained by his inability to bring his years of trade union expertise into his essay on present-day poverty. He did not feel comfortable with the pragmatic approach of playing to the rules of the game, which seemed to require him to simply juxtapose data from different sources and to eschew personal knowledge.

Writing across courses: 'structure and argument'

We examine here a 'telling case' (Mitchell, 1984) of the problems that these differences in understanding the writing requirements of specific courses can lead to. A first-year history student had a strikingly different response from his tutors to an anthropology essay and to a history essay written during the same period in his first year of study. For the history essay, in which the emphasis had been on content and factual information, he received positive feedback, but when he attempted an essay for anthropology using a similar format, he was subject to strong criticism. He felt, however, that he had written a successful essay in both cases. The feedback from the anthropology lecturer suggested that his difficulties were with general essay-writing skills, although feedback and grades in both history and politics at the same time, as well as his pre-university A level experience, had led him to believe that he could handle academic writing requirements with no real difficulties. The tutor in anthropology was particularly critical of his 'lack' of 'structure and argument' in the anthropology essay. The student, however, could not understand how the essay lacked structure and felt that he had presented a coherent argument in his writing.

We would suggest that the explanation for this divergence of opinion and response lies at a deeper level than the surface features of 'writing' to which the anthropology tutor refers. Rather, the cause of the poor assessment of his essay can be traced, we suggest, to the student's lack of familiarity with the subject matter of anthropology, which was not his major, and to his greater ease with history, which he had studied successfully at A level and was now taking as his major: his experience with writing in history led him to attempt to break down and categorise some factual aspects of his knowledge in his anthropology essay, without attention to some of the implicit ways of writing knowledge in his anthropology, and in particular the need to abstract theory rather than attend to factual detail as evidence, as was required by at least some tutors in that discipline. In our analysis, we attend particularly to the tutor's comments in the margins of the essay, and on the feedback sheet attached to the end.

The essay was on the question: 'Must governments, in order to survive, always claim to be "better" than ordinary people?' In attempting to answer this question, the student had written in one paragraph about 'Principality' – one of the forms of government listed by Aristotle, whom he quoted at the outset. 'Principality', he writes, 'represents the pinnacle of this domination and therefore demands absolute government control'. He gives an example of how individuals may break away from dominant groups, such as those defined by caste and lineage, and assert that they are 'better' (as called for in the title) by being a member of another clan. The paragraph concludes that this 'is evidence of their survival depending on their repressive claim to power through blood/lineage'. The next paragraph opens: 'As in all forms of government "authority" must secure as wide a measure of popular support as it can …' The following paragraph commences: 'Religion is the most powerful tool with which to obtain "popular support" and therefore survival'. The tutor has written in the margin between the first two paragraphs *'Linkage'* (tutor comments in italics here for clarity, but in handwriting in the original) and between the second two paragraphs: *'Too many unlinked facts here, I can't see any argument'*.

The student, however, might well assume that the linkage is there but given by the paragraph 'structure' of his essay and by lexical reference back to the title – 'better', 'survive'. In the first section, he had listed Aristotle's 'six forms' of government. Each section of the essay that follows starts with a reference to one of these forms, e.g. 'Principality', 'Tyranny', 'Aristocracy'. The paragraphs cited above refer to 'Principality', and in keeping with this interpretation of the student's organisation of the essay, the term is the first word in the initial paragraph. The next paragraph, commencing 'Religion is a powerful tool', could be seen as intended to link with the account of 'Principality'. The student refers to anthropological data on the role of clans among the Bemba people, which could be taken as empirical evidence with respect to the question of 'survival' of forms of government: this is summarised in the phrase, 'Religion is the most powerful tool with which to obtain "popular support" and therefore survival' – a further reference to the title.

As the essay progresses, different forms of government are indicated: one paragraph begins, 'Principality's downfall is secured by Tyranny'; another, 'Machiavelli saw the constant successional threat of aristocracy in 16th century France in these terms'. The tutor has put a question mark in the margin beside this sentence, presumably further indicating his general concern on this page with 'linkage' and 'argument'. However, the markers of cohesion, such as the use of connectives ('these', 'such', 'therefore') and the repetition of key terms from the title ('survival', 'better', 'government') could be seen as intended to indicate the flow of such an 'argument' – that forms of government attempted to gain support in order to survive but gave way to other forms, which have their ethnographic and empirical correlates in accounts of the Bemba and Shilluck, which are classic cases of political formations in the anthropological literature. The final paragraph states: 'In conclusion irrespective of whether governments claim to be better than ordinary people, their survival will eventually be undermined by the next form of government'. Here the student has made direct reference back to the title, presumably to create an ending to his essay that is coherent with the opening question.

The tutor's comments in the margins and at the end regarding lack of 'linkage' indicate that these attempts at 'argument' and cohesion have not been recognised. The tutor writes at the end: 'You really have a problem with this essay, mainly for the reason that it is so incoherent. It has no beginning, middle and end, no structure, no argument'. The student is advised to go the university study centre 'and make enquires about essay-writing clinics'. The pathologising of his writing and the references to 'lack' of key components of 'good writing – 'structure', 'argument' – suggest that the student's 'problem' is to do with generic features of essay writing. And yet the same student received excellent grades and comments for another essay – in history – written in the same week in much the same style and manner. Again, the writer uses standard cohesive ties (Hatch, 1995), such as the conjunctions 'therefore' and 'yet' and repetition of key terms from the title, 'economy', 'society', in order to link the conclusion with the initial question and with the flow of the argument. In this case, the tutor has implicitly recognised the work of cohesion and writes: 'I like your conclusion to what is a carefully argued and relevant essay'.

If we interpret the attempts at structure and argument in the way suggested above, then what appears to be at stake can be analysed at two levels. Firstly, the linguistic features of structure and argument are clearly open to interpretation, and what may indicate argument for one person (e.g. cohesive ties, juxtaposition, reference, connectives) may not appear so to another. In this case, the anthropology tutor is looking for analysis of each area of content and does not notice the linguistic and structural devices this student has used for indicating 'argument'. Secondly, and following from this last point, what may be at stake is determination of what is involved in a particular discipline – the tutor in this case may see anthropology as requiring different conceptions of knowledge and more to be done with linkage and analysis of concepts, than did the history tutor for whom clear summary of the facts in appropriate sequence was sufficient evidence of a 'carefully argued and relevant essay'. The anthropology tutor's comments, however, are couched in terms of writing problems, so such epistemological presupposition regarding academic disciplines is hidden beneath more technical attention to supposedly generic features of 'academic writing': 'May I suggest very strongly that you go to the study centre and make enquiries about essay-writing clinics'.

We suggest that the contrast we are making between such writing-focused comments on the one hand, and the deeper epistemological issues associated with knowledge in different disciplines, on the other, might be applied to other examples of staff–student relations in connection with the writing process. Such an approach might open up areas of inquiry and reinterpretation that would revalue much student writing, shift attention from surface features of 'literacy' to deeper features of epistemology and of authority, of the kind indicated above, and perhaps explain much of the miscommunication between tutors and students that is coming to be documented as researchers focus on academic literacies.

Understandings of plagiarism

A similar area of conflict between different perspectives on the writing process amongst tutors and students concerns the concept of 'plagiarism'. We found reference to 'plagiarism' was identified surprisingly often in the interview comments of both tutors and students, and frequently in the documentation available for students as advice on assignment writing and other course documentation. In both universities, there appeared to be an unquestioned assumption that both tutor and student would share the same interpretation and understanding of 'plagiarism'. Our evidence, in common with Ashworth et al. (1997), would suggest that we cannot assume this to be the case. Students often expressed anxieties about plagiarism in terms of their own authority as writers. They were unclear about what actually constituted plagiarism and yet at the same time were concerned about how to acknowledge the authority of academic texts. Their overriding concerns were that the texts they read were authoritative and that they as students had little useful to say. They were confused, not only about the conventions for referencing, but more importantly they found it difficult to understand the implicit relationship between acknowledging the source of the text and acknowledging the authority of the text. Their concerns lay more with the latter and how they as novice students could write anything that they had not read in an authoritative source:

> I don't know anything about the subject other than what I've read in books so how on earth could I write anything which was not someone else's idea?

For this student, as with others, the relationship between plagiarism and correct referencing was not transparent and he was worried that he would plagiarise unknowingly. For academics, the issue of referencing sources seems clear; for students, the boundary between their sources and their own account is less certain as they feel, like the student quoted here, that all of their knowledge is implicated in others' texts. Indeed, some tutors did express concern during the interviews about student interpretations of plagiarism that recognised this uncertainty.

However, at an institutional level, plagiarism was treated as clearly definitive and unquestionable. In one particular instance, a standard feedback sheet for tutors to comment on student essays gave considerable attention to plagiarism in a document that was necessarily constrained for space and where the choice of topic in relation to student writing is therefore highly significant. Even if the emphasis on plagiarism evident here could be construed as a valid aspect of a document offering advice and feedback to students learning to write, the discourse here is that of the law and authority rather than of tutor and student engaged in the learning practices of educational discourse:

> PLAGIARISM is an assessment offence (see section 3.7–3.9 of University Assessment Regulations pp. 26–27 in Student regulations). A student who knowingly allows his/her work to be copied, either verbatim or by paraphrasing, will be guilty of an assessment offence.

In this same university, whilst interviewing tutors, we observed notices warning against plagiarism on the walls of tutors' offices and on the notice boards in corridors. Whatever the formal and legal issues involved, as a social practice, this focus upon the term plagiarism itself and the legalistic discourse in which it is embedded affirms the disciplinary and surveillance aspects of the writing process. This discourse reinforces the relations of tutor to student as those of authority, backed by the heavy weight of an institution with boards, regulations and, ultimately, legal resources.

Student writing: interpreting feedback

So far, we have attempted to outline some of the indications in the research data for conceptualising variety in the different interpretations and understandings of student writing we encountered. These variations exist within and across courses, subjects and disciplines – and between students and academic tutors in many different contexts. They are constituted both in the linguistic form of the texts – the written assignments and the accompanying feedback – and in the social relations that exist around them – the relationships of power and authority between tutor and student – and they are manifest in the divergent literacy practices surrounding written texts. Central to our understanding of both the varieties of academic literacy practices which students engage in across the university and the relations which surround text production is an examination of the ways in which written feedback is interpreted by staff and students.

As we have illustrated, the research has been concerned with a textual examination of tutor-written feedback on student work – both on standard feedback sheets and in the margins of assignment – and with students' interpretations of the meanings that they attach to this feedback, both in general and in relation to a specific piece of written work. This analysis has raised questions about the relationship between feedback and epistemo-logical issues of knowledge construction. How is feedback being used to direct students to develop and write their academic knowledge in very specific ways within particular courses which are implicitly presented as 'common-sense ways of knowing'? We have already illustrated a feedback genre within which the use of descriptive categories – such as 'structure' and 'argument' – may embed contrasting conceptual understandings. As we have suggested, such terms tend to be rather elusive, particularly for students, and may be more usefully understood in their gatekeeping role or at a more complex ideological level within an institutional hierarchy than as the unproblematic generic requirements of student writing.

One useful way of examining the relationships surrounding texts may be to start by examining the feedback that staff give to students as a genre. By examining some of the genres of students' written work and the genre of staff feedback on it, we may be able to make more sense of the complex ways in which staff and students construct appropriate ways of knowing and reproduce appropriate forms of disciplinary and subject knowledge. There is a dynamic within the feedback genre, for instance, which works both to construct academic knowledge and to maintain relationships of power and authority between novice student and experienced academic. Assumptions about what constitutes valid knowledge may be inferred by analysing feedback but frequently such assumptions remain implicit, as in the feedback on the essay analysed above.

The ways in which a speaker or writer indicate their implicit commitment to the truth of what is being said – what linguists refer to as 'modality' – varies with types of text and social relations. Tutor comments frequently take the form of what we term categorical modality, using imperatives and assertions, with little mitigation or qualification. The first page of the essay analysed above has the following comments: 'Explain', 'A bit confused', 'Linkage?', 'Too many unlinked facts here. Can't see argument'. This categorical modality is also expressed here and frequently in the essays we have seen, by means of orthographic marks such as '?', '!' or '(', that indicate disagreement, doubt, criticism. The question mark frequently indicates not a genuine question which tutor and student are engaged in explicating, but rather is used as a kind of expletive, or as a categorical assertion that the point is not 'correct'. In the essay in question, there are seven unattached question marks, many with this function, and six bracket signs indicating links that should have been made, in the space of 31 pages. One has only to imagine other kinds of modality that could be expressed in this context to recognise the conventional and categorical nature of this usage: mitigated comments such as 'you might like to consider', 'have you thought about', 'in my opinion …', 'perhaps', and open-ended questions such as 'could this be interpreted differently?', 'is there a link with other comments here?', would evoke a different modality (more provisional or mitigated), create a different genre and evoke a different interpersonal relationship between student as writer and tutor as marker than that indicated by the comments we have described above. In making these comments, the tutor clearly and firmly takes authority, assumes the right to criticise directly and categorically on the basis of an assumed 'correct' view of what should have been written and how. Students, however, may have a different interpretation of feedback comments. For the anthropology student in question, he could not understand how to make sense of the feedback comment 'Meaning?' on his text. For him, both the meaning of what he was saying and the development of the argument in his own text was clear. Even where students indicate in interviews that they did not understand the comment, thought it unfair or even disagreed with it, few if any challenge the tutor's right to make such comments. It appears, then, that written feedback on student work, is not merely an attempt at communication, or at learning a 'discipline', or at socialisation into a community – although it clearly has elements of all of these – but is also embedded in relationships of authority as a marker of difference and a sustainer of boundaries.

Additionally, institutional procedures were implicated in the ways in which students were able to read, understand and make use of feedback on their work. In the new university, where a fully modular system was in operation, it was reported to us by both staff and students alike that in many instances, students did not receive feedback on assessed written work until they had completed their studies for this module. Inevitably, students found that they were unable to benefit from receiving feedback in this manner. Since they generally found feedback comments to be specific to a particular piece of work, or at the least to the module being studied, they reported that such feedback frequently bore no relationship to their studies in the subsequent module. Academic staff reported that they were unable to make best use of standard feedback sheets because these were received by students after module completion:

> The problem with the modular system is that every piece of work they [the students] do is for assessment purposes. It is not until they are well into the second module that they get the results from the first. Effectively there is no feedback.

Evidence such as this has led us to suggest that we consider the analysis of writing in the university as an 'institutional' issue and not just a matter for particular participants. The institution within which tutors and students write defines the conventions and boundaries of their writing practices, through its procedures and regulations (definitions of plagiarism, requirements of modularity and assessment procedures etc.), whatever individual tutors and students may believe themselves to be as writers, and whatever autonomy and distinctiveness their disciplines may assert.

Future directions

Our research indicates the variety in both the writing practices that students engage with as part of their university courses and the complex nature of the feedback they receive from tutors. These writing practices and genres are not simply concerned with technical matters in which 'appropriate' skills are acquired and novices become members of an expert community, as in the first two models described in the appendix. The third model, that of academic literacies (from which we are viewing these data), suggests a more complex and contested interpretation in which the processes of student writing and tutor feedback are defined through implicit assumptions about what constitutes valid knowledge within a particular context, and the relationships of authority that exist around the communication of these assumptions. The nature of this authority and the claims associated with it can be identified through both formal, linguistic features of the writing involved and in the social and institutional relationships associated with it.

During the course of the research, we have identified three thematic categories originating from both students and staff as ways of looking at students' writing. The first is focused on the student and suggests that students lack a set of basic skills that can be dealt with primarily in a remedial study skills or learning support unit. This takes no account of the interaction of the student with institutional practices and is based on the underlying principle that knowledge is transferred rather than mediated or constructed through writing practices. The second, identified most clearly by students, is derived from the interaction of student and tutor and is concerned with issues such as student and tutor assumptions and understandings of assignment titles, tutor feedback on students' written work and, for the students themselves, the importance of their own 'identity' as writers rather than simply the acquisition of skills in becoming an academic writer. The third theme is at a broadly institutional level and concerns the implications of modularity, assessment and university procedures on student writing.

We suggest that these three themes, focused broadly on students, student–tutor interactions, and the institution, need to be examined more fully against the changing 'fields of study' and student 'course switching' to which we have referred. All three, we argue, are located in relations of power and authority and are not simply reducible to the skills and competences required for entry to, and success within, the academic community. The current movement away from traditional academic disciplines and subject areas, within which academic staff have conceptualised their own and their students' writing practices, makes a broader perspective critical in understanding the 'problems' being identified in student writing. Without such a perspective, such problems tend to be explained mainly with respect to the students themselves or seen as a consequence of the mass introduction of 'nontraditional' students. From an academic literacies perspective, such explanations are limited and will not provide the basis for reflection on learning and teaching in higher education that the Dearing Report and others are calling for. Exploration of these themes within an academic literacies perspective may provide, we suggest, a fruitful area for research and for teacher education in higher education in the coming years.

References

Ashworth, P., Bannister, P. & Thorne, P. (1997) Guilty in whose eyes? University students' perceptions of cheating and plagiarism in academic work and assessment, *Studies in Higher Education*, 22, pp. 187–203.

Baker, D., Fox, C. & Clay, J. (1995) *Challenging Ways of Knowing in Maths, Science and English* (Lewes, Falmer Press).

Barton, D. (1994) *Literacy: an introduction to the ecology of written language* (Oxford, Blackwell).

Baynham, M. (1995) *Literacy Practices* (London, Longman).

Bazerman, C. (1988) *Shaping Written Knowledge: the genre and activity of the experimental article in science* (Madison, University of Wisconsin Press).

Berkenkotter, C. & Huckin, T. (1995) *Genre Knowledge in Disciplinary Communication* (New York, Lawrence Erlbaum Associates).

Cohen, M. (1993) Listening to students' voices: what university students tell us about how they can learn, paper presented to Annual Meeting of the American Educational Research Association, Atlanta, GA.

Fairclough, N. (1992) *Discourse and Social Change* (Cambridge, Polity Press).

Gibbs, G. (1994) *Improving Student Learning: theory and practice* (Oxford, Oxford Centre for Staff Development).

Green, J. & Bloome, D. (1997) Ethnography and ethnographers of and in education: a situated perspective, in: J. Flood, S. Brice Heath & D. Lapp (Eds) *Handbook of Research on Teaching Literacy through the Communicative and Visual Arts,* pp. 181–203 (New York, Simon & Schuster, Macmillan).

Gumperz, J. (1982) *Discourse Strategies* (Cambridge, Cambridge University Press).

Hatch, E. (1995) *Discourse and Language Education* (Cambridge, Cambridge University Press).

Hounsell, D. (1988) Towards an anatomy of academic discourse: meaning and context in the undergraduate essay, in: R. Saljo (Ed.) *The Written World. Studies in literate thought and action,* pp. 161–177 (Berlin, Springer-Verlag).

Ivanic, R. (1998) *Writing and Identity: the discoursal construction of identity in academic writing* (Amsterdam, John Benjamins).

Lea, M. (1994) 'I thought I could write till I came here': student writing in higher education, in: G. Gibbs (Ed.) *Improving Student Learning*: *theory and practice*, pp. 216–226 (Oxford, Oxford Centre for Staff Development).

Lea, M. & Street, B. (1997a) Models of student writing in higher education, paper presented to Higher Education Funding Council for England, Social Anthropology Teaching and Learning Network workshop, 'New forms of student writing', June 1997, University of Sussex.

Lea, M. & Street, B. (1997b) *Perspectives on Academic Literacies: an institutional approach* (Swindon, Economic and Social Research Council).

Marton, F., Hounsell, D. & Entwistle, N. (Eds) (1997) *The Experience of Learning* (Edinburgh, Scottish Academic Press).

Mitchell, C. (1984) Case Studies, in: R. Ellen (Ed.) *Ethnographic Research: a guide to general conduct*, pp. 237–241 (London, Academic Press).

Stierer, B. (1997) *Mastering Education: a preliminary analysis of academic literacy practices within master-level courses in education* (Milton Keynes, Centre for Language & Communications, Open University).

Street, B. (1984) *Literacy in Theory and Practice* (Cambridge, Cambridge University Press).

Street, B. (1995) Academic literacies, in: D. Baker, C. Fox & J. Clay *Challenging Ways of Knowing in Maths, Science and English,* pp. 101–134 (Lewes, Falmer Press).

Taylor, G., Ballard, B., Beasley, V., Hanne, B., Clanchy, J. & Nightingale, P. (1988) *Literacy by Degrees* (Milton Keynes, Society for Research in Higher Education/Open University).

Appendix. Models of student writing in higher education

Study skills:

Student deficit

- 'Fix it'; atomised skills; surface language, grammar, spelling.
- Sources: behavioural and experimental psychology; programmed learning.

Student writing as technical and instrumental skill.

Academic socialisation:

Acculturation of students into academic discourse

- Inducting students into new 'culture'; focus on orientation to learning and interpretation of learning task, e.g. 'deep', 'surface', 'strategic' learning; homogeneous 'culture', lack of focus on institutional practices, change and power.
- Sources: social psychology; anthropology; constructivism.

Student writing as transparent medium of representation.

Academic literacies

Student's negotiation of conflicting literacy practices

- Literacies as social practices; at level of epistemology and identities; institutions as sites of/constituted in discourses and power; variety of communicative repertoire, e.g. genres, fields, disciplines; switching with regard to linguistic practices, social meanings and identities.
- Sources: 'new literacy studies'; critical discourse analysis; systemic functional linguistics; cultural anthropology.

Student writing as meaning-making and contested.

Part 5

Transforming Practice

17

Dyslexia and Adult Literacy: Does Dyslexia Disempower?

Hugo Kerr

> ... the history of dyslexia research is littered with theories that were once widely sup-
> ported but now lie abandoned on the scrap heap ... It is vital that we should continue
> to treat everything as questionable and to regard nothing as beyond dispute. Certainty
> is for tele-evangelists, not scientific researchers or teachers. (Ellis et al., 1997: 13–14,
> their emphasis)

A small survey of adult basic education (ABE) providers

In 1998, an in-depth questionnaire survey was carried out among 12 professional
providers of ABE, exploring their attitudes towards, and behaviour in respect of, developmental dyslexia (hereafter simply dyslexia) in their students (Kerr, 1999). The sample was small but this research appears to be the first of its kind and particular interest
is thereby claimed for it though such a preliminary piece of research can only be suggestive and exploratory. All respondents were on the same M. Ed. distance learning
course as was the author, forming therefore a straightforwardly 'convenience sample'.
All respondents taught, or had until recently taught, ABE. Two had become managers,
one managing workplace literacy initiatives, the other ABE and family literacy provision county-wide. The remainder all taught ABE as follows: two worked in the prison
service, one as a volunteer tutor with elderly people in the USA and the remaining seven
with the general 16+ population in, or through the auspices of, colleges. My sample
population was reasonably representative of ABE provision. Eight of the respondents
held teachers' certificates and four held City and Guild certificates relevant to ABE
(9282 or 9285 or both).

Results were interesting but disconcerting. The most outstanding finding was variance
among, even within, respondents' opinions, overtly recognised by almost every respondent.

From: Hamilton, M., Tett, L. and Crowther, J. (eds) *Powerful Literacies*, pp. 69–79 (Leicester:
National Institute of Adult Continuing Education, 2001).

There was almost universal, and very considerable, confusion as to what dyslexia might be, what might indicate it, what might cause it, what to do about it and even whether it existed at all. Almost all respondents were muddled and insecure on the subject of dyslexia, but recognised this clearly and overtly in their questionnaire responses. There was a considerable tendency to use the term 'dyslexia' very loosely; to mean simply 'difficulty with literacy', irrespective of aetiology (the assignment of causation). The spread of opinion among respondents was substantial. One respondent estimated the prevalance of dyslexia, for example, at over 25 per cent, another at under 5 per cent. One respondent considered six times as many signs to be indicative of dyslexia as did another. Intelligence/achievement discrepancies were overwhelmingly chosen as pathognomic for dyslexia (as that sign which, absolutely and alone, indicates dyslexia beyond doubt). Five respondents could not provide a definition when asked and only one coherent definition emerged. Many respondents accepted extremely wide variation in possible aetiologies and effects. Emotional problems were suggested by eight respondents as a commonplace, alternative explanation for poor literacy skills. Five respondents stated that they did not believe psychometric tests were useful or reliable, particularly in ABE. Six respondents claimed to consider dyslexia when assessing students, but six said they did not. Only two respondents routinely screened for dyslexia, one by performance assessments adopted from Klein (1993) and one using a battery of psychometric tests. Four responses claimed that the apparent effect of a diagnosis on a student could be positive (e.g. 'relief') but two that it could be negative (e.g. 'doom'). A quarter of the sample stated that they were fully persuaded that dyslexia existed, [while] another quarter were absolutely sure that it did not. Half the sample were uncertain, and said so.

Perhaps the most practically important finding was that respondents almost universally showed marked signs of disempowerment, or learned helplessness, in respect of students with the diagnosis. Faced with a 'dyslexic' student, respondents' language grew grey and pessimistic. Only two respondents confidently expected progress. The remainder considered that progress would be unlikely or uncertain and would take much longer, with an increased tendency to regress. Any progress made would, most respondents wrote, be very insecure, with learned skills much less likely to be applied outside the 'classroom'. The language of respondents in respect of their tuition policy, faced with a student diagnosed as dyslexic, became abruptly behaviourist. Almost all respondents dramatically altered tuition under these circumstances. What they said they offered a 'dyslexic' student was repetitive, highly structured and controlled, depersonalised and skill-focused. Methodologies and expectations were instantly and drastically restricted, according to respondents' own accounts, following a diagnosis of dyslexia. Only two respondents were satisfied with such an approach, but nonetheless almost all felt obliged to adapt their tuition in these ways. These findings suggest that it is important to review what we know of dyslexia; to review what the evidence says and perhaps particularly what it does not say.

Why review this issue?

The most important purpose of education may be the inculcation ... of a deep, even raucous, scepticism. (J.K. Galbraith, 1969)

The term *dyslexia* is used, by most of us, very casually. We use it without properly defining it, or we define it so broadly as to be next to pointless. We apply the term even when we are perfectly well aware that we have no clear definition of it, or explanation for it. The word is commonly used to mean nothing more scientifically exact than a difficulty with written language which appears to be inexplicable. We tend to use the term to denote a problem with reading and/or writing and/or spelling (and sometimes much more besides) which we find hard to understand – especially where there appears to be a discrepancy with what we would otherwise expect from a particular person. We find such discrepancy so peculiar, so personally threatening, so deeply and intimately offensive that we are driven to believe, almost to hope, that there is something constitutionally wrong with the victim, that the cause must be a specific neurological deficit, beyond blame, safely located among all the other medical conditions beginning with 'dys-'.

Dyslexia is sometimes sought after as an empowering diagnosis, in that it may open particular educational opportunities. The diagnosis may also be considered to be desirable as preferable to the alternative, which may simply be considered unintelligent. There is an established dyslexia industry and very considerable vested interest in it. There seem to be as many wonderfully special assessment methods, remedial schemes and distinguished gurus as the market will carry. There are illogicalities and inconsistencies in much of the reported science (and see later). Weird and colourful creatures appear fleetingly through the muddied waters – are they fish, fowl or beast? Mostly, they soon disappear again. None of this seems to *bother* us nearly enough.

Why all the fuss? Does it matter whether there really is such a syndrome, so long as people who need appropriate help get it? I suspect that it matters fundamentally, and for several reasons. Much discussion about dyslexia is careless, or at least carefree. Many are willing to make the diagnosis, though rather fewer are qualified so to do. And what about those students who don't achieve the label? Are they simply (and publicly) to be designated as stupid? And then, we do not see over or around dyslexia; once the diagnosis has been invoked we stop looking for other aetiologies. Simpler, more everyday, scientifically duller (and much less lucrative) explanations are not sought once a diagnosis of dyslexia has been made. While dyslexia may be aspired to as a more socially acceptable and politically powerful aetiology, it may also prove extremely disconcerting. 'That was another big shock, finding out you're disabled!' cried one student (Whitehouse, 1995). Dyslexia is accepted as a disability by the DfEE, and the law. In the face of a diagnosis, we may act and believe differently – we may perceive a need for deficit-focused and limited practice, and we may experience abruptly depressed expectations. This is, indeed, almost inevitable once we have attributed a student's problems to a single, conceptually simple (albeit imperfectly understood), seemingly innate and fundamentally unalterable cause. This is classic soil in which to grow another important disability – 'learned helplessness' – and assuredly not only in the student (Agne *et al,* 1994; Butkowsky and Willows, 1980; Chan, 1994, 1996; Fang, 1996; Holt, 1984a, 1984b; Johnston, 1985; Kerr, 1999; Maier and Seligman, 1976; Peterson *et al,* 1993; Westwood, 1995).

Some science

To begin at the beginning, with definition.

Definitions of dyslexia are notoriously varied and no single definition of dyslexia has succeeded in gaining a scientific acceptance which even approaches unanimity … Definitions … soon become muddied when the researcher or clinician is confronted with a variety of adult cases exhibiting highly heterogenous profiles. (Beaton *et al,* 1997: 2)

Writers often feel free to define very loosely, or give up altogether without a blush.

The fact that no exact definition [of dyslexia] has yet been produced is of little consequence … *there is another quite distinct group* who have difficulty with reading yet are very able in other ways … for convenience we refer to them as being *dyslexic* or having *dyslexia*. Parents, teachers and others understand these words and find them to be an easy form of verbal shorthand to describe the children with whom we are concerned. (Doyle, 1997: 82, his emphasis)

Assessment varies, depending on who does it and to what end. There are many assessment schemes designed for practitioners in literacy teaching, based on assessment of performance on a variety of skills involved in, or said to relate to, literacy (see Klein, 1993; Miles, 1983; Nicolson and Fawcett, 1997). Such schemes are intended for dissemination to educationalists specifically to enable them to diagnose dyslexia on the run, for immediate educational purposes, with the implicit (indeed often explicit) presumption that both tuition and expectations will differ importantly should the syndrome be found. It remains unclear, though, to what degree the measurement of literacy or related skills measures anything other than these skills themselves; in particular, it is not at all clear whether such performance tests are able to tell us anything whatsoever about the aetiology of literacy failure.

Assessment for dyslexia for the purposes of scientific research continues to regard the intelligence/achievement discrepancy criterion as the single pathognomic indicator of dyslexia and researchers use it themselves, or rely for diagnosis on educational psychologists who use it. Diagnosing dyslexia simply on a finding of a particular discrepancy between measured IQ and performance on norm-referenced literacy tasks is problematic on two counts. The first is the increasingly frequent finding that a population defined as dyslexic by IQ/achievement discrepancy may not, in the event, differ reliably or importantly from the general population (see Miles and Miles, 1999; Samuelsson *et al,* 1999; Siegel and Himel, 1998; Stanovich and Stanovich, 1997). IQ/achievement discrepancy certainly indicates the existence of a problem (it is a discrepancy after all) but the measure probably says nothing useful about its aetiology. Much frontline scientific theory, however, rests on the definition of sample populations as distinct, different and dyslexic by invocation of this criterion (e.g. Brooks and Weeks, 1998; Fisher *et al,* 1999; Hanley, 1997; Hogben, 1997; Hynd *et al,* 1995). Such studies may thus be fundamentally, perhaps even fatally, flawed.

The second, and perhaps more basic, difficulty lies in the concept of IQ itself. As Stanovich (1991: 9) says, '… one would be hard pressed to find a concept more controversial than intelligence in all of psychology'. Some writers (e.g. Turner, 1997) claim to measure IQ in a multitude of different cognitive domains and with great precision, though even Turner himself says that:

It has often been said that the best indicator of dyslexia in young children is the performance of the father on a reading test. As 80% of cases may be identified in this way, it would compare favourably with more elaborate screening exercises (1997: 224)

The gene for dyslexia?

There is much interest in the 'gene for dyslexia' (e.g. Cardon *et al*, 1994; Fisher *et al*, 1999). This strand to the argument raises fundamental questions. Biologically speaking, there can be no gene(s) for literacy per se. The first literate acts (clay tablet invoices) were only about 6,000 years ago. This is some 94,000 years too short a time for a skill or aptitude to be encoded into our DNA. It would be about as sensible to propose genes for driving ability as for literacy per se. However, it is feasible to imagine that a gene or genes affecting a skill or skills related to literacy might have evolved. That is to say, dyslexia, if it exists at all, will never show itself as pure literacy failure – it will be accompanied by consistent failure at a fundamental, related ability or abilities. The 'dyslexic' who is absolutely 'normal' in every other respect is, in other words, mythical. The search for consistent diagnostic signs (ranging widely, e.g. from perceptual defects through postural weakness to postmortem neuropathology) other than literacy failure per se continues, with extremely variable result and no sign of consensus (Everatt, 1997; Galaburda, 1993; Hulme and Snowling, 1997; Nicolson and Fawcett, 1999; Pumfrey and Reason, 1991; Rack, 1997).

The incidence of dyslexia is consistently reported to be three to four times greater in boys than in girls, and yet a genetic sex-linkage has not been demonstrated. It should be simple to do this if such a linkage existed. This is a wobble and not a trivial one; as Stein and Talcott (1999: 60) say, it is 'surprising' and 'still lacks an explanation'. The pure 'gene for dyslexia' theory is considerably flawed at this point.

What might innate deficits which related to literacy consist of? They might be genetically determined deficits, or deficits induced *in utero* or at birth or thereabouts. A number of interesting candidates have been considered for such deficits. (It should be noted that studies considered in this section define 'dyslexics' by invoking the IQ/achievement discrepancy criterion, as does almost all such research.)

First, a tentative dip into the phonological awareness debate. There is good evidence that 'dyslexics' have relatively poor linguistic phonological skills (Ellis, 1993; Goswami, 1997; Snowling, 1995; Snowling and Nation, 1997). There is also the finding that literacy training in an alphabetic system rapidly improves phonological awareness. This is an important carts and horses question that has been well aired in the literature (Goswami and Bryant, 1990; Perfetti and Zhang, 1995; Smith, 1994; Taft, 1991; Thompson, 1999). Given the phenomenal, phonological fuzziness of spoken language, however, it is not astonishing that those with poor literacy skills have poor phonological skills, nor that the latter swiftly improve with targeted tuition, nor that such improvement supports subsequent spelling performance. There is circularity here: learning literacy (in English) causes phonological awareness, something only rather good spellers have.

The 'magnocellular deficit' is an interesting proposal (Eden *et al*, 1996; Hogben, 1997; Stein and Talcott, 1999; but also Goulandris *et al*, 1998; Johannes *et al*, 1996). Magnocells, as a result of the speed at which they conduct stimuli, play an important part in the control of rapid, accurate eye movements (e.g. saccades) and the stabilising of eye fixations. A magnocellular deficit will clearly affect reading. It will, though, similarly affect all those other activities for which magnocellular systems were evolved. Diagnostic signs, in neurological fields unrelated to literacy, should be consistently obtained. However, findings are generally contradictory and contradicted.

Different brains?

Brain scans show exciting, if crude, differences between 'dyslexics' and 'normals' (Duara et al, 1991; Eden et al, 1996; Larsen et al, 1990). However, the normal and literate brain inevitably differs from the normal but less literate brain in important functional ways. This is absolutely unremarkable – they have had radically different experiences (e.g. Castro-Caldas et al, 1998). The Matthew effect (the differential effect on ability or performance of variation in the quantity of practice – see Stanovich, 1986 and Matthew, XV: 29), naturally enough, eventually shows up as a difference in functional organisation on brain scan; how could it be otherwise? We need not invoke neuropathology to explain these findings.

Geschwind and Galaburda (1987) proposed a general, overarching theory of 'anomalous cerebral dominance' (which they suggested was primarily due to a testosterone imbalance *in utero*). This theory, which can only be described as grand, links a vast array of syndromes and conditions such as most language disorders, including dyslexia, and many immune disorders. Evidence is wildly mixed and the theory remains disputed (Bryden et al, 1994). Problems of measurement and definition bedevil the elucidation of this theory, and findings frequently contradict previous findings.

In other studies, the macro-anatomy of brains is measured and far-reaching conclusions drawn (e.g. Hynd et al, 1995). Unusual symmetry of the planum temporale (a part of the brain which, on the left side in most people, deals with much language management), for example, has been claimed as diagnostic (Galaburda et al, 1985, 1994). It is not clear how far this 'weights-and-measures' approach takes us. Sample sizes are often very small and 'dyslexics' are discrepancy defined. Brain micro-anatomy likewise, some research claims, shows a plethora of different abnormalities in 'dyslexics' (e.g. Galaburda, 1993). How abnormal such macro- and micro-abnormalities really are is uncertain and so is how, if at all, they relate to observed abilities or behaviours (e.g. Pumfrey and Reason, 1991).

To say that this theoretical area is unresolved is an understatement. No theory has reached anything like consensus and theories which have been intensively researched are frequently not supported, or not strongly supported.

Is the diagnosis benign?

Learned helplessness (Butkowsky and Willows, 1980; Maier and Seligman, 1976) refers to an unconsciously mediated mental state characterised by reduced confidence, lowered motivation, diminished expectation and passivity. In the educational context, it is frequently engendered by maladaptive attribution (the attribution of an effect – such as poor literacy – to a cause which is debilitating – such as low ability, or in this instance to an innate, neurological defect). Learned helplessness is disempowerment.

Is a diagnosis of dyslexia a neutral thing? May it have a subtle but malign influence? Learned helplessness, or disempowerment, as a result of maladaptive attributions, is well recognised among ABE students (Charnley and Jones, 1981; Du Vivier, 1992; Levine, 1986; Mace, 1979; Wallis, 1995). Occasionally it is consciously apparent.

> I was very unhappy. I was told I'd never be able to read or write – I was told this by an educational psychologist. (Open Learning Project, nd: 37)

Also:

> Dyslexia is a disability or specific learning difficulty which needs to be identified and clarified with the student. This is not because of some desire to label students, but because students need to understand that their difficulties will not go away with tuition, practice, hard work, etc. (Klein, 1993: 54)

My own research, though, in addition, appears clearly to demonstrate a strong disempowerment effect among *providers* of ABE tuition, in respect of students with a diagnosis of dyslexia (Kerr, 1999).

Given the clear maladaptive attribution that a diagnosis of an innate, irreversible, neurological handicap inevitably entails, how could it be otherwise? (Bar-Tal, 1984; Chan, 1994, 1996; Fang, 1996; Johnston, 1985; Muthukrishna and Borkowski, 1995; Peterson *et al,* 1993; Stanovich, 1986). Maladaptive attribution inevitably engenders learned helplessness. Dyslexia, whatever else it may or may not be, is clearly a maladaptive attribution. A diagnosis of dyslexia, to the precise degree it is accepted, may therefore function on a conscious level as a politically powerful, socially acceptable and hence desirable explanation for poor literacy skills, on a less conscious level as a potent, but generally unnoticed, impediment to learning those skills – and developmental dyslexia itself may yet prove to be non-existent.

Dyslexia is politically powerful: '... the media have accepted (why I wonder?) that the case is proven ... .' (Martin, 1989: 19). The teacher of literacy works in an environment where public, student and management firmly believe that dyslexia is real. As Galbraith ironically asserted, in a different context, 'Anything so convenient must be right' (J.K. Galbraith, 1969). Dyslexia is nothing if not convenient; it blames the victim, which is such a comfort to everyone else. If only because of the highly particular political convenience of the syndrome presently sweeping us all along, dyslexia surely demands our deep, even raucous scepticism.

References

Agne, K.J., Greenwood, G.E. and Miller, L.D. (1994) 'Relationships between teacher belief systems and teacher effectiveness', *Journal of Research and Development in Education*, 27, pp. 141–52.

Bar-Tal, D. (1984) 'The effect of teachers' behaviour on pupils' attributions – a review in Barnes, P., Oates, J., Chapman, J., Lee, V. and Czerniewska, P. (eds), *Personality, Development and Learning*. Milton Keynes: Open University Press.

Beaton, A., McDougall, S. and Singleton, C. (1997) 'Humpty Dumpty grows up? Diagnosing dyslexia in adulthood', *Journal of Research in Reading,* 20(l), pp. 1–12.

Brooks, P.L. and Weeks, S.A.J. (1998) 'A comparison of the responses of dyslexic, slow-learning and control children to different strategies for teaching spellings', *Dyslexia,* 4(4), pp. 212–22.

Bryden, M.P., McManus, I.C. and Bulman-Fleming, B. (1994) 'Evaluating the empirical support for the Geschwond-Behan-Galaburda model of cerebral lateralisation', *Brain and Cognition,* 20, pp. 103–67.

Butkowsky, Irwin S. and Willows, Dale, M. (1980) 'Cognitive-motivational characteristics of children varying in reading ability: evidence for learned helplessness in poor readers', *Journal of Educational Psychology,* 72(3), pp. 408–22.

Cardon, L.R., Smith, S.D., Fulder, D.W., Kimberling, W.J., Pennington, B.F. and De Fries, J.C. (1994) 'Quantitative trait locus for reading disability on chromosome 6', *Science,* 266, pp. 276–9.

Castro-Caldas, A., Peterson, K.M., Reis, A., Stone-Elander, S. and Ingvar, M. (1998) 'The illiterate brain: learning to read and write during childhood influences the functional organisation of the adult brain', *Brain,* 121, pp. 1053–63.

Chan, L.K.S. (1994) 'Relationship of motivation, strategic learning and reading achievement in grades 5, 7 & 9', *Journal of Experimental Education,* 62(4), pp. 319–39.

Chan, L.K.S. (1996) 'Combined strategy and attributional training for 7th grade average and poor readers', *Journal of Research in Reading,* 19(2), pp. 111–28.

Charnley, A.H. and Jones, H.A. (1981) *The Concept of Success in Adult Literacy.* London. ALBSU.

Doyle, J. (1997) *Dyslexia: An Introductory Guide.* London: Whurr.

Du Vivier, E. (ed.) (1992) *Learning to be Literate: A Study of Students' Perceptions of the Goals and Outcomes of Adult Literacy Tuition.* Dublin: Dublin Literacy Scheme.

Duara, R., Kutseh, A., Cross-Glenn, K., Barket, W., Jallad. B., Pascal, S., Lowenstein, D.A., Sheidon, J., Rabin, M., Levin, B. and Lubs, H. (1991) 'Neuroanatomic differences between dyslexia and normal readers on magnetic resonance imaging scans', *Archives of Neurology,* 48, pp. 410–16.

Eden, G.F., Van Meter, J.W., Rumsey, J.W., Maisong, J. and Zetlino, T.A. (1996) 'Functional MRI reveals differences in visual motion processing in individuals with dyslexia', *Nature,* 382, pp. 66–9.

Ellis, A.W. (1993) *Reading, Writing and Dyslexia: a Cognitive Analysis.* Hove: Lawrence Erlbaum Associates.

Ellis, A.W., McDougall, Sine J.P. and Monk. A.F. (1997) 'Are dyslexics different? IV. In defence of uncertainty', *Dyslexia,* 3(1), pp. 12–14.

Everatt, J. (1997) 'The abilities and disabilities associated with adult developmental dyslexia', *Journal of Research in Reading,* 20(1), pp. 13–21.

Fang, Z. (1996) 'A review of research on teachers' beliefs and practices', *Educational Research,* 38(1), pp. 47–65.

Fisher, S. F., Marlow, A.J., Lamb, J., Maestrini, E., Williams, D.F., Richardson, A.J., Weeks, D.E., Stem, J.F. and Monaco, A.P. (1999) 'A quantitative-trait locus on chromosome 6p influences different aspects of developmental dyslexia', *American Journal of Human Genetics,* 64, pp. 146–56.

Galaburda, A.M., Sherman, G.F., Rosen, G.D., Aboiz, F. and Geschwind, N. (1985) 'Developmental dyslexia: four consecutive cases with cortical anomalies', *Annals of Neurology,* 18, pp. 222–33.

Galaburda, A.M. (ed.) (1993) *Dyslexia and Development: Neurological Aspects of Extra-Ordinary Brain.* Cambridge, MA: Harvard University Press.

Galaburda, A.M., Menand, M.T. and Rosen, G.D. (1994) 'Evidence for aberrant auditory anatomy in developmental dyslexia', *Proceedings of the National Academy of Science of the U.S.A,* 91, pp. 8010–13.

Galbraith, J.K. (1969) *The Affluent Society.* London: Penguin.

Geschwind, N. and Galaburda, A.M. (1987) *Cerebral Lateralisation.* Cambridge (Mass.): MIT Press.

Goswami, U. and Bryant, P. (1990) *Phonological Skills and Learning to Read.* Hove: Lawrence Erlbaum Associates.

Goswami, U. (1997) 'Learning to read in different orthographics: phonological awareness, orthographic representations and dyslexia', in Hulme, C. and Snowling, M. (eds), *Dyslexia: Biology, Cognition and Intervention*. London: Whurr Publishers.

Goulandris, N., McIntyre, A., Snowling, M., Bethel, J. and Lee, J.P. (1998) 'A comparison of dyslexic and normal readers using orthoptic assessment procedures', *Dyslexia*, 4(1), pp. 30–48.

Hanley, J.R. (1997) 'Reading and spelling impairments in undergraduate students with developmental dyslexia', *Journal of Research in Reading*, 20(1), pp. 22–30.

Hogben, J.H. (1997), 'How does a visual transient deficit affect reading?', in Hulme, C. and Snowling, M. (eds), *Dyslexia: Biology, Cognition and Intervention*. London: Whurr Publishers.

Holt, J. (1984a) *Hon Children Fail*. London: Penguin.

Holt, J. (1984b) *Hon Children Learn*. London: Penguin.

Hulme, C. and Snowling, M. (eds) (1997) *Dyslexia: Biology, Cognition and Intervention*. London: Whurr Publishers.

Hynd, G.W., Hall, L.J., Novey, E.S., Eliopolus, D., Black, K., Gonzales, J.J., Edmonds, J.E., Riccio, C., and Cohen, M.J. (1995) 'Dyslexia and corpus callosum morphology', *Archives of Neurology*, 52, pp. 32–8.

Johannes, S., Kussmaul, C.L., Munte, T.F. and Mangun, G.R. (1996) 'Developmental dyslexia: passive visual stimulation provides no evidence for a magncellular processing defect', *Neuropsychologia*, 34(11), pp. 1123–27.

Johnston, P.H. (1985) 'Understanding reading disability: a case study approach', *Harvard Educational Review'*, 55(2), pp. 153–77.

Kerr, H. (1999) *Dyslexia in ABE: Beliefs and Consequences*, M.Ed. Dissertation: Sheffield University Library.

Klein, C. (1993) *Diagnosing Dyslexia: A Guide to the Assessment of Adults with Specific Learning Difficulties*. London: ALBSU (BSA).

Larsen, J.F., Hoien, T., Lundberg, L., and Odegnard, H. (1990) 'MR: evaluation of the size symmetry of the planum temporale in adolescents with developmental dyslexia', *Brain and Language*, 39, pp. 289–301.

Levine, K. (1986) *The Social Context of Literacy*. London: Routledge and Kegan Paul.

Mace, J. (1979) *Working with Words*. London: Writers and Readers Publishers Cooperative.

Maier, S.F. and Seligman, M.E.P. (1976) 'Learned helplessness: theory and evidence*', Journal of Experimental Psychology: General*, 105, pp. 3–46.

Martin, T. (1989) *The Struggles*. Milton Keynes: Open University Press.

Miles, T.R. (1983) *The Bangor Dyslexia Test*. Wisbech, Cambs: LDA.

Miles, T.R. and Miles, E. (1999) *Dyslexia One Hundred Years On*. Buckingham: Open University Press.

Muthukrishna, N. and Borkowski, J.G. (1995) 'How learning contexts facilitate strategy transfer', *Applied Cognitive Psychology*, 9, pp. 425–46.

Nicolson, R.I. and Fawcett, A.J. (1997) 'Development of objective procedures for screening and assessment of dyslexic students in higher education', *Journal of Research in Reading*, 20(1), pp. 77–83.

Nicolson, R.I. and Fawcett, A.J. (1999) 'Developmental dyslexia: the role of the cerebellum', *Dyslexia*, 5(30), pp. 155–77.

Open Learning Project (undated) '*We've Tried – you Try!*' Lancaster: the Literacy Research Group and London: Goldsmiths College.

Perfetti, C.A. and Zhang, S. (1995) 'The universal word identification reflex', *The Psychology of Learning and Motivation*, 33, pp. 159–89.

Peterson, C., Maier, S.F. and Seligman, M.E.P. (1993) *Learned Helplessness: a Theory for the Age of Personal Control*. Oxford: Oxford University Press.

Pumfrey, P.D. and Reason, R. (1991) *Specific Learning Difficulties (Dyslexia): Challenges and Responses*. London: Routledge.

Rack, J. (1997) 'Issues in the assessment of developmental dyslexia in adults: theoretical and applied perspectives', *Journal of Research in Reading,* 20(1), pp. 66–76.

Samuelsson, S., Bylund, B., Cervin, T., Finnstrom, O., Gaddlin, P., Leijon, I., Mard, S., Ronnberg, J., Sandstedt, P. and Warngard, O. (1999) 'The prevalance of reading disabilities among very-low-birth-weight children at 9 years of age', *Dyslexia,* 5(2), pp. 94–112.

Siegel, L.S. and Himel, N. (1998) 'Socioeconomic status, age and the classification of dyslexics and poor readers: the danger of using IQ scores in the definition of reading disability', *Dyslexia,* 4(2), pp. 74–90.

Smith, F. (1994) *Understanding Reading.* Hove: Lawrence Erlbaum Associates.

Snowling, M. (1995) 'Phonological processing and developmental dyslexia', *Journal of Research in Reading,* 18(2), pp. 132–38.

Snowling, M.J. and Nation, K.A. (1997) 'Language, phonology and learning to read', in Hulme, C. and Snowling, M. (eds), *Dyslexia: Biology, Cognition and Intervention.* London: Whurr Publishers.

Stanovich, K.E. (1986) 'Matthew effects in reading: some consequences of individual differences in the acquisition of literacy', *Reading Research Quarterly,* 21, pp. 360–406.

Stanovich, K.E. (1991) 'Discrepancy definitions of reading disability: has intelligence led us astray?', *Reading Research Quarterly,* 26, pp. 7–29.

Stanovich, K.E. and Stanovich, P.J. (1997) 'Further thoughts on aptitude/achievement discrepancy', *Educational Psychology in Practice,* 13(1), pp. 3–8.

Stein, J. and Talcott, J. (1999) 'Impaired neuronal timing in developmental dyslexia – the magnocellular hypothesis', *Dyslexia,* 5(2), pp. 59–77.

Taft, M. (1991) *Reading and the Mental Lexicon.* Hove: Lawrence Erlbaum Associates.

Thompson, M.E. (1999) 'Subtypes of dyslexia: a teaching artefact?', *Dyslexia,* 5(3), pp. 127–37.

Turner, M. (1997) *The Psychological Assessment of Dyslexia.* London: Whurr Publishers.

Wallis, J. (199S) '"You can't write until you can spell". Attitudes to writing among adult basic education students', in Mace, J. (ed.), *Literacy, Language and Community Publishing: Essays in Adult Education.* London: Routledge.

Westwood, P.S. (1995) 'Teachers' beliefs and expectations concerning students with learning difficulties', *Australian Journal of Remedial Education,* 27(2), pp. 19–21.

Whitehouse, G. (1995) 'Dyslexia: an FE student's experience of assessment', *RaPAL Bulletin,* 27, pp. 19–21.

18

Effects of the Home Learning Environment and Preschool Center Experience upon Literacy and Numeracy Development in Early Primary School

Edward C. Melhuish, Mai B. Phan, Kathy Sylva,
Pam Sammons, Iram Siraj-Blatchford and Brenda Taggart

[…]

Many research studies document the relationship of socioeconomic status (SES) to cognitive development and academic achievement (e.g., Bloom, 1964; Feinstein, 2003), as well as other aspects of children's development (e.g., Davie, Butler, & Goldstein, 1972), although the strength of such relationships may vary widely between cultures (OECD, 2004). In terms of which aspects of SES relate most strongly with academic achievement, there is long-standing evidence (e.g., Mercy & Steelman, 1982; Sammons et al., 2004) that parental education is the best predictor, with maternal education being most potent in the early years. However, SES explains only a limited amount of difference in academic achievement – about 5% according to a meta-analysis of studies by White (1982). Thus, other factors are necessary to explain variation in academic achievement. The issues related to how to alleviate poor academic achievement are increasing in importance partly because a country's economic success is increasingly tied to the knowledge and skills of its workforce.

The extent and persistence of deficits in academic achievement associated with low SES (and minority ethnic status) led to policy initiatives in the United States such as the Elementary and Secondary Education Act of 1965 and the recent No Child Left Behind Act of 2001. Similar thinking also applies to policies in other countries aiming to improve schooling outcomes for disadvantaged children. However, several studies indicate that lower school achievement among disadvantaged children is presaged by preschool cognitive differences (e.g., Denton, West, & Walston, 2003). Indeed the relationship between SES and cognitive development is present from infancy on (McCall, 1981). Such evidence suggests that the causes of poor academic achievement may partly lie in experiences and development during the preschool years. For example, Heckman and Wax (2004) recently proclaimed, 'Like it or not, the most important mental and behavioral patterns, once established, are difficult to change once children enter school' (p. 14). This may be overstated, but the importance of the early years is clear.

From: *Journal of Social Issues,* 64 (1), 2008, pp. 95–114.

One approach to ameliorating this early inequality has been to consider the benefits for disadvantaged children of high-quality preschool childcare or education. Barnett (2001) showed how the deficits in emergent literacy for lower SES children can be reduced by preschool education. There is now ample evidence of the benefits of preschool education for children generally and not just the disadvantaged (e.g., Magnuson, Meyers, Ruhm, & Waldfogel, 2004; Sammons et al., 2004; Sylva et al., 2004; Melhuish et al., 2006). Such evidence has influenced the 2004 introduction of state-funded universal part-time pre-school education for 3- and 4-year-olds in the United Kingdom, the universal state-funded preschool education for 4-year-olds in some American states (e.g., Oklahoma, Georgia), as well as increased state preschool provision in several other countries (Melhuish & Petrogiannis, 2006).

Parenting also matters. Typically, for cognitive outcomes, the effect sizes for preschool childcare are only about a half to a third as large as those for parenting (NICHD ECCRN, 2006). Parenting varies with SES. Parcel and Menaghan (1990) found that mothers with more intellectually stimulating jobs provided more support and stimulating materials for their children, which was, in turn, linked to children's verbal skills. The argument linking low SES to lack of stimulation and lower cognitive development has a long history and has regularly been supported by evidence (e.g., Bradley, Corwyn, Burchinal, McAdoo, & Coll, 2001; Brooks-Gunn, Duncan, & Aber, 1997).

Parenting practices such as reading to children, using complex language, responsive-ness, and warmth in interactions are all associated with better developmental outcomes (Bradley, 2002). This partly explains links between SES and developmental outcomes, in that higher SES parents use more developmentally enhancing activities (Hess et al., 1982). Stimulating activities may enhance development by helping children with specific skills (e.g., linking letters to sounds), but also, and perhaps most important, by developing the child's ability and motivation concerned with learning generally. Additionally, it is possi-ble that a feedback loop is operating whereby parents are influenced by the child's level of attainment, which would lead to children with higher ability possibly receiving more parental stimulation.

Better understanding of the factors influencing children's preparedness for school and capacity for educational achievement has implications for (a) theories of educational achievement and (b) educational policy and practice. A theory of educational achievement must account for influences before schooling starts if it is to be worthwhile, and this study considers modifiable factors in the early years that can influence school readiness. Such evidence may be useful to governments wishing to maximize educational achievement and indicates appropriate steps to facilitate children's preparedness for school. Such policy changes may operate locally although enabling policies may need central government planning (Feinstein & Peck, 2008). Findings from studies such as this may indicate the appropriate focus of such policies.

The study aims to advance research on parenting and preschool by considering aspects of the home environment and preschool composition as partial explanations for why home and preschool environments produce effects upon children's literacy and numeracy. To such ends, this study aims to demonstrate that an interview-based measure of the home environ-ment is associated with academic achievement at the start of school and in later years, to determine the influence of the child's preschool center upon academic achievement, and to identify whether preschool center composition is pertinent to developing literacy and numeracy during the first years of school. Groups with unexpected levels of attainment (not achieving as expected on the basis of demographic characteristics) were examined using multilevel modeling to examine performance at the level of both individuals and preschool centers. Thus, this study investigates sources of unexpected performance that are linked to the immediate environment (meso-level) rather than due to individual or more macro-level variables.

Method

Participants

One hundred and forty-one preschool centers were randomly chosen in six local authorities, identified as having a demographic make-up similar to that of England overall. From these 141 centers, 2,857 children were recruited into a longitudinal study. Children already in preschools were recruited when they became 3 years old; children starting preschool after their third birthday were recruited at entry to preschool. Their mean age at entry to the study was 3 years 5 months (SD = 4.6 months). Full data exist for 2,603 children and families at 3 and 5 years and 2,354 at 3, 5, and 7 years.

Measures

When children entered the study, they were assessed with four subscales from the British Ability Scales II (BAS II; block building, picture similarities, verbal comprehension, and naming vocabulary) (Elliot, Smith, & McCulloch, 1996) to give a general cognitive ability (GCA) score. Upon entering primary school at age 5, children were assessed again with the BAS II. In addition, literacy was assessed by combining the Letter Recognition Test (Clay, 1993) and subscales on the Phonological Awareness assessment (Bryant & Bradley, 1985); numeracy was assessed by the Early Number Concepts subscale of the BAS II. At the end of the third school year (7+ years), nationally standardized, teacher-conducted, national assessments of the children's achievement in reading and mathematics were obtained.

Shortly after initial child assessments, one of the child's parents or guardians was interviewed (usually the mother). Most questions in the semistructured interview were precoded, with some open-ended questions coded post hoc. The interview covered parents' education; occupation and employment; family structure; ethnicity and languages used; the child's birth weight, health, development, and behavior; the use of preschool provision and childcare history; and significant life events. The parental interview included questions concerning the frequency that children engaged in 14 activities: playing with friends at home; playing with friends elsewhere; visiting relatives or friends; shopping with parent; watching TV; eating meals with the family; going to the library; playing with letters/numbers; painting or drawing; being read to; learning activities with the alphabet, numbers/shapes, and songs/poems/nursery rhymes; as well as having a regular bedtime. Frequency of activities was coded on a 7-point scale (0 = *not at all;* 7 = *very frequent*). A selection of these activities was used in the construction of a home learning environment (HLE) index as described later.

Analytic strategy

Children and families are clustered by preschool center, and data are hierarchical. Using standard regression with such data can lead to inaccurate error variance estimates. Potentially, there is greater similarity between participants within the same centers so the independence of measurement assumption is violated, and mis-estimating of levels of significance is likely. Hence, we used multilevel modeling (Goldstein, 2003) to overcome such problems and to provide estimates of center effects, thus allowing the identification of preschool centers that were particularly effective or ineffective in fostering children's development.

Analyses focused on four outcomes: literacy and numeracy achievement at age 5 (start of primary school) and reading and mathematics achievement at 7+ years. First, multilevel models of age 5 outcomes were run to assess the extent of reliable variation in age 5 outcomes across preschool centers and to produce child and center residuals after controlling for family and background characteristics. These multilevel models estimate the proportion of variance not only between children within centers but also between centers. Children's predicted achievement in school was based on age, gender, birth weight, ethnic group, health, developmental or behavioral problems, mothers' and fathers' education, highest social class of mother and father (family socioeconomic status [SES]), number of siblings, deprivation (eligible for free school meals or not), household income, and duration of preschool attendance. Several predictors were categorical (because the interview provided categorical answers) with a reference category (lowest usually, but for ethnicity white U.K. group as reference), and other predictors were continuous variables (i.e., birth weight, age, and duration of preschool).

Second, using multilevel model residuals at the individual level, three groups were formed: unexpected overachieving, expected, and unexpected underachieving. Analyses explored how the 14 individual home activities influenced the probability of children performing better or worse than expected. Using the results from these analyses, 7 of the 14 home activities were selected to create a HLE index. Also, using multilevel model residuals at the center level, the analyses explored how center composition predicted centers that had higher or lower scores than expected. The categories of over-achievers, average, and underachievers were calculated using the individual-level standardized residuals from the multilevel model. A child was considered to be performing below expectation if the child's standardized residual was more than one standard deviation below the mean of zero, above expectation if the standardized residual was above one standard deviation from the mean, and as expected if the child's score was within one standard error of the mean. Center effects were similarly categorized from the center-level standardized residuals, which provided a measure of the extent to which the children attending a particular center were performing above or below expectation. Multinomial models assessed the effect of the HLE index on children's level of achievement as well as the effect of compositional effects (i.e., percentage of children with highly educated mothers, and average level of children's ability in centers) on the levels of achievement at the center level.

Third, new multilevel models were constructed that included the HLE and preschool center variables. Using these models, the effect sizes of the variables, SES, mother's education, father's education, household income, and HLE were computed for the outcomes at 5 and 7 years of age. For the age 5 outcome models, children are treated as clustered within preschools and in the age 7 outcome models, clustering is within schools. In order to take account of preschool center effects at age 7, preschool composition variables and a measure of preschool effectiveness derived from the 5-year outcome models are used as individual-level predictors.

Results

Achievement at age 5

Children's characteristics and family background were included in the demographic multi-level model to predict children's age-adjusted achievement. From these models, three categories of performance (unexpected overachievers, expected, and unexpected underachievers) for literacy and numeracy were constructed based on child residual scores deviating by at least ± 1 standard deviation. Each category of unexpected over- or underachievement is a nominal outcome variable with *average achieving* children as the reference category. Sixteen percent of children were achieving higher than predicted from their background in both literacy and numeracy, and a similar proportion (16% literacy, 15% numeracy) were achieving less well than would be predicted. The age 5 multilevel model produced residuals at the center level, identifying centers as *over-* and *underachieving* centers in the same way (e.g., overachieving centers produce children having higher-than-expected scores given intake characteristics). Greater proportions of centers fall into these categories than children – about one third (33% literacy, 29% numeracy) overachieving and underachieving (28% literacy, 29% numeracy).

Quantifying the home learning environment

Each of the 14 home activity items was regressed in separate equations on the individual categorical variables of over- or underachievement. The seven social/routine activities (play with friends at home, and elsewhere, visiting relatives/friends, shopping, TV, eating meals with family, regular bedtime) were not significant for under- or overachievement in literacy and numeracy at age 5. Conversely, the seven activities providing clear learning opportunities (frequency read to, going to the library, playing with numbers, painting and drawing, being taught letters, being taught numbers, songs/poems/rhymes) had significant positive effects on unexpected achievements. Since the items are conceptually and statistically linked, a combined measure, the HLE, was created. The frequency of each of the seven activities was coded on a 0–7 scale (0 = *not occurring*, 7 = *very frequent*) and the seven scores were added to produce an index with a possible range of 0–49, which was normally distributed with a mean of 23.42 ($SD = 7.71$).

Center composition

Center composition was considered in terms of the level of [the] mother's education and average child cognitive ability in [the] center at age 3. The percentage of children with a mother with a degree in each center was standardized about the median to account for a negative skew, with a mean of .31 ($SD = .94$). Center average ability was constructed as the standardized average of children's 3-year-old cognitive ability score, with a mean of −.04 ($SD = 1.00$). Center mothers' education and center child ability are highly associated ($r = .58$).

Predicting under- and overachievement at the start of school (age 5)

The multilevel models for age 5 outcomes treated children as clustered by preschool center, allowing the estimation and separation of residuals into individual and center variance, and estimation of the amount of variance explained by adding parameters to the model in stepwise fashion (see Table 18.1). For age 5 literacy and numeracy, family and background characteristics explained significant individual variation between children in centers: 16% for literacy and numeracy scores. Thus, most variation in children's achievement was not due to family or background characteristics but to other unmeasured factors not considered in the demographic model.

It was hypothesized that variations in predicted achievement based upon family and background characteristics (i.e., unexplained individual-level variance) would be partially accounted for by the home learning environment and by center composition. Firstly, the categories of over- and underachievement for children and centers were examined for a relationship with [the] home learning environment at the child level, and with center composition, at the center level. The mean HLE scores for the overachieving (mean = 26.44, SD = 7.26), average (mean = 23.61, SD = 7.45) and underachieving (mean = 21.62, SD = 7.83) groups of children appear to vary systematically for the demographically adjusted levels of achievement (i.e., unexpected overachieving, expected, and unexpected underachieving) in literacy. Multinomial logistic regressions confirm, as hypothesized, that children with a higher HLE are more likely to be overachievers (p < .0001), while lower HLE scores are associated with underachievement (p < .0001). For numeracy, the effects were also significant but not as strong as for literacy. Children with higher HLEs had a greater likelihood of overachieving in numeracy, and those with lower HLE had a greater likelihood of underachieving in numeracy.

Next, the hypothesized link between center composition and differences at the center level in predicted achievement was considered. The mean center child ability varied for the overachieving (mean = 2.86, SD 7.39), average (mean = –.06, SD = 5.68), and underachieving (mean = –4.09, SD = 6.08) categories in literacy. For numeracy, mean center child ability also varied for the overachieving (mean = 3.26, SD = 6.53), average (mean = –0.94, SD = 6.51), and underachieving (mean = –2.69, SD = 6.65) categories. The mean center percent of mothers with a degree also varies for the overachieving (mean = 18.89, SD = 23.79), average (mean = 8.76, SD = 17.91), and underachieving (mean = .80, SD = 10.31) categories in literacy and for numeracy (overachieving mean = 13.14, SD = 2.92; average mean = 11.08, SD = 18.55; and underachieving mean = 4.88, SD = 17.20). Multinomial logistic regressions confirm that over- and underachievement for centers is significantly associated with center composition. Center average ability differentiated overachieving centers from average-achieving centers for literacy and numeracy, but only differentiated underachieving centers from average-achieving centers for literacy, with the difference for numeracy not statistically significant. Center levels of degree-educated mothers increased the likelihood of overachievement and reduced underachievement for literacy, but the differences for numeracy were not significant.

To support the conclusions that the HLE and center composition added to the prediction of achievement over that provided by family and background characteristics for children, new multilevel models for literacy and numeracy were created. These models included HLE and either center average ability or center percentage of mothers with a degree as predictors in addition to the significant family and child background factors (see Table 18.1). By adding the HLE to the demographic model, the explained variance at the child level showed a 21% increase for age 5 literacy and an 18% increase for age 5 numeracy.

Table 18.1   Fixed and random effects at child and center levels for the prediction of age 5 literacy and numeracy achievement (standard deviations in parentheses)

	Random effects	Demographic model	Add home learning environment	With center ability	With center % mothers with degree
1.1: Literacy achievement at age 5					
Intercept	.04 (.40)	-1.27 (.97)	-1.07 (.96)	-1.06 (.95)	-1.80 (1.00)
Home learning environment	—	—	1.72*** (.17)	1.83*** (.17)	1.80*** (.62)
Center cognitive ability	—	—	—	1.89*** (.27)	—
Center % mothers with degree	—	—	—	—	1.77*** (.28)
Random effects					
Individual error variance (δ)	74.08*** (2.07)	61.69*** (1.77)	58.89*** (1.69)	58.81*** (1.68)	58.79*** (1.65)
Center error variance (T)	18.06*** (2.68)	6.38*** (1.26)	7 49*** (1.41)	4.87*** (1.03)	5 32*** (1.08)
Interclass correlation	.196	.094	.113	.076	.083
Explained variance between centers		16.7%	20.5%	35.07	29.0%
				(center level)	(center level)
1.2: Numeracy achievement at age 5					
Intercept	.04 (.38)	-.17 (1.08)	.03 (1.07)	-.002 (1.06)	-.52 (1.07)
Home learning environment	—	—	1.43*** (.19)	1.54*** (.19)	1.50*** (.19)
Center cognitive ability	—	—	—	1.40*** (.28)	—
Center % mothers with degree	—	—	—	—	1.20*** (.29)
Random effects					
Individual error variance (δ)	92.08*** (2.49)	77.63*** (2.22)	75.718*** (2.16)	75.572*** (2.16)	75.61*** (2.16)
Center error variance (T)	15.24*** (2.49)	4.67*** (1.13)	5.18*** (1.20)	4.00*** (1.02)	4.35*** (1.07)
Interclass correlation	.142	.057	.064	.050	.054
Explained variance between centers		15.7%	17.8%	22.8%	16.0%
				(center level)	(center level)

Statistically significant * $p < .05$, ** $p < .001$, *** $p < .0001$.

Although the magnitude of random variance between centers was relatively small compared to that between children, after accounting for the potentially selective effects of family background on the choice of preschool centers in the demographic model, variation in literacy and numeracy scores at the center level were significantly reduced. For example, center variance in age 5 literacy scores showed a 52% decrease due to selection effects. With HLE in the model, center variance for literacy was 11%. Adding center composition into the multilevel models separately led to a 33% reduction in center-level variance with center ability added and a 27% reduction with center percentage of mothers with degree added. With HLE in the model, center variance for numeracy was 6%. Adding center composition into the multilevel models separately led to a 22% reduction in center-level variance with center ability added and a 16% reduction with center percentage of mothers with degree added. While including center composition reduces unexplained center level variance, there was still significant center-level variation remaining, suggesting that further unmeasured characteristics of preschool centers need to be explored.

Predicting under- and overachievement at age 7

The multilevel models for age 7 outcomes treated children as clustered within schools. The demographic multilevel models were used to produce three groups of children that vary in relation to expected performance (unexpected overachieving, expected, and unexpected underachieving) using the 7-year-old scores of reading and mathematics. The groupings based on child-level residual scores indicates more homogeneity at 7 than at 5 years, with most children achieving at the expected levels in reading (76%) and mathematics (80%), which may be partly due to the relative lack of precision and differentiation of the national assessments administered in classroom groups by teachers at age 7 compared with the one-to-one standardized psychometric assessments used at age 5 and administered by the research team. HLE scores for the overachieving (mean = 23.81, *SD* = 7.89), expected (mean = 24.22, *SD* = 7.40), and underachieving (mean = 20.37, *SD* = 7.93) groups indicate lower HLE for the underachieving group but little difference between the average and overachieving groups in reading. Also, for mathematics, the HLE scores for the overachieving (mean = 23.38, *SD* = 7.32), expected (mean = 24.13, *SD* = 7.50), and underachieving (mean = 20.40, *SD* = 8.21) groups of children indicate lower HLE for the underachieving group but little difference between the average and overachieving groups. Multinomial logistic regression confirmed that links between HLE and achievement level at age 7 were significant in only one direction: Unsupportive home learning environment was associated with increased likelihood of underachievement for reading and mathematics. Supportive home learning environment did not have a statistically significant effect on overachievement at age 7 relative to predicted achievement.

To further examine the effects of HLE and preschool variables on the prediction of achievement over that provided by family and background characteristics for children, new multilevel models for reading and mathematics at age 7 were created that added the HLE, then preschool center effectiveness (derived from age 5 demographic models), and subsequently either center average ability or center percentage of mothers with degree as predictors in addition to the significant family and child background factors (see Table 18.2). Comparison of models indicates a significant contribution of the HLE to children's attainment. Adding the HLE to the demographic model, the variance explained increased by 10% for reading and 6% for mathematics. Recall that the increased explanation given by HLE on age 5 achievement scores

Table 18.2   Fixed and random effects at child and school levels for the prediction of age 7 reading and mathematics achievement (standard deviations in parentheses)

	Random effects	Demographic model	Add home learning environment	With center effect/ness	With center ability	With center % mothers with degree
2.1: Reading attainment at age 7						
Intercept	.073*** (.018)	−.208* (.086)	−.166 (.085)	−.164 (.085)	−.163 (.085)	−.16 (.085)
Home learning environment		—	.125*** (.015)	.123*** (.015)	.121*** (.015)	.123*** (.015)
Preschool effectiveness	—	—	—	.022* (.007)	.015 (.008)	.022* (.008)
Center cognitive ability	—	—	—	—	.042* (.019)	—
Center % mothers with degree	—	—	—	—	—	−.005 (.019)
Random effects						
Individual error variance (δ)	.452*** (.015)	.356*** (.012)	.344*** (.011)	.343*** (.011)	.342*** (.011)	.343*** (.011)
School error variance (T)	.064*** (.011)	.035*** (.008)	.036*** (.008)	.035*** (.008)	.036*** (.008)	.035*** (.008)
Interclass correlation between schools	.124	.088	.095	.094	.095	.093
Explained variance		21.7%	23.9%	24.1%	24.4%	24.1%
2.2: Mathematics attainment at age 7						
Intercept	.052* (.016)	−.066 (.072)	−.032 (.069)	−.031 (.069)	−.031* (.069)	−.035 (.069)
Home learning environment		—	.087*** (.013)	.086*** (.013)	.085*** (.013)	.085*** (.013)
Preschool effectiveness	—	—	—	.028* (.009)	.025* (.009)	.026* (.009)
Center cognitive ability	—	—	—	—	.018 (.016)	—
Center % mothers with degree	—	—	—	—	—	−.014 (.019)
Random effects						
Individual error variance (δ)	.342*** (.011)	.286*** (.009)	.282*** (.009)	.281*** (.009)	.281*** (.009)	.281*** (.009)
School error variance (T)	.047*** (.008)	.025*** (.006)	.026*** (.006)	.025*** (.006)	.025*** (.006)	.026*** (.006)
Interclass correlation between schools	.121	.081	.084	.083	.083	.084
Explained variance		16.5%	17.5%	18.6%	18.6%	18.7%

Statistically significant *$p < .05$, **$p < .001$, ***$p < .0001$.

Table 18.3   Effect sizes for socioeconomic status (SES), mother's and father's education, income, and HLE on 5- and 7-year outcomes

	5 year		7 year	
	Literacy	**Numeracy**	**Reading**	**Mathematics**
SES	.29	.43	.37	.39
Mother's education	.35	.23	.33	.33
Father's education	n.s.	n.s.	.19	.16
Earned income	.31	.28	.15	.15
HLE	.73	.65	.60	.50

Note: n.s. = not significant; HLE = Home Learning Environment.

was 21% and 18%, respectively. Hence, the HLE's effects on children's achievement were reduced by age 7 but were still significant. Preschool center effectiveness has significant effects for both 7-year reading and mathematics attainment. Adding center average ability reduced this effect to insignificance for reading but had no impact for mathematics. The educational level of mothers of children in a center had no significant effect for reading or mathematics.

Effect sizes for child-level variables

The final multilevel models allow for the calculation of effect sizes for an independent variable having allowed for the influence of all other variables in the model. Effect sizes are calculated for the HLE variable and also the main aspects of social class (i.e., family SES, mother's and father's education, and household income); these are shown in Table 18.3. For 5-year-old literacy achievement, the effect size for HLE (bottom 10% compared with top 10%) was greater than that for any of the variables reflecting social class. For 5-year-old numeracy, HLE again had the largest effect size followed by SES, then household income and mother's education. For both 7-year-old reading and mathematics, the largest effect size was still for HLE, followed by SES, mother's education, father's education, and household income.

Discussion

The results clearly support the importance of the HLE, and the influence of the HLE was over and above that of standard proxy measures of parental education and SES. The results also demonstrate that this interview method is useful for identifying variability in parenting. While other family factors such as parents' education and SES are also important, the extent of home learning activities exerts a greater and independent influence on educational attainment.

The comparison of over-, average, and underachieving groups indicates that at age 5 the HLE is effective in differentiating both over- and underachieving groups from children achieving as expected (i.e., across the ability range). However, by age 7, the HLE for both reading and mathematics achievement only differentiates underachieving children from average and overachieving children, with no difference between average and overachieving children, indicating that its effects are more localized on the lower ability range. The changes in effect size by age 7 could be due to several reasons: (a) age 5 assessments are more precise and have better differentiation in the upper ability range than those at age 7; (b) over time, earlier experiences become less influential, losing their developmental significance; or (c) new sources of influence, especially schooling, affect children's development. Possibly, the continuing effects at age 7 of the HLE, measured 4 years previously, is to be expected from continuity over time in the relative standing of homes on developmentally enhancing activities (i.e., it is concurrent effects of the HLE rather than earlier experience producing longer term effects upon development). However, the interpretation that earlier home experience matters is supported by NICHD study evidence (Belsky et al., 2007) indicating that parenting sensitivity at 4.5 years predicts cognitive development at age 10 with current parenting controlled. Also, the importance of early parenting variables is further supported with adolescent educational achievement reported by Englund, Egeland, and Collins (2008). Developmental versus environmental continuity issues pervade longitudinal research and require ongoing attention.

With regard to preschool center effects, the significant center-level variance at 5 years of age for both literacy and numeracy indicates that specific preschool experiences matter. The addition of either preschool composition variable to the 5-year model significantly reduces the preschool center-level variance, but this reduction is greater for center composition in terms of average ability of children in a center rather than in terms of the educational level of mothers using a center, for both literacy and numeracy. However, these effects leave much preschool center variance unexplained indicating that yet further characteristics of preschools, such as quality of provision, need to be considered to understand more completely how specific preschools influence children's development. One approach is to use qualitative case studies to explore quantitatively defined effective and ineffective preschools (e.g., Sammons et al., 2005; Siraj-Blatchford et al., 2003). At age 7, the measure of preschool center effectiveness derived from the 5-year models significantly contributes to explaining both 7-year reading and mathematics attainment. However, adding average ability of children in a center reduces this effect to insignificance for reading. Hence, preschool composition in terms of average ability of children in a center has a persisting effect on 7-year reading (but not mathematics) while the educational level of mothers of children in a center no longer has a significant effect. Such specific preschool effects are further evidence of the importance of preschool education for children's school readiness.

The home learning environment is important for school readiness in addition to benefits associated with preschool. The home learning environment is only moderately associated with SES and parents' educational levels (correlations = .28 −.32), indicating that low SES homes sometimes score highly and, conversely, high SES homes sometimes score poorly on the HLE measure. In studies using the Home Observation for the Measurement of the Environment (HOME), the correlations between HOME and maternal education or SES are in the range 0.36 to 0.50 for differing social and ethnic groups. Generally, HOME measures are significantly associated with social and cognitive development after controlling for demographic factors (Bradley et al., 2001). Others have found that the affective quality of mother–child interactions predicts cognitive skills (e.g., Estrada, Arsenic, Hess, & Holloway, 1987). Such findings led Conger et al. (1992) to conclude that between 20–50% of the variance in child outcomes can be accounted for by differences in parenting.

The effects of the home environment and parenting upon children's development may partly be due to the teaching and learning of specific skills (e.g., letter–sound relationships).

However, the multiplicity of learning opportunities included in the HLE suggests that the effects may be related to more generalized and motivational aspects of child development (e.g., learning to learn). Also, children may internalize aspects of parental values and expectations (implicit in the activities of the HLE) as they form a self-concept of themselves as a learner. Such a perspective is congruent with Vygotsky's (1978) theory that children learn higher psychological processes through their social environment and specifically with adult guidance operating within a child's 'zone of proximal development' (stimulation within the child's comprehension) and reinforces the idea that children acquire cognitive skills such as literacy through interaction with others who aid and encourage skill development.

It is quite possible that the strong relationship between home learning environment and cognitive scores is mediated by some intervening unmeasured factor. Those parents, who answer the questions in a way leading to a high score, may have other characteristics that lead their children to have higher cognitive scores. Even if this were so, the HLE would still be an efficient proxy measure of such unmeasured factors.

Whatever the mechanisms, the influences of parenting upon child development are pervasive. Research involving 0- to 3-year-olds from the evaluation of the Early Head Start (EHS) program, which provided combinations of home visits and center childcare intervention for disadvantaged families, found that the intervention increased both the quantity and quality of parents' interaction with children, as well as children's social and cognitive development (Love et al., 2005). A review of early interventions concluded that, to gain the most impact, interventions should include both parent and child together with a focus on enhancing interactions (Barnes & Freude-Lagevardi, 2003). Such work indicates that parenting behaviors are learnable, and changes in parenting are associated with improved child development. Similar conclusions derive from a study by Hannon, Nutbrown, and Morgan (2005) in the United Kingdom, where children showed better literacy progress when parents received a program on ways to improve child literacy during the preschool period.

With primary school children, similar links between parenting and academic achievement occur. DeGarmo, Forgatch, and Martinez (1999) found that the effects of parent education upon primary school achievement were primarily mediated through parents' provision of opportunities for building intellectual skills. Reviewing studies, Mason and Allen (1986) concluded that the quality and quantity of interactions, not just reading materials and a storytime routine, shaped early literacy. Similarly, Zellman and Waterman (1998) found parent–child interaction more important than other family variables for primary school children's success in reading or mathematics.

With secondary school children, similar effects are detectable. In the United States, Siu-Chu and Willms (1996) analyzed data for 24,000 14-year-olds and found that parental involvement was linked to academic achievement over and above the effects of family demographics; in particular, parent–child interaction seemed most important. Similarly, in the United Kingdom, Feinstein and Symons (1999) found that indicators of parental interest and involvement with child learning were more important in predicting academic achievement at age 16 than parental education and social class.

Such research indicates the importance of school readiness, and there is mounting evidence that demonstrates the role of parenting for children's school readiness skills and ongoing achievement. Academic achievement in adolescence and beyond can be linked to academic skills at school entry (Alexander, Entwisle, & Horsey, 1997), and school entry ability can, in turn, be linked to preschool abilities (Agostin & Bain, 1997). Possibly, preschool experience matters because behavior is more susceptible to the environment earlier rather than later in childhood or because starting school is a critical social transition when ability predicts longer term achievement through creating expectations.

The influences upon parenting and how parenting may influence educational achievement are not simple matters. Poverty, parental education, culture, ethnicity, parental age, health, and other factors are all likely to be important, and multiple factors will interact complexly as shown by Messersmith and Schulenberg (2008) for college students. However, it is clear that parenting is influenced by poverty. For instance, NICHD ECCRN (2005) reported that families in chronic poverty have less stimulating home environments but that the home environment improves as families move out of poverty. Also, families exposed to transient poverty appear to manage to maintain adequate home stimulation despite restricted resources. Wachs and Camli (1991) noted that crowding, the number of people coming and going in the home, and noise level may have adverse effects on parenting and child development via a reduction in maternal involvement, verbal stimulation, and maternal responsivity.

Poverty is linked to poorer child outcomes as well as poorer parenting (Brooks-Gunn et al., 1997). Children in persistent poverty have greater cognitive and behavioral deficits at age 5 than those exposed to transient poverty, who in turn have more deficits than children in nonpoor families (Korenman, Miller, & Sjaastad, 1995). Some deficits can be attributed to health problems associated with poverty, but the greatest part can be explained by reduced emotional support and less cognitive stimulation from parents (McLoyd, 1998).

Such findings suggest that policies for disadvantaged parents that encourage active parenting strategies can help to promote young children's literacy and numeracy and facilitate later academic achievement. However, responsibility should not be placed solely on parents. The provision of good quality preschool education from 3 years of age is likely to produce further benefits, particularly when the preschool center works closely with parents. Studies of successful preschools by Siraj-Blatchford et al. (2003) indicate that preschools that promote activities for parents and children to engage in together are likely to be most beneficial for young children, and this has implications for strategies to help disadvantaged children start school with more academic skills and maintain their educational achievement. Studies as described in this [chapter], and other work on preschool education, have been influential in the formulation of early years policy in the UK as evidenced in the Children Act (2004) and the U.K. government's Ten Year Childcare Strategy (HM Treasury, 2004; see Sylva & Pugh, 2005). Additionally, this work has influenced the guidelines developed by the U.K. government for Children's Centres, which provide integrated services including childcare, preschool education, and parent support in disadvantaged areas, and has attracted interest from policy makers in several countries such as China, Malaysia, Australia, and Canada. With regard to the United States, Heckman (2006) argued that later compensation for deficient early family environments is very costly, and that early intervention is the only cost-effective route to take to simultaneously promote social justice and economic productivity. Finally, it is noteworthy that several countries such as China appear to be recognizing the importance of preschool experience and early years education as an essential part of the infrastructure for economic development (Melhuish & Petrogiannis, 2006).

References

Agostin, T.M., & Bain, S.K. (1997). Predicting early school success with developmental and social skills screeners. *Psychology in the Schools, 34,* 219–228.

Alexander, K.L., Entwisle, D.R., & Horsey, C.S. (1997). From first grade forward: Early foundations of high school dropout. *Sociology of Education, 70,* 87–107.

Barnes, J., & Freude-Lagevardi, A. (2003). *From pregnancy to early childhood: Early interventions to enhance the mental health of children and families.* London: Mental Health Foundation.

Barnett, W.S. (2001). Preschool education for economically disadvantaged children: Effects on reading achievement and related outcomes. In S. Neuman & D. Dickinson (Eds.) *Handbook of early literacy research* (pp. 421–443). New York: Guilford Press.

Belsky, J., Vandell, D.L., Burchinal, M., Clarke-Stewart, K.A., McCartney, K., Owen, M.T., & the NICHD Early Child Care Research Network (2007). Are there long-term effects of early child care? *Child Development, 78,* 681–701.

Bloom, B. (1964). *Stability and change in human characteristics.* New York: Wiley.

Bradley, R. (2002). Environment and parenting. In M. Bornstein (Ed.) *Handbook of parenting* (2nd ed). Hillsdale, NJ: Lawrence Erlbaum.

Bradley, R.H., Corwyn, R.F., Burchinal, M., McAdoo, H.P., & Coll, C.G. (2001). The home environments of children in the United States Part II: Relations with behavioral development through age thirteen. *Child Development, 72,* 1868–1886.

Brooks-Gunn, J., Duncan, G., & Aber, L. (Eds.). (1997). *Neighborhood poverty: Context and consequences for children, Vol. 1.* New York: Russell Sage Foundation.

Bryant, P., & Bradley, L. (1985). *Children's reading problems.* Oxford, UK: Blackwell.

Clay, M. (1993). *An observation survey of early literacy achievement.* Portsmouth, NH: Heinemann.

Conger, R.D., Conger, K., Elder, G., Lorenz, F.O., Simons, R.L., & Whitbeck, L.B. (1992). A family process model of economic hardship and adjustment of early adolescent boys. *Child Development, 63,* 526–541.

Davie, R., Butler, N., & Goldstein, H. (1972). *From birth to seven: A report of the National Child Development Study.* London: Longman.

DeGarmo, D.S., Forgatch, M.S., & Martinez, C.R. (1999). Parenting of divorced mothers as a link between social status and boys' academic outcomes. *Child Development, 70,* 1231–1245.

Denton, K., West, J., & Walston, J. (2003). *Reading – Young children's achievement and classroom experiences* (NCES) 2003–070. Washington, DC: U.S. Dept. of Education.

Elliot, C., Smith, P., & McCulloch, K. (1996). *British Ability Scales Second Edition (BAS II).* Windsor, UK: NFER-Nelson Publishing Company Limited.

Englund, M.M., Egeland. B., & Collins, W.A. (2008). Exceptions to high school dropout predictions in a low-income sample: Do adults make a difference? *Journal of Social Issues, 64,* 1–20.

Estrada, P., Arsenio, W.F., Hess, R.D., & Holloway, S.D. (1987). Affective quality of the mother–child relationship: Longitudinal consequences for children's school-relevant cognitive functioning. *Developmental Psychology, 23,* 210–215.

Feinstein, L. (2003). Inequality in early cognitive development of British children in the 1970 cohort. *Economica, 70,* 73–97.

Feinstein, L., & Peck, S.C. (2008). Unexpected educational pathways: Why do some students not succeed in school and what helps others beat the odds? *Journal of Social Issues.*

Feinstein, L., & Symons, J. (1999). Attainment in secondary school. *Oxford Economic Papers, 51,* 300–321.

Goldstein, H. (2003). *Multilevel statistical models* (3rd ed.). London: Arnold.

Hannon, P., Nutbrown, C., & Morgan, A. (2005). *Early literacy work with families.* London: Sage.

Heckman, J., & Wax, A. (2004, January 23). Home alone. *Wall Street Journal,* p. 14.

Heckman, J.J. (2006). Skill formation and the economics of investing in disadvantaged children. *Science,* 132, 1900–1902.

Hess, R.D., Holloway, S., Price, G., & Dickson, W.P. (1982). Family environments and the acquisition of reading skills. In L.M. Laosa & I.E. Sigel (Eds.), *Families as learning environments of children* (pp. 87–113). New York: Plenum.

HM Treasury (2004). *Choice for parents: The best start for children. A ten year childcare strategy.* Available at http://www.hm-treasury.gov.uk/media/B/E/pbr04childcare_480upd050105.pdf

Korenman, S., Miller, E.J., & Sjaastad, E.J. (1995). Long-term poverty and child development in the United States. *Children and Youth Services Review*, 17, 127–155.

Love, J.M., Kisker, E.E., Ross, C., Constantine, J., Boller, K., Chazan-Cohen, R., et al. (2005). The effectiveness of Early Head Start for 3-year-old children and their parents: Lessons for policy and programs. *Developmental Psychology*, 41, 885–901.

Magnuson, K., Meyers, M., Ruhm, C., & Waldfogel, J. (2004). Inequality in preschool education and school readiness. *American Educational Research Journal*, 41, 115–157.

Mason, J., & Allen, J. B. (1986). A review of emergent literacy with implications for research and practice in reading. *Review of Research in Education*, 13, 3–47.

McCall, R.B. (1981). Nature–nurture and the two realms of development: A proposed integration with respect to mental development. *Child Development*, 52, 1–12.

McLoyd, C.V. (1998). Socioeconomic disadvantage and child development. *American Psychologist,* 53, 185–204.

Melhuish, E., & Petrogiannis, K. (Eds.) (2006). *Early childhood care and education: International perspectives on policy and research.* London: Routledge.

Melhuish, E., Quinn, L., Hanna, K., Sylva, K., Siraj-Blatchford, I., Sammons, R., et al. (2006). *The effective preschool provision in Northern Ireland Project, Summary Report.* Belfast, N.I.: Stranmillis University Press.

Mercy, J.A., & Steelman, L.C. (1982). Familial influence on the intellectual attainment of children. *American Sociological Review*, 47, 532–542.

Messersmith, E.E., & Schulenberg, J.E. (2008). Can we expect the unexpected? Predicting educational attainment when it differs from previous expectations. *Journal of Social Issues,* 64, 195–211.

NICHD Early Child Care Research Network (2005). Duration and developmental timing of poverty and children's cognitive and social development from birth through third grade. *Child Development,* 76, 795–810.

NICHD Early Child Care Research Network (2006). Child care effect sizes for the NICHD study of early child care and youth development. *American Psychologist,* 61, 99–116.

Organisation of Economic Cooperation and Development (2004). *Messages from the Programme for International Student Assessment.* Paris: OECD Publications.

Parcel, T., & Menaghan, E. (1990). Maternal working conditions and children's verbal facility: Studying the intergenerational transmission of inequality from mothers to young children. *Social Psychology Quarterly,* 132–147.

Sammons, P., Elliot, K., Sylva, K., Melhuish, E.C., Siraj-Blatchford, I., & Taggart, B. (2004). The impact of pre-school on young children's cognitive attainments at entry to reception. *British Educational Research Journal,* 30, 691–712.

Sammons, P., Siraj-Blatchford, I., Sylva, K., Melhuish, E., Taggart, B., & Elliot, K. (2005). Investigating the effects of pre-school provision: Using mixed methods in the EPPE research. *International Journal of Social Research Methodology,* 8, 207–224.

Siraj-Blatchford, I., Sylva, K. Taggart, B., Sammons, P., Melhuish, E., & Elliot, K. (2003). *The effective provision of pre-school education (EPPE) project: Intensive case studies of practice across the foundation stage.* London: DfEE/Institute of Education.

Siu-Chu, H.O., & Willms, J.D. (1996). Effects of parental involvement on eighth-grade achievement. *Sociology of Education,* 69, 126–141.

Sylva, K., Melhuish, E., Sammons, P., Siraj-Blatchford, I., & Taggart, B. (2004). *Effective pre-school provision.* London: Institute of Education.

Sylva, K., & Pugh, G. (2005). Transforming the early years in England. *Oxford Review of Education, 31,* 11–22.

Vygotsky, L.S. (1978). *Mind in society.* Cambridge, MA: Harvard University Press.

Wachs, D., & Camli, O. (1991). Do ecological or individual characteristics mediate the influence of physical environment upon maternal behavior? *Journal of Environmental Psychology, 11,* 249–264.

White, K.R. (1982). The relation between socioeconomic status and academic achievement. *Psychological Bulletin, 91,* 461–481.

Zellman, G.L., & Waterman, J.M. (1998). Understanding the impact of parent school involvement on children's educational outcome. *The Journal of Educational Research, 91,* 370–380.

Index